European and Muscovite

Russian Research Center Studies, 68

European and Muscovite

Ivan Kireevsky and the
Origins of Slavophilism

Abbott Gleason

Harvard University Press
Cambridge, Massachusetts
1972

To
Mary Eleanor Abbott Gleason
Sarell Everett Gleason

Contents

Illustrations

Acknowledgments

I should first like to thank my parents, who in the deepest kind of way made a historian of me. This book is dedicated to them. I owe my initial enthusiasm for Russian history primarily to two men: Professor Martin Malia of the University of California at Berkeley and particularly Professor James Billington of Princeton, who took extraordinary pains with me when I was a feckless and undisciplined undergraduate. Professor Richard Pipes of Harvard University directed the doctoral dissertation upon which this book is based and gave me a sympathetic and helpful reading at a later stage in its development. I should also like to thank the following colleagues and friends for their advice, criticism, and encouragement: Daniel Field, Edward Keenan, Barrington Moore, Jr., and Norman Rich. My wife, Sarah, helped this study along in every way and at every stage.

Brown University, through its program of summer grants, and the American Philosophical Society helped to finance the metamorphosis of thesis into book. Above all, however, my debt is to the Russian Research Center of Harvard University. The Center not only helped finance this study from its inception, but also — and more significantly — it provided a place where a young historian could steep himself in the history and culture of a country which is in so many ways inaccessible today, particularly to one who, like myself, has no familial connection with it. To all those with whom I talked at so many lunches, whose privacy I so often invaded, and whose brains I picked for every kind of information — to all of them I express my gratitude for the education they gave me.

Finally, I would like to express my appreciation to two distinguished European scholars. Professor Andrzej Walicki of the University of Warsaw introduced me to the writings of Karl Mannheim and the sociology of knowledge and in general helped me to realize what kind of history I wanted to write and how. His book, *W kręgu konserwatywnej utopii*, embodies his own conclusions about "utopian thought" in nineteenth-century Russia, and I believe that it will long remain preeminent in the field. Dr. Eberhard Müller of the University of Tübingen, himself the author of a learned and fascinating study of Kireevsky's thought (*Russischer Intellekt in europäischer Krise: Ivan V. Kireevskij, 1806–1856*), was kind enough to make available to me a number of microfilms, through the *Institut für osteuropäische Geschichte und Landeskunde* of the University of Tübingen, but I am even more beholden to him for the stimulation which his book afforded. In conclusion, I am grateful to Professor J. Thomas Shaw of the University of Wisconsin for permission to quote from his English translation of the letters of Alexander Pushkin.

Abbott Gleason

Providence, R.I.
February 1971

European and Muscovite

Introduction

*I have no imagination, properly speaking, only
memory.*
— Ivan Kireevsky, in a letter to his mother

For the relatively small number of readers who have already done
some exploring into prerevolutionary cultural history, it should
not be necessary to set forth the reasons why there should be a
biography of Ivan Kireevsky in English, despite the fact that he
was not an original thinker of the first rank. For other readers a
word or two may not be out of place. Kireevsky was one of those
useful and often fascinating men who transmit ideas from one
culture to another, who translate them into a form in which they
can become available to people who could not themselves have
gone to the fountainhead, or even have used these insights, perhaps, in their original form. Ivan Kireevsky served in this fashion
as a transmitter of a number of important ideas and intuitions
which first received coherent form in the intellectual counterrevolution in Europe that began in the last years of the eighteenth
century. Probably the richest and most varied expression of these
irrationalist and reactionary impulses emerged from the German
culture of the early nineteenth century.

In the period which spans the lives of J. G. Herder and Hegel,
that is, roughly from the 1770's to the 1830's, German culture
went through a remarkable period of productivity and achievement. German philosophy and literary criticism, German ideas on
the nature of society and the writing of history came gradually

1

to dominate the thinking of Europeans, to occupy the place which had formerly been held by French classicism. By 1830, France itself was succumbing; but nowhere were German ideas more eagerly received and more hotly debated than in central and eastern Europe. Only the English-speaking world remained to some degree isolated from the triumphal march of German culture.

These developments are of course well known, and the fact that at this late date it is not absolutely redundant to remind American readers of them testifies to the degree to which America — and England — managed to escape their influence — or at least to remain unaware of the source of a good many powerful and influential ideas.

A great deal has been done in recent years to bridge the gap (which still exists) between Anglo-American and German culture. Our philosophers have begun to take the German philosophical tradition seriously, both as a central historical fact and as an important contemporary influence on their own ideas. From the most various standpoints and with the most divergent motives, Americans are discovering the philosophy of Hegel and the intellectual tradition of which he was, in a sense, the culmination.

German thought in this period, however, was much more than just a preamble to Hegel, or to Hegel and Marx. For a variety of reasons, the conservative response to the French Revolution found its most able spokesmen in Germany,[1] although France, too, produced a number of astute critics. German political romanticism, the major current of intellectual hostility to Enlightenment thought, had an enormous effect on European intellectual life. Its influence, furthermore, extended far beyond men and movements which we now think of as "conservative." The whole genesis of sociology, for instance, was crucially affected, if not absolutely defined, by "counterrevolutionary" thought. In a real sense, men could not even conceive of "society" until the hegemony of eighteenth-century rationalism had been at least partially shattered. Then, too, the nascent socialist movement was deeply influenced by the critique of Enlightenment and liberal values provided by romanticism — in both its political and nonpolitical forms. If "community" was discovered by the right, it was quickly taken over by the left.

In the English-speaking world, too, the currents of thought emanating from Germany had their spokesmen, interpreters, and sometimes plagiarists. In England, there were — most obviously — Coleridge and Carlyle; in the United States there was Emerson and perhaps Poe. The stature and achievement of the men who spread German romantic ideas throughout the rest of the world varies considerably, but they were united in a fundamental way by their missionary role. To some extent they were all writing what Mme. de Staël called *De l'Allemagne*. Ivan Kireevsky belongs to this group.[2]

There is, of course, an important difference between the situation of Carlyle or Emerson in the English-speaking world and that of Kireevsky in Russia. The former were relatively isolated: German thought remained only one intellectual current among many. In Russia, however, the situation was quite different. Between the 1820's and the 1860's — roughly — German philosophy utterly dominated the views and opinions of Russian intellectuals as they attempted to answer key questions about the essence of the Russian people, the historical evolution of the Russian state, and the current situation of Russian culture. In a sense, the debate between the Slavophiles and Westerners was little more than a reworking, in Russian terms, of the arguments which conservative followers of Herder and Schelling were having with Hegelians and particularly with Left Hegelians.[3]

Ivan Kireevsky was thus only one of a number of Russians who used German ideas in an attempt to unravel what subsequently came to be known as the "cursed questions," but he was one of the most significant. He was a member of the first Russian "circle" devoted to German philosophy, the so-called "Lovers of Wisdom," which met for several years before the Decembrist Revolt of 1825. And — more significantly — he was the most important theoretician, or myth-maker, of Russian Slavophilism, a movement which attempted to define the essence of Russia's historical development and destiny with reference to a counterrevolutionary model of idealized communal social forms.

The Slavophiles made up one party, although far from a unified one, in the great debate of the 1840's with the so-called "Westerners," likewise a less than monolithic group. But Slavophilism was more than an interesting and dramatic moment in Russian intellectual history. The ideas and attitudes of Kireevsky, A. S. Khomiakov, and their younger friends and colleagues had a long and pervasive influence on virtually every area of Russian culture. Slavophilism was the form in which the ideas of the romantic counterrevolution entered Russia's bloodstream. History, literature, folklore, political theory, theology — none escaped its influence. Even the revolutionary movement, against the early stages of which Kireevsky struggled so valiantly, was vitally affected by several of "his" ideas, in particular the notion of Russia's essential uniqueness and the central place of the peasant commune in the Russian body social.

The Slavophiles can be properly termed "reactionaries" — and not only in a strictly Marxist sense of the term. Kireevsky was reactionary in that he rejected the major social and intellectual developments of his time: rationalism and secularism, in the broadest sense of those terms, and the industrial revolution. He came to oppose not only the obviously "left" phenomena of political and economic liberalism, but the bureaucratic absolutism of Nicholas' Russia as well. Russia in his time, he felt, had nearly lost its religiously based, communal social order, and the political institutions which corresponded to it had been thoroughly perverted by the ruling dynasty ever since the time of Peter the Great. In other words, the state had been *the* revolutionary force in Russian life until Kireevsky's own time, and their perception of this fact made the Slavophiles an oppositional force in Russian intellectual life — whether they liked it or not. Their view of the relations which ought to obtain between state and society, their essential hostility to an activist, rationalizing, modern state, was nearly as repugnant to the Russian government as the eclectic radicalism of the Westerners.

How Ivan Kireevsky came to occupy this unhappy position, and what he made of it, is the subject of this book. In the jargon of the day, it might be called "the making of an aristocratic conservative." Any analysis of this process involves a further undertaking: a description of the special form that aristocratic and reactionary views took in pre-Emancipation Russia. To address oneself to these questions is also to generalize, to some degree, about the political and social position of the estate to which Kireevsky belonged — the Russian gentry. Finally, the history of Ivan Kireevsky provides another illustration of the deep similarities between those who criticized the emerging world of nineteenth-century Europe with reference to the values of the past — in an idealized form — and those who fought against their age by trying to look beyond it.

I. Family and Childhood

*Every man carries within himself a world made
up of all that he has seen and loved; and it is to
this world that he returns incessantly, though
he may pass through, and seem to inhabit, a world
quite foreign to it.*
— Chateaubriand, *Voyage en Italie*

If one wishes to maintain that Ivan Kireevsky's writings are
basically a defense of a kind of life that he knew and loved
against forces and events which seemed to threaten it, the importance of his childhood is immediately obvious. With men
like Herzen and Tolstoy, one is principally concerned to discover
what kind of milieu helped to create such rebellious spirits. But
Kireevsky wanted to defend his parents, not to repudiate them,
to preserve their way of life, not to destroy it. Thus what small
information we have on the Kireevsky family is of the greatest
value.

The Kireevsky traditions were religious and conservative, and
the family itself had been based in the Belëv-Kozel'sk* area,
where they owned "numerous properties," since at least 1600.
According to Peter Kireevsky (Ivan's brother), Vasily Semënovich Kireevsky, a nobleman (*dvorianin*) of Belëv, received his
former *pomestie*, the village of Dolbino, as a *votchina* "in the
early seventeenth century." [1] We may assume that he performed
some notable service for one of the tsars during the Time of
Troubles. Both the sons of Vasily Semënovich took part in the
tortuous military and diplomatic campaigns in the Ukraine against

---

* The Russian soft sign (*miagkii znak*) has been retained in translitera-
tion and is indicated by an apostrophe.

7

Hetman Doroshenko and the Poles. The elder, Ivan Vasil'evich, died a monk in the Kirilo-Belozersky monastery. His son, Ivan Ivanovich, was a *stol'nik* under both Aleksei Mikhailovich and Fëdor Alekseevich. He left an indignant memoir behind him, criticizing Peter the Great, who had made him shave his beard.[2] Ivan Ivanovich's grandson, Ivan Vasil'evich, was the first Marshal of the Nobility in the Kozel'sk district of Kaluga province. He married Elizaveta Afanas'evna Tyrtova, and they had two children: a girl who died mad, some time after 1812, and Vasily Ivanovich, the father of Ivan and Peter, who was born in 1773.[3] Thus, however "rootless" many service gentry families may have been, the Kireevsky family was certainly characterized by a long and intimate relationship to a circumscribed geographical area.

Our knowledge of the important events in Vasily Ivanovich's life is, to say the least, skeletal. During Paul's reign, when Vasily Ivanovich was in his middle twenties, he retired from the guards with the rank of "second-major" and went to live at Dolbino. In 1807 he took part in the mobilization of the militia, but before things had gotten very far Alexander I signed the Treaty of Tilsit. In 1812, with the French in Moscow, Vasily Ivanovich moved his family to the Kireevskaia Sloboda near Orël.[4] There, entirely on his own initiative, he simply took command of the local hospital, which was in the last stages of chaos and disintegration, and in which the patients were mostly wounded French soldiers. After heroic labors of reorganization and actual doctoring, he died of typhoid on November 1, 1812.[5]

About his character, opinions, and style of life we are rather better informed, and the agreement among those who knew him was substantial. "Severe," "pious," "melancholy," and "eccentric" are words which occur again and again. K. D. Kavelin (whose parents had known Vasily Ivanovich personally) thought him "peculiar to the point of strangeness," and noted that his hatred of Voltaire was such that he used to seek out his works in Moscow bookstores and burn them.[6] Shortly after Vasily Ivanovich's marriage to the sixteen-year-old Avdot'ia Petrovna Iushkova, the governor of Kaluga province stopped at Dolbino on a tour, expecting to spend the night. But because he had brought a "young woman" with him, his host refused to entertain them, not even allowing the girl to come in to fix her hair and wash. His will was unshakable, as it always seems to have been in what he regarded as matters of religion and morality.[7]

His puritanism, however, did not entail a mean or uncomfortable style of life. At his beloved Dolbino he "built a new house, magnificent, according to his contemporaries, of wood faced with marble, surrounded by splendid gardens."[8] His pride and joy was an English garden, and he loved English literature and what he knew of English life and "liberty." His bred-in-the-bone Russian patriotism blended with his sense of duty and noblesse oblige into something approaching an ideal of citizenship, which prompted him at one point to draw up an elaborate project for the Emperor on the control of epidemic disease, with particular reference to the peasantry.[9] And "having been elected a judge in his district, he rapidly won general esteem by his justice and inflexible honesty, as well as provoking general terror by his severity."[10]

His love of learning was enormous and encompassed both the arts and the sciences. His rich library included books in Russian, German, French, English, and Italian. In his youth he had translated and apparently even published a number of novels and tales, but at the time of his marriage the natural sciences were occupying him ever more completely.[11] He built a chemistry laboratory at Dolbino — a nice complement to the English garden. He studied medicine with genuine seriousness and apparently had a considerable, if informal, medical practice. The atmosphere of learning at Dolbino extended even to the serfs. Of the fifteen male house servitors, six were literate and "enthusiastic readers," according to Alexander Peterson, who was thoroughly familiar with life at Dolbino.[12]

Vasily Ivanovich's character and style of life make one think immediately of Freemasonry, and although we have no evidence that he had ever actually joined a lodge, Ivan subsequently told Peter Ivanovich Bartenev that his father had been "of Novikov's persuasion." [13] Ivan Lopukhin, a famous Freemason and devotee of the "Invisible Church," stood godfather to Ivan and sent him books.

With reference to the childhood of Ivan Kireevsky, the question of the relations between master and man, between the *barin* and the "people" at Dolbino, deserves particular attention. One of the principal contentions of the defenders of the traditional order in early nineteenth-century Europe was that the introduction of abstract notions of "equality" destroyed an existing harmony in the name of intellectual constructions which had nothing to do with "life." In looking for the origins of Ivan Kireevsky's complex attitude toward the "people," one must begin insofar as possible where he began: with Vasily Ivanovich's benevolent paternalism at Dolbino.

According to Peterson, Vasily Ivanovich's peasants were all reasonably well off and "many were prosperous." On one occasion, peasant representatives from a neighboring estate came to see Vasily Ivanovich.

"Buy us, Batiushka," they said. "We want to be yours and nobody else's." "Brothers," Kireevsky said to them, "I don't want to enlarge my estate; I can't do it for your pleasure. I haven't the money on hand." Several days later . . . the representatives were back: "Good *barin*, take us for yours. Since you don't have enough money, we bring you ours. We want to belong to you." Vasily Ivanovich bought [them]. After their installation, they invited him, along with the little *barin* [Ivan], to an entertainment. It went splendidly; there . was even ice cream; a cook was hired and crockery rented from the neighborhood of Belëv. The leader of the peasants was a dealer in skins named Drykin.

It is difficult to believe that events like these were not important in forming the attitudes of the young *barin.*

There was no sort of corporal punishment [continued Peterson] no cudgels or birch rods. The principal punishment at Dolbino was prostration before the icon, forty times and more (depending on the offense) and the Chair. This chair was a heavy oak block, a stump weighing two or more puds, upon which one could sit. . . . The guilty party was manacled to it by a long chain on one hand.[14]

The importance of moral disapproval and religious atonement is the more striking in a country and class so addicted to the knout. In this respect too, Vasily Ivanovich was an unusual man.

On Christmas Eve, Peterson reported,

certain of the house serfs gathered in the master's hall — one would be dressed as an ordinary rooster or as an Indian cock, another as a crane; there was a bear with his comical keeper, a mounted horseman, *baba-yaga* in a mortar with a pestle and broom. . . . The would-be crane put a sheepskin coat over his head and walked bent over with his hands behind his head, now pecking on the ground, now raising his head and calling drolly like a crane. Sometimes complicated masks appeared. Kireevsky's valet was in the habit of appearing as Aesop; he would recite from memory a fable of Khemnitser, with comical asides. Another house serf came on in the vestments of a bishop, and setting a lectern down in front of him, began to preach a sermon — humorous, but decent in tone and content. Nevertheless, Vasily Ivanovich stopped him and sent him out of the room (he was very pious).[15]

It is clear that Vasily Ivanovich's peasants, like nearly everyone else, regarded him with a mixture of affection and awe, or even fear.

The question of "wholeness" was subsequently to occupy Ivan Kireevsky a great deal — wholeness and harmoniousness in cul-

ture and in the individual personality. At the root of this preoccupation, at least in part, was the contrast, even collision, between the microcosm of Dolbino and the macrocosm of the
Russia of Nicholas I, between the kind of patriarchal and traditional order we have been describing and a frequently brutal
bureaucratic absolutism. Life at Dolbino was an integrated life,
in the sense that the "contradictions" within the traditional order
were not yet apparent. As Koyré shrewdly pointed out, Vasily
Ivanovich's broad culture, his love of England, in no way dimin-
ished his "Russianness" — or so, at any rate, it must have appeared to his eldest son.[16] There was no apparent contradiction
between Vasily Ivanovich's preoccupation with chemistry and his
firm religious convictions. One may, perhaps, go a bit further.
Ivan Kireevsky was subsequently to construct an ideal of medieval Russia: a land of autonomous, communal organizations,
"ruled," if that is the right word, by a monarch who judged, or
even regulated, but who adhered to tradition and was never an
innovator. Surely this model is related to life at Dolbino in the
time of Vasily Ivanovich.

   The austere piety of his father was far from being Ivan's only
exposure to religion. Christianity must have seemed to the boy
inextricably involved with the society around him, with the
people and their life. The village church at Dolbino was famous
for the miracle-working icon of the Assumption of the Mother of
God. "Toward Assumption Day," Peterson recalled,

a multitude of people began to arrive from neighboring villages and
towns, and in front of the church building a fair took place, sump-
tuous by village standards. Merchants put up a vast array of tents,
with splendid wares of all kinds; there were long rows of stalls jammed
together, offering fruit and berries. . . . But Vasily Ivanovich would
not permit the sale of vodka. Even on the day of the fair the pur-
veyors of vodka (*otkupshchiki*) could not cope with him, or even
defend their right to reign over the tavern. There were no police
present at all, but everything went off happily and in an orderly way.[17]

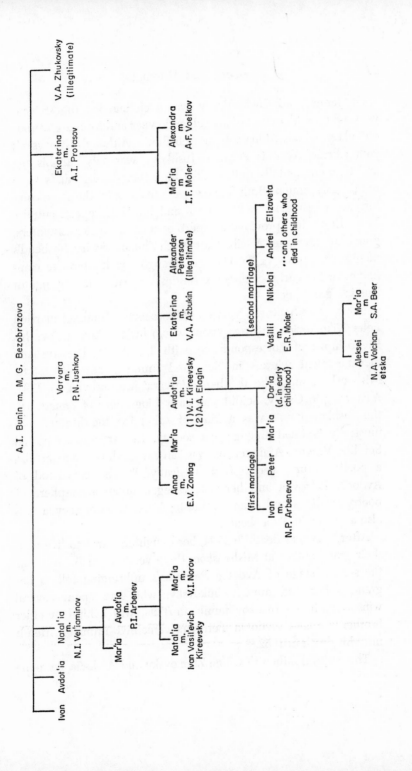

A.I. Bunin m. M.G. Bezobrazova

Ivan

Avdot'ia
Natal'ia
m.
N.I. Vel'iaminov

Mar'ia
Avdot'ia
m.
P.I. Arbenev

Natal'ia
Ivan Vasil'evich
Kireevsky

Mar'ia
m.
V.I. Norov

Anna
m.
E.V. Zontag

Mar'ia

Avdot'ia
m.
(1)V.I. Kireevsky
(2)A.A. Elagin

Ekaterina
m.
V.A. Azbukin

Alexander
Peterson
(illegitimate)

Varvara
m.
P.N. Iushkov

(first marriage)
Ivan
m.
N.P. Arbeneva

Peter

Mar'ia

Daria
(d. in early
childhood)

(second marriage)
Vasilii
m.
E.R. Moler

Nikolai

Andrei

Elizaveta

...and others who
died in childhood

Aleksei
m.
N.A. Volchan-
etska

Mar'ia
m
S.A. Beer

Ekaterina
m.
A.I. Protasov

Mar'ia
m
I.F. Moler

Alexandra
m
A.F. Voeikov

V.A. Zhukovsky
(illegitimate)

On January 13, 1805, Vasily Ivanovich married the sixteen-year-old granddaughter of a local landowner and former governor of Tula province, Afanasy Ivanovich Bunin. Although Kireevsky's young bride, Avdot'ia Petrovna Iushkova, was only half his age and temperamentally quite unlike him, their backgrounds were remarkably similar. Both families were marked by the same combination of Russian traditionalism and broad European culture. Mme. Bunin had provided a superb education for her daughters, granddaughters, and Vasily Andreevich Zhukovsky, her husband's illegitimate son by a Turkish girl brought back from the campaigns of the early seventeen-seventies, and subsequently one of Russia's great poets.

Ivan's grandmother, Varvara Afanaseevna Bunina, married Peter Nikolaevich Iushkov, about whom little is known save his friendship and correspondence with Lavater.[18] The Iushkov ménage spent winters in Tula and summers at their estate, Mishenskoe, until the death of Varvara Afanaseevna in 1794. According to Carl v. Seidlitz, an early biographer of Zhukovsky, the Iushkov house was a kind of salon for the literary and musically inclined among Tula society. In particular, reported Seidlitz, Varvara Afanaseevna was "an extraordinary personality, a poetic nature, very gifted musically."[19] The childhood of Avdot'ia Petrovna and her sisters began in an atmosphere of poetry readings and chamber music; Varvara Afanaseevna was also a power in Tula theater.

After Varvara's death in 1794, her daughters came to live with their grandmother at Mishenskoe, three versts from Belëv. Thus the second stage of Avdot'ia Petrovna's upbringing fell to her grandmother and aunts. Zhukovsky, who had spent several winters with the Iushkov family in Tula, was a kind of elder brother; he and Avdot'ia Petrovna remained intimate friends until his death in 1852.[20]

The cultural milieu in which Zhukovsky and Avdot'ia Petrovna found themselves at Mishenskoe was "at once Russian and French."[21] Of Avdot'ia Petrovna's governesses, we know only Mme. Dorer by name, a Frenchwoman "of quality" — on one authority a countess[22] — in flight from the Revolution. She and her unknown colleagues did their work well, for in spite of Avdot'ia Petrovna's subsequent role as grande dame of the Slavophile salon, her favorite writers remained French.[23] It is probable that Racine and Fénelon were introduced to Avdot'ia Petrovna by the governesses, while Rousseau and Bernardin de St.-Pierre must have come later, through the agency of Zhukovsky and his university friends. Her Russian tutor was a curious and attractive provincial intellectual named Filat' Gavrilovich Pokrovsky, who ran the school in Tula. His interests ranged from Russian literature to political economy and geology, and he signed his occasional articles in *Passing Time Pleasantly and Usefully* (*Priiatnoe i poleznoe prepovozhdenie vremeni*) "the Philosopher of Alaun Mountain, Living at the Foot of Mount Utla."[24]

The Iushkov family spent a number of winters in Moscow, where Avdot'ia Petrovna met Zhukovsky's friends the Turgenevs and the Sokovnins. Literary taste, of course, continued heavily French; Nicholas Karamzin, a relation of Mme. Bunin and a frequent guest in the house, was also greatly admired, as was the poetaster I. I. Dmitriev.

By 1803, Zhukovsky had translated Gray's "Elegy in a Country Churchyard" and discovered that the English had a sentimental literature that might bear comparison with the French, but of his circle only Andrei Turgenev was a real convert to German literature. It was not until 1806 that Zhukovsky did his first "imitation" of Schiller, and not until 1809 that he translated Goethe. It is probable that Avdot'ia Petrovna knew little enough of German literature before her marriage.

Life with the austere Vasily Ivanovich Kireevsky must have

been difficult for her at first; she was a gay and whimsical child
and had not been consulted about her bridegroom. Zhukovsky,
for one, seems to have been against the marriage at first, and
the two saw less of each other in the years immediately following. Nevertheless, things seem to have proceeded well enough,
and if Vasily Ivanovich "reinforced" her religiosity (as Koyré
perhaps euphemistically put it), she brought him her love of
literature, art, and flowers. Perhaps she was even able to soften
somewhat his powerful sense of duty.

But however compatible and happy they may, on the whole,
have been, Vasily Ivanovich's unworldliness, untidiness, and
eccentricity must have been hard for a totally inexperienced
sixteen-year-old to cope with. According to the historian, Gershenzon, Vasily Ivanovich was

extraordinarily slovenly in his appearance. He read a great deal, and
loved to read locked up in his room, lying on the floor. Around him
on the floor stood the dirty cups — tidying up his study was forbidden,
as was sweeping or dusting. After his marriage . . . guests who had
stayed with them reported that the only clean object in the house
was the young hostess. In ordinary matters of daily life he was as
naive as a child. Thus, living in Moscow with a wife who was little
more than a girl, he would leave the house in the morning without
giving her money for the shopping; she had no idea how to feed her
considerable domestic establishment. Having spent the day in some
bookstore or other, he would come home late with a heap of books,
or sometimes with a heap of old china, which he was continually
and zealously hunting.[25]

Four children were born into this curious household: Ivan, on
March 22, 1806, Peter, on February 11, 1808, and Mar'ia, on
August 8, 1811. A second daughter, Dar'ia, died in early childhood.[26] Winters were spent in Moscow, summers at Dolbino.
Vasily Ivanovich managed his estates, worked in his laboratory,
read voraciously (if sporadically), and indulged his passion for
china. Avdot'ia Petrovna was apparently not wholly absorbed

with her growing family and household management; she found time, in 1808–09, to help Zhukovsky with the correspondence arising from his editorship of the *Messenger of Europe* (*Vestnik Evropy*) and in certain matters of translation as well.[27]

But in spite of the lightness and gaiety which Avdot'ia Petrovna initially brought to Dolbino, various "dark forebodings and passions came to dwell there," according to Gershenzon. "The family chronicle of the Kireevskys and their relatives is full of all kinds of mystical stories, unexpected coincidences, and miracles. The spirits of certain old women who had died a hundred years ago appeared in the house at Dolbino. It is said that at the time of Vasily Ivanovich's death . . . he arrived at Dolbino in a carriage, went into the house, and shouted for his man. All the house serfs saw him and heard his voice."[28] Everyone in the family had prophetic and revelatory dreams, and all were prey to an intense concern about matters of health. Neither Ivan nor Peter was ever free from this anxiety. Gershenzon believed that the extraordinary closeness of the family, an almost neurotic sensitivity to each other's emotional nuance, was the salient feature in the childhood of all three young Kireevskys.[29] The death of Vasily Ivanovich and the isolation of the mother and three children at Dolbino must have fostered this intimacy, particularly in view of the relative closeness in age between mother and children. It is tempting to try to account for the vivid reality of the supernatural phenomena which Gershenzon describes in terms of Vasily Ivanovich's religiosity, with its possible component of occult Freemasonry, and Avdot'ia Petrovna's aestheticism and sensitivity to the natural world, but these are at best reasonable speculations. What is certain is that the Kireevsky family milieu must have been fertile soil for a variety of mysticisms. German idealism was one way of ordering and systematizing such perceptions and experiences.

Napoleon's invasion and the death of Vasily Ivanovich in the hospital at Orël in 1812 drastically altered the life of the Kire-evsky family. The young widow took her children and moved in with her aunt, Ekaterina Afanaseevna Protasova, at Muratovo, near Orël. Zhukovsky was there too, and there she recovered from her grief.

One is tempted to say that it was only with Vasily Ivanovich's death that Avdot'ia Petrovna became an adult; that this seems so to us is in large measure the result of circumstances. Between 1813 and 1817 we see her, not as the child bride or the young mother, but primarily as an important protagonist in a bitter and protracted family drama: Zhukovsky's unsuccessful courtship of Mar'ia Andreevna Protasova. In Avdot'ia Petrovna's relations with the principal actors — Zhukovsky himself, his half-sister, Ekaterina Afanaseevna Protasova, and the latter's daughter, Mar'ia Andreevna, we perceive her directly for the first time. We see that she is passionate in her defense of Zhukovsky, that she is impulsive, that she is loving, that she is not always patient. We see that she is the sort of person who gets involved in other people's lives, and not merely because her own is, for the moment, not very interesting.

Briefly, the story of Zhukovsky's unhappy involvement with Mar'ia Andreevna is as follows.[30] In 1802 Zhukovsky left Moscow, after a very brief stint in government service, to devote himself to self-cultivation and poetry, in a rural setting. He lived briefly at Mishenskoe, then in Belëv, and finally bought a modest estate near Muratovo, where Ekaterina Afanaseevna Protasova, who had just been widowed, was bringing up her children. Both his sympathy and his pedagogical bent were easily aroused, and he was soon tutoring Mar'ia and her younger sister, Alexandra. Soon thereafter he found his feelings for Mar'ia Andreevna changing and realized (this was still in 1805) that he was falling in love.[31] He was twenty-two and she was twelve. He kept this development a secret until 1811, when his conviction that Mar'ia

Andreevna shared his feelings led him to confide in Mme. Protasova. Her refusal was immediate and direct. Although illegitimate, Zhukovsky was, she felt, Mar'ia's uncle — at any rate in the eyes of God. Ekaterina Afanaseevna never wavered in her opposition, although most of the family, and many friends, took Zhukovsky's part.

This was the situation in 1812, when Avdot'ia Petrovna became a widow. At the end of 1814, the Protasov family moved to Dorpat, where Alexander Voeikov, Alexandra's husband, had just received a professorship, thanks to the good offices of Zhukovsky and Alexander Turgenev. Zhukovsky, meanwhile, continued to pursue his suit until, in November 1815, Mar'ia Andreevna decided to accept an offer of marriage from a Professor Moier of the University of Dorpat. She was certainly not in love with him; she merely wished to make an end to the incessant emotional strain and periodic strife which the situation had imposed on the entire family, and Moier seems to have been a kindly man, who could promise peace and stability. Zhukovsky, initially beside himself, adapted, one feels, almost too readily; his behavior seems to have been a truly Rousseauian mixture of deeply felt emotion, clumsy naiveté, and rhetorical highmindedness. He continued to spend a great deal of time with Mar'ia Andreevna after her marriage, although somewhat less as time passed. The whole rather miserable affair terminated with her death in childbirth early in 1823.

Avdot'ia Petrovna was very closely involved, particularly until 1817, when she married a second time. She and Zhukovsky had been intimate friends from a very young age,[32] and Mar'ia Andreevna adored her: the girl had trees in her garden named for all the Kireevskys, and subsequently found one for Elagin,[33] Avdot'ia Petrovna's second husband. Avdot'ia Petrovna initially supported Zhukovsky, but subsequently urged him to abandon his suit. Their friendship was of such a passionate intensity at this

point as to rouse the suspicions of the reader of their correspondence, but apparently Avdot'ia Petrovna was never really more
than a dear sister to Zhukovsky.

These relationships, then, were often tense. Avdot'ia Petrovna
would become impatient with Mar'ia Andreevna's sentimental
effusions, scold her for being insufficiently loyal to Zhukovsky —
and then Zhukovsky would reproach Avdot'ia Petrovna for her
"severity." A curious sidelight on the whole affair is provided by
the passion of Mar'ia Andreevna for Avdot'ia Petrovna, who
seems to have served as a kind of symbol of her happy and
tranquil childhood, when Zhukovsky was a kind of revered and
learned elder brother, rather than an emotionally exhausting
suitor.

Early in the summer of 1813, Avdot'ia Petrovna decided that
she should leave Muratovo and go back to Dolbino with the
children. Zhukovsky urged her to postpone this step. He felt
that her decision to return was really only a morbid attempt to
reactivate her grief by returning to the scenes of her married life.
Displaying an insight which he often lacked with regard to his
own emotions, he told her that she regarded her grief as a kind
of moral obligation which she must continue to fulfill.[34] It may
also be that Zhukovsky felt the need of an ally in the household
at Muratovo. In any case, the return was postponed until the
spring of 1814.

Soon thereafter Zhukovsky joined her; he had renewed his
pleas to Mme. Protasov in the summer of 1814 and had again
been refused. At the end of August he took refuge at Dolbino for
several months. The Kireevsky estate was both a physical and a
spiritual sanctuary for him, despite the fact that Avdot'ia Petrovna
was now urging him to drop his suit. His particular fondness for
Ivan and little Peter appears to date from this period; they
appear frequently in his so-called "Dolbino poems," delightful

and often humorous verses which present something of a contrast to the air of literary melancholy more usual to him.[35] This
was Zhukovsky's only period of real closeness to Ivan and Peter;
he saw them only fleetingly over the next sixteen years. Ivan
was eight and Peter was six in 1814. This fact needs to be
stressed, since there has been a tendency among historians —
based on Kireevsky family tradition — to attribute to Zhukovsky
a very major role in Ivan's personal and intellectual development.[36] Zhukovsky never lost interest in the two brothers, ex-
horted their mother about this or that tutor (none of whom was
actually taken on), sent them lists of books, and rendered them
both important services later in their careers. But as far as direct
influence is concerned, it is difficult to maintain that Zhukovsky
did more than reinforce in the boy the feeling that literature was
a vital part of the life of the individual, and, perhaps more important, that the creation of a high literary culture in Russia
was a sacred task that one owed to the Fatherland. Although
Zhukovsky is rightly known as one of the most important bearers
of German literature to the Russians, it must not be forgotten
that he had almost no interest in or understanding of philosophy
and that his literary sensibility was that of late eighteenth-
century sentimentalism.[37] He could produce a beautiful translation of *Der Erlkönig*, but Goethe's thought — to say nothing of
Schelling's aesthetics — was a closed book to him.[38] He urged that
Ivan attend a German university in the course of his education,
but it is difficult to imagine a young man of Ivan's interests
studying elsewhere in Europe.[39]

Avdot'ia Petrovna remained at Dolbino from 1814 until 1821,
when the family moved to Moscow for the sake of the children's
education. How successful she was at managing the Kireevsky
estates, with their "thousands of souls," [40] we do not know. In
1815 Avdot'ia Petrovna was able to lend Zhukovsky 2,000 rubles

for the printing of his poems, although he noted guiltily in a letter that he was afraid that she needed the money for her "debt" and for "constructions" at Dolbino.[41] Nevertheless, there was obviously no major financial crisis.

We know almost nothing about the life of the family at Dolbino in this period. Zhukovsky's voluminous letters to Avdot'ia Petrovna, our principal source, reflect his life and adventures almost exclusively. Only rarely do we get real news of her. One such exception was a letter of 1815, in which we learn that a certain S. M. Sokovnin was "seeking the hand" of Avdot'ia Petrovna.[42] But nothing is said about the origins or development of his courtship or why it came to nothing.

Zhukovsky received another blow in the fall of 1815, when he received word of Mar'ia Andreevna's betrothal to Moier, the Dorpat professor. The decision to take this step was made even more agonizing for her by Avdot'ia Petrovna's reproachful letters. Early in February, Mar'ia Andreevna wrote to Avdot'ia Petrovna that she was simply desperate to see her and talk matters over. Avdot'ia Petrovna, presumably hoping to prevent the betrothal at the eleventh hour, simply packed her bags and set out for Dorpat, a journey of well over 1,250 versts. But only 50 versts from Dolbino her carriage fell through the ice while crossing a lake; she nevertheless continued on to Moscow, where she was obliged to remain, having come down with what was apparently pneumonia.[43] It was some time before either Dolbino or Dorpat discovered what had happened. Zhukovsky was horrified, but the lecture he administered had an undercurrent of admiration. "Such an angel-demon," he concluded his recitation of her sins, "could only be you." [44]

This incident was oddly prophetic of another adventure which took place almost a year later. According to Gershenzon,

on the eleventh of January, 1817, on Avdot'ia Petrovna's birthday, the wedding of her best friend, Mar'ia Andreevna Protasova, was sched-

uled to take place in Dorpat. . . . For some reason the wedding did
not take place on that date and was postponed until the fourteenth
of January. Avdot'ia Petrovna hurried from Dolbino, but the ice in
the Oka caved in under her carriage and she nearly drowned, caught
a terrible cold, and had to remain for a considerable time in Kozel'sk.
There she became close to her third cousin . . . Aleksei Andreevich
Elagin, with whom she soon [on July 4, 1817] made her second
marriage.[45]

Elagin emerges from the memoir literature of the period as a
rather indistinct figure, always in the background, always overshadowed by his more brilliant family. According to Khomiakov,
he appeared "coarse and uncouth" but was in fact warm-hearted
and intelligent.[46] Elagin had fought in the Napoleonic wars and
in the process spent some time in Germany, returning to Russia
with a copy of Kant's *Critique of Pure Reason* in his knapsack.
Shortly thereafter, through his friend Vellansky, a professor at
Moscow University, he became intensely interested in the philosophy of Schelling, which he had first encountered in Germany.
To while away the evenings at Dolbino, he eventually undertook
the translation of Schelling's *Philosophical Letters on Dogmatism
and Criticism,* an important early work. His philosophical outlook
seems to have been considerably more latitudinarian than that of
Vasily Ivanovich Kireevsky, for Locke and Helvétius were also
represented in his library. According to his son, Nikolai Alekseevich Elagin, Ivan's philosophical orientation began here.[47]

As with so much else about life at Dolbino at this time, we
know very little about Ivan's early education. We do, however,
have some intriguing indirect evidence, in the form of a few
leaves from the diary of Ivan's younger sister, Mar'ia Vasil'evna,
in which she describes the progress of her studies. Her account
dates from the 1820's, but presumably the formidable curriculum
which she outlined was not so very different from what Ivan and
Peter had gone through a few years earlier.

Fr. [she noted]: translate Socrates, grammar and read Voltaire's tragedy. Ger.: grammar, read 1 volume of the History of the Netherlands, translate Undine. Eng.: read Lalla Rookh. Russ.: translate Fénelon's Educ. des Fillis [sic], learn 100 pp. of poetry, 3 pp. a day. Read 5 volumes of Karamzin thoroughly and 4 volumes of Sismondi. In addition to other pieces, learn Ries's concerto by heart.

Fr. Once a week on Monday trans. 6 pp. from 11 to 1. Germ. 3 times a week, Tuesday, Thursday, Saturday. Translate 10 pp. each time and read 25, morning until 1. Eng. once, Monday evening. Russ. twice a week: Wednesday, Friday, 15 pp. a time; 9 pp. of poetry each time. 3 times a week read Karamzin from 5 to 7 after dinner. Twice a week Sismondi from 9 to 11.[48]

All this, of course, is only a statement of good intentions. Nevertheless, given the family's seriousness about culture, it is a fair assumption that all three children had a regime of this kind laid out for them and more or less adhered to it — with impressive results. No wonder both Kireevsky brothers were among the best-educated men of their time.

The question of a suitable tutor for the boys was a frequent subject of discussion in Zhukovsky's letters to Avdot'ia Petrovna after his departure from Dolbino at the end of 1814. It was difficult to find someone who knew French, German, Latin and Greek, mathematics, and history — particularly when he had to have a congenial personality as well and not mind living in the country. By the fall of 1816, Zhukovsky appears finally to have produced a candidate — a German by the name of Cedergren, whom he had met in Dorpat. Just as he was writing Avdot'ia Petrovna to this effect, she hired a man named Wagner (also a German), who, curiously enough, had come to Dolbino on business, but stayed on to be a companion to the boys. Zhukovsky was rather annoyed, since Wagner knew no history and no Greek, while Cedergren was allegedly accomplished in both.[49] According to N. A. Elagin, Ivan Kireevsky's half-brother, Wagner was hired largely to provide "practice in German conversation."

He was also obligated to "dress the children, to walk with them
— in a word, all that was incumbent upon a guardian (*diad'ka*),
but he was never either a *gouverneur* or a tutor." [50] Elagin goes
on to discuss Ivan's intellectual gifts and development in the
following terms: "In 1813 he had already mastered the game
of chess to such a degree that the captive general Bonamy could
not play with him, being afraid to lose to a seven-year-old boy;
he would follow the child's play with interest for several hours,
as he easily beat the other French officers. At ten years old,
Kireevsky was thoroughly acquainted with all the best productions of Russian literature and so-called classical French literature; at twelve he knew German well." [51] Of course "all the best
productions" of Russian literature and "classical French literature" might be defined in such a way as to make the actual
number of books read quite manageable, but even so, it is clear
that by the time the Elagins moved to Moscow late in 1821,
Ivan's education was well under way, to say the very least.
Furthermore, he had already become interested both in writing
and in philosophy while the family was still at Dolbino, as a
letter from Zhukovsky to Avdot'ia Petrovna makes clear:

Apropos of your letter, I hasten to say one thing: I am convinced
that Vania might become a good writer. He has all that is necessary:
a passionate spirit, the head of a thinker, a noble character, the
talent necessary for a writer. He needs to acquire more knowledge
and to acquaint himself further with language. To achieve the former
— study; for the latter, the habit of writing. I can say to him only:
study and write. Bring honor to Russia and you will not have lived
in vain. It seems to me that it would be better not to think of government service as the main thing; he should dedicate himself to being
a writer. His talent will tell him what to write. Let him study
Russia and Walter Scott to develop true patriotic feeling; then let
him familiarize himself with moral writers and English philosophers.
We are not yet ready for the profound philosophy of the Germans;
we need a simple, manly, practical moral philosophy, not dry and

materialistic, but founded on what is lofty — but at the same time clear and appropriate for application to real life.[52]

The writers which Zhukovsky recommended to Ivan were Shakespeare, Walter Scott, Adam Smith, David Hume, and the Scottish philosophers Dugald Stewart and Thomas Reid. "This," he concluded, "is sufficient for life."

II. The Lovers
of Wisdom

The Elagin family's move to Moscow was dictated primarily by the necessities of the children's education. The departure from the scenes of his childhood must have been an emotional moment for the fifteen-year-old Ivan. In his *Childhood*, Tolstoy has left us a poignant account of such a move, with all the sadness of growing up and putting away childish things, mingled with the excitement of exploring the unknown. The family moved first into the so-called "Pomerantsev House," near the Sukharev Tower on Basmannaia Street, but soon purchased a rambling mansion near the Red Gates (*Krasnye Vorota*), just off Sadovaia Street and around the corner from the Church of the Three Redeemers. Avdot'ia Petrovna spent twenty years in this house, with its vast, shaded gardens and its "almost rural spaciousness." [1] It was a famous house in its time, one of the principal meeting places of not only the Slavophiles and Westernizers, but of virtually the entire intellectual elite of Moscow. Avdot'ia Petrovna's remaining children — Nikolai (1822), Andrei (1823), and Elizaveta (1825) — were born in the house on Three Redeemers Lane.

Ivan did not "attend" Moscow University, which was still almost entirely the preserve of the *raznochintsy*, or, more properly, a mix of the sons of the lower gentry, preparing for a career in the bureaucracy, and the offspring of priests, lawyers, and other "professional men." The Elagins, like most other cultivated middle and upper gentry families, were prepared to exploit the facilities of the university — to send their sons to lectures and to employ professors as tutors — but not actually to put their children on the rolls. When Alexander Herzen, six years younger than Ivan, decided to become a university student, a fearful row with his father ensued. He had his way, however, and the situation began to change significantly around 1830.[2]

Ivan studied Latin and Greek with Professor Snegirev, more famous as a folklorist (he also studied Greek with a resident national named Bailo); when he came to be interested in reading the Church Fathers in the original, he was to regret that he had not worked harder. His literature teacher was Zhukovsky's old friend, A. F. Merzliakov, subsequently to be castigated by Ivan and his Germanophile friends as a slave to all things French. Mirsky thought Merzliakov an "eclectic follower of senescent classicism,"[3] but according to Herzen, he was among the very few Russian (as opposed to German) professors of the day who was respected by his students.[4] Another was the conservative authority on Roman law, L. A. Tsvetaev, who tutored Ivan in law and political economy.[5]

Of far greater importance than these rather academic — one suspects — tutorials was his exposure to the seductive doctrines of German idealism, which, in the 1820's, meant the philosophy of Schelling.[6] Ivan was, as we have seen, exposed to Schelling early. Professor D. M. Vellansky, of the University of St. Petersburg, was a family friend, and was doubtless responsible for Aleksei Elagin's interest in Schelling, which was passed along to Ivan.[7] No doubt Ivan was something of a "Schellingian" even before he began to attend Professor M. G. Pavlov's lectures in Moscow.

Pavlov had, in the words of Alexandre Koyré, "an absolutely remarkable gift of vulgarization."[8] While the chair in philosophy at the University of Moscow was eliminated, for reasons of state security, in 1826, Pavlov gave his philosophy lectures in the guise of an introduction to physics and agriculture — subjects which in fact Pavlov easily made into a rather simplified and schematized version of the *Naturphilosophie* of Schelling.[9]

The *Naturphilosophie*, with its system of "identity," or correspondence between the unconscious life of nature and the conscious life of the human mind, was a stage in Schelling's lifelong attempt to resolve the epistemological problems raised by Kant. From the standpoint of the history of philosophy, Schelling's break with Fichte over the question of "subjective" or "objective" idealism in 1801 was a matter of some importance.[10] Among the Master's enthusiastic but inexperienced Russian disciples, however, the distinction between Fichte's "the ego is everything" and Schelling's "everything is the ego" tended, not surprisingly, to be lost. Thus, the development from Schelling's *Ideen zu einer Philosophie der Natur* (1797) to the *System des transcendentalen Idealismus* (1800) passed unnoticed; his "Jena period" was interpreted as a unitary whole.

Schelling first set forth his "solution" to the Kantian dilemma in his *Philosophical Letters on Dogmatism and Criticism*, published in 1795 and translated into Russian, it will be recalled, by Ivan's stepfather. Schelling attempted to bridge the abyss between the Absolute and the knowing subject, or ego, by positing a kind of "intellectual intuition," by which the ego discovers the eternal *within itself* through immediate and uncaused experience. In this experience, the intuiting ego becomes "identical" with the intuited, and this "absolute identity" annihilates space, time, and consciousness.

Between 1795 and 1797, Schelling further elaborated this breakthrough into a metaphysics of extreme subjectivity, closely related to that of Fichte. The complex structures of physical nature, of "reality," were regarded as merely derivative accidents of the all-powerful "Absolute Ego" which determined them and which was the ultimate ground of all reality.

By 1800, Schelling, in his concentration on the philosophy of nature, had surpassed even Fichte in his subjectivity; the latter still endowed the world of nature with a residue of limited objectivity, while Schelling, in effect, identified mind and nature completely in the *System des transcendentalen Idealismus.*

The philosopher and the artist were particularly exalted beings in Schelling's idealist system; they were, through their creative activity, most closely in touch with the Absolute Ego and the highest expression of the identity which underlay mind and nature. It was the philosopher who advanced the self-consciousness of the Absolute by penetrating the mysteries of the natural world, which lay behind its temporal veil. Since the self-realization of the Absolute was in fact divine creation, the status of the philosopher was quasi-divine.

After his meeting with Franz Baader and his discovery of Jakob Boehme in 1806, Schelling moved away from the "philosophy of identity," having come to feel that this static, quasi-pantheist doctrine failed to account for the creation and actual existence of the world, failed to account for the dynamic, both in human affairs and in the life of nature. Pavlov, however, like the other first-generation Russian Schellingians, remained a devotee of the *Naturphilosophie;* with a certain amount of "empirical digression," he presented a "clarified" version of the system which Schelling had elaborated between 1797 and 1803. The intoxicating doctrines that he preached, the skill with which he simplified them, and his spellbinding style made his lectures famous. He became both a social and an intellectual lion.

Ivan Kireevsky was spiritually even better prepared for idealism than most of his contemporaries. The sentimental literature with which he grew up was pregnant with pantheistic suggestion. His mother was particularly prone to a quasi-religious love of nature and identification with it, while his father's interest in "natural science" may also have played a role. The Kireevsky-Elagin belief in miracles and in dreams of communication and prophecy predisposed Ivan toward Schelling's view that the forces of nature were not "mechanical" in the old, Newtonian sense, but attractive forces, analogous to divine love — and that nature and mind are ultimately one. Intuition was deified, and empiricism — reliance on "experience" — tended to mean mysticism. "By intellectual or rational intuition, real and ideal, being and thought, object and subject were seen as identical, so that experience and speculation were harmonized." [11]

Perhaps even more important for Ivan was Schelling's aesthetics: his cult of artistic creation and the artistic genius. Except for the philosopher, only the artist, in Schelling's view, could grasp and in part depict something of that ultimate harmony, the reconciliation of opposites in the Absolute.[12] It was his high calling to depict the eternal ideas behind the particular forms of physical nature.

In view of Ivan's own experience, his own literary gifts and ambitions, his tendency toward aristocratic idealism, what could be more natural than to elevate the artist to this position of preeminence? His childhood had been saturated in culture, as we have seen. While Herzen's father was complacently planning to provide for his bastard son by ensuring him a comfortable slot in the civil service, Avdot'ia Petrovna was anxiously conferring with Zhukovsky as to whether Vania might "make a writer." Even the religious and national aura surrounding "the artist" was a commonplace of their discourse. The creative artist, for Zhukovsky, was a species of national-cultural Moses; no higher vocation could be imagined. Ironically enough, Zhukovsky never saw that the kinds of attitudes he had done so much to foster led, for a young man of Ivan's generation, straight to Schelling's aesthetics. He had "nothing against metaphysics," Zhukovsky wrote to

Avdot'ia Petrovna from Dresden in the winter of 1824, but Vania should read some English philosophy and clear his head. "Even in Germany they don't understand Schelling," he complained.[13]

The romantic cult of individual genius, in Schellingian or other form, was a common enough phenomenon in early nineteenth-century Europe. In the Russia of the 1820's, it was accompanied by other ideas, equally "romantic" and more specifically German in origin: notions of the "organic" character of the nation and, in particular, the "organic" relationship between the nation and its culture.[14] Herder, of course, was the author of the first profound attack on cultural cosmopolitanism, most notably in his *Ideen zur Philosophie der Geschichte der Menschheit.* Russians of Ivan's generation had a certain familiarity with Herder, but it was largely through Fichte and the popularizers of idealism that Herder reached Russia.[15]

The critique of cosmopolitanism launched by Herder and continued by the romantics was a vital factor in the national-cultural identity crisis which Russia began to undergo in the 1820's.[16] As long as culture was not directly related to the spiritual essence and power of the nation, Russian imitativeness in this sphere did not imply any sort of national sterility. Enlightenment thinkers had calculated the statistical likelihood of genius and believed that certain social institutions were clearly better able to develop it than others.[17] But as soon as culture became truly "national" culture, a direct emanation of the "national spirit" or soul, cultural imitativeness had clear — and frightening — implications about Russian society. Furthermore, the triumph of romanticized forms of Herder's ideas took place in the period following the victory of Russian arms in Europe, when the spectacle of Russian material power coexisting with the lack of any particular cultural achievement was already disturbing to cultivated Russians, whose awareness of the triumphs of other literatures was unique at the time. Where was Russian literature? What was the matter with

the Russians, that they did not have a literature? Where was
the great literary figure who would vindicate the Russian spirit
and life and found the great national literary culture?

In the Russia of the 1820's, the answers to these and other
questions — personal, social, aesthetic — were passionately sought
for in German idealism. In a sense, Herder taught the Russians
to ask questions, and they turned to Schelling and later to Hegel
for answers. Why, one may ask, did this happen? Why did Russia,
rather than learn from England and France, seem intent on
parodying Germany? Martin Malia has set out to answer this
vexing question with the help of some of the axioms of the
sociology of knowledge.[18] The most important of these is Karl
Mannheim's "law" for the transplanting of ideas into new surroundings. According to Mannheim, when intellectual groups take
over a body of ideas which they cannot put into practice, they
tend to project them onto a higher plane of abstraction, where
their ultimate implications are laid bare through a study of their
"purely logical implications."[19] One way of discussing German
idealism, as Malia, following Mannheim, has pointed out, is to
treat it as the working out of the principles of the French Revolution in a purely philosophical arena — Germany being too backward, politically and economically, for these principles to have
application "in the real world." Russia, of course, was less advanced even than Germany, and this fact may account, in part,
for both the crudity of the Russian efforts to assimilate idealism
and the passion, greater even than that of their German cousins,
with which the Russians substituted philosophy for politics and
other pursuits and satisfactions of the real world.

What is particularly striking, with reference to these developments, about Ivan Kireevsky and those of his friends who made
up the so-called "Lovers of Wisdom" (*Liubomudry*) was that
they foreshadowed tendencies and attitudes which became widespread only later.[20] It is from the failure of the Decembrist up-

rising that one must date the real feast of Schellingian reason in Russia, of which the *Liubomudry* were the most important premonition.

Shortly after the arrival of the Elagins in Moscow, Ivan met and became friendly with Alexander Ivanovich Koshelëv, a young man of almost exactly his own age and of a very similar family background. The two young men were near neighbors and met at the house of Professor Merzliakov, with whom both were studying Russian and European literature. "We frequently walked home together," wrote Koshelëv, "and our friendship grew and became fast." As to their intellectual interests, Koshelëv described himself as particularly interested in "political subjects, but Kireevsky inclined toward literature and aesthetics; both of us, however, felt the need of philosophy." [21]

The philosophy that the two young men read together at this time was not merely the "wisdom" of the Germans, however; Locke and Helvétius were also on the agenda. The former may have been part of Zhukovsky's head-clearing program, while Helvétius, we know, was in the Elagin library. "The simplicity and clarity of his exposition charmed us," wrote Koshelëv of Locke;[22] Ivan has left us a fuller account of his early encounter with French materialism in a letter to Koshelëv, written some ten years later.

I think I should be of the same opinion as you [that is, hostile] if I were to read him now. But ten years ago he had a completely different effect on me. I confess that he then seemed to me not only intelligible, clear — the sort of thing that would seem perfectly sensible to the common man — but also moral, despite his preaching of egoism. This egoism seemed to me merely an imprecise expression, because by it might be meant patriotism, too, and love for humanity, and every virtue. That same thought, that virtue is not only a duty for us, but also a happiness, seemed to speak very well for Helvétius. Likewise, the example of his own life contradicts reproaches of immorality.[23]

We cannot all be *Schöne Seelen,* and Ivan's view may have been that Helvétius might help the vulgar to escape from the opposition of morality and happiness, while the elite utilized Schiller and Schelling to the same end.

Koshelëv, unlike Ivan, had enrolled in the university in 1822, but due to a dispute about lecture requirements, he departed again in 1823. "At this time," wrote Koshelëv, "my friendship with I. V. Kireevsky was particularly useful; we studied together and inspired and encouraged each other." [24] It was just at this time, according to Koshelëv, that German philosophy, especially Schelling, began to achieve its hegemony over their other intellectual preoccupations. Together with the gifted poet and critic, Dmitry Venevitinov, they engaged in passionate evening discussions, "which continued long after midnight, and turned out to be much more fruitful for us than all our lessons with the professors." [25] Soon the trio became a group: N. M. Rozhalin, subsequently a close friend of the whole Elagin family, Prince Vladimir Odoevsky, already something of a literary and philosophical luminary, V. P. Titov, S. P. Shevyrëv, N. A. Mel'gunov are the names mentioned by Koshelëv. To them must be added that of Avdot'ia Petrovna, who, as far as their collective existence was concerned, may have been the most important of all. Koshelëv paid glowing tribute to her extraordinary cultivation and her equally extraordinary loving heart; it was, in fact, with these talented young men that her gifts as a highly literate and sympathetic hostess for a semipermanent salon were first realized.

In November 1824, Ivan took the so-called "committee examination," obligatory under a law of 1809 for entry into the state service. He then went to work in the archives of the Foreign Ministry in Moscow, with Zhukovsky smoothing his path. Nothing could be easier than to arrange such an appointment, Zhukovsky wrote to Avdot'ia Petrovna early in 1824; he only wished that something more difficult were involved, since nothing could give him more pleasure than to talk about "Vaniusha."[26]

Ivan was accompanied into the archives by ten or a dozen of his friends. They were nominally engaged in the discovery, analysis, and cataloguing of ancient documents; in practice the demands made on them were almost nonexistent, and this gilded youth passed its days with such diversions as the collective writing of humorous tales and conversation, sometimes lofty, on a variety of subjects. They became known as the "Young Men of the Archives," and the phrase was subsequently immortalized by Pushkin in *Evgeny Onegin*.[27]

Although the "Young Men of the Archives" seem to have spent their days largely in delightful idleness, their evenings were given over to higher and more serious things. Two overlapping intellectual constellations were drawn largely from this personnel: the "Raich circle" and the "Society of the Lovers of Wisdom" (*Obshchestvo liubomudriia*), to both of which Ivan belonged. Late in 1822, the former group gathered around S. E. Raich, a well-known classical scholar who had translated Virgil. Their meetings were public and often frequented by prominent literary or governmental figures, such as the Governor-General of Moscow, Prince D. Golitsyn.[28] "[Raich] then lived," M. A. Dmitriev subsequently recalled, "in the house of the Lanskoi family, in the capacity of tutor to their children. Here, on the side street which runs from the Nikitsky monastery to the Predtechensky gates, on the ground floor of a great stone house . . . a small circle of his friends gathered once a week and occupied themselves with literature. They read their own translations, criticized them, and thus formed a small literary society. Usually present at their meetings were S. P. Shevyrëv, D. P. Oznobishin, A. I. Pisarev, I. V. and P. V. Kireevsky . . . I remember with real pleasure these peaceful discussions of literature, to which all conceit and passion were foreign."[29]

Although the works of "the best Russian authors" were sometimes discussed at these gatherings, the bulk of the communal energy was expanded on translations. As Raich himself recalls it, "we read and discussed, according to the reigning laws of aesthetics, the works of the members and translations from Greek, Latin, Persian, Arabic, English, Italian, German, and occasionally French." [30] As this passage would suggest, the intellectual ambitions of the Raich circle were gargantuan. "We intend, incidentally, to translate all the Greek and Latin classics and to translate the best books on education (*vospitanie*) from every language," wrote the historian Pogodin with characteristic solemnity, "and we have already begun Plato, Demosthenes, and Titus Livius." [31]

The "Society for the Lovers of Wisdom" was a different sort of organization. If it was not actually secret, as Koshelëv maintained, the membership was at any rate restricted. The group evolved, apparently, from literary afternoons at Professor Merzliakov's apartment,[32] but philosophy soon came to dominate the group's discussions, and an atmosphere of mystery — if not mystification — developed. With Odoevsky and Venevitinov the moving spirits (president and secretary, respectively), the society convened in Odoevsky's rooms. Folio and quarto volumes covered the walls, lay heaped on chairs, and overflowed into all corners of the room. A skeleton hung near the door; on its skull was written: *Sapere aude.*[33] "German philosophy was master there," wrote Koshelëv, "that is, Kant, Fichte, Schelling, Oken, and Görres." [34] Both in the discussions and in the much less frequent readings of "original" work, the goal was always "principles (*nachala*) on which all human knowledge could be founded." Christianity was considered suitable solely for the mob; only through Schelling's "system of identity" or his disciple Oken's similar doctrine of "correspondences" could one conquer the intractable external world.

Gone were Kant's epistemological barriers; the secrets of the universe seemed wholly unveiled. Given the "identity" of the world and the Ego, self-analysis became analysis of the external world. "I owe to Schelling," wrote Odoevsky to Titov in 1823, "the habit I now have of *generalizing* the least events and the most insignificant phenomena which I encounter." [35] The flower was found to "correspond to the circle, and the fruit to the ellipse." Mathematical symbols, the four elements, the three Graces — all were furiously manipulated to provide this specious mastery of man over his environment through symbolic correspondence.

Carl Schmitt has suggested in a brilliant essay that the substitution of "occasionalism" for causality is at the very heart of romanticism: concrete reality becomes merely the jumping-off place for aestheticism or fantasy.[36] The real world is merely the occasion for something else. Or, as Malia puts it, "Nothing is easier for novices in abstract thought than thinking by analogy; nor does any device make the universe seem easier to comprehend. It is a 'method' that admits of no permanent enigmas, which leaves no areas of uncertainty or doubt. It is, in short, a device for people who cannot afford to face reality as it is and yet who are in a hurry to make the world over in the image of the heart's desire, a shortcut to understanding and to an illusive feeling of mastery over experience." [37]

In their isolation from the outside world, in the fusion of exalted intellectual interests with passionate friendship, the *Liubomudry* were an archetypal "circle." This was, for them, the *Gemeinschaft* of the Romantics, and it was Ivan's first direct participation in the joys of the collective.

The magus, or seer, was the ideal of the *Liubomudry*. Knowledge — real knowledge — was, by its very nature, the attainment of the few; the rest might make do with Christianity or some other surrogate. This spiritual elitism was a very basic feature of the *Liubomudry*, and it links them with their masonic predecessors. There we find the same air of secrecy, a like notion of all "real" knowledge as in some sense "esoteric," a similar manipulation of symbols, and essentially the same belief that the philosopher was a kind of magician. Even the name *Liubomudry* came to Odoevsky and his friends from Freemasonry, via A. F. Labzin.[38]

The principal contrast between these young idealists and their masonic predecessors — or some of them — would seem to be the lack in the former of the critical and humanitarian spirit which animated Novikov and certain of his contemporaries. If one views the activity of the *Liubomudry* and the Freemasons as, in part, sublimated politics, it is at any rate certain that the *Liubomudry* sublimated more deeply. "Nothing is more characteristic," according to Koyré, "of the mentality of the generation of the twenties, nothing marks the difference between . . . its spirit and that of its elders more profoundly than this 'apoliticism'."[39]

Nevertheless, the mood of the last years of Alexander's reign, and particularly the events of the year 1825, had a considerable impact on these "apolitical" young men. Koshelëv recalled an evening in February or March, 1825, which he spent at the house of his third cousin, M. M. Naryshkin. Present were

Ryleev, Prince Obolensky, Pushkin, and several others subsequently sent to Siberia. Ryleev read his patriotic *dumy,* and everyone spoke freely about the necessity — *d'en finir avec ce gouvernement.* This evening made a very strong impression on me, and on the following morning I conveyed everything I had heard to Ivan Kireevsky, and together we went to see Dm. Venevitinov, with whom Rozhalin then lived. . . . We talked a great deal about politics that day, and about the necessity of bringing about a change in the form of government in Russia. After this, we applied ourselves with particular avidity to the works of Benjamin Constant, Royer-Collard, and other French political writers, and for a while our interest in German philosophy receded.[40]

The formal disbanding of the *Obshchestvo liubomudriia* was the direct result of the events of December 14. To cite Koshelëv once more: "How well I remember Prince Odoevsky calling us together after that unhappy date, and with particular solemnity committing the statutes and protocols of our *Obshchestvo liubomudriia* to the flames in his fireplace." [41] No doubt a simple fear that the police might think that their "secret" organization was part of the conspiracy motivated, in part, the breakup. But Koshelëv also states that their philosophical conversations were "cut short" because "all our attention was concentrated on political events." [42] Moreover, "we, German philosophers, forgot Schelling and company, went every day to the *manège* and the *salle d'armes* to learn riding and fencing and thus to prepare ourselves for the activity for which we were destined." [43] Rather quixotic, no doubt, even comical, but obviously these young men felt that this was the real thing. Their drastic, albeit brief, alteration of the agenda further suggests the degree to which the "mastery" over the external world provided by idealism might be replaced by a more direct and less complex relationship with "reality."

A largely passive sympathy for the Decembrists was of course widespread, in particular among the Moscow aristocracy. Odoevsky's cousin had been involved, and all the *Liubomudry* had friends or relatives among the insurgents. Avdot'ia Petrovna wrote to Zhukovsky, pleading with him to intervene on behalf of G. S. Baten'kov, a close family friend, who was to spend twenty years in the Fortress of St. Peter and St. Paul.[44] Other conspirators were also the object of her concern and sympathy. Prominent among the men for whom she wrote letters (and for whose wives and children she tried to provide at least information) were M. A. Fonvizin and I. D. Iakushkin. Both had been deeply involved from early on, although both could be described as "moderates"; Iakushkin had in fact been one of the founders of the

Union of Salvation.[45] There was of course very little that Zhukovsky could do in an affair of this magnitude, and he soon modified his efforts, out of a natural concern for his own position at court. "Tomorrow the tsar will arrive in Moscow," Avdot'ia Petrovna wrote to Zhukovsky after the sentences had been handed down, "and I shall see your tutee [Zhukovsky had been the imperial tutor for several years]; how I should have rejoiced! But the severe sentence has broken my heart; all around me are despair and groans; mothers, wives, brothers — all are in bitter sorrow." [46]

There is little doubt, then, that the revolt, trial, and sentencing of the Decembrists shook the whole family very deeply. Nevertheless, it would be a mistake to say — on the basis of evidence now available — that Ivan's stepfather or even his mother actually approved of the uprising. The distinction between vague personal sympathy and real political agreement is not always an easy one to make, and some Soviet historians, anxious to find "progressive" lines in the Kireevsky-Elagin family, have been less than discriminating on this important point. Avdot'ia Petrovna's response involved outrage at the severity of the sentences, but this was the closest that she came to a political utterance. Nor do we have any indication that Elagin seriously "supported" his old friend Baten'kov's involvement in the conspiracy.

Our knowledge of how Ivan and Peter felt is not much more extensive. Koshelëv's memoirs give us leave to assume at least a passing sympathy which was more thoroughgoing and "political" than that of their mother and foster father. Both young men probably also shared the feelings of their parents that the social group to which they belonged had undergone a catastrophe. But was there anything more?

Certainly Ivan's initial feelings of out-and-out sympathy were quickly spent. Nevertheless, one can discern certain traces, over the next few years, of a mildly oppositional mentality. There is,

for example, his poem on the Ukraine, written in the album of a
certain N. A. Markevich, a "well-known Ukrainian historian,
ethnographer, and poet":

> When you read me your verses
> About the happy years
> Of holy Ukrainian freedom —
> Consumed with love for antiquity,
> I listened to you sadly
> And said: Ukraine!! Where are you? [47]

There is also the fact that Peter Kireevsky expressed in print his
detestation of the regime of King Ferdinand in Spain, although
this really does not give the Soviet historian Soimonov the right
to refer to his "democratic views." [48]

But whatever Ivan's awareness of lost liberty in the Ukraine
(or in Russia), or Peter's view of the Spanish government, it
would certainly be a mistake to conceive of the two brothers as
straightforward "liberals," let alone protorevolutionaries. What
Russia needed, Ivan vaguely felt, was a kind of national regeneration, and in this he would play a major role through literature,
which he felt to be his vocation.

In 1827 he wrote to Koshelëv, defending himself from charges
of idleness and self-indulgence with which Koshelëv had responded to his decision not to enter the service. "To serve," he
asked, "but with what end in view? Can I render some significant
service to the fatherland in the government service?" The answer
to this rhetorical question was — obviously not. "But do not think
that I have forgotten that I am a Russian," Ivan went on, "and
that I do not consider myself bound to act for the benefit of my
native land. No! All my powers are consecrated to it. . . . I can
be a man of letters, and is not working for the enlightenment of
the people the greatest service I can perform for them? . . .
Since the principal goal of my life has been to educate myself,
can I not be a force in literature? I can," he continued vehe-

mently, "and I will give literature its direction." After appealing
to Koshelëv and Titov to be his "helpers" in this great task, he
presented his program: "We will restore the rights of true religion, reconcile the elegant with the moral, excite love for truth,
exchange a stupid liberalism for respect for the laws, and elevate
purity of life above purity of style. What can limit our influence?
Where will you set a boundary, saying *nec plus ultra?*" [49]

This is indeed the most ambitious kind of total culture, having
little to do with either art or the free play of intellect for its own
sake. The Decembrist spirit, too, is notably absent.

Here, then, is essentially Zhukovsky's old program, touched
with the Schellingian view of the philosopher/artist as the man
in touch with the Absolute. Ivan would bring the divine fire to
the Russians. As to the question of who would set a boundary
to his influence, the answer was, in part, he himself. For this
letter also gives us an early hint of that combination of physical
weakness and spiritual passivity which played so central a role
in defining the contours of his career and limiting his achievement. "If I am, at the moment, doing nothing," he continued to
Koshelëv,

the cause, unhappily, is more than sufficient. I have so shattered my
health this winter that any mental effort is bad for me. Certain
circumstances even give us reason to fear consumption. . . . Even
the coffee, which you so attack, I have had to give up for chocolate,
à la santé. My pipe has not yet left me, only because it does me no
harm. By the way, my regimen is most monotonous. I spend morn-
ings in my room, reading novels, poems, and whatever does not
demand much effort. After dinner I sleep, and ride in the evenings.
I make no new acquaintaces, and see almost no one but Rozhalin,
Polevoi, Mickiewicz, and Sobolevsky, with whom, in a group, I go
about Moscow.[50]

Ivan's lifelong tendency toward hypochondria and extreme nervousness about matters of health in general was very much a family problem, which Gershenzon diagnoses as stemming originally

from the marriage of Vasily Ivanovich Kireevsky's severity and Avdot'ia Petrovna's nervous excitability.[51] Be that as it may, this occasion was by no means the last on which ill health would serve Ivan as an excuse for inaction or as justification for the withdrawal from some enterprise. Emotionally vulnerable to the challenges and shocks that the world provides, he became increasingly prone to withdrawal into melancholia or illness.

The man who more directly limited Ivan Kireevsky's influence, however, was Nicholas I. In July 1827 a perfectly innocent letter from Koshelëv and Titov to Ivan was intercepted by an agent of the Third Section. Although unable — as seems often to have been the case — to make out what the letter was about, Benckendorff, the chief of the Third Section, wrote "très intéressant" in the margin and opened a dossier on all three. It was the beginning of Ivan's long involvement with the political police.[52]

III. The Literary Aristocracy

*Democratic literature is always infested with a tribe
of writers who look upon letters as a mere trade;
and for some few great authors who adorn it,
you may reckon thousands of idea-mongers.*
— Alexis de Tocqueville

In 1830, the literary war between Pushkin and Viazemsky (with
their adherents) and Bulgarin escalated into a more ferocious
stage.[1] One of the most interesting developments in this fascinating feud was a polemic over the term "literary aristocracy," which
had been used by Bulgarin — with pejorative intent — to describe
Pushkin and his friends in an article in the *Northern Bee*
(*Severnaia pchela*).[2] It is significant that although both Viazemsky and Pushkin furiously denied Bulgarin's charge that they,
together with Zhukovsky, were the leaders of a literary clique,
admission to which was a matter of genealogy, they essentially
accepted the notion of their "aristocracy" in a somewhat broader
sense.

In 1825, Pushkin had written to A. Bestuzhev that "our writers
are recruited from the highest social class. With them aristocratic
pride is linked with their literary ambition. We do not want to be
patronized by equals. That is what the rascal Vorontsov does not
understand. He imagines the Russian poet appearing in his
anteroom with a dedicatory poem or ode, but this poet appears
with a lineage of six hundred years and with a demand for respect
— there is a devilish difference. . . . Our poets do not solicit the
protection of gentlemen; our poets are gentlemen themselves.

Among us there are no ragged abbés whom a musician would take off the streets to write him a libretto." [3]

Viazemsky was no less unequivocal about the connection between social position and disinterested literary values. "We *gentlemen*," he wrote to Zhukovsky in 1823, "as a literary chorus, have allowed the lackeys and little boys into the drawing room, while we play at knucklebones in the courtyard. Who if not we will *tenir la haut bout de la conversation?* Of course our audience will understand little, whatever we may say, but *literary integrity* will be maintained." And again: "Who will be independent, then, if not we — we who are driven to write by a noble ambition, out of a selfless necessity of the soul? The value of the writer depreciates here every day, and if the chosen few do not maintain it, [literature] will become a kind of state service, a branch of the police, or what is even worse, merely a department of the Ministry of Education. Independence is the power we should serve." [4] Viazemsky was quite explicit: the threat to the integrity of literature (or to "aristocratic" literary values) came not only from a kind of democratic vulgarity, but also from the bureaucratic autocracy. Zhukovsky, too, referred expressly to an "aristocratic direction" in literature, of which he believed himself a part.

Thus we see that it can hardly be maintained, as Pushkin and Viazemsky did in 1830, that their notion of "literary aristocracy" had nothing to do with genealogical aristocracy. [5] Nevertheless, as a recent biographer of Viazemsky has pointed out, [6] it is a fact that a priest's son, P. A. Pletnëv, [7] was a member of the "aristocracy," while Bulgarin proclaimed, loudly and often, his membership in the Polish nobility. A patent of nobility did not automatically entitle a writer to membership in the aristocratic party (which included Baratynsky, Iazykov, Odoevsky, with Karamzin and Dmitriev frequently claimed for it as well), but its members did basically believe that in Russia the kind of independence and integrity necessary for serious literary achievement was confined largely to the gentry.[8] Viazemsky undoubtedly believed in the "aristocracy of talent," of which he so often spoke in his polemic with Bulgarin,[9] but since in Russia "the highest class is also the most cultivated," [10] Russian culture was inevitably aristocratic.

The quarrel over the "literary aristocracy" terminated its public phase, at any rate, later in the year (1830), when Benckendorff forbade Del'vig to discuss the matter further in his columns. Since the *Literary Gazette* was then the only journal open to the aristocrats, public discussion was at an end. Henceforth they were simply the "Poets' Party," as Mirsky called them.[11]

The whole question of the "literary aristocracy" is generally considered merely an episode in lower-level literary history, the occasion for some of Viazemsky's and Pushkin's brilliant and epigrammatic invective. A Soviet literary historian, N. L. Stepanov, thought otherwise. Noting the reprimand to Del'vig which ended the public controversy, he wrote that in fact

government circles stood on Bulgarin's side, seeing in the activities of the *Literary Gazette* a defense of oppositional tendencies, the establishment of the independence of the progressive gentry from the police-monarchical system . . . The heroic history of the Russian people is embodied, for Pushkin, in the names of his forefathers, as well as in the "plebeian names" of the Nizhni Novgorod *meshchanin* Minin, and Lomonosov. It is precisely these names which he opposes to the "barbarity, cheapness, and ignorance" of Nicholas' Russia, to the new *notables,* base and trivial, to the snobbish rabble, fawning on the Tsar, but devoid of real patriotism, alien and hostile to the people . . . At the beginning of the thirties, the group of writers united around the *Literary Gazette,* only recently linked, to a significant degree, with the Decembrist movement, was the expression of progressive ideas and tendencies.[12]

This is clearly both overstated and in some respects simply false. It distorts Pushkin's pride in his six-hundred-year ancestry into a kind of "democratic" attitude. And it is only in a very special and qualified sense that Pushkin's and Viazemsky's social (as opposed to intellectual-literary) attitudes might be called "progressive." Nevertheless, it is perfectly true that Bulgarin was, in large part, an instrument of the autocracy, and that Pushkin was bitterly hostile not only toward Bulgarin and Grech, but toward the "new *notables*," who had been, since the eighteenth century, the instruments of the autocracy, and who were embodied, for Pushkin, in the figures of Benckendorff and Bulgarin. "Whom do our journalists attack?" inquired Pushkin bitterly. "Not the new *dvorianstvo*, constituted by Peter I and the emperors, which largely makes up our elite, our true, rich, and powerful aristocracy — *pas si bête*. Our journalists are polite to extremes before this aristocracy. It is the ancient *dvorianstvo* that they attack, who now, by virtue of their fragmented estates, comprise here a kind of middle order (*sostoianie*), a venerable, hardworking, and enlightened order, an order to which the greater part of our writers belongs." [13]

Stepanov is not wrong in linking such sentiments to 1825; several years later Pushkin wrote in his diary: "What then does our ancient nobility signify, well educated, its estates destroyed by endless depredations, hating the great aristocracy, yet retaining all its pretensions to power and wealth? There is no such terrible element of revolt in Europe. Who was out on the square on December 14? Nobles only. How many of them will be involved in the first new uprising? I do not know, but I think many." [14] Pushkin's feelings of solidarity with the Decembrists seem to have been based largely — at least at this later date — on such considerations; here we see the historical link which unites 1825 with the aristocratic attempt to limit the monarchy in 1730.

In addition to its importance for literary historians, the *petite histoire* of the "literary aristocracy" would seem to be of interest to the sociologist and historian as well, for here we see a group, with some pretensions to the status of *noblesse de race,* fighting a pathetically ineffective rearguard action against the bureaucratic, absolutist state. Bulgarin can be viewed as, among other things, a kind of parody of the "king's man," raised from nothing by the monarch. As Bulgarin enthusiastically put it, "one of the most salutary aspects of monarchical rule is that the monarch can, in spite of circumstances, raise a man from the dust, place him on the step next to the throne, and crush the sceptre of his power if he uses it for evil." Elsewhere he wrote that "before the autocratic monarch, as before God, all subjects are equal." [15]

A consistent Marxist would, in fact, have to admit that the views of the "aristocrats" had a definite reactionary cast. *Pace* Stepanov, Bulgarin's greatest sin in the eyes of the "aristocrats" — aside from his frequent denunciations of competitors — was that for him, literature was basically a commodity, to be "produced," bought, and sold — a most bourgeois attitude.[16] Polevoi, the vodka merchant who edited the Moscow *Telegraph,* was no better, and in spite of Viazemsky's early collaboration with him, he was the object of the prince's biting wit nearly as often as Bulgarin.[17]

Despite the fact that Ivan Kireevsky has not generally been considered a member of the Pushkin-Viazemsky group, there are good reasons for considering his career as critic and editor under this rubric. It was a pathetically brief career, which ended with the suppression of the *European* in 1832. Not only was he a protégé of Zhukovsky, but, in the words of Pushkin's most notable biographer, "in these years [i.e., 1826–1832], of all the young *Liubomudry,* Ivan Kireevsky was closest to Pushkin," who warmly admired his small output of criticism, as did Viazemsky.[18] Kireevsky's family background was similar to theirs, as were his fundamental attitudes and values; it is worth noting that he used the term "literary aristocracy" as an accolade a year before the controversy between the *Literary Gazette* and the *Northern Bee* erupted.[19] He also shared their enemies. Polevoi linked him with the "aristocrats." [20] Bulgarin denounced him and appears to have played a major role in the demise of the *European*.[21] That journal, in fact, became the organ of the "aristocrats," following the closing of Del'vig's *Literary Gazette*. "Kireevsky is editing the *European*," wrote Pogodin to Shevyrëv in December 1831, "and all the aristocrats are with him." [22]

Given the rapt and heavy-breathing quality of the intellectual life of the *Liubomudry*, one might have expected that Kireevsky's literary criticism would be permeated with Schellingian aesthetics, or even resemble the visionary incoherence of Novalis' writings on poetry. This is far from the case. Nor did Ivan Kireevsky — as did, for example, Coleridge in England — adapt the writings of German idealism to the end of technical literary criticism. Sensitivity to language, a good feeling for structure (undoubtedly strengthened by the idea of the work of art as an "organic" whole), and a range of reading little short of amazing in a man of twenty-three — these were the qualities which gave "Something on the Character of Pushkin's Poetry" and particularly the "Survey of Russian Literature in 1829" their considerable success with the "Poet's Party." Even after a century of Pushkin criticism and Pushkinolatry, they stand up well, so much so that Mirsky can maintain that "almost the best criticism of Pushkin's work is to be found in the works of his younger contemporaries, especially of Ivan Kireevskii." [23] But what is perhaps most striking today, particularly to the intellectual historian, is the developed historicism of these essays.

Mirsky also found Kireevsky's style akin to that of both Karamzin and Pushkin, but Kireevsky seldom, in these early works, attained anything approaching Pushkin's condensed and terse prose.[24] His elegance is more fragile and more rhetorical, and there are a few passages which, even by the standards of

that day, are downright florid. One such flight occurs in his exposition of Zhukovsky's historical place in Russian literature. "The
ideal (*ideal'nost'*)," he wrote, "purity and depth of feeling; the
sanctity of the past; belief in the beautiful and in the im-
mutability of friendship, in the dignity of man and the plenitude
(*blagost'*) of Providence, the striving for the transcendental; indifference to everything ordinary, to all that is not spirit, to all
that is not *love* — in a word, the whole of life's *poetry*, the very
heart of the spirit, if one may put it so, appeared to us in one
being, taking shape in the captivating form of Zhukovsky's
muse." [25] Typically, however, this rhetorical effusion was followed by the shrewd observation that "love for the past" is the
"dominant tone of Zhukovsky's lyre." Zhukovsky's foremost
biographer considers this lack of range — both intellectually and
with regard to sensibility — his greatest limitation as a poet.[26]
There is a fastidious wit in these pieces, too, although Kireevsky
never attained to the chilly mordancy of Viazemsky.

Ivan Kireevsky's first published piece, "Something on the
Character of Pushkin's Poetry," appeared in the *Moscow Messenger* in 1828. The *Messenger*, as originally conceived, was to
be the organ of what was left of the *Liubomudry* group. Pogodin
— hardworking, honest, unimaginative — was the obvious choice
for editor; he suffered least from that aristocratic dilettantism
which was so marked a feature of these young men. But then an
event took place which increased not only the inherent interest
of the *Messenger*, but also its potential readership and commercial
viability: it cemented an alliance with Pushkin.[27]

In September 1826, Pushkin had returned from exile on his
father's estate in Pskov province; after his celebrated interview
with Nicholas he took up residence in Moscow.[28] There he
rapidly became friendly with the gifted young poet and critic,
Venevitinov, and through him with the remaining *Liubomudry*.
On October 12, Pushkin read *Boris Godunov* aloud at Veneviti-

nov's apartment.[29] Ivan and Peter Kireevsky were there, as well as Khomiakov, Pogodin, Shevyrëv, Rozhalin, and several others. This seems to have been Kireevsky's first meeting with Pushkin, although Pushkin's poems had been eagerly read at the Elagin house for some years; manuscript copies in some quantity have been found among the family papers.[30] *Boris* was ecstatically received and, amid the general euphoria, Pushkin promised to help with the projected journal. Within a few days, Pogodin had explained matters to Pushkin in detail, and something in the nature of a formal "treaty" of alliance was agreed upon.[31] On October 24, the birth of the new journal was celebrated at a dinner given by Khomiakov; among those present were Pogodin, Shevyrëv, the Kireevsky brothers, Raich, Mal'tsov, Titov, Baratynsky, the Venevitinovs, Rozhalin, Sobolevsky, Richter, Prince Obolensky, Pushkin, and Mickiewicz.[32] In essence, the guest list was the bulk of the old *Liubomudry* group, plus Pushkin and several of his closest friends.

The "alliance" was not without its strains; a certain flavor of *mariage de convenance* was evident from the start. Pushkin had been extremely dissatisfied with the Moscow journals, regarding Polevoi's *Telegraph* "as a radical, even a Jacobin journal." [33] The *Messenger* filled an obvious need. A Soviet literary historian has even suggested that Pushkin contemplated a coup d'état against Pogodin which would make the *Messenger* truly his organ.[34] Pushkin's principal objection to the *Messenger* (as to the *Liubomudry* in general) was its preoccupation with German philosophy. "God knows how I hate and despise it," he wrote to Del'vig on March 2, 1827, "but what am I to do? The warm and ingenuous youngsters have gathered together. The priest has his and the devil his. . . . The 'Moscow Messenger' sits in the ditch and asks: what is truth?" [35] Even Kireevsky was never quite forgiven for Schelling; it was Pushkin's only reservation about his criticism.[36] On the other hand, not only did Pushkin, for the time being, need the *Messenger*, but it was impossible not to be flattered by the "warm and ingenuous youngsters" who had such a high opinion of poets and clearly regarded him as *the* Russian poet.

The title of Kireevsky's *Messenger* piece — "Something on the Character of Pushkin's Poetry" — is significant. The word "character" indicates that the emphasis will not fall on purely aesthetic, formal analysis. "Character" obviously relates to the German, and, as with, for example, *Volkscharakter*, intimates the progressive unfolding or developing of a preexisting essence. This was in fact Kireevsky's approach to Pushkin's poetry. He began by modestly noting that it was only the total lack of any useful discussion of Pushkin's major work which gave him the right to undertake the task: "with us [in Russia] no one's voice is superfluous." [38]

The problem to which he first addressed himself was the diversity — in tone, style, and viewpoint — of Pushkin's work up to that time. Under what common rubric could one discuss the gaiety and wit of "Ruslan and Liudmila," the "gloomy coldness" of the first five chapters of *Onegin*? The "Captive of the Caucasus" and "The Gypsies" were likewise "wholly distinct." It was not until the "Survey of Russian Literature in 1829" that Kireevsky fully devleoped his historicist scheme, but here too he met the problem by dividing Pushkin's work into three stages.

The first period — with "Ruslan and Liudmila" the chief exemplum — was that of "pure poetry." Pushkin was the "creator-poet," setting before us a world wholly of the imagination, a world of his own creation. Surely there is an echo of Schelling and Novalis in Kireevsky's phraseology here. The dominant influence and the tone of Pushkin's work was Italian-French. In this early poetry Pushkin

carefully avoids anything pathetic, anything that might strongly affect the reader, for strong feeling is out of place when one aspires to the marvelous and comic; it can live only with the marvelous and sublime. Only the charming can entice us into the kingdom of enchantment, and if, among the enchanting possibilities, something strikes us seriously, compelling us to return to ourselves — then good-bye to belief in the unbelievable. . . . In general, one may say of Ruslan and Liudmila that if stringent criticism can find in it some weaknesses, some inconsistencies, it will not, of course, find anything superfluous, anything out of place. Chivalry, love, sorcery, feasts, war, water nymphs — all the verses of a magical world here combine into one creation, and the motley parts notwithstanding, everything is harmonious, consonant, *whole*.[39]

The second period in Pushkin's *oeuvre* was the "Byronic," and here Kireevsky considered "The Captive of the Caucasus," "The Fountain of Bakchisarai," "The Gypsies," and the first chapters of *Eugene Onegin*. Pushkin was now, perhaps somewhat to his surprise, the "poet-philosopher," and his poems had undergone an invasion of reality. Dealing with the phenomenon of Byron's influence, Kireevsky was, by and large, discriminating and historically accurate. He observed that the general mood, tone, even *Weltanschauung* of these poems owed much to Byron, that the narrative form was directly traceable to Byron, and that many of Pushkin's characters had obvious models in the works of the British poet. On the other hand, the precision of the descriptive passage, their naturalness and "truth," and above all the "originality of the language" throughout was pure Pushkin.[40] Kireevsky laid great stress on the emerging *samobytnost'* (individuality) of Pushkin, but did not attempt to minimize Byron's influence, seeing it as "one of the two contending directions of our time," and regarding Pushkin's submission to it for awhile as inevitable.[41]

"The Gypsies" represents the culmination of the Byronic period; it is the greatest of the Byronic poems, but also the least successful. In it one sees the new, *narodnyi* (popular-national) Pushkin struggling to be born. Kireevsky even went so far as

to attribute "all the inadequacies in 'The Gypsies' " to the opposition of two different aspirations: "one indigenous (*samobytnyi*),
the other Byronic." This same conflict is even more apparent,
he said, in the first chapters of *Onegin*. Pushkin has attempted
to create a Russian Childe Harold and has failed, because such a
creature is not native to Russia, cannot take root in Russian soil,
and Kireevsky's optimistic spirit, fired with pictures of Russia's
greatness, could not envisage a Russian Childe Harold. "May
God grant," he added fervently, "that the time never come." [42]
He shrewdly pointed out the differences between Onegin and the
typical Byronic hero: "The favorite dream of the British poet is
an extraordinary, lofty creature. Not poverty, but an over-
abundance of inner force makes him cold toward the world around
him. . . . Thus Childe Harold has nothing in common with the
ordinary crowd: his sufferings, his dreams, his pleasures are unintelligible to others; he exchanges secrets only with lofty moun-
tains and bare cliffs." [43] On the other hand, Onegin is a "completely ordinary, trivial being." It is not "bitterness" which makes
him cold and indifferent to those around him, but a simple "inability to love." Like the Byronic hero, Onegin has thrown over
the social world, but not in order to find himself in solitary medi-
tation. He is simply bored.

Kireevsky's pages on "The Gypsies" and *Onegin* reveal a
moralizing tendency which looks backward toward Rousseau and
in a curious way anticipates Tolstoy. Kireevsky did indeed show
that Onegin differs in certain essential respects from the "typical"
Byronic hero. But it is difficult to agree with him that Onegin's
shallowness seriously mars the poem. And his assertion about the
incompatibility of the "Byronic hero" and Russian culture is most
charitably passed over in silence. In "The Gypsies," too, Kireevsky criticized Pushkin's content. Pushkin, he felt, was trying to
portray the gypsies as representatives of a golden age, "where
people are just without laws, where passions never exceed the

bounds of the proper, where everyone is free, but no one destroys
the general harmony, and inner perfection is the result not of
laborious cultivation, but of the happy innocence of nature's perfection." [44] The inconstancy of the gypsy women, which brought
about Aleko's downfall, is, however, incompatible with this Rous-
seauist vision, and Pushkin was charged with a major philosophical inconsistency. This kind of criticism is perfectly consonant
with the Schellingian tendency to consider poetry and philosophy
as basically the same revelation, but it makes difficult reading
today.

Nevertheless, Kireevsky concluded that "the inadequacies of
Onegin, it would appear, are Pushkin's last tribute to the British
poet." [45] Already in Lensky and Tat'iana, in the description of
the landscape in "The Gypsies," and in certain scenes from *Boris
Godunov*, Kireevsky detected the presence of a new stage in
Pushkin's work: the "Russo-Pushkinian" period, as he not altogether felicitously called it. The "principal features" of this
period he found to be "picturesqueness, a certain lightearted-
ness, a certain pensiveness, and finally something inexpressible,
intelligible only to the Russian heart, for how can we name that
feeling, exuded by the melodies of Russian folk songs . . . ?" [46]
This period in Pushkin's work is also characterized, Kireevsky
found, by his "ability to forget himself in surrounding objects and
in the present moment," a quality characteristic of the Russian
people as a whole and a source of both national strengths and
weaknesses. In general, the "Russo-Pushkinian" period was
sweepingly and rather vaguely characterized as *"narodnyi"*;
Kireevsky did note that Pushkin, in *Boris Godunov*, showed a
remarkable grasp of the historical milieu, the "character of the
century." But it was not until his "Survey of Russian Literature
in 1829" that he was able seriously to discuss Pushkin's new
"objectivity" and historical orientation and put them, in turn, into
historical perspective.

"Something on the Character of Pushkin's Poetry" made a favorable impression on Pushkin himself and on Zhukovsky. This young critic's piece in the *Messenger*, Pushkin noted, had "focused on him the attention of the small number of observers who can truly appreciate talent." [47] In April 1828 Zhukovsky wrote to Avdot'ia Petrovna that he had "read Vaniusha's article on Pushkin in the *Moscow Messenger*, and rejoiced with all my heart. I bless him for writing intelligent, rich, philosophical prose. Let him now work with his head and furnish it properly — I tell you he'll have a splendid language for his thought." [48]

Nevertheless, the piece is clearly the work of a young man, and suffers somewhat by comparison with the "Survey," written less than two years later. The three-stage development of Pushkin's poetry is more fully worked out and more concisely expressed in the later article, abetted by a more developed historicism. Too often, in the earlier piece, the discussion of the poetry tends toward an impressionistic slackness. There is little analysis and almost none of the pithy and shrewd characterization in which the "Survey" abounds. The discussion of Byronism, although intelligent in places, is often moralistic and imprecise; as Tomashevsky has noted, Kireevsky had a tendency to "blame" Byron for what he felt were Pushkin's philosophical failures.[49]

"Something on the Character of Pushkin's Poetry" is, however, an important document in the development in Russia of what Belinsky called the "Age of National Character." Pushkin is cast in the role of The Poet — less Schelling's seer in touch with the Absolute than he who will most fully express the essence of the national soul. "To be *narodnyi*," wrote Kireevsky, "it is necessary to be bred, so to speak, at the center of the life of one's people, to share the hopes of one's native land, its efforts and failures; in a word, to live its life and to express that life unconsciously in the process of self-expression." [50] This sounds like Herder, and it is significant that one of Kireevsky's "projects" in 1828 was to read "all of Herder." [51] And yet, in 1828, Ivan Kireevsky cannot define Russian *narodnost'* or *samobytnost'* in terms more precise than "the ineffable quality of Russian folksongs." He saw before anyone else that Pushkin was to be the great national poet. As Pushkin entered upon the third stage of his development, Russian culture came of age with him, ceasing to be merely a recipient of the accumulated riches of Europe and becoming a contributor. For Kireevsky and his contemporaries, this was a crucial moment. But the only hint Kireevsky gave us here as to what Pushkin's *narodnost'* actually involved was the notion that Pushkin, like the Russian people, had a tendency to yield himself up to the immediacy of experience. Slavophilism was to provide one answer to this question and to make possible the formulation of other answers.

"The Survey of Russian Literature in 1829" was a more mature and more successful article than the Pushkin piece.[52] Kireevsky was prevailed upon to write it by M. A. Maksimovich, favorite pupil of Pavlov and Ivan's former colleague in the Archives, who in 1829 decided to publish an "almanac," which he called *Dawn* (*Dennitsa*).[53]

In accord with his view of himself as a purifying agent in Russian letters and a molder of public opinion, Kireevsky opened the substance of the "Survey" with some sharp remarks about the low quality of Russian journals (their "indecent critics, their barbarous tone, their strange personalities, their rustic manners"), which are like the "disordered movements of an unswaddled child." [54] But he found hope for improvement, in part because of the liberalization of the censorship law, a development upon which he dilated at some length.

He then turned to the question of the "prevailing direction of our literature as a whole," which he conceived in the form of a dialectical triad, the first stage of which embodied by Karamzin. As a kind of preface to the first "stage" he paid a glowing tribute to Novikov, who had done so much to further the development of Russian culture and had presided over the birth — at any rate — of an educated public opinion. Novikov was important to Kireevsky, who saw himself as the heir of the great philanthropist, whom he also identified to some degree with his father. Contemporary Russia was rebuked for having forgotten one of the most illustrious of her sons. The historical essence of Karamzin's early work Kireevsky found to be a "philanthropical way of thinking," which represented a fusion of the dominant intellectual trends of that time: mysticism and the ideals of the French Enlightenment. Karamzin's great achievement and influence led, in turn, to a further strengthening of French literary culture in Russia.

In this first period of modern Russian culture, one could already detect the Russian tendency to seek philosophy in poetry. As this tendency became stronger, the Karamzinian "way of thinking" — and here Kireevsky meant its emphasis on the "social" — began to seem merely a "wallowing in everyday life," which gave insufficient scope to the "better side of our existence, to the ideal, the dreamy side." [55] Thus a second stage in the triad arose, a stage explicitly German and philosophical, a stage identified with the attempt to express the "whole man" in literature. In spite of Zhukovsky's personal hostility toward idealist philosophy, the second stage bore his name. The third stage, into which the two previous principles had "fused" (*sovpadalis'*), is the "striving for a better reality," and Pushkin, of course, is the poet of contemporary Russian culture. Pushkin's own work, as in Kireevsky's earlier discussion of it, is also viewed dialectically. First came a naive, gay period of "trusting hopes," followed by a gloomy period of "Byronic indignation toward the existing." Thus, Pushkin's "radicalism," or at any rate his sympathy for the Decembrists, is implicitly linked with his Byronism. Chronologically, at any rate, this is quite accurate. The third, synthetic stage is a kind of optimistic historicism, in which the "seeds of the *desired future*" are seen to be "contained in *present* reality"; Providence, said Kireevsky, is in necessity. Here we see historicism playing the role it has so often played in periods of reaction or social quietism. This capacity to console is a source of the doctrine's great power, particularly in its vulgar Marxist form. How comforting it is to believe that the "seeds of the desired future" are "contained in present reality"!

This attitude of "respect for reality," which is the focal point not only of contemporary Russian culture, but that of Europe as well, led Kireevsky to his final general point: the current historical direction, not only of literature narrowly conceived, but of all European culture. Thiers, for example, in order to defend certain proposals in the French parliament, ends up writing a history of France. Pushkin's *Poltava* is only one of the many examples of literary men turning to history. The historical preoccupation is evident in politics, philosophy, even in mathematics — but above all in poetry, that "expression of the totality of the human spirit."

Turning to the literature of the past year, Kireevsky delivered an impassioned tribute to the final volume of Karamzin's *History of the Russian State*. The closer Karamzin came to the present, according to Ivan, the greater his power and intelligence. Karamzin's critics, to whom a good deal of space was devoted, were divided into three categories. First, there were those who rummaged through the archives and found the small mistakes, inevitable in a work of such scope, which they triumphantly laid before the public. Their failure was in their pettiness, their unawareness of Karamzin's great achievement. Pogodin was rebuked for publishing several such articles in the Moscow *Messenger*.[56] To the second group, those who criticized the "plan" of the *History* (largely from the standpoint of the predominance of political history), Kireevsky replied that this limitation was the prerequisite of Karamzin's success; obviously other histories could be written with different emphases and organizing principles.[57] His severest strictures, however, were for the "know-nothing" critics, whose motivation for base and slanderous attacks on Karamzin remains obscure, although such attacks, he clearly implied, had been published by Bulgarin.

Kireevsky then turned to Pushkin's *Poltava;* this section is perhaps the most successful of the "Survey," in that the over-arching historicist schema seems to grow naturally out of the text itself. He began the discussion by noting that certain critics have been discussing *Poltava* as if it were a historical work, and he dismissed those who had nothing better to do than to argue and dispute as to whether Pushkin "correctly" depicted the historical events. Nevertheless, Pushkin was *not,* he thought, in a higher sense, always faithful to "reality." There are in *Poltava* instances of a conflict between an atmosphere of reverie (*mechtatel'nost'*), ultimately traceable to French sentimentalism, and the kind of "substantiality" (*sushchestvennost'*) which is characteristic not only of Pushkin's present work but of European literature as a whole. And we find, in *Poltava,* "bursts of feeling, incompatible with that Shakespearian condition in which the creator must find himself, in order that he may see the external world as wholly the reflection of the internal."[58] Furthermore, Pushkin fails to maintain the "unity of interest." The first part, basically the drama of Mazepa and his goddaughter, is romantic in conception and execution (and, as Mirsky notes, is an extension of the world of the Southern poems).[59] The second half, dealing with Peter, Charles of Sweden, and the Battle of Poltava, is so insufficiently related, thematically and in its treatment, as to seem an entirely different work. Nevertheless, in its compression, clarity, and control, *Poltava* points the way to even greater achievements than one had hitherto expected from Pushkin.

Turning to some of the lesser works of 1829, Kireevsky had high praise for Zhukovsky's Schiller and Homer translations. In delicacy and nuance of language, he maintained, Zhukovsky's rendering of "Das Siegesfest" surpassed the original. Kireevsky dealt with Khomiakov, Tiutchev, and Shevyrëv under the rubric of the "German school" and linked them with Zhukovsky. He hedged on Khomiakov's tragedy *Ermak*, which he had not seen on the stage, and passed over Tiutchev (who only published one poem in 1829) in silence. Shevyrëv, he noted, lacks "finish," but he does have talent, and with the acquisition of experience and polish he will surely take his rightful place in the "literary aristocracy." He had high praise for the Decembrist Kuchelbecher's *Izhorsky*, published, thanks to Pushkin, under the colophon of the Third Section. Kireevsky tactfully preserved the author's anonymity.

Kireevsky's encomium to the late Dmitry Venevitinov again demonstrates his historicist way of thinking and his view of poetry and philosophy as vitally linked, not only to each other, but to the totality of the social organism. Venevitinov's personality, said Kireevsky, with typical romantic insistence, was his most beautiful "song"; Venevitinov was a philosopher and a philosophical poet, whose heart and intellect were perfectly in harmony. "But that which Venevitinov would have achieved, had it not been for his early end, will achieve itself, though perhaps not so quickly, not so fully, not so beautifully. We *must have* philosophy; the whole development of our mind (*um*) demands it. It alone can breathe life into our poetry and inspire it." [60] German philosophy is a first step only — our philosophy must be our own — but its acquisition is an important first step. This, as Herbert Bowman has observed, is Mme. de Staël's famous paradox: imitate a foreign model to become original. [61]

In discussing the French and German "directions" in poetry, Kireevsky observed that one could best see how used-up and sterile French models now are for the Russian writer by examining the work of obvious second-raters. The work of the French epigones is totally worthless, while the imitators of German literature almost always say something of value. It is, he continued, another matter with talented writers, and Viazemsky is the most witty and gifted of the "French school"; his poetry is an "always clever, always felicitous, brilliant *intellectual game.*" But his work is most successful when "the voice of the heart" makes itself heard over that of the mind. Baratynsky, like Pushkin, is no longer "French," but European. Kireevsky aptly characterized his lightness, precision, and "dandyism." He saw, as in the case of Pushkin, his greatest triumphs before him.

Apropos of Del'vig's translations from the classical poets, Kireevsky gave a sophisticated and historical justification for a free "imitation" (*podrazhanie*). Our love of the poem, our direct response to it, is the starting point for any good translation. But think, he urged, of all that has happened to European culture since the ancients wrote: the religious feeling "for which we are beholden to Christianity," romantic love (a gift of the Arabs and barbarians), the melancholy of our own Northern climate, the primacy of thought over feeling, and, finally (here is an intimation of things to come), the fanaticism which has resulted from centuries of European disorder and struggle. A translation of Greece's "simple note" must now sound a "chord." In its rather overstated way, this passage obviously relates to Schiller's *On Naive and Sentimental Poetry* and the critical discussions, stemming from it, by Friedrich Schlegel, Jean Paul, and other German critics.[62]

Kireevsky characterized Del'vig's poetry in general as a fusion of clear, light, "Hellenic" sweetness with Northern melancholy. But, he continued, "the delicate beauty of [his Attic muse] could not have borne the cold of the gloomy North, if the poet had not clothed it in our native dress, if upon its classical forms he had not draped the *sheepskin jacket of modern melancholy.*" Ivan's friends, including Pushkin, smiled at this unfortunate phrase, but Bulgarin, whose recent novel, *Ivan Vyzhigin,* Kireevsky had found to be characterized by "emptiness, tastelessness, soullessness, and moral sententiousness," found the "sheepskin jacket" a windfall.[63] He fell on the phrase with delight and signed his counterblast in the *Northern Bee* "Porfirii Ushegreikin" (*dushegreika* 'sheepskin jacket').

The area of Russian literary culture which Kireevsky found to be in the poorest shape of all was the theater. Russians continue to imitate the French in their dramatic literature, he found — excepting those qualities which made the French theater great: taste, wit, purity of language. The stage was not a "mirror of our life," but a preserve for lackeys and buffoons. Fonvizin and Griboedov remain Russia's only two comic geniuses. On the other hand, he found the large number of good translations of first-rate foreign writers a hopeful sign. Goethe, Schiller, Shakespeare, Byron, Moore, and Mickiewicz have all been extensively done into Russian, "a happy sign for the future," except for "our love of Moore . . . which belongs to those curiosities of our literary taste which earlier gave rise to our unconditional adoration of Lamartine." Kireevsky's tribute to his friend Mickiewicz is particularly grateful: not only has Mickiewicz given Poland a "voice among the intellectual deputies of Europe," but his achievement has made it possible for Polish literature fruitfully to influence Russian literature. He is, in fact, the Polish Pushkin.[64]

Kireevsky concluded the substantive part of the survey with brief characterizations of the principal journals of the day. He broadmindedly observed that Polevoi's *Telegraph* was richer than any other journal in "good, serious articles"; it also gave the public the most interesting items from foreign journals. The *Northern Bee,* he remarked acidly, had the "freshest" political news. In general, he found that all the Russian journals tended to be atrociously written, in a style frequently worse than that of the pre-Karamzin period. That was one reason why Russian journals were not read by educated people!

In closing, Kireevsky turned again to the larger questions of Russian and European culture and the destiny of Russia. What, he asked rhetorically, from our literature, is of general European significance? Some of Derzhavin's odes, Karamzin's *History*, some poems by Pushkin and Zhukovsky, some fables by Krylov, and a few scenes from Fonvizin and Griboedov. That is all. But Russia's comparative backwardness is her great hope — and here Kireevsky invoked that argument from backwardness, which in its many guises — cultural, political, and economic — was to have such an enormous vogue in nineteenth- and twentieth-century Russia. "The crown of European enlightenment," he wrote,

has been the cradle of our culture, born as other states are already completing the cycle of their intellectual development, and where they end, we begin. . . . Look now, at all the European peoples: each of them has already fulfilled its mission (*naznachenie*), each has expressed its character, lived out its particular tendency, and not one is still living a separate existence. The life of Europe as a whole has swallowed up the independence of all the *individual* states. But in order for the *whole* of Europe to be formed into a harmonious, organic body, a particular focal point is necessary, a people which will dominate the others politically and intellectually. The whole history of modern culture demonstrates the necessity of such an ascendancy: there has always been one state which is, so to speak, the *capital* of the others, the *heart* from which the blood issues forth and to which it returns.[65]

England and Germany are now in that position, but their "influence cannot be lifegiving, for their inner life has already completed its development"; they now exhibit the "one-sidedness of maturity." Hence the "kind of torpor" which we see in Europe today.

There are only two states which have not participated in the development of European culture (and hence are available as future "capitals"): Russia and the United States of America.[66] But the United States, seemingly young and vital like Russia, is in fact already "one-sided," thanks to her relationship with England, and is, in any case, too far away. But if Russia is to achieve this preeminence, upon which the future of Europe depends, her cultural development is vitally important: "the destiny of Russia is contained in her culture."

Kireevsky's "Survey" caused considerable stir. Not long after its appearance, Andrei Turgenev wrote to Viazemsky from Paris, inquiring about the author and asking to have a copy sent. He was happy to hear that the piece contained a long-overdue tribute to Novikov. Was Kireevsky, as he had heard, studying in Munich? [67] Pushkin was so taken by the "Survey," its philosophical tendency notwithstanding, that he devoted an entire article (in Del'vig's almanac, *Northern Flowers*) to summarizing and excerpting from it. He disagreed, at least in print, only with Ivan's characterization of the Russian theater as a sink of literary iniquity. Kireevsky, said Pushkin, "renders the condition of the stage with such humorousness that although we do not share his opinion entirely, we still cannot help quoting this original passage." And quote it he did. Pushkin seems not to have entirely grasped Ivan's concluding remarks about Russian culture's present poverty and glorious future. "We smiled," wrote Pushkin, "reading this melancholy epilogue. But we observe to Mr. Kireevsky that where a twenty-three-year-old critic can write such an entertaining, such an eloquent *Survey of Literature* — there is literature, and its maturity is not far distant." [68] Tomashevsky has pointed out, as well, how much Pushkin liked Kireevsky's designation of him as the "poet of reality," although one may doubt whether the two men understood the phrase in precisely the same way.[69]

Of Kireevsky's friends and admirers, only Zhukovsky expressed a negative view. His curious response revealed, above all, that he belonged to an earlier generation. In January 1830, on his way to Germany, Kireevsky visited the Imperial Tutor in St. Petersburg and showed him the "Survey." He described Zhukovsky's response in a letter to his parents. "On the following day he said that he did not like it. Again the Procrustean bed, he says [meaning philosophy]. Where did you find literature? What the devil kind of life is there in it? What do we have of our own? You talk about us as one can talk only about the Germans, the French, etc. The sheepskin jacket (*dushegreika*) did not please him, nor about Baratynsky; in a word, he praised almost nothing. He says, though, that the article is as well-written as the first." [70] Zhukovsky's response revealed (in addition to his chronic aversion to philosophy) the feelings of inferiority that a Russian writer of his generation still had vis-à-vis Europe.

Ivan Kireevsky's friends and well-wishers were not the only ones to take note of the "Survey." Bulgarin could not fail to respond to Kireevsky's cutting remarks about *Ivan Vyzhigin*. In the eleventh and twelfth numbers of the *Northern Bee* for 1830, Bulgarin bitterly assailed the "born critic, who, in a word, has bestowed immortality on all his friends and mowed down, with the cannonballs of thought and the grapeshot of his enlightening touch, all those whom his friends do not like." He dwelt at length on the *dushegreika*, as well as Del'vig's "Greek muse," and other highflown notions. The poet Iazykov, insulted for Kireevsky and planning at the time to put out an almanac of his own, wished to call it *Dushegreika*.[71]

But Bulgarin, as was his wont, did not confine himself to replying in print. He immediately wrote a letter to Benckendorff, attempting to justify his bad review of Zagoskin's *Iurii Miloslavsky* (which Nicholas, unfortunately for Bulgarin, had liked), and attacking the critics of Vyzhigin. All the reviews were bad, he (quite truly) said. "I will give you one short example, the piece by Kireevsky, the nephew of the tutor to the heir to the throne. You will see that it is not only I who am abused, but all those who read 'Vyzhigin'." He concluded with a denunciation of Kireevsky and his "friends," after complaining of how Zhukovsky was ceaselessly working against him at court.[72] He also appended a letter from a prominent Polish scholar (who did not know Russian), saying how much he had loved the book. This letter, according to Bulgarin, was "proof" that Kireevsky and his friends were writing nonsense.[73] Bulgarin was not, at that moment, in very good odor at court, and no action was taken against Kireevsky. Nevertheless, it lengthened his dossier and probably played some part in the suppression of the *European*.

Historians have tended, perhaps inevitably, to read Kireevsky's criticism largely in the light of his subsequent Slavophile views. Koyré even went so far as to say that in these first critical articles the young man "gives us, already, the basis of his thought," which according to Koyré, was the idea that the "civilization of humanity" is entering a new stage, a stage in which Russia will play the leading role.[74] The West has already fully expressed its essence and spirit and is exhausted.

Andrzej Walicki, however, has acutely observed that there is, in the "Survey," more "occidentalism" than might appear at first glance. On the one hand, Kireevsky derived real culture from the people, from their way of life, from their "essence." On the other hand, he asserted that all of Russian culture is "something imported, the joint effort of all the peoples of Europe." Kireevsky was a historicist, a theoretician of the "organic continuity of popular life" — and yet he admitted, at least by implication, that everything in Russia began with the great Tsar-Jacobin, Peter the Great.[75]

This contradiction is of great importance to the relationship between Kireevsky's world view and his subsequent Slavophilism. Perhaps the most striking and obvious disagreement between the

Slavophiles and the "Official Nationalists" was their estimate of Peter the Great and his reforms.[76] Nor was Nicholas wrong in regarding the Slavophile distaste for Peter as hostility toward himself; his own static and bureaucratic absolutism was the lineal heir of the Petrine monarchy, and no less alien to the type of patriarchal conservatism which was the basis of Slavophilism. Kireevsky's attitude toward the achievement of Peter and toward Western culture had to undergo a drastic change before the mythology of Slavophilism could emerge.

This conflict had deep sociological roots.[77] On the one hand, Ivan Kireevsky was from a family of the old nobility, which owed its "social position" not to Peter's Table of Ranks, but to the "organic process of history," a family which was conscious of, and set great store by, its long tradition. On the other hand, he was a Europeanized intellectual, who fully realized how much of Russia's culture resulted from Peter's rupture with the past.

Also to this period belongs the prose sketch, *Tsaritsyn Night,* which Kireevsky composed, at Viazemsky's behest, for a literary evening at Princess Volkonskaia's.[78] It is really only a brief conversation in a romantic landscape — the abandoned palace at Tsaritsyn — among a closely knit group of young men, obviously patterned on the *Liubomudry.* Ivan stressed their openness with one another, their naiveté and inexperience — life had not yet provided them with that "experience" which chills idealism and chokes frankness. Kireevsky obviously believed, too, that this group of young idealists would one day be a force to reckon with in Russia.

Their conversation reflected the mood and preoccupations of the *Liubomudry* period. Particularly revealing were the opening remarks about the Time of Troubles. Imagine, said Vladimir (one of the principal conversationalists), a young man living at the time of the final struggles of Boris. However capable that Tsar may have been, the young man believes him to be a regicide. The falseness of the Pretender's claim is apparent. This situation must have forced on such people their first intuition of something called *Russia* — the beginnings of national self-consciousness. It was only in the name of this new ideal that men like Minin and Pozharsky could have acted, and acted successfully. What Vladimir is driving at is clear from the ensuing discussion: Russia is going through a similar period of national questioning and self-definition today. As indeed she was. Amid the romantic surroundings — the decaying palace, the small ponds, surrounded by gardens running to seed, the conversation of the group "turned to dreams of the future, the purpose of man, the secrets of art and life, to love, one's own destiny, and finally to the destiny of Russia. Each of them still lived on hope, and Russia was the favorite object of their conversations, the knot which held their alliance together, the burning focus of the clear glass of their hopes and desires." [79] The evening concluded with champagne and a poem by the poet of the group, Vel'sky. *Tsaritsyn Night* provides, in very short compass, an admirable introduction to the *Gedankenwelt* of Ivan Kireevsky and his friends. The moonlit communion, the self-conscious purity and youth, the involvement of their own destinies with the larger destiny of Russia, struggling to take possession of her glorious future — it is all contained in this brief sketch.

In general, Kireevsky lived a pleasant life in Moscow between 1826 and 1830, in which the literary and the social combined harmoniously. His propensity for enjoying a kind of melancholy solitude is already evident from his letters, but he had overcome what busy, active people like Koshelëv and Zhukovsky thought of as his "laziness" sufficiently to produce two important articles. His reading, obviously, was vast; it is difficult to think of a Russian contemporary who had Kireevsky's knowledge of both his own and foreign literature.

As noted above, both Kireevsky brothers had taken part in

the founding of the Moscow *Messenger,* but despite Ivan's having published his Pushkin piece in that journal, his relations with editor Pogodin were anything but harmonious. The events which highlighted their personal incompatibilities and gave rise to their frequent altercations were various and sometimes rooted in trivial events about which we are unlikely ever to know very much.[80] Their disagreement over Karamzin's *History* was one of the clearer episodes. Kireevsky regarded Karamzin, a distant relative and close personal friend of Zhukovsky and other members of his family, as a tremendous literary force and influence. Karamzin's services to Russian culture were such that they summed up a whole era and put him, in a real sense, beyond criticism. This we know from the "Survey." If not actually a member of the "literary aristocracy," he was its greatest forerunner, even its founding father, for it was from the Arzamas group that the "Poets' Party" and the "literary aristocracy" developed. The continuity, both of personnel and literary attitudes was very great. Karamzin, it must be remembered, was also the great spokesman for the special relationship between the autocrat and the gentry.[81] When Pogodin published an attack on Karamzin's *History* by a young historian, N. S. Artsybashev, ridiculing Karamzin's style and accusing the great man, in a very unpleasant and personal way, of having been virtually indifferent to scholarship, a battle began immediately in the salons and journals of Moscow.[82] Viazemsky led the counterattack against both Artsybashev and the *Messenger.* Pogodin, showing more spirit than one might have expected, replied that "men of the world" looking for casual reading had no real right to take part in the discussion.[83] Kireevsky had his public say, on Karamzin's behalf, in the "Survey."

Kireevsky and Pogodin had already been at odds, however, at the beginning of 1827, over Titov's and Odoevsky's attempt to make Shevyrëv co-editor of the *Messenger.*[84] The two quarreled again a few months later, and things were not smoothed over for a whole year.[85] In November, 1829, they again fell out, again over Karamzin.[86] Pogodin was foolish enough to write to Kireevsky (then in Petersburg, about to go abroad), asking him, in the manner of adolescents: what do you really think of me? "All right," wrote Kireevsky in answer, "there is, in the essence of your being, something so spoiled, so foolish — or, to put it better, immature, undeveloped, and crude (*dikii*), that it is impossible to remind you of your faults too often. Incoherence, thoughtlessness, extravagance, together with a very good heart and a mind which is often one-sided — that is what you are, both as a litterateur and as a man." [87] Only a devoted and discriminating circle of friends can improve you, he continued. With regard to their common struggle for Russian culture, Kireevsky declared that acting on his own, Pogodin would "of course" do much that was good. But "truly, you will also perform many what can only be called *dirty deeds.* Watch out for them!" [88] Coming at the end of a long period of sporadic quarreling, this harsh statement was undoubtedly, as Kireevsky would have put it, "one-sided," and hardly represented his real feelings about Mikhail Petrovich. Nevertheless, the temperamental incompatibilities between the plodding, hard-working, intellectually limited Pogodin and his melancholy, dreamy friend, with his many bootless "projects," his passion, and his spirituality, were very great. They were friends, to be sure, but when the coarse-grained plebeian Pogodin dared to lay hands on the "aristocrat" Karamzin, Ivan rallied instinctively and passionately to the latter's side. This conflict sheds light not only on the relations between the "gentlemen" of the Poets' Party and the plebeian journalists, but also, less directly, on the gulf which would separate the Slavophiles from the "Official Nationalists." [89]

Of Ivan Kireevsky's life and activities in the period before his trip to Germany, it remains to mention his friendship with the

Polish poet in exile, Adam Mickiewicz. There is almost nothing in Kireevsky's correspondence about this interesting subject, but we know from Lednicki and other Mickiewicz scholars[90] that Kireevsky was among the poet's closest friends and that he spent a good deal of time in the Elagin household. At the farewell dinner for Mickiewicz, early in 1828, his Russian well-wishers presented him with a silver goblet with their names inscribed. Ivan Kireevsky read a poem about this memento, which, he said, was far from an ordinary cup. It was to be a magic talisman, a living bond between Mickiewicz and those he left behind in Russia.[91]

It had always been assumed, since the days at Muratovo and Dolbino when Zhukovsky and Avdot'ia Petrovna planned the education of her children, that Ivan and Peter would complete their education with several years in a German university. On July 5, 1829, Avdot'ia Petrovna wrote to Zhukovsky that Peter had decided to go to Munich.[92] Zhukovsky "gave his blessing," but was obviously irritated not to have been seriously consulted about the actual decision. Ivan's decision, shortly thereafter, also to go to Germany, resulted not primarily from a burning desire to hear the German philosophers at first hand, but from the rejection of a proposal of marriage made to his second cousin, Natal'ia Petrovna Arbeneva. Rather unexpectedly, his correspondence sheds absolutely no light on his falling in love or on the initial stages of his courtship.[93] The Arbenev family's refusal, it is clear, was based largely on the blood relationship — what echoes of Zhukovsky's blighted hopes must have been conjured up! Predictably enough, perhaps, his mother was not pleased with his choice and also opposed the marriage. "The whole [Arbenev] family inspired little faith in her; she considered the girl an unsuitable spouse for her son, who in her opinion was blindly infatuated with a cold and clever person who had turned his head." Zhukovsky, his own past notwithstanding, tended to credit Avdot'ia Petrovna's view of things.[94] Then, as now, a trip abroad was one of the obvious answers to such a misfortune; the doctors urged it as well, fearing for Ivan's health. It was decided that he would follow Peter to Germany, but to Berlin, rather than Munich.[95] He left Moscow for St. Petersburg and points west early in January 1830.

IV. Germany

*One should read Germany, meditate it, play it on
the piano — but ride across it by rail from end
to end in one day.*

— Alexander Herzen

Ivan and Peter Kireevsky were among the first young Russians
to visit German universities in search of the elixirs of idealist
philosophy. A bare list of those pilgrims provides the most eloquent testimony to the power of Germany philosophy over the
minds of Russians who were young in the 1830's and 1840's. Most
of those who did not actually visit the home of German philosophy redoubled their efforts to assimilate it from a distance
through study, or simple osmosis, while envying their more fortu-
nate friends.

Berlin was the usual destination of the Russian students, since
it remained, even after Hegel's death, the capital of Hegelianism;
for some reason, the number of students who went to Munich to
hear Schelling was smaller, even when his popularity in Russia
was at its height. The flood began in the thirties: Nicholas Stankevich and the historian, Timothy Granovsky, were in Berlin in
the mid-thirties, while Michael Bakunin, Ivan Turgenev, and
Michael Katkov — sometime liberal and eventually an influential
right-wing publicist — arrived at the end of the decade. These
were only the most prominent; there was also the distinguished
professor of law, Peter Redkin, as well as Stankevich's friend,
Ivan Neverov, and Nicholas Ogarëv.[1]

Ivan's way west ran, appropriately enough, through St. Petersburg, where he was to spend several days with Zhukovsky. While renewing his relationship with the older man and seeing something of the capital and its literary life, Ivan also took advantage of Zhukovsky's familiarity with the German university world and Berlin society.

Still, the departure from Moscow was hard. Late in the evening of his first day in St. Petersburg, Ivan wrote to his parents after Zhukovsky had gone to bed. "How did you spend today?" he inquired. "I began it miserably and ended it sadly; it will be better from now on." In leaving Moscow, he continued, he had left "everything," and he begged his family somewhat histrionically to forgive him the weakness which had made the trip necessary. The following day, feeling somewhat calmer, he continued the letter. Zhukovsky had left a note for him at the stagecoach depot and they had spent the evening together. Zhukovsky had urged him to go first to Berlin, "even if only for a month." "When you are on the spot," he advised, "you'll see what to do: stay in Berlin or go on to Paris." The latter option, Kireevsky observed, "evidently did not please him." [2] So he dutifully promised to spend a month in Berlin going to lectures and meeting the "notable people," and, if he found the city to his liking, to stay longer.

Zhukovsky then turned to the young man's literary aspirations. "You will be a writer in time," he said, "if you work at it. It's early to think about it now. Your character is in your style, insofar as I have read your work. You're obviously a thoughtful person, if still a young one, who has confined his thought to a Procrustean bed. But in time this quality may be useful, since it shows you're in the habit of thinking. But now you must observe, simply and disinterestedly. When facts are few, theory is merely harmful. . . . By the way," he said again, "your style pleases me. Do you know who taught you to write? Your mother. I know no one who writes better than she. There's a trio for you — she,

Mar'ia Andreevna, and Aleksandra Andreevna. Aleksandra Andreevna wrote beautifully, *il y avait du genie dans son style.*" [3]
At this point a visitor arrived and Zhukovsky excused himself briefly. Kireevsky went into his room and jotted down a description of the furnishings and pictures in Zhukovsky's apartments, which, as he noted in the letter to his parents, gave one an excellent impression of the man. The pictures tended to be romantic landscapes, full of graveyards and moonlit nights. A much-cherished painting of Zhukovsky, Alexander Turgenev, and his brother (Zhukovsky's dear friend, who had died in 1803), hung in a place of honor. Kireevsky also took note of a Raphael madonna and a beautiful table, the gift of the Prince of Prussia.

When Zhukovsky's visitor had gone, the conversation turned to literature again. The poet spoke contemptuously of Bulgarin and his novels, but praised Zagoskin's *Iury Miloslavsky.* Then, reported Kireevsky, "I showed him the children's journal [entitled *Midnight Nonsense*][4] and works. He read *everything* with great pleasure, laughed, and particularly enjoyed the tale, which he praised at almost every word." [5] Then Zhukovsky went off to bed with Ivan's "Survey" — which he liked much less.

Kireevsky spent the next few days exploring St. Petersburg in the company of Titov, Koshelëv, and Odoevsky. In the evenings, joined by Zhukovsky, they sat up talking until the small hours. They visited Smirdin's bookstore and found that Nikolai Rozhalin's translation of *Werther* was sold out, as was the latest volume of Polevoi's *History* and *Iury Miloslavsky.*[6] Maksimovich's *Dawn* was on the stand, however, and the format delighted Kireevsky. "Tell that to Maksimovich," he wrote, "to whom everyone sends their best, and I in particular." [7]

Pushkin came over twice, on the fourteenth and sixteenth, and on both occasions Zhukovsky read aloud from the children's journal, with which Pushkin was much taken. According to Kireevsky's report, he "laughed at every word and was pleased with everything. He was amazed, ooh-ed and ah-ed, and kept jumping up." Even pleasanter to report was the "barrel of compliments" he paid Kireevsky on his articles.[8] Pletnëv, Krylov, and Ivan's younger friends were also present on the second evening, a farewell dinner for Kireevsky, which turned into a regular literary soirée. Polevoi's historical views were critically discussed, as was Zagoskin's novel, and Zhukovsky held forth at length on eighteenth-century literature and literary gossip, talking of Derzhavin, of "Sumarokov's quarrel with Lomonosov," and about how it came about that Potëmkin ceased to receive Fonvizin.[9]

These days in Petersburg marked Kireevsky's first extensive contact with Zhukovsky since his childhood; as far as the Elagin family was concerned, and Avdot'ia Petrovna in particular, Zhukovsky embodied the Artist, with a large pinch of fairy godfather thrown in. Despite the nature of the family relationship, the young man's attitude toward Zhukovsky was an independent one; he showed no particular tendency toward hero worship. On his last evening in St. Petersburg, the two sat up until one o'clock, arguing about Flemish painting. "It seems," wrote Kireevsky ruefully to his parents afterward, "that I have left him with the same opinion of me that he had after our first meeting in '26. But I hid nothing; the sooner we get to know each other the better." Zhukovsky read some of his early occasional poems aloud, and Kireevsky did not care for them. "*Cette profanation de genie m'a choqué,*" he wrote to his parents. "Now he is writing nothing, and so much the better. The cause of poetry (*poeticheskoe delo*) is more important than poetic verses." Zhukovsky, he concluded, had given him a "heap" of letters to people in Berlin and Paris, and had promised to write a reassuring letter to the Elagins after he departed. "Write to me in Berlin everything that he says about me. For many reasons I shall be extremely interested." [10]

The following day Zhukovsky, as he had promised, wrote to
the Elagins. "Today, at ten o'clock, I sent our dear traveler on
his way, healthy, and even cheerful. I drove him to the stagecoach depot, where we said goodbye." After detailing the various people in Riga, Berlin, and Paris (Turgenev) to whom he
had written letters about Ivan, he continued: "To me he was a
dear, short-lived appearance, a representative of a past both clear
and melancholy, but in both respects precious — and a happy
image of the future, for judging by him and by the editors of
our domestic journal (especially the author of the remarkable
Catilinian conspiracy), not to mention our bearcub in Munich,
you have a whole dynasty of talented writers in your family —
send them all my way! They will do well. Vania is a very pure,
good, intelligent, and even philosophical creature. It's been delightful to know him a bit." After going over their activities in
brief and gently teasing Avdot'ia Petrovna for worrying, Zhukovsky concluded: "I did not touch the wound of which you know.
The road will begin to heal it." [11]

After an uneventful journey, Kireevsky arrived in Riga on
January 26. The streets were full of Germans — a *Vorschmack*,
as he put it, of the Germans he was traveling to meet. He stayed
with *Prokuror* Peterson, a friend of Zhukovsky, about whom he
wrote home enthusiastically ("dear, respectable, stout, good,
Peterson"). He did not have the chance to call on anyone in
Dorpat, since the coach stopped there only briefly in the middle
of the night, but he made a sentimental journey to Ekaterina
Afanaseevna's house. In Königsberg he spent the evening with a
philology professor named Struve, whose simplicity and candor
made a very agreeable impression on him.

Kireevsky's letters from Berlin were, as one would expect, a
mixture of impressions of the city, its population and intellectual
life, together with worries about the health of his family (a

recurring note) and requests for news about Moscow friends. As with many travelers who have left a tightly knit circle at home, he gave the impression of trying to live in two places at once.

Oddly enough, his initial favorite among the professors at the university was the geographer Ritter, for whose lectures he forsook those of Hegel, which were scheduled at the same hour. He also heard the historians Friedrich von Raumer and Peter Stuhr, the former on the "modern period," the latter on the eighteenth century. He soon came to the conclusion, however, that the "history lectures here aren't worth a cent," not because the men were not good scholars, but because their performance in the lecture hall was so bad. Stuhr, he reported, "reads the history of the eighteenth century from notes, really mediocrely written, with great pretensions to eloquence, hence, badly. Raumer, the great scholar Raumer, fills the entire lecture with military dispatches and other extracts from the public lists. These dispatches and extracts are mostly in French; imagine how agreeable they sound on German lips." [12] So bad was the situation that in this age of history, the lectures of the historians drew only about forty students.

The juridical faculty was different.

Savigny, Gans, Klenze, and others have achieved European renown, even more for their lectures than for their books. I have heard Gans several times; this student of Hegel is lecturing on natural law, positive law, and Prussian civil law. He is extremely eloquent, clever, and pleasant on the podium, despite the fact that he is a baptized Jew. But this Jew has spent many years in France, in Paris, and this is evident in his every word: in his propriety, in the brilliance of his style, and in the superficiality of his knowledge. In his lectures you seldom learn a new fact (aside from Jewish law, where he has said much that is interesting), hence the constant retreat to generalities, an inappropriate retreat, and one which would be tiresome, were he not able to embellish them with the fire and gift of the word.[13]

In a letter of March 3/15,* Kireevsky again wrote to his parents of Gans: "Today, he lectured on canon law, wholly in a Roman Catholic spirit, which in its novelty was extremely interesting for me, particularly in that this Roman Catholic spirit was completely subordinated to the spirit of Hegelian philosophy, and consequently, this catholicism was not Jesuitical, but, if one may put it so, catholicism of the newest Protestantism." [14]

Shortly after this, Kireevsky transferred his allegiance back from Ritter to Hegel, giving as his reason the fact that "the industrious Ritter will probably put out a new *Erdkunde,* in which his system will be set forth in full." Hegel, on the other hand, "is old, will soon die, and then there will be no chance of learning what he thinks of all the newest philosophies." [15] Still, Hegel was disappointing at first, for "in his lectures he adds almost nothing to his *Handbücher.* He speaks unbearably, coughs at almost every word, swallows half the sounds, and scarcely gets the rest out in a trembling, weeping voice." [16]

The only professor at the university whom Kireevsky at the time thought comparable to Ritter was Friedrich D. E. Schleiermacher. Having heard him in the pulpit — the arena where his genius had perhaps freest play — Ivan referred to Schleiermacher as "the glorious translator of Plato, one of the most eloquent preachers in Germany" and, significantly, as "a man having a very strong influence on the highest class of this capital," and on all Protestant Germany.[17] Schleiermacher's lectures on the life of Christ pleased him less, and indeed the figure of Christ presented special theological difficulties to the theologian of "feeling."

Kireevsky's objections to Schleiermacher's lecture on the Resurrection — the only lecture on which he reported in detail — were basically two. In the first place, instead of seizing the great,

* Dates are given here according to both the Julian and Gregorian calendars. The Julian calendar was used by Russians until 1917.

miraculous moment in Christianity and dealing with it as the focal point of man's spiritual destiny, in all its metaphysical irreducibility, Schleiermacher skirted the issue by dealing with such lesser — and scholastic in a bad sense of the word — questions, as whether Jesus was entirely dead, prior to the Resurrection, or whether a spark of life still remained in his body. Kireevsky's objections to this particular lecture seem well taken, always providing he did not misunderstand Schleiermacher in some important way. In reading his account of the lecture, one is reminded of the aversion to the miraculous which Schleiermacher inherited from the Enlightenment, as well as the perceptible tendency toward naturalism in his treatment of the figure of Christ. It is perhaps these crucial elements in Schleiermacher's theology, so well brought out by Karl Barth in his history of Protestant theology in the nineteenth century, that are at the root of Kireevsky's objections.[18]

His second and even more fundamental criticism of Schleiermacher was that, in the last analysis, he "tried to believe" with his heart, but thought with his head; "philosophy" and belief were not united in a single, unified system.[19] Here Kireevsky seems close to Barth's view that it was only Schleiermacher's deep personal piety which kept his theology from turning into a combination of individual psychology and Church history.[20] Kireevsky's discussion of Schleiermacher is of particular interest, because it is the first recorded instance of his taking up the problem of the relationship between religion and philosophy, a problem which, in various guises, occupied him for the rest of his life.

On March 14/26, Kireevsky wrote his last Berlin letter to his parents. "After midnight," it begins. "Just back from Hegel's, and I hasten to write you, to share with you my impression of today — although I don't know how to express this mood, never experienced before, which has so strongly mastered my thoughts, almost as if by magic. I have been surrounded *by the first-class minds of Europe!*" [21] He had, he said, debated with himself for some time as to whether he should pay a call on Hegel. But in spite of dire premonitions of a chilly and awkward five-minute visit, he had finally pulled himself together and written the great man an "extremely polite note," which "cost me much, since it had been so long since I had written to anyone in German." This admission tells us something of Kireevsky's social habits in Berlin. To his relief, Hegel replied the same day in a "very cordial and worldly, French way," inviting him to his house on the following evening. The occasion was a success, conversation being, as Kireevsky put it, "interesting, deep, but very free notwithstanding." Hegel involuntarily "turned every subject of conversation toward the universal; everything suggested the whole system of the newest thought, Hegelian thought." [22]

On the following day, Hegel invited Kireevsky to spend another evening with him, any evening, save only that the "Herr Professor möchte aber es voraus wissen, denn es werden dazu noch mehrere Andere eingeladen." This was the occasion that Kireevsky wrote home about in such excitement. The guests were Gans, who turned out to be "just as amiable in society as he is eloquent on the podium, which is saying a good deal," C. L. Michelet, the philosophy professor, who gave Ivan a copy of his dissertation signed "Nobilissimo viro Jean V. Kireiwsky," and Hotte, a professor of German literature. The dramatist Raupach and a traveling American, of whom Kireevsky took no notice, rounded out the company. Raupach, whom Ivan had previously admired, made some remark about the Russians not having sufficient "energy," and a lively dispute ensued, with Gans taking the Russian side. "What did we talk about, you are asking," wrote Ivan to his mother. "About politics, philosophy, religion, poetry, etc., but I can't describe the conversation in detail because everything was particulars, of interest only then and in passing." He was quite scornful of Michelet, who seemed to him rather a slavish follower of Hegel; Michelet kept ending their discussions by saying "Ja wohl! Sie können vielleicht Recht haben, aber diese Meinung gehört vielmehr zu dem Schellingischen als zu dem Hegelischen System!" [23]

As a result of this pleasant evening, Kireevsky's opinion of both Hegel and Gans improved dramatically. The former ceased to be the superannuated old dodderer of the early letters and became, again, one of Europe's great philosophers. Gans, who had been particularly cordial, was no longer regarded as merely a Frenchified Jew who was too clever by half. Kireevsky, at first defensive and skeptical, was won over — personally if not intellectually — by a dinner party. This is a perfectly understandable reaction, with which one can sympathize. More difficult to explain — and more important as well, one feels — was his virtual detestation of the German civilization he encountered in Berlin and Munich. By contrast with Peter, he went only a few times to the theater, finding the plays (including Goethe's *Tasso*) uninteresting and the actors bad. As far as the "public" was concerned, he found that "despite the great education of the Germans, they are, in the mass, just as soulless and stupid as their opposition numbers who fill our theaters." The audience missed everything "true, simple [and] natural," and applauded mindlessly and all the time. The adulation lavished on the actors by the public revolted him; even when they "were making fools of themselves in the most simple-minded way," actors were regarded as being "from the other world." [24] So much for Berlin theatergoers.

As for the "simple people on the street," they love to joke, but their joke is always the same one, told to them by some "verrückter Kerl" (a term of high praise, Kireevsky noted disapprovingly, both in middle-class and lower-class circles). "There is nothing stupider than a laughing German, and he laughs incessantly," Kireevsky concluded. "Nevertheless," he added in a burst of fairmindedness, "where is the people not stupid? Where

is the crowd not a crowd?" [25] By mid-summer, his attitude toward the surrounding world of Germans was even more exacerbated. "On the whole terrestrial globe," he exploded in a letter
written in July, "there is not a worse, more soulless, blinder, or
more vexing people than the Germans! Bulgarin, by comparison
with them, is a genius! . . . We have had a bellyful of Germany." [26]

How does one set about explaining Kireevsky's negative attitude toward a civilization to which he owed, intellectually speaking, so much? A great deal may be accounted for by his extraordinary closeness to a small circle of friends and, of course, to his
family; he was now, for the first time, separated from this warm
nest by several thousand miles. Perhaps even more important is
the fact that university life in Biedermeier Germany provided a
particularly sharp contrast with his life in Moscow; it was, for
both Kireevsky brothers, appallingly bourgeois. [27] A small indication of this may be seen in the adjectives which Ivan applied to
the Germans again and again: "soulless," "stupid," "narrow" —
to which Peter added "cold" and "calculating." [28] Even distinguished professors tended to speak French badly, and their conversation seemed to Kireevsky quite uncivilized. This was his first
— really his only — brush with a way of life which was unabashedly middle-class, and aristocratic disgust lay at the root of his
complaints about the Germans, rather than ordinary insularity
or chauvinism.

This reaction to life in Germany was — to a greater or lesser
degree — characteristic of most of the scions of the Russian gentry
who spent student years there. We find Michael Bakunin, for
instance, complaining to Herzen shortly after his arrival in Berlin
that "the Germans are terrible philistines. If the tenth part of
their rich spiritual consciousness were realized in their life, they
would be a splendid people. Up to now, though, they are — oh!
— a most ridiculous people." It was not merely in Germany that

Russian gentry travelers had this kind of reaction. Speaking of the French, as he came to know them in the Paris of the 1820's, Khomiakov confided to his brother: "I do not care for the people. They are neither one thing nor another. Their government is not in agreement with their spirit, and a kind of striving for commercial turnover, or more precisely for money (the result of their constitution) is so awkwardly mixed up in the French soul that they . . . have lost their natural character. They themselves feel this and complain about it, but they are scarcely able to correct it." [29]

Nor did Kireevsky have any fellow-feeling for the majority of the Russian students in Berlin, "of whom the greater part are drawn from seminaries," he wrote to his mother, "and will return to Russia just as unwashed as when they arrived." [30] On the other hand, Baron Maltitz made a good impression on him, and he was greatly attracted to Joseph von Radowitz, the Prussian aristocrat who subsequently played such an important role in German politics. Kireevsky liked him "most of anyone in Berlin," and felt that he united "a firm, rich, many-sided erudition with an ardent spirit, original thoughts, and a German good-heartedness." [31]

At the end of March, Kireevsky set off for Dresden and Munich, planning to spend only a few days in each place before going on to Paris. As matters turned out, he was still in Munich in the fall, when the cholera epidemic led to the return of both brothers to Russia. In Dresden, he stayed with his mother's protégé, Nikolai Rozhalin, who went on with him to Munich. The reunion of the brothers was a happy one. Ivan found Peter more sure of himself, more accustomed to moving among people outside his intimate circle. Peter found Ivan "just the same," only now "a European, that is, energetic." The trip, Peter felt, was "the best medicine" for Ivan. Reassuring his worried parents, he wrote them that Ivan "wants to struggle with the torment of his feelings and he will overcome it." Ivan was more frank with Peter about his state of mind than with his parents, discussing with his brother his struggles to achieve "firmness" and "independence of the character from the heart." [32] The immediate context, of course, was his attempt to subdue his feelings for Natal'ia Arbeneva, but one senses here, as well, an awareness of his own melancholy and passivity, problems which went well beyond his rejected suit.

Despite Peter's reassuring words to his parents on Ivan's state of mind, the correspondence of both brothers reveals an exacerbation of their temperamental tendency toward solitary inactivity, their propensity for long periods of daydreaming, together with a growing homesickness. The fact that they could now fall back on each other undoubtedly facilitated their withdrawal from the society around them. One feels increasingly, with Koyré, that the family was one large organism, whose life was greater than that of any individual member, and one feels equally that the source of the organism's vitality was Avdot'ia Petrovna.[33] An increasing part of Ivan's correspondence was given over to wondering what his mother was doing at the moment, worrying about not having received a letter, etc.[34] He dreamed constantly about life at home. "My Berlin activity has run aground here," he wrote from Munich on June 2. "Instead of busying myself with what is near at hand, I let my thoughts go far away, and hence spend a third of the day in bed." [35] To make matters worse, the Tiutchevs, who had provided Peter with a home-away-from-home during the winter and spring, left for a lengthy visit to Russia at the end of May.

Ivan did attend Schelling's lectures and spent several evenings at the house of the great man. On May 21/June 2, he wrote to his parents that "Schelling's system has so ripened in his head since the time that he stopped publishing, that like ripe fruit, it has simply dropped off the branch on which it formed, and lies in a heap, like glossy apples, between History and Religion." [36]

It is perhaps indicative of Ivan's state of mind that he never described to his foster father — that old Schellingian — what made Schelling's new system so interesting, but confined himself to elaborate and lapidary generalities.

The following month, by contrast, he wrote to his parents that he had stopped writing up notes on Schelling's lectures, since "the spirit is more interesting than the letter." [37] He really would rather be talking about Schelling with his stepfather in Russia, he confessed, than hearing him in the flesh at the University of Munich. Nevertheless, the Kireevskys' last evening at Schelling's house was, apparently, an interesting occasion. Peter reported that "Schelling was very pleasant; Brother asked him to explain much of his new system, and an extraordinarily interesting conversation ensued, which Brother has surely described to you in detail." [38] Alas, he does not appear to have done so.

In July, Pushkin's great friend, Sergei Aleksandrovich Sobolevsky, arrived for a visit of several weeks, bringing with him a breath of the outside world. He spent "the better part of the day lying on the divan in his dressing gown, describing, in stentorian voice, the balls, evenings, and good tone of Paris society." Neither Sobolevsky's worldly gossip nor his horseplay appealed much to the trio. After seeing him off to Turin, Peter wrote that although "I love him and respect him for many things, I am not sorry, between us, that he is gone." [39]

Despite his playful and frivolous disposition, Sobolevsky was an acute observer, and his impression of Ivan Kireevsky is worth noting. "As for him, my friend," he wrote to Shevyrëv in Rome, "sad to say there is nothing good to report. His health is no good at all; he is sallow, thin, and coughs incessantly, but for all that he has not abandoned his bad habits — sleeping during the day, not sleeping at night, smoking, and drinking coffee incessantly; he takes no sort of care of himself and does the devil knows what." [40]

Sobolevsky very sensibly tried to persuade Ivan to join him in Switzerland for the sake of his health, rather than submitting himself first to the inferno of an Italian summer and then to the dampness of Paris. What he needs above all is "diversion," wrote Sobolevsky, prescribing, perhaps, the medicine which always worked for him. "I hope that Kireevsky falls in love with some decent Roman girl. That would cure him once and for all." [41]

And so the summer dragged on. Both brothers wanted to get out of Germany, and travel plans were endlessly discussed. Ivan was studying Italian, and there was much talk of Italy's "sapphire sky." [42] Should they go first to Italy, then on to Paris? Or spend the winter in Rome with Shevyrëv? Or go straight to Paris? The last option was finally discarded, but not, as Ivan wrote home in some heat, because of the revolution and its disorders; he even found that his mother's alarms about revolutionary Paris "smelled of Bulgarin." [43] It was inertia that kept them in Munich.

Ivan had, as usual, a number of "projects" in the course of his ten months abroad. He wrote to Zhukovsky in March that he would like to do a piece on the "religious disputes" in Germany for Del'vig's *Literary Gazette,* but nothing came of it.[44] He failed to send Pogodin so much as a line for the *Messenger.* Iazykov's projected almanac never materialized, but if it had, there would have been no piece by Ivan Kireevsky, despite much rumination as to what he should write.[45] In a letter to his mother, he confessed to a deep envy of his hard-working, productive friends. Speaking of Shevyrëv's letters from Rome, he wrote: "How much friendship there is in them, and how much enviable youthful fire. Yes! For me, youthfulness is already an alien and enviable quality, and I look upon any kind of feverish excitement with the same feelings with which the legless invalid looks upon the daring movements of his comrades. Shevyrëv's movements are in fact daring. The more he works, the stronger he gets, and instead of fatigue he accumulates more and more enthusiasm and spirit. In his life he is like a fish in water." [46]

Judging from his letters, the only activities in which Kireevsky indulged with any deep enthusiasm in Munich were looking at pictures in the city's fine galleries and reading Italian literature. Some of his observations on his experiences in the gallery are worth quoting at length, for they reveal a good deal about his sensibility, and about his knowledge of himself as well. "The art gallery has completely mastered me," he wrote to his family on April 26.

Sometimes it seems to me that I was born to be a painter, if only taking pleasure in art meant having any capability for it. More frequently, however, it seems to me that I will never have any sense (*tolk*) for painting, and am even incapable of understanding it, since it is just those pictures which make the greatest impression on me that grip me the least in themselves. As yet I have not been able to accustom myself, when looking at a picture, to see in it only what is there. I usually begin with the image itself, and the more I look at it, the more I tend to wander from the picture to that ideal which the artist wished to depict. Here the field is broad, and before I manage to collect myself, the imagination has taken the bit in its teeth, and, like St. Anthony's devil, carried it away so fast, that before you can contrive to tip your cap it is already a thousand versts away. Only when the material presence of the picture recalls me to it, do I realize that I've been far away, almost always there, where the sun rises. I recognize the absurdity of my ability to take delight in that which is not in the picture, and I am most aware of the entire strangeness of this quality, which, to be completely *consequent*, should most enjoy a golden frame around an empty space. It is even stranger for me to see this quality in myself, where it does not even take the place of imaginative creativity, for I have no *imagination*, properly speaking, only memory instead. Just imagine, it often happens that I look at one picture for a long time, thinking about another which is hanging on the opposite wall; when I approach the other, I again think about the first. This is not innate, and I know very well whence it comes. [47]

In this passage we see again the Kireevsky tendency to undisciplined mental association, as well as that concern with the "ideal," an almost platonic attitude, which seems to have been part and parcel of idealism. And in this concern with the ideal, and the concomitant indifference to material reality, we may perhaps even detect an essential attitude of what came to be called Slavophilism. Ivan Kireevsky was unfair to himself when he said that he had "no imagination," but there can be no question of the enormous role which memory played in his "imagination" — memory and the "ideal" which he found in his family and their past — and subsequently in the past of Russian society.

Kireevsky's attraction to Italy, its culture and landscape, was another theme of that summer in Munich. True, he never managed to get beyond the Brenner Pass, and it might be argued that in his heart of hearts he was perfectly content to remain in Munich, meditating about the landscape which he saw in quattrocento paintings, seeing that "sapphire sky" in his mind's eye, and reading Ariosto, Petrarch, and Dante.[48] In any case, it is characteristic of Kireevsky that he never managed to visit Shevyrëv in Rome or even to slip down into Tuscany for a few days; an actual trip to Italy proved beyond him. The curious inertia and passivity which we have seen so clearly, particularly during his months in Munich, kept him there until the cholera galvanized his homesickness sufficiently to take him back to Moscow. Nevertheless, he seems to have had a case of that Italian sickness which has been such a familiar ailment among Northern European men of letters, particularly Germans.

In the summer of 1829, the cholera reappeared in Russia after a hiatus of six years. Unlike the Astrakhan' outbreak of 1823, the epidemic this time did not remain localized, but moved outward from Orenburg. By September 11, 1830, Moscow had been swept by a "rising tide of panic" over the approach of the disease; the first officially recognized case appeared in the city on September 14.[49] Avdot'ia Petrovna first mentioned the epidemic in a letter of September 8; like many other Russians, she seems to have thought at first that it was plague.[50] Kireevsky inquired about it anxiously in a letter written early in October; on October 30 he wrote that if he did not hear from his family in short order he would leave Munich, not for Italy, but for Moscow. On November 11, he wrote them from Warsaw, announcing his imminent arrival. Peter, who had been with Rozhalin in Vienna, arrived a few days after Ivan, who was in Moscow on November 16.[51] Ivan's *Wanderjahre*, against all expectation, lasted only about ten months.

To what general conclusions can one come about his sojourn in Germany, or, to be more precise, how did it affect his spiritual development? Earlier writers like Koyré have seen Kireevsky's detestation of Germany — and his corresponding achievement of a more "just" appreciation of Russia — as important in the development of the Slavophile opposition of Russia and "the West." [52] But as we have seen, this "opposition" is already clearly visible in the conclusion of the "Survey of Russian Literature in 1829," and, as Andrzej Walicki has pointed out, Kireevsky's next important article, "The Nineteenth Century," was in a variety of ways *more* favorably disposed toward Western culture than the "Survey." [53]

Eberhard Müller sees the primary importance of the trip as having brought Kireevsky into closer touch with European intellectual developments and European culture as a whole. "The experiences of this year were to bear fruit in the *European*," he concludes.[54] That the experiences of the year were to some degree "broadening" for Kireevsky cannot be denied, and yet it is hard to tell from his letters how much new intellectual ground he broke in Germany. The lectures he heard do not appear to have been major stimuli for him, even those of Schelling, which, it will be recalled, he stopped writing up, since "the spirit is more interesting than the letter." [55] He certainly did not explore even his immediate university environment with any thoroughness; he seems not to have heard Franz von Baader at all. His reading, on the other hand, was considerable — this becomes quite clear when we see him as an editor and journalist in 1832. Feeling, memory, and the printed word were always more important to Kireevsky than his physical environment. In a sense, he never left Moscow at all.

Kireevsky's letters from Germany are most useful to a biographer for the insights they provide into such important parts of his life as family relations, personal values and judgments, way of life, and, most important of all, his own reflections on his psyche and his personal problems. In these letters, which he himself — significantly — thought of as a kind of diary, we see the man more intimately than we will ever see him again.

V. *The* European

The Decembrist uprising in 1825 seems to us now so obviously the moment at which the celebrated "abyss" opened between the Russian gentry and the government (or, at any rate, became visible), that the fact has often been overlooked that the most reactionary and stagnant period of Nicholas' regime began only five or six years later. The revolutions of 1830, the Polish revolt, and the bloody insurrection in the military colonies kept Nicholas' fears of a new conspiracy of the Decembrist sort at a fever pitch. The closing down of virtually all the independent Moscow press was but one indication of what the decade of the 1830's was to bring. The Moscow *Messenger* died a natural death in 1830, but early in the following year Del'vig was forbidden to take part in the publication of the *Literary Gazette*. In 1832, Kireevsky's *European* was suppressed after one issue, and Polevoi's Moscow *Telegraph* followed in 1834. N. I. Nadezhdin managed to keep afloat until the end of 1836, despite denunciations by Bulgarin and the sporadic hostility of Uvarov, who had become Minister of Education in 1833. The demise of Nadezhdin's *Telescope*, of course, was the direct result of the appearance of Chaadaev's famous "First Philosophical Letter" in its columns.

A less mechanical index of the quality of life in Russia in the 1830's may be had by examining the intellectual biographies of some of the principal members of what we may loosely call the *intelligentsiia.* Herzen was either in prison or in exile from 1834 until 1840, and in the first years of his exile he went through his disembodied, epistolary love affair with his future wife Natal'ia. Under the influence of his Viatka "Virgil," Alexander Witberg (whom Herzen subsequently compared to Kireevsky),[1] Herzen's reading went from Schiller to Swedenborg, Paracelsus, Eckhartshausen, and Neoplatonic mysticism.[2]

Vissarion Belinsky moved, in the course of the 1830's, from a position of criticizing Russian life or "reality" (using what snippets of German idealism were available to him) to his famous "reconciliation with Reality." In his articles of 1839, Belinsky seemed, in Bowman's words, "to be announcing an unqualified patriotism, a mystique of Russian life in which national faults become almost national virtues."[3] Bakunin, at about the same time, was equally well-disposed toward things as they were. "Let us hope," he wrote in the *Moscow Observer* for March 1838, "that the new generation will reconcile itself with our beautiful Russian reality."[4]

In this decade of repression — in what seems an almost Freudian sense of the word — of mysticism, of withdrawal and passivity, Slavophilism was born. Ivan Kireevsky's *European* adventure marks the high tide of his "occidentalism," as Andrzej Walicki calls it. His hostility to Germany and the "West" in general receded somewhat, in the early 1830's, and his aristocratic disgust at the vulgarity of Russian life reached its apogee. At the same time, his belief in the coming of a new epoch of "realism" — both in Russia and the West — brought him into contact with the radical critics of Young Germany: Heinrich Heine, Ludwig Börne, and Wolfgang Menzel.

The suppression of the *European,* on the other hand, was a crucial step in the formation of his Slavophile views. Kireevsky withdrew from "Russian reality" in the thirties, as did Herzen.

He sought solace in a whole new attitude toward religion, toward Orthodoxy, which became the basis for his new view of Russian culture, first formulated in 1838. But Kireevsky, unlike Herzen, did not return to "Russian reality" in the 1840's. Nothing could have been more out of keeping with his subsequent views than the vision of the new realism which he proclaimed so confidently in 1832.

Early in 1831, we find Pogodin writing to Shevyrëv, then still in Rome: "I do not understand Kireevsky. He lies around and sleeps; perhaps he is thinking something over. Unlikely." [5] Koshelëv's impression was similar. "On the very day of my arrival [from St. Petersburg] I saw Kireevsky. His condition disturbs me. The melancholy of his spirit has plunged him into passivity. All he can do is sleep and eat, eat and sleep. I am trying to bring him back to his family, for now even his mother sees him only rarely. A good, splendid fellow, but a wonderfully odd one." [6] Clearly, the Munich lassitude was not cleared up immediately by the bracing Moscow air. [7]

While Kireevsky was readjusting to Russian life, important events were taking place in the journalistic world. Del'vig, who had just been separated from his journal, the *Literary Gazette*, by the Third Section, died on January 14, 1831. [8] His friend Pletnëv attempted to carry on, but Pushkin and Viazemsky had at the time little to contribute, and the journal folded in July. This meant, of course, that the "Aristocrats" were without a literary organ.

Exactly what convinced Ivan Kireevsky to try to fill the gap left by the *Literary Gazette* we do not know, but of course the idea of a journal of his own was a natural outgrowth of his belief in the importance of public opinion and of himself as Novikov's heir. [9] In September he approached the Moscow Censorship Committee, asking permission to edit a journal to be called the *European*, beginning the following year. [10] On October 13, the

Main Administration of the Censorship granted him the necessary permission; six days later there was a victory celebration,
where, according to Alexander Turgenev, "the *European* was
christened with champagne. They got the poet Iazykov drunk
on the same, and listened until three in the morning to his poems
about the dear *unforgettable one* and so on." [11]

A week before the permission came through, Kireevsky wrote
to Zhukovsky in great excitement, asking his blessing on the
enterprise, but allowing that if Zhukovsky thought him still too
immature for such an undertaking, he would abandon the idea.
If, with Zhukovsky's approval, he went forward, he hoped that
the

next year of my life will not be without advantage to our literature, if
only because my journal will compel Baratynsky and Iazykov to write
more; they have both promised me their active participation. Furthermore, journalistic activities would be useful for me as well. They
would force me to directed activity and train me in it; they would
surround me *mit der Welt des europäischen wissenschaftlichen Lebens,*
and they would give to this faraway world the power and influence
over me of what is near at hand. In some wise, this may take the
place of a trip for me.[12] Subscribing to all the best nonpolitical
journals in three languages, going deeply into the most outstanding
works of the best writers of the present time, I would make of my
study a lecture hall of the European university, and my journal, like
the notes of an industrious student, would be useful to those who
themselves do not have the time or means to take lessons at first
hand. Russian literature would enter into it only as a supplement to
European, and with what delight could I speak of you, of Pushkin, of
Baratynsky, of Viazemsky, of Krylov, of Karamzin — on pages not
sullied with the name of Bulgarin, before a public which will not
buy the journal for the fashion plates, remembering only those readers
who do not think and feel by rote, whose participation will enhance
the activity, forgetting that others exist in the world.[13]

Here is a spirit very different from that with which Kireevsky had
endured his university lectures in Berlin and Munich; we see

again how important for him was an active role. It is interesting
to observe, as well, how his exclusively Russian orientation has
receded. It is the "European university," in the largest sense,
that is at issue here, and Russian literature is only a "supplement"
to European.[14] The impulse which led to the foundation of the
journal was in large part to open the doors of the cultural treasury
of Europe to the thinking minority in Russia, in order to create
that cultural elite on which the destinies of Russia depended.

Not all of Kireevsky's friends and collaborators liked the idea
of calling the journal the *European,* clearly as that title followed
from his conception. "As far as the name is concerned," wrote
Baratynsky to Kireevsky on October 8, "it seems to me that it
would be best to choose something which would mean precisely
nothing and make no sort of claim. The *European,* besides being
completely unintelligible to the public, would be understood by
the journalists in an offensive sense, and why arm them betimes?
Isn't it possible to call the journal the *Northern Messenger,*
Opinion, or something at once capricious and meaningless, like
The Yellow Dwarf, which the Bonapartists published under Louis
XVIII?"[15] But the name had already been given the censors,
and it was too late to reconsider, or so the editor alleged.

Among the first, very naturally, to whom Kireevsky wrote about
the *European* was Pushkin.[16] His letter attests to the great importance which he placed upon Pushkin's collaboration, and the
rather strained imagery indicated nervousness and veneration.
On October 25, he wrote to him in the following terms:

Yesterday I was authorized to edit a journal in the coming year, 1832,
and I hasten to recommend it to you, as a recruit who is consumed
with impatience to serve and fight under your command, as a woman,
still innocent, who wants to belong to you body and soul, as a cleric
(*dukhovnaia osoba*), who asks you to confirm him as pastor of the
literary flock, and, finally, I recommend my journal to you as a
European — for so it is called. I have called it that not, as you must
know, because I hoped to make it of European significance (I do

not yet know to what degree I may hope for your participation), but
because I propose to fill it with articles relating more to Europe in
general than to Russia. However, if at some point Feofilakt Kosichkin[17]
wishes to do my journal the honor of horsewhipping Bulgarin in it,
then of course in that case Bulgarin would be Europe in the full sense
of the word. . . .

My journal will consist of five parts: (1) scholarly disciplines
(*nauka*), where pride of place will be given to philosophy; (2) belles-
lettres (*iziashchaia slovesnost'*); (3) biographies of notable contemporaries; (4) analyses of foreign and Russian books, criticism,
etc.; (5) miscellany. Every month two booklets (*knizhki*) will appear.[18]

The principal problems which confronted Kireevsky from the
outset — aside from the purely financial — were getting contributions from the Russian writers whose participation he desired and getting his hands on the wide range of European periodicals he needed to document the exciting and complicated
intellectual life of Western Europe. His principal collaborator on
the editorial side was the poet N. M. Iazykov, who worked tire-
lessly, badgering their mutual friends for contributions and seeing
to the wearisome business of supplying the *European* with its
vital journalistic links with Europe.[19]

Pushkin, of course, was their principal hope; he had been loud
in his proclamations of the need for a journal to replace the
Literary Gazette. Disconcertingly enough, however, he did not
answer either Kireevsky's letter or Iazykov's until November 18,
when he wrote to Iazykov: "I cordially thank you, dear Nikolai
Mikhailovich, both you and Kireevsky, for the friendly letters
. . . ; if you had added your addresses as well, I would have been
completely content. I congratulate the brotherhood upon the
birth of the *European.* As for me, I am ready to serve you with
whatever you please, with prose and poetry, in conscience and
against conscience. Feofilakt Kosichkin is touched to tears by the
attention which you vouchsafe him." [20]

This ringing declaration notwithstanding, Pushkin contributed nothing to the first two booklets. "For some reason Pushkin is looking down his nose at Kireevsky," wrote Iazykov to his brother on January 6, 1832, "hasn't given the poems, and only promises everything, everything." [21] Viazemsky, too, provided no real support. On January 11, Avdot'ia Petrovna wrote to Zhukovsky that "Viazemsky promised much and has given nothing, likewise Pushkin. The editor is left with his own things and is terribly embarrassed." [22] It appeared that "balls and evening parties" were to blame. On the following day Viazemsky wrote airily to his wife: "When you see Kireevsky, tell him that the European [the first booklet of which had just appeared] is tricked out in too Asiatic a fashion. The paper it is printed on is really too ugly. I was particularly struck by this, because I saw it for the first time on a fashionable coffee table at Mr. Lavalle's . . . on the day of a ball, surrounded by the glittering legions of both sexes of Petersburg society. I have not read the *European* because I do not have it, but I hear that the first number has pleased everybody." [23]

Under the circumstances, the literary wheelhorses of the first two booklets were Zhukovsky, Baratynsky, and Iazykov. Zhukovsky contributed his *Tale of the Sleeping Princess* (*Skazka o spiashchei tsarevne*) to the first booklet, and a fragment of the *War between the Mice and the Frogs* to the second; his *Divine Justice* (*Bozhii sud*) would have appeared in the third part, had it been permitted to appear. Baratynsky was represented by three poems ("Elegy," "The Signet Ring" [*Persten'*], and "To N. M. Iazykov") in the first two parts, and Iazykov by five, including his beautiful "Elegy."

In addition, Iazykov, as mentioned above, took upon himself the time-consuming task of getting hold of as much contemporary periodical literature as possible. Due to the great distances involved, Ivan and Iazykov were forced to content themselves, for

the first two booklets, with the *Revue des deux mondes,* the
Revue britannique, the *Revue germanique,* the *Revue de Paris,*
and the *Foreign Quarterly Review,* all ordered from Gref, a
dealer in St. Petersburg. To these were added the *Morgenblatt
für gebildete Stände* and Wolfgang Menzel's *Literatur-Blatt,* both
of which were, according to Eberhard Müller, part of Kireevsky's
regular reading in Moscow.[24] The dearth of periodicals upon
which to draw for the all-important translations in the first issues
was a source of great disappointment to the young editor in the
hectic months before the first number appeared, as was the fact
that as late as December 16 there were no subscribers. "It seems,"
wrote Avdot'ia Petrovna to Zhukovsky, "that the announcement
was too modest, and the unknown name of the editor attracts
nobody." [25] The liberal Catholic *L'Avenir* could not be had, for
reasons of censorship, nor could some desirable English journals.
When the first issue appeared, there was a total of only fifty
subscriptions.[26]

In what has survived of Ivan Kireevsky's correspondence from
1830–1831, he scarcely mentions the revolution in France. The
explanation for this may lie, in part, in the fact that almost all
the letters which we have are written to his parents; such letters
are obviously based on what the writer is "doing," geared to the
details of the daily round, rather than the events of the larger
world. The reader is also struck by a characteristic of Kireevsky
which was to become more pronounced as time passed: the degree to which he experienced and "understood" what we think of
as politics on the level of philosophy, literature, and *Geistesge-
schichte.* For Kireevsky was far from unaware of what had happened in 1830. On the contrary — the contents of the *European,*
and, more particularly, of his own long article, "The Nineteenth
Century," reveal that he had an extraordinarily keen grasp of
what was going on. But — characteristically — it was not the

politics of 1830 which excited his interest, but the intellectual currents that emanated from them.

Almost from the moment of the revolution, perceptive Europeans recognized that the period in which they were living marked an important divide in history, the end of one era and the beginning of another. For Germans, the change was highlighted almost as significantly by the deaths of Friedrich Schlegel, Hegel, and Goethe as by the July revolution.

Subsequent political, social, and literary historians have almost all accepted 1830 as a watershed. Arnold Hauser, in what is an extreme but far from untenable view, has written that "the nineteenth century, or what we usually understand by that term, begins around 1830. It is only during the July monarchy that the foundations and outlines of this century are developed, that is to say, the social order in which we ourselves are rooted, the economic system, the antagonisms and contradictions of which still continue, and the literature in whose forms we on the whole still express ourselves today. The novels of Stendhal and Balzac are the first books concerned with our own life, our own vital problems, with moral difficulties and conflicts unknown to earlier generations." [27]

To speak somewhat more narrowly and politically, the period 1830–1832 marked the accession to political power of a significant portion of the upper bourgeoisie in England, France, and Belgium. In itself, this development was only "revolutionary" in a rather narrow and technical sense; the government of Louis-Philippe was faithful at home to its numerically small constituency, while piously eschewing "liberationist" activity abroad. Nevertheless, there was now a genuine line of demarcation between those three Western nations and the rest of Europe. Social strife became endemic in Spain and Portugal, while the governments of the Restoration period remained thoroughly in control in central and eastern Europe.

Despite — or perhaps because of — this very limited triumph
of a portion of the wealthy bourgeoisie, the period after 1830 saw
a very considerable upsurge in critical and radical thought —
and, to a much lesser degree, organization and action. With the
shattering of the conservative unity of Restoration Europe, the
united front of its enemies also came unstuck. In France, a left
romanticism finally triumphed over the ruins of French classicism.
"Romanticism," proclaimed the converted Victor Hugo in his
famous preface to *Hernani*, "is liberalism in literature." [28] But
romanticism in France was to be little comfort to the "liberal"
government of Louis-Philippe. Balzac, Stendhal, Eugène Sue,
and Georges Sand all attacked the plutocratic society of the July
monarchy; all were strongly marked by romanticism (and its
offspring, "realism"), and all except Balzac were basically men
of the left. Conversely, radicalism in France and elsewhere took
on certain "romantic" qualities, quite alien to its eighteenth-
century origins: nationalism and the view of society as properly
"organic."

At the same time, spokesmen for the new liberal and national
movements all over Europe began contrasting "life" with "art,"
and most chose the former. A good many German men of letters
moved to the left and became, to varying degrees, Francophile
and political. Heinrich Heine, Wolfgang Menzel, and Ludwig
Börne all professed to be ultimately for "life" and "politics,"
rather than art; Heine liked to think of himself as — in the last
analysis — "a soldier in the war of humanity." [29] All three were
represented in the "European University" of Kireevsky, and
Menzel, a romantic nationalist and admirer of Schelling, influenced Kireevsky's view of European intellectual developments
over a considerable period.[30]

The year 1830, then, marked an important stage in the pol-
iticization of European intellectual life, a process which had been
under way since 1789. As Kireevsky was to point out dolefully

more than once in his career, not only was literature becoming increasingly tendentious, but the lines between politics, literature, and journalism were blurring in the most disconcerting way. The age which was emerging in the early 1830's, finally, was clearly an age of prose, and Kireevsky, with Lamartine, foresaw the decline of poetry for an indefinite period.

This is the intellectual context within which Kireevsky's remarkable article, "The Nineteenth Century," must be discussed. Writing in 1831, he saw, with a clarity and depth unequaled in Russia, that 1830 was a major divide. Almost twelve years later, Alexander Herzen reread the *European* and wrote in his diary: "Ivan Kireevsky's article is remarkable. He anticipated the contemporary direction of Europe itself; what a healthy, powerful intelligence, what talent, style . . . and what has become of him? Despotism has squeezed him and squeezed him and he is finally broken." [31]

"The Nineteenth Century" was the core of the *European*.[32] With the exception of the poetry, the content of the journal — Heine, Börne, Menzel, Villemain, et al. — flowed from Kireevsky's central idea of the "new era" in Europe and European literature.[33] They — and he with them — were in fact the new era itself.

As the nineteenth century develops, Kireevsky began, so too does our understanding of it. We are like the traveler moving along the road; at every turning he looks back whence he has come, and with every change in his own position, the road he has traveled looks different too. Formerly it took a man of genius to chart the direction of the times; nowadays, every "thinking person" is devoting himself to this end, and the necessary material is being frantically collected. Hence, Kireevsky observed modestly, all that is required is attention and a bit of dispassionate calculation. The principal difficulty in the operation is the now vastly accelerated rate of change. Whatever the differences of opinion within them, generations and eras were a leisurely affair in the old days. Now we see that men who were formed by the era before 1789 are really different from the children of the French Revolution, who differ in turn from those who grew up in the Napoleonic era, or in the post-Napoleonic period.

Having set the stage in his usual graceful and intelligent way, Kireevsky then turned to the history of present-day Europe, beginning with the Englightenment, whose "spirit" he found to be destructive and profoundly materialistic. Its ideals — liberty, equality, humanity — have no positive content, but merely negate the ideas and institutions of the *ancien régime.* As Kireevsky discusses the simple-minded, head-counting democracy, the imitation of nature in the arts, the materialism in philosophy, the identification of religion with its abuses, his aversion becomes increasingly evident. Nevertheless, the dominant feeling is historicist — all this had to happen, one feels. The period of negation culminated, of course, in the French Revolution.

These developments created, in men's minds, their opposite, the "counterrevolutionary direction." This is described much as one would expect: the basic manifestation was conceived as an artificial and one-sided drive for "unity," among the important symptoms of which were systematic philosophical speculation (as opposed to the empiricism of the previous period), mysticism, and the re-creation of the former ostentatious "society."

At present, continued Kireevsky, European culture finds itself in a transitional stage, an artificial equilibrium, marked by the dominance of the historical spirit. The literature of the present time is characterized by the attempt to "reconcile imagination with reality, rightness (*pravil'nost'*) of form with freedom of content, perfection (*okruglënnost'*) of artifice with depth of naturalness — in a word, that which we uselessly call classicism with what is even less properly known as *romanticism.*" [34] Walter Scott (one cannot help wanting to push him back into the preceding period) and Goethe, who contains within himself the complex fusion of classicism and romanticism, illustrate this equilibrium period in literature, while Schelling's system of identity has replaced the strife of materialism and idealism.

But this momentary stasis is already giving way to the true synthesis. Scott's popularity is being sapped by a new art, marked by crudity and sensationalism, dramatic contrasts and a general stylistic vulgarity. Public taste increasingly demands literature characterized by (1) "enthusiasm," rather than "sensitivity," (2) the love of the shocking, without regard for artistic considerations, (3) an imagination stimulated largely by "reality in all its nakedness." [35] This is a pretty fair start (from a somewhat hostile point of view, to be sure) at a definition of literary "realism," and Kireevsky went on to ask whether, given the obvious and growing taste of the public for "real life," the great age of poetry had not passed. Again he was prophetic.

In philosophy, he went on, idealism has until very recently swept all before it. The systems of Fichte, Oken, Hegel, and Schelling have passed for the last word in "science." But "this same Schelling, who first created the system of identity, has now revealed a new goal and indicated a new road for philosophy. True knowledge, he says, positive, living knowledge, constituting the final goal of all the strivings of our mind, does not consist in the logical development of the necessary laws of reason. It is *outside* the logical process of the school, and hence *living*; it is higher than the understanding of eternal necessity, and hence positive; it is *more essential* than mathematical abstraction, and hence *individual-certain, historical*." [36] The systems of idealism, by contrast, are based on "purely logical convictions," on the "abstract understanding of the laws of our reason, and not on the "living understanding of the essence of things and existence (*byt*)." [37] Thus the essential difference between idealism and materialism, so insisted on by the idealists themselves, is gone.

Both are ultimately based on logic, or mental processes, and the knowledge they can provide is ultimately "negative." Schelling has told us that philosophy, too, must be historical, must have that crucial connection with life and reality.

Kireevsky was thoroughly attuned to the religious revival which had come with the Restoration. We have seen, he wrote, how in the counterrevolutionary period Voltairian skepticism was opposed by a kind of dreamy mysticism. Nevertheless, "free-thinking" could not be overcome by mysticism, limited as it was to a small elite. Now, thanks to the spread of "enlightenment (*prosveshchenie*) in general," religion seems to be everywhere on the ascendant. The only disturbing fact was that in spite of this religious revival, a certain "indifference" was everywhere observable, an indifference which Kireevsky suggested was related to the fact that educated people tend to regard religion as either simply the sum of ritual and ceremony or as a purely individual conviction about certain truths. But religion is neither of these things, for its ultimate development demands the "full conformity of a people's ideas, consecrated by glowing memories, developed in harmonious traditions, imbued with the order of the state, embodied in the uniquely significant national (*obshche-narodnyi*) order, united by one positive principle and attuned to all civil and familial relationships." [38] Unless these conditions be met, there cannot be religion, properly speaking. In the face of his Herderian rhetoric, one wonders whether Kireevsky would actually have claimed that the early Christians had no "religion." This truth — as he would have it — Kireevsky found particularly evident at the present time. All the religious "parties" of Europe, Catholic, Protestant, and Saint-Simonian, are united in the demand for a "larger fusion of Religion with the life of people and peoples": [39] religion, too, is seeking "life."

Having sketched out this picture of contemporary Europe and its recent history, Kireevsky turned to the great question: what is Russian culture, and how does "the life of enlightened Europe act upon it?" First of all, he observed, despite the heroic efforts of Peter and Catherine, something like a Chinese wall still stands between Russia and the rest of Europe. "How can it be destroyed? Will the level of our culture soon rise to that which has been achieved by the enlightened states of Europe? What ought we to do to achieve this goal or to promote its development? Ought we to adopt our culture from our own inner life or receive it from Europe? And what kind of principle should we develop within our own life? And what ought we to borrow from those who have become enlightened before us?" [40] Thus, here we have the questions of the 1820's again, the questions of Viazemsky, the questions of Venevitinov. Europe or *samobytnost'*? And what is our *samobytnost'*?

Again Kireevsky went over the familiar ground, noting that although Russia's past is long indeed, Russian culture has barely begun. Nor has this culture, he continued, been "the fruit of our previous life, the necessary result of our inner development." It came to us from Europe and was introduced, in part, by force. Hence, "its external form is still, to this day, in contradiction with the form of our nationality."

Why has Russia lagged behind for so long? What is it in our *byt*, in our history, that is responsible? Here Kireevsky introduced the famous cultural formula, taken from Guizot,[41] alleged to account for the unique lines of Western European culture: Christianity, the "character, culture, and spirit" of the barbarian peoples who destroyed the Roman Empire, and the heritage of ancient Greece and Rome. It was, of course, the final member of the triad which Russia lacked: the heritage of Roman law, of Roman institutions.

Here for the first time, a key element of the subsequent Slavophile world view was introduced — but standing on its head, as it were. Roman law was incessantly attacked by nineteenth-century conservatives for its abstractness, its encyclopedic, rationalizing tendency, its intolerance of concrete, "irrational" survivals from a feudal past; for the Slavophiles, Rome was to become the great enemy. But Kireevsky saw the matter very differently in 1832.

This Roman legacy in Europe, he went on, had a strong impact on the civilization created by the barbarian peoples, but its most vital influence was on the urban commercial centers of Western Europe. There is no real Russian equivalent for these towns. We have, to be sure, Novgorod and Pskov, but their essential spirit was so opposed to that of the rest of Russia (Kireevsky supposed their institutional structure to have been heavily influenced by commercial foreigners), that they had no real impact on the rest of the country at all, did not affect, as he put it, "the totality of our *byt.*"

Even more important than the influence of the Roman spirit on the towns of Western Europe was its influence on the Roman Catholic Church. Kireevsky was quite specific as to what this "influence" was, and his attitude toward it was one of approval: it was the "civil authority" of the clergy which Catholicism owes to Rome. Behind this phrase looms the enormous temporal power of the medieval Church, that power which Kireevsky was subsequently to condemn so passionately. To be sure, even in "The Nineteenth Century" he found the Russian Church "purer" and "holier," but lacking the political power of the Church of Rome, it was a far less effective force for unity in a time of feudal disintegration. It could not animate the various political bodies with "one soul" as did the Church of Rome. This spiritual-national failure had important consequences for Russia in the long struggle with the Tatars, for, being unable to unite spiritually against them, the Russians had to be united "physically," a process which took place over several centuries and had the most serious effects on national development. Thus, with typical monistic unfairness, Kireevsky attributed both the initial Tatar success and the subsequent Tatar influence on Russia to her lack of a classical heritage. Divide Russia into these appanages again, he wrote, and new Tatars will undoubtedly appear, although this time they may come from Europe.

The purely material Russian unification and liberation from the Tatar yoke was so slow and arduous a business that for many centuries it left the country little time or energy to devote to the creation of a culture. In the West, the Renaissance, the voyages of discovery, and all the ferment of the fifteenth century were born from the Roman Catholic culture of the fourteenth, even though the men of the Renaissance broke away from the church to some degree and sought to establish a more direct bond with classical antiquity. Both in Russia and the West a struggle for national unity and independence took place, but in the West, religious and political thought had so developed that they were able to define the aims and goals of the national movements. In Russia, on the other hand, "the place of thought was taken by the *individual,* the private event, the pretender." [42]

Real Russian culture began to develop long before Peter—in the time of Minin and Pozharsky, in fact, "when our history permitted us a rapprochement with Europe." One should bear in mind, at this point, that Kireevsky felt Russian national consciousness — or at any rate its beginnings — to have been the product of the Time of Troubles, or, more properly, to have arisen in that dark hour against a backdrop of the collapse of the older patrimonial-monarchical ideal.[43] And culture, in his definition, had to be accompanied by this national consciousness, to which it was intimately related. Western influences increased during the seventeenth century, but the whole process of rapprochement (*sblizhenie*) was so drastically accelerated under Peter that he deserved the title of "founder of our new life" and "father of our intellectual development." [44]

In support of Peter the Great and against his detractors — and Peter Kireevsky may well be meant here — Ivan Kireevsky advanced a quasi-Hegelian, cosmopolitan argument against their version of Herder. Those who accuse Peter I of breaking the organic, national lines of development would be justified, he observed, if the culture of each nation were simply the sum of its own national experience or the development of its national essence. But Peter's critics are wrong in making this assumption, he claimed, and he proceeded to advance a skeletal, despiritualized version of Hegel's idea of the world-historical nations. The stress in his exposition fell on the notion that as each of these nations achieved its temporary cultural hegemony, it further developed the "culture of all humanity," as Ivan put it, not merely its own national culture. Hence, "the culture of each people comprises not the sum of its own knowledge (*poznanie*), not the refinement and complexity of that which we call civil society — but only its participation in the culture of all humanity, that place which it occupies in the general course of human development." [45] Cultures which develop in isolation, cultures like that of China — another Hegelianism — are inevitably doomed by their isolation: there is no life in them, for there is no progress.

Peter's detractors would have us return to pre-Petrine times, to our *samobytnost'*. They forget that even the search for nationality is a foreign idea, a European idea. Furthermore, a European may turn to his past with some hope of finding something there, but for us it is folly, for we have no culture there to discover. Lacking crucial elements, where will we find them if not in Europe? The culture of Western Europe is based on the culture of classical antiquity, and it is the culture of humanity.

Russia's hope, Kireevsky concluded, lies in the radical break in European culture which came in the middle of the eighteenth century. This new stage, of course, followed from the old, as its

negation, but nevertheless "exists independently," or "autochthon-
ously" (*samobytno*). For this reason, "a people, beginning to
develop itself (*obrazovyvat'sia*), can adopt it directly and install
it at home without what went before, applying it directly to one's
own real *byt*. This is why in both Russia and America, enlightenment began to develop conspicuously only in the eighteenth and
particularly in the nineteenth century." [46] Europe is — and is to
be — for Russia, what antiquity was for Europe.

In terms of the evolution of Ivan Kireevsky's own ideas on the
question of Russia and Europe, the most striking feature of "The
Nineteenth Century" was the author's reassessment of the cultural vitality of Europe and his greater caution, if not pessimism,
about Russia's future. Gone was the talk of the "exhaustion" and
"torpor" of Europe, as was the idea that the cultural hegemony
of England and Germany might pass to Russia in the future. And
with the help of Guizot's triad, Kireevsky made real efforts to
describe the unique evolution of Western culture.

This question of what Andrzej Walicki calls "Kireevsky's evolution toward occidentalism" has been much discussed and has been
generally laid to the influence of Peter Chaadaev, author of the
remarkable *Philosophical Letters*, written between 1827 and
1831. [47] Unfortunately, hard information on Kireevsky's relations
with Chaadaev in the period immediately following his return
from Europe has yet to be uncovered, although it seems fair
to presuppose a general familiarity on Kireevsky's part with
Chaadaev's ideas. [48] Thus, the case for Chaadaev's influence on
Kireevsky — best made by Alexandre Koyré — has remained a
matter of the comparison of ideas and systems. "The simple
analysis of their respective work," wrote Koyré, "reveals several
points of contact: universalism is one, and the insistence with
which Kireevsky speaks of the impossibility of an isolated civilization (*à la chinoise*) certainly recalls Chaadaev. The latter, it
is true, speaks not of China, but of Japan and Abyssinia. It is

from Chaadaev, in all probability, that Kireevsky borrows his new conception of the role of Russia's territorial greatness; the tone is different, Kireevsky does not have the bitter sarcasm of Chaadaev, but the idea is the same. It is to Chaadaev that he owes his explanation of the Mongol yoke, as well as the evident sympathy for the Catholic church and the social conception of Christianity." [49]

Eberhard Müller strongly disagrees and has recently provided a thoroughgoing critique of Koyré's case.[50] Müller admits that certain ideas are common to the work of the two men — most significantly, Russia's isolation and failure to contribute to the "culture of humanity." But Kireevsky felt that Russia's failure to experience classical antiquity was the primary factor in her isolation, while Chaadaev viewed Western Catholic Christianity as a self-sufficient entity, with its own social, cultural, and moral consequences, quite apart from any tie with the ancient world. Chaadaev's ideas came out of French traditionalism, while Kireevsky was a child of German idealism. Chaadaev wanted a "new Middle Ages," had no faith in any kind of progress, and believed that Russia's salvation lay in returning to the Christian world that she had left at the time of the Great Schism. Chaadaev loathed the Renaissance and the French Revolution as interrelated heretical disasters, while Kireevsky, sharing many of Chaadaev's feelings about the French Revolution, nevertheless saw both events as "necessary" stages on the way to the modern world. The opposition was basically Bonald vs. Hegel.

All of what Müller says is quite true and very trenchantly presented. More specifically, one could well argue that the idea of Russia's "Chinese" isolation is specifically Hegelian and much more likely to have come directly from that quarter than from Chaadaev's analogous notions about Japan and Abyssinia. Nevertheless, it is likely that here, as elsewhere, Müller has given a Russian thinker credit for a theoretical consistency which he does not merit. When discussing Hegel and Bonald, it is by and large right to speak of systems of thought, and in so doing to rule out the possibility of certain kinds of reciprocal "influence." But the Russians of Kireevsky's generation thought nothing of taking bits and pieces of the most diverse philosophies and ideologies and piecing them together into their own "systems." To rule out the possibility of Chaadaev's influencing Kireevsky on basically structural grounds is naive. On balance, it seems likely that Kireevsky was struck by Chaadaev's general line of argumentation, preoccupied as he was by the same general problem; one feels the presence of conversations with Chaadaev, particularly when the role of the Roman Catholic Church is at issue, even if specific "borrowings" are difficult to pin down.

In retrospect, it is clear that the great tension in "The Nineteenth Century" has to do with the question of whether national culture is to be conceived fundamentally in Herder's terms, as a developing organic totality, or not. Kireevsky, in "The Nineteenth Century," tried to have his cake and eat it too. On the one hand, European culture, in itself, was organically conceived, each stage growing dialectically out of that which had preceded it. But as far as Russia was concerned, the organic development of European culture was shattered by the Enlightenment; the fact that the second half of the eighteenth century marked an entirely new stage in European culture meant that Russia could adopt it directly "without what went before." [51] As Andrzej Walicki has shrewdly pointed out, if one had high hopes for Russia's role in the new civilization, one had to resign oneself to the fact that this civilization would not have organic ties to the past, but would have to be constructed by a nonhistorical, "rational" method. [52] In the course of the 1830's, Chaadaev was to come to this conclusion: the hope for Russia, he wrote in the "Apology of a Madman," lay in the fact that she was a tabula rasa, free from all tradition and from the past.[53] An essential fact of Slavophilism was the rejection of this notion. Kireevsky, in spite of a certain hedging, chose the "organic" idea. His attitude toward antiquity had to be revised, and, consequently, the mixture of Christianity and classical paganism was replaced by the "pure" Christianity of eastern Orthodoxy.

Just as "The Nineteenth Century" made the high-water mark of Kireevsky's attraction toward the West — and, one might add, the contemporary world — the publicistic venture of the *European* marked his closest approximation to a "left" political position. In the first place, simply to chart the direction of contemporary Europe and say that Russia must become part of it was, in Russia, a political act. The Europe of Heine, Börne, and (to a lesser extent) Menzel was a radical Europe. The idea of "realism" was inseparable from the period of bourgeois ascendancy in Europe. Kireevsky even had a few kind words for industrialism: whatever the initial chaos and suffering brought by the invention of the steam engine, there can be no doubt that the end result will be of the greatest benefit to the human race.

The acceptance — albeit with a certain lack of enthusiasm — of the politicalization of literature and the invasion of religion and philosophy (as well as art) by "life" led Kireevsky to his most political critique of his own country. Observing, at the beginning of "A Survey of Russian Literature for 1831," that "affairs of state" are the focal point of European culture today, he contrasted that culture with Russia. "In our country," he remarked ironically, "the indefatigable care of a sagacious Government relieves private individuals of the necessity of occupying themselves with politics, and thus the only index of our intellectual development remains literature." [54]

In the selections from Heine and Börne — mutilated as they were to pass the censor — art and literary criticism were always on the borderline of politics.[55] The Heine selection was taken from his review of the Paris *Salon* of 1831 which originally appeared in the Saint-Simonian *Globe*. Toward the end we read:

My old prophecy of the end of the artistic period which began at Goethe's cradle and will end at his coffin seems to be near fulfillment. The art of today must perish, because its principle is still rooted in the moribund *ancien régime*, in the Holy Roman Imperial past. Therefore, like all the faded relics of this past, it stands in irremediable contradiction with the present. It is this contradiction and not the tendency of the times that is so damaging to art; on the contrary, this tendency of the times must be advantageous [for art], as was the case in Athens and Florence, where even in the wildest alarms of wars and parties, art produced her most splendid blossoms. . . . Meanwhile, the new age will also bring forth a new art, which will be in inspired harmony with itself, which need no longer borrow its symbols from a faded past, and which will even bring forth a new technique, altogether differing from that which preceded it.[56]

The summaries and translations of Menzel and Börne likewise relate to the new era;[57] in Germany the touchstone was one's attitude toward Goethe, and by this criterion, Menzel, no less than Heine and Börne, stood on the Left. As Müller put it, what was the government to think "of the *European's* opinion of the Parisian experiments of the year 1830?"[58] Having added "The Nineteenth Century" to a mélange of German radical criticism, Kireevsky should not have been surprised that the government of Nicholas was not pleased.

Kireevsky's views, in 1832, were in fact tantalizingly close to the Left romanticism of a figure like Mazzini. For both men, the vague but passionately felt vision of a "national regeneration" was at the heart of the desired future. In 1834, "Young Europe" proclaimed that "every people has its special mission which will cooperate towards the fulfillment of the general mission of humanity. That mission constitutes its nationality. Nationality is sacred."[59] Mazzini saw a special role for Italy in realizing the "general mission of humanity," as Kireevsky did for Russia, but the Russian could certainly have joined the insurgent Young Europeans in the general statement.

On the other hand, Russia and Italy were in very different situations, in terms of the politics of the day, and this fact helps to explain why the two men's ideas of the "national regeneration" became so different. A rather flippant formulation would be that the Italians lacked a state, and the Russians lacked everything else — or believed that they did. In Italy, that "geographical expression," romantic nationalism was bound to be disruptive and likely to be radical. In Russia, the range of possibility for romantic ideas of "nationality" was very different. The real alien presence in Russia, Kireevsky was to decide, was what he called "Western rationalism," which he was to oppose in the same way Mazzini opposed Metternich.

The suppression of Kireevsky's *European* symbolized the postponement for a decade of Russia's participation in the intellectual world of "Young Europe." When a kind of "Young Russia" did come into existence in the 1840's, it was divided into two halves. The Slavophiles took up the national component of the program, while the Westerners sponsored the radical side. Both, however, were in fundamental agreement in their alienation from the Russia of their day — an agreement which neither party fully understood.

It would not do, however, to go too far in identifying Kireevsky's views at the time of the appearance of the *European* with the views of "Young Europe." Although Walicki is quite mistaken in saying that Kireevsky was only interested in the European past, he is right in observing that, even in 1831–1832, Kireevsky's basic intellectual affinities remained with conservative rather than liberal thinkers.[60] His pronounced antipathy for the Enlightenment and all its works never wavered, despite his acceptance of it within a historicist framework. His aristocratic fastidiousness

continued to manifest itself in diatribes against "the crowd" and
their revolting manners, as in his review of "Woe from Wit" on
the Moscow stage.[61] Nor did this aristocratic elitism really take
a form explicitly hostile to Nicholas' autocracy; it often degenerated into sterile admiration for a parody version of the German
idea of *Bildung*, as in the fragment of a novel, "Two Lives,"
written in 1832.[62]

Even the new European spirit, of which Kireevsky was the
proud prophet in Russia, was by no means unambiguously "left."
To the "realism" of Young Germany Kireevsky added the "realism" of Schelling. This is no place for a general exposition of
Schelling's philosophical development after 1809, but since the
subject continued to interest Kireevsky, a brief summary may
be in order.

The starting point for Schelling's later philosophy was his
growing conviction that "reality" could not be grasped by the
purely intellectual — or "rational" — processes of traditional metaphysics. In moving to this new position — which, as Kireevsky
readily grasped, was quite in tune with the times — Schelling
abandoned a basic presumption, not only of the idealism of Hegel
and Fichte, but of his own earlier metaphysics as well.

What disturbed Schelling was basically the all-encompassing
and increasingly grandiose subjectivism which had characterized
German philosophy since Kant. It had reached its culmination,
Schelling felt, in Hegel's ontology, and almost all of Schelling's
later philosophy was, in one aspect, a polemic with Hegel. To
express Schelling's viewpoint in the simplest possible way, he
came to deny the notion that one can in any sense "know"
reality by knowing one's own mind. To use a somewhat more
philosophical vocabulary, Schelling denied that Reason could
have itself as content. Hegel's ontology was merely "negative,"
that is, it could comprehend only "potential being," never breaking through to the real world. In Karl Löwith's paraphrase,

"Pure thought cannot result in true movement or in any vital perception of the world, because there is no empirical basis for the deliberate lack of preconditions in its imminent movement. The synthesis of 'becoming' out of pure being and nothingness is an illusion. An 'abstraction of an abstraction,' such as pure and vacuous being, can never proceed from itself, go toward something, and return to itself, or even give itself up to nature. This can only be done by something that really is, something positive." [63]

Not surprisingly, when Schelling decided that what he termed "rationalism" was inadequate to apprehend reality, he turned to empiricism. But he specifically rejected the traditional kind of empiricism, whose authority was sense experience, as well as several varieties of "mystical" empiricism. Instead he turned directly to history, which he conceived, after 1809, as the drama of God's development, his achievement of complete self-expression. "The birth of the spirit," wrote Schelling, "is the realm of history." [64]

Philosophy, then, became a process by which one entered into history and traced in it the evolution of God. This, roughly speaking, is what Schelling meant by the "positive science of existence," or a "positive philosophy." Human freedom, as evidenced in history, no longer had to be reconciled in some artificial way with divine omnipotence: it became an essential part of the development of God in history, became, as it were, "part" of God.

There is no question that Schelling's later philosophy had a significant influence on Kireevsky's Slavophile formulations. Most obviously, Kireevsky's subsequent view of Hegel as representing the apogee of the long development of Western rationalism was obviously closely related to Schelling's view of Hegel and the development of idealism in general. It is also likely that Schelling's attack on rationalism in philosophy and his advocacy of "positive," or "living," knowledge impressed his young Russian student. But, as we shall see, Kireevsky's "living" knowledge was not the same as Schelling's, and the "rationalism" which he fought was much less narrowly and philosophically defined than the excesses of metaphysical subjectivity which drew the wrath of Schelling. Nevertheless, there is no doubt that Schelling's formulations in this area were of continuing interest to Kireevsky and played something of a role in his rather murky Slavophile epistemology; on the other hand, there is relatively clear evidence that Kireevsky was never more than mildly interested in Schelling's elaborate historical metaphysics, his Philosophy of Mythology and Philosophy of Revelation.

In the short run, Kireevsky's response to Schelling's new work was baffling. It will be recalled that he gave up taking notes on Schelling in July 1830, after concluding that "the mountain has brought forth a mouse. In sum, it appears that as against his system of previous years, there is not much new." [65] Nevertheless, in "The Nineteenth Century," Kireevsky saw at least the general direction of Schelling's new work, its putative opposition to earlier idealism, and he related Schelling's insistence on "living" knowledge to the new direction of European thought.

Schelling's later philosophy had, ultimately, the most varied intellectual consequences. On the one hand, it culminated in his Berlin lectures of 1841, where the all-out attack on Hegel helped the young Left Hegelians and Kierkegaard to emancipate themselves from the tutelage of the master.[66] On the other hand, Friedrich Julius Stahl, a young *privatdozent* in Munich, built his authoritarian philosophy of the state on the first gleanings of the new Schelling.[67] Interpreting Schelling's stress on the "real" and "historical" in terms that recall Burke and Savigny, he launched a full-dress attack on the rationalism of Hegel, the revolutionary implications of whose doctrine he fully grasped.

Kireevsky must have known Stahl's ideas, at least at second

hand, for the first volume of the latter's *Philosophie des Rechts* had appeared in 1830. Yet, significantly, he did not immediately exploit Schelling's new ideas for an attack on Hegel, as did Stahl, but followed Schelling himself in claiming that the new "positive" knowledge did not come to destroy idealism, but to fulfill it. Only later would Kireevsky come to see the philosophy of Hegel as the culmination of the one-sided development of "reason" in Western European culture.

However narrowly and selectively Stahl used Schelling, there can be no doubt that the latter's late philosophy pointed toward irrationalism and political conservatism and illustrates another facet of the new European attitude toward the "real" and "living." When the *European* appeared, Ivan Kireevsky could report and to some extent order the new developments in the intellectual life of Europe. He could not see where all of these ideas would lead — and who can blame him for that? His own views, like those of the European actors about whom he reported, remained a battleground of liberal and conservative ideas in a new and political environment.

VI. Suppression

In order fully to understand the traumatic effects of the suppression of the *European* on Ivan Kireevsky, one must bear in mind the enormous store he set by this enterprise, intimately related as it was to his whole notion of service to Russia and Russian culture through the creation of a broadly educated public opinion.[1] One historian found proof of Kireevsky's ardor in the fact that in spite of his "ineradicable laziness," he wrote no less than five articles for the first two booklets.[2] To this primary output must be added the heavy editorial burdens, including extensive translating, summarizing, and annotating. All in all, it was an immense undertaking for a dreamy young man with little direct experience of this sort of thing and a comparatively low level of animal vitality.

From our perspective, the most striking aspect of the *European* remains Kireevsky's diagnosis of the new intellectual scene in Europe (both in his own work and in the translations) and the historical relationship of Russia to it. These analytic and prophetic elements were what Herzen found so impressive, looking back on "The Nineteenth Century" from the 1840's. In 1832, however, Kireevsky's constituency was more literary than historical or philosophical, and it was as a vehicle for an extraordinary amount of fine literature and criticism that the *European* was primarily admired. Perhaps even more important in this regard was the fact that only the first half of "The Nineteenth Century" appeared in the *European*. The conclusion was scheduled for the third booklet, which never appeared.

Pushkin, to take an obvious example, sufficiently overcame his mysterious feelings of annoyance at Kireevsky to write to him on February 4, 1832, in the following terms:

Forgive me magnanimously for not having thanked you until now for *The European* and for not having sent you my humble tribute-payment. The blame for this lies in the distractions of Petersburg life, and also on the almanacs, which have completely exhausted my treasury, so that I do not even have a couplet left for a rainy day, except for a tale which I have saved, a fragment of which I am forwarding to your journal. God grant many years to your journal! If one may conjecture by the first two issues, *The European* will be long-lived. Until now our journals have been dry and insignificant, or intelligent and dry; it would seem that *The European* will be the first to combine intelligence and the ability to interest. Now a few words about journal economy: in your first two issues you published two capital pieces by Zhukovsky and a world of verses by Yazykov; such extravagance is out of place. There should have been at least three issues between "The Sleeping Tsarevna" and "Stepanida the Mouse." Two pieces by Yazykov would have been plenty. Save him for a rainy day. Otherwise what you'll do is squander what you have and you will be compelled to live on Raich and Pavlov. Your article about *Godunov* and *The Concubine* gladdened all hearts; at long last we have lived to see true criticism. N.B.: avoid learned terms, instead try translating, that is, paraphrasing them. That will be both pleasant for the ignoramuses and useful for our language, which is still in the stage of infancy.[3]

Pushkin wound up the letter with a discussion of Baratynsky's answer to criticisms of his "Concubine."

Even as Kireevsky was reading Pushkin's letter, however, the Third Section was on the move. On February 5, Benckendorff directed General A. A. Volkov, the commander of the Moscow

Gendarme District, to get hold of as much information as he could in a short time as to Kireevsky's "behavior, way of life, thoughts, and connections," with particular reference to his recent European trip.[4] "Evidently," wrote the historian Lemke, "the information was necessary for the drawing up of a formal indictment, where mention would be made of the damage to the mind and character of Kireevsky resulting from his travels in turbulent Europe."[5] Before turning to the actual suppression, it may be well at this point to review the strange history of Kireevsky's relations with the Third Section.

If such things can be said to have a "beginning," the Kireevsky case began in the summer of 1827, when Koshelëv and Titov wrote a letter to Ivan from St. Petersburg. "The undersigned," this curious missive began, "not having received any sort of answer from Mr. Kireevsky to the repeated representations made to him, find themselves, to their extreme regret, obliged to declare to him that if, in the course of fifteen days, dating from the 6 July, they do not receive a satisfactory answer from His Lordship, they will (1) break off all relations with him, (2) curse him, and (3) expunge him from the list of *ours*." The letter was signed "A. Koshelëv" and "V. Titov" and dated July 6.[6]

On that very same day it was in the hands of the Third Section, in all probability delivered by a servant in one or another of Kireevsky's friends' houses. In the margin Benckendorff wrote: "Cette lettre est très intéressante a ce qu'il parroit voyer s'il est possible de savoir qui sont les individu [*sic*] et ce que cela peut être." Still on the same day, July 6, Benckendorff wrote to Volkov that, "due to circumstances too grave to be ignored," he had to know who Ivan Kireevsky was, who his friends were, and what was his general reputation.[7] There can be no doubt that Benckendorff believed Titov's and Koshelëv's piece of foolery, presumably relating to Kireevsky's habit of not writing letters, to have deep conspiratorial significance. The government was still haunted by the Decembrist revolt. "Ours," Benckendorff probably thought, meant a secret society.

On August 9, Volkov's reply was in. "He is from the Orël nobility, very well brought up, has acquired broad information, is solid and even considered deep." There followed a résumé of Kireevsky's recent history (the Archives), his circle of friends, the family's economic circumstances (1,500 souls), and a few other scraps of information. Of all Kireevsky's friends, Sergei Alexandrovich Sobolevsky seemed to Volkov the most suspicious. "He comes to Kireevsky's house almost every day," wrote Volkov, "and they frequently go out together on horseback; from this it may be concluded that they are keeping something secret from the others, the more so, as when other visitors come to call, he, Kireevsky, and Sobolevsky frequently leave the others and talk together in a special room." Volkov also noted that in view of Kireevsky's "modest way of life," kindness to his "people," and "excellent education," it was extraordinarily hard to get anything on him. He frequently read far into the night — but only, apparently, "the works of the best writers." He went out, from time to time — but only to the houses of his friends or to the theater. Occasionally Volkov detected "the liberal spark" in Kireevsky's conversation, but he was, in general, "very cautious." [8] In spite of this most discouraging initial report, Kireevsky and his two friends were put under observation.

On September 12, 1827, "Volkov wrote to Benckendorff that he 'most sincerely wished to discover the secret bond' of those under observation, but he had 'already exhausted all means and pretexts, one of which being, in the guise of procuring a rich bride for Kireevsky, the striking up of an acquaintance, and even a friendship, with his valet.'" [9] But despite Volkov's best efforts, Kireevsky's "secret" remained in obscurity. Volkov pleaded with Benckendorff for "more daring" measures; the friendship with Kireevsky's valet, it is clear, was placing an increasing strain on the general. But the policy continued, for the moment, unchanged.

There remains one grisly footnote to the first chapter of the Kireevsky case. In July 1828 Nikolai Rozhalin's brother Vasily attempted suicide, apparently as the result of a desire to escape the repeated indecent advances of his stepmother. Kireevsky wrote to Titov, telling him about the affair in some detail, and of course the letter was read by the Third Section. After it had been circulated around from von Vock to Dibich to Benckendorff, it was discovered that Kireevsky's account of the matter was completely circumstantial and no action was taken.[10]

With all this in his dossier — not to mention Bulgarin's denunciation of 1830 — the fact that Kireevsky was given permission to put out a magazine at all has an aspect of the miraculous about it. It is very likely that Zhukovsky was able to sway Prince Lieven, the head of the Ministry of Education, whose relations with the Third Section were not always harmonious;[11] even so, a certificate was required from the police as to Kireevsky's "loyalty."

The developments of early 1832 — which led to the suppression of the *European* after only two booklets had appeared — are far from clear. There is, for instance, the question of whether Bulgarin added a second denunciation of Kireevsky to Benckendorff's files. Pushkin thought not: "The denunciation, so far as I have been able to find out, struck not from Bulgarin's dung heap, but out of the cloud," he wrote to Kireevsky the following July.[12] Zhukovsky, on the other hand, was inclined to believe that Bulgarin was directly responsible.[13] Regardless of Bulgarin's possible initiating role, it is clear that Kireevsky's satirical remarks on foreigners in Russia, in the closing paragraphs of his review of "Woe from Wit," inflamed Benckendorff, who was keenly sensitive about his own inability to master the Russian language.[14]

Two days later, however, when Benckendorff wrote to Lieven, matters had developed considerably. "The Sovereign Emperor," Benckendorff wrote,

having read the article "The Nineteenth Century," in the journal published in Moscow by Ivan Kireevsky under the name of the *European*, has deigned to turn his particular attention upon it. His Majesty has deigned to find that the entire article is in fact a discussion of high policy, in spite of the fact that the author himself asserts at the beginning that he is speaking not about politics, but about literature. One has only to supply a certain amount of attention to see that the author, allegedly discussing literature, has something entirely different in mind: that by the word *enlightenment* he means *liberty* (*svoboda*), that the *activity of the mind* means *revolution* for him, and that the *skillfully contrived middle ground* is nothing else but a *constitution*. His Majesty therefore deigns to find that this article ought not to have been permitted in a literary journal in which it is forbidden to insert anything about politics, and furthermore, the naiveté of this article notwithstanding, it is written in a most disloyal spirit, and the censor ought not to have permitted it. Furthermore, in this same booklet of the *European*, the Soverign Emperor deigns to observe a most indecent and improper canard (*vykhodka*) against foreigners living in Russia, for the permitting of which the censor is most guilty.

His Majesty commands that I communicate to Your Eminence these remarks, to the end that you may deign to apply the legal penalty to the censor who passed the aforementioned booklet, the *European*, and in order that this journal may be forbidden in the future, since the editor, Mr. Kireevsky, has shown himself to be a disloyal and untrustworthy person.[15]

Between February 5 and 7, then, the initial notion of making the case against Ivan in terms of insulting foreigners had turned into the far more serious charges of preaching sedition and revolution, with the remarks in the "Woe from Wit" review tacked on merely for good measure. How extraordinary that Nicholas' government should resort to these fanciful interpolations, when the pervasive and generalized radicalism of many of the contributors, particularly the foreign ones, would, from the government point of view, have more than justified the suppression. And yet this method of verbal correspondences — "activity of the mind" as a code word for "revolution," and so forth — was the style of Nicholas' government. It may well be that no one read the Heine translation; he was, after all, just some German writing about French pictures. In the future, the Emperor decreed in conclusion, there should be no new journals without the personal, Imperial permission.

We do not know when Kireevsky first got wind of the suppression, but it was considered a *fait accompli* in St. Petersburg no later than February 10. On February 20, we find Iazykov writing wanly to a friend that "for the time being there is no official suppression." [16] It came, with proper ceremony, two days later.[17] Meanwhile, Zhukovsky had swung into action, as much on his own behalf as for the sake of his protégé. According to Avdot'ia Petrovna, as soon as Zhukovsky heard what was in the wind, he approached Nicholas directly, saying that he would vouch for Ivan personally. "And who will vouch for you?" replied his Sovereign. At which Zhukovsky took to his bed. Only after the Empress had intervened did Nicholas approach Zhukovsky, saying: "Well — time to be reconciled." [18] Avdot'ia Petrovna herself went to bed with what Pogodin described as a "bilious fever." [19]

Knowing the system as he did, Zhukovsky did not confine himself to personal appeals to Nicholas. To D. V. Golitsyn, the Governor-General of Moscow (a man of a certain independence of mind, who enjoyed excellent relations with Nicholas), he wrote, *inter alia,* "I ask nothing for [Kireevsky] from Your Excellency save your attention; all the rest I leave to you, to your intelligence, inseparable from your convictions, to your noble heart, in which modest innocence will always find a true defender and impartial judge." Recommending Kireevsky, Zhukovsky swore that he was worthy "in thought and deed" of Golitsyn's protection.[20]

To Benckendorff, Zhukovsky wrote a long letter, full of controlled fury. Had Kireevsky, he began, been confronted with these charges and asked to defend himself, he could no doubt have done so. As this had not happened, he, Zhukovsky, found himself obliged to say a few words, not on behalf of the journal, which had already been destroyed, but on behalf of an innocent man, who had now been branded as disloyal before the world. "There is not a line," he wrote, "however simply it may be written, which could not be construed in the most ruinous manner if, instead of the words used by the author, you invent others, and, presupposing the author's ill intent, compel him to say not what he thought, but what you compel him to think. There is no prayer which could not thus be turned into blasphemy." [21]

To slander the intention is easy and always advantageous for the slanderer, for how can one defend oneself? "One may simply say: *I did not have that intention which was ascribed to me*, but who will take your word, and where is the evidence for it to be found?" This propensity to believe the slanderer rather than his victim is, of course, wholly irrational, but it is a fact which must be taken into account. Zhukovsky wrote the same letter to Nicholas, albeit in very much milder language. Nevertheless, it was daring enough under the circumstances, and one may concur with Lemke when he wrote that "all Russian society" was speaking through Zhukovsky.[22]

To Kireevsky, Zhukovsky wrote tenderly:

My dear "European," I embrace you for your dear letter. Today I am going with it to Benckendorff, and I will add my own written and oral declaration to it. You on your side must do what I advised you: write to Benckendorff yourself. But in your letter, rather than trying to show that an injustice has been done you, try to vindicate your innocence. Act less for your journal than for yourself . . . Talk about your desire to be useful, as the government conceives it, about your desire to spread, through your writing, those ideas which the government finds generally useful, and about how the suspicion which is bound to fall upon you with the suppression of your journal will take from you the means to translate your devotion into deeds.

To attack them for their unjust behavior, Zhukovsky stressed, would be a grave tactical error. Don't do it! "I have already written to the Emperor," he went on,

both about your journal and about you. Gave my opinion as to your innocence. I haven't had an answer and probably won't have one, but what had to be said has been said. From this whole business it is clear that there are some good people here, probably scoundrelly writers, who have injured you out of personal malice, but in injuring you they wish to confuse the government about all those who write with good intentions. They are slandering these intentions, and I am sure that the government is convinced that there is a secret agreement among writers of a certain rank, in which I am probably included, to disseminate destructive and revolutionary opinions. Given the existence of such thoughts, it is scarcely surprising that the government looks upon us with suspicion and sees, even in the most innocent things, that which is not, and cannot, be there.[23]

There is no doubt that Zhukovsky was right. The government in fact saw the "literary aristocracy" (or, in Zhukovsky's words, "writers of a certain rank") as potential heirs to the unfinished business of December 14. Neither Polevoi nor Nadezhdin, the two leading "plebeian" journalists, was able to keep operating in the atmosphere of the thirties, but it was a gentry *fronde* that Nicholas' government feared above all. Zhukovsky concluded by underlining, as he had in the other two letters, the spectacular difficulty of their situation: how is a writer to vindicate the purity of his "intentions?" Nevertheless, he urged Ivan again to lose no time in writing to Benckendorff.

The general reaction in society to the closing of the *European* was a kind of hopeless bitterness. By February 10, the news of Benckendorff's letter had reached the censor and university professor, A. V. Nikitenko. "Confound it," he wrote in his diary, "and what are we supposed to do, after all is said and done, in Russia? Drink and brawl? It's terrible and shameful and sad!" [24]

The reaction in Kireevsky's more immediate circle was of course even sharper. "Probably you know," wrote Pushkin to Dimitriev, "that the journal *The European* has been suppressed in consequence of a denunciation. Kireevsky, kind and shy Kireevsky, has been represented to the government as a madcap and a Jacobin. Everybody here [St. Petersburg] hopes that he will succeed in justifying himself and that the slanderers — or at least the slander — will be abashed and unmasked." [25] Baratynsky wrote to Kireevsky to say that he couldn't get over "the suppression of your journal. There is no doubt that an unjust, hidden, and foul informer has been at work here, but there is little consolation in that. How is he to be brought to justice? After this, what can one undertake in a literary way? Like you, I have been deprived of a strong inducement to literary work. The suppression of your journal depresses me, and judging by your letter, you are feeling melancholy yourself. What is to be done? We'll think in silence and leave the field to Polevoi and Bulgarin." We must confine ourselves to a small circle of believers, like the early Christians, Baratynsky concluded, and perhaps one day we shall triumph too. [26]

Viazemsky, in a series of letters which he sent to Kireevsky through his wife, gave the same advice that Zhukovsky had given: do not try to resurrect the journal, or even say that you were "right." Concentrate on making the government believe in your "honor." Viazemsky, too, wrote to Benckendorff, who he said was not evil, merely without character and "weakminded." [27]

Thanks to Zhukovsky's good offices — and perhaps to those of Viazemsky — Kireevsky was not arrested. Nevertheless, his situation was bad enough. He was publicly declared to be "disloyal and untrustworthy"; his name could not appear on the title page of any journal, and he continued under police supervision. The responsible censor, Sergei Aksakov, father of the Slavophile brothers, was given a severe reprimand.[28]

In the face of this disaster, Kireevsky remained, as nearly as can be ascertained, almost wholly passive. Zhukovsky, as we have seen, urged him to bestir himself and write to Benckendorff. In a letter written in early February, Kireevsky promised Zhukovsky that he would do so, as soon as the suppression became official. In this relatively brief note, Ivan declared his complete innocence of the government charges: he may have entertained mistaken opinions, he wrote, but what he said was there for all to see; there were no hidden meanings or innuendoes. In a second letter to Zhukovsky, apparently written in mid-February, Kireevsky discussed in more specific terms the government charges and expressed his bewilderment as to how, precisely, such accusations were to be answered, beyond a straightforward — and presumably futile — denial. He also asked for Zhukovsky's advice as to the proper tone to adopt "in a polemic with the Sovereign," a difficult question indeed. In closing, he asked if he might send his statement to Zhukovsky to be edited before it went to Nicholas. At this stage, Kireevsky was still confident that the journal might be resurrected.[29]

The letter to Benckendorff, however, appears to have remained unwritten. On March 28, Viazemsky wrote to his wife and asked why Kireevsky had not written this letter.[30] As late as the following July, Pushkin wrote to Kireevsky, urging his own defense upon him.

The suppression of your journal has produced a great impression here [St. Petersburg]; everybody has been on your side; that is, on the side of complete innocence. . . . Zhukovsky has stood up for you with his ardent straightforwardness; Viazemsky has written Bencken-

Fig. 1. Ivan Kireevsky (probably in the 1840's).

Fig. 3. *Avdot'ia Petrovna Kireevskaia (Elagina) in 1812.*

Fig. 2. *Peter Kireevsky in the 1840's, from a portrait by E. A. Dmitriev-Mamonov.*

Fig. 5. Makary's cell (foreground) in the Optina Monastery.

Fig. 4. Vasily Zhukovsky, from an engraving, circa. 1830.

Fig. 6. A street in Belëv in the mid-nineteenth century.

dorff a courageous, intelligent and convincing letter. You are the only one who has not acted, and in this instance you are completely wrong. As a citizen you have been deprived by the government of one of the rights of all subjects; you should have justified yourself out of self-esteem, and, I even dare say, out of esteem for the Sovereign; for attacks by him are not attacks by Polevoy or Nadezhdin. I do not know whether it is too late, but if I were you, even now I would not hesitate to make this justification. Begin your letter by saying that "having been long awaiting an inquiry from the government, you have been silent up to now, but," etc. I swear that wouldn't be too much for you to do.[31]

But apparently it was. "Ivan has still not been able to pull himself together and take hold. He plans to go to the country and devote himself to agriculture," his mother wrote to Zhukovsky in April.[32] And following his removal to Dolbino, toward the end of the year, he was subject to harassment by the Kaluga provincial officialdom.[33] Avdot'ia Petrovna's few words inform us of what was to become obvious later: this was a real crisis in the life of her son. Furthermore, he was — significantly — unable to defend himself in any way. He might have simply said, as his brother confessed in the middle of his own struggle with the imperial government and its censor: "I am a bad fighter." Rather than fighting, he retired from the field, turned within himself — and eventually repudiated, as best he could, the title of his journal.

Nevertheless, the letter to Benckendorff which Zhukovsky, Viazemsky, and Pushkin urged upon Kireevsky was in fact written, although not, apparently, by Ivan himself. During the latter part of 1832, a most interesting document, entitled "Mémoire au comte Benkendorf," was circulated in Moscow; whether it was ever actually presented to anybody in the government remains, like much else about it, obscure.[34] Prince I. S. Gagarin, the editor of the first published collection of Chaadaev's works,[35] believed it to have been his work, and appended to it the following note:

"Mr. Ivan Kireevsky had founded a journal, entitled the European. It had been suppressed after the second number. Peter Chaadaev, who was closely linked with Ivan Kireevsky, although he did not share all his ideas, drew up a memoir, which was to have been presented by Kireevsky to Count Benckendorff . . . We will only remind the reader that Chaadaev, taking up the pen for his friend, and not speaking in his own name, may not be held responsible for all the ideas which are here found. One must recognize, however, that he is undertaking in this piece to set forth that aspect of Kireevsky's ideas which most closely approaches his own." [36]

In a letter to Khomiakov in 1844, Kireevsky stated that not only was he not the author of the "Mémoire," but that it did not express his "thoughts," nor was it circulated at his behest.[37] Nor, in fact, do we have any real evidence, aside from Gagarin's note, that Chaadaev was the author, although no one has hitherto seriously disputed it. One may perhaps surmise that Kireevsky chose Chaadaev for an advocate because of the older man's ties with Benckendorff, whom he had known since his schooldays. Having discussed the matter with Chaadaev and given him certain directions as to how to set about the letter, Kireevsky eventually withheld his approval from the finished product, which was nevertheless circulated without his imprimatur. This, of course, is merely a hypothesis, but there is reason to believe that the author, whoever he may have been, had assistance from Kireevsky or from a member of his family, as an examination of the text reveals. The memoir begins:

His Majesty has deigned to glance at the journal of which I was the editor. He has there noted certain ideas which he has found deserving of censure, and he has found the entire tendency of the journal to be such that the authorities cannot suffer it to be published. He has therefore commanded that it be shut down; I have incurred the greatest misfortune that a faithful subject and a good citizen can incur in a monarchy, that of having been blighted in the opinion of the sovereign. You have permitted me, general, to address to you an apologia for my ideas; I take advantage of this favor with the profound obedience owing to so lofty a decree, and with confidence in the justice and wisdom of my august judge, in the hope that he will deign to take cognizance of my defense. I believe, general, that I can do no better by way of demonstrating how different my real opinions are, I dare say, from the sense which the Emperor has attached to the terms which I employed to express them, than by submitting to you the totality of my opinions on the subject which I only touched upon in my journal.[38]

This is certainly the tone which Zhukovsky and Viazemsky had urged Kireevsky to take: flowery, submissive, and misunderstood. All thought of resuscitating the journal has been abandoned: the author's only concern is to vindicate his intentions in the eyes of Benckendorff and Nicholas. One can well envisage Kireevsky's collaboration in this formulation, but more suggestive of his hand (or that of someone close to him) is a subsequent passage. "For a writer beginning his literary career," it runs, "the first concern is naturally that he should be read; but who would have read me, general, if I had spoken a language to which I alone had the key?"[39] This echoes a passage in Zhukovsky's letter to Benckendorff, in which he argues against the likelihood of a revolutionary propagandist using what later came to be known as "Aesopian" language. "Why should an article be written," Zhukovsky inquired rhetorically, "in which you read one thing but must understand another? The reader must have a key, but where is that key to be found?"[40]

If these passages suggest Kireevsky's involvement in the composition of the "Mémoire au comte Benkendorf," there are a number of opinions expressed therein which are not his. In setting forth the "totality of his opinions," the author of the memoir argues strongly for the emancipation of the serfs. We have no direct evidence as to how Kireevsky felt about this matter in 1832, but in the discussions of the later 1840's, he was strongly opposed to an emancipation until certain key internal reforms had been carried out.[41] Furthermore, as Koyré has pointed out, the author of the memoir urged that Russia assimilate pre-eighteenth century European culture — not that of the modern period.[42] In both these cases, the views expressed correspond to those of Chaadaev rather than Kireevsky.

In sum, one may conclude, taking into account style and content, that the author of the "Mémoire au comte Benkendorf" was in all probability Chaadaev. There are some grounds for believing that either Kireevsky or someone familiar with the correspondence between him and Zhukovsky participated in drawing it up. Why Ivan withheld his approval from it, we have no way of knowing, but he may well have felt that there was too much Chaadaev in it, and not enough Kireevsky.

In the period immediately following the Revolution of 1830 in France, the intellectual assault on romanticism, idealism, and the "Restoration" in general began in earnest. At first the center of these new tendencies was France, even though Germans like Heine and Börne played a major role; it was not until the accession of Frederick William IV in 1840 that the radicalism which was to lead to 1848 was truly launched in Germany. At about this time, certain tremors began to be felt even in Russia. Ivan Kireevsky's *European* provided, for the more wide-awake of his contemporaries, a fascinating look at an early stage of this process, at that turning to "reality" which was beginning to characterize European thought.

VII. The "Conversion" of Ivan Kireevsky

In the course of the six years which followed the closing of the *European*, Ivan Kireevsky virtually ceased to be a significant figure in the Russian intellectual life of the period, such as it was. He wrote little and published less, and although he never really made good his declared intention of burying himself in the country and "devoting himself to agriculture," he did spend more time at Dolbino than he had previously. At the end of 1833, Zhukovsky wrote testily to Avdot'ia Petrovna: "What is Ivan doing? I fear that he is doing nothing, and that gets one nowhere. His journalistic failure is no justification; it is really only an excuse for his laziness. Peter spoke to me at some point about his intention to translate Shakespeare; that is the business of a whole lifetime, and what a service to the Russian language! Why doesn't Ivan think of some similar work? And it is not everything to write for publication. Work so that the soul matures and does not grow shallow. But that's not the custom with us in Russia." [1]

Kireevsky's melancholy and — if Zhukovsky is right — slothful existence was altered in the most significant way by his marriage, an important event not only from a purely biographical standpoint, but in relation to his "conversion" to Orthodoxy and Slavophilism as well. It will be recalled that the Arbenev family had formally refused Kireevsky's suit in early September 1829 on the grounds that he and Natal'ia Petrovna were second cousins. Another factor, presumably, in the failure of the marriage plans was Avdot'ia Petrovna's expressed distaste for her prospective daughter-in-law: she considered Ivan's cousin cold, calculating, and generally unsuitable.[2]

Then, in 1831, Natal'ia Petrovna's mother died, and the girl went to live with her married sister, Mar'ia Petrovna Norova. Late in 1833, some kind of "unpleasantness" occurred between Natal'ia Petrovna and her sister's husband, presumably the result of an awkward *ménage à trois,* and Natal'ia Petrovna sought assistance from her future mother-in-law.[3] A reconciliation soon followed, for Avdot'ia Petrovna always found it hard to hold out against anyone who needed her. The denouement came speedily. On March 6, 1834, Avdot'ia Petrovna wrote to Zhukovsky, asking him to "bless Ivan and Natasha. The whole five-year accumulation of misunderstandings, partings, reasonableness, etc., crumbled at a glance. On the first of March, after a five-year separation, he saw her for the first time; for two hours, surrounded by alien guests, he looked at her from afar, and, as she was getting up to go, fell under the sway of some invisible power. On the porch, a single word, a single glance made everything clear. On the following day I gave my blessing to a daughter." [4] The marriage took place on April 29, with Zhukovsky Ivan's best man *in absentia.*

Natal'ia Petrovna was beautiful, witty, malicious, very pious, and never one to lose sight of her own interests or those of her immediate family. Gershenzon referred to her "meanness and cupidity," [5] vis-à-vis the division of family property which took place between 1835 and early 1837, and Zhukovsky was moved to protest against the "sacrifice" of the interests of the Elagin children which he saw taking place.[6]

On the other hand, Natal'ia Petrovna could charm the birds from the trees when she so desired. On one occasion, Avdot'ia Petrovna gave a birthday party for Prince Odoevsky, who neglected hostess, party, and guests and spent all his time talking to young Mme. Kireevsky.[7] The historian T. N. Granovsky described her to a friend in 1840 as "young, pretty, agreeable, and mocking." Her wit, he added, was of a very special sort, "excessively original and sometimes really wounding. There are persons who fear her; I have had the temerity to defy her, and now we get on very well." But, he added, "several years ago I would not have dared to approach her." [8]

As far as the evolution of Kireevsky's views is concerned, however, Natal'ia Petrovna's religiosity and her clerical connections are of particular importance. It was through her, in fact, that Ivan's close connection with the monks of the Optina Monastery came about, a connection which was closely related to his Slavophile evolution. What appears to be Natal'ia Petrovna's own account of her influence on her husband is given in a curious document entitled "The Story of the Conversion of Ivan Vasil'evich." [9] Written in the hand of Koshelëv, it was found among Kireevsky's papers and is, according to Gershenzon, "undoubtedly in the words of . . . Natal'ia Petrovna Kireevskaia," although Gershenzon gave no indication of how he could be so sure.[10] It runs as follows:

I. V. Kireevsky was married in 1834 to a girl, Nat. Petr. Arbeneva, who had been brought up according to the dictates of strict Christian piety. In this period immediately following the marriage, her performance of the rites and customs of our church struck him unpleasantly, but with his customary patience and delicacy, he in no way hindered her in this observance. She, on her part, was even more sorrowful to observe his absence of belief and complete neglect of all the customs of the Orthodox Church. There were conversations between them which ended in an agreement that he would not hinder her in the fulfillment of her obligations. He was to be free in his own actions, but promised her not to scoff at sacred things and even to put a complete stop to those conversations of his friends which were so unpleasant for her. In the second year of their marriage, he asked his wife to read Cousin.[11] She did this eagerly, but when he began to ask her opinion about this book, she said that there was much in it that was good, but she found nothing new, for all of it was set forth in a much deeper and more satisfying way in the writings of the Church Fathers. He smiled and was silent. He began to ask his wife to read Voltaire with him. She declared to him that she was ready to read any serious book which he recommended to her, but that raillery or any kind of scoffing at the sacred was alien to her, and she could neither listen to nor read such things. Sometime after that they began to read Schelling together, and when his great, luminous thoughts were at an end, and I. V. Kireevsky turned to his wife, expecting her to be surprised, she answered him forthwith that these thoughts were known to her from the writings of the Church Fathers. More than once she pointed things out in the works of the Church Fathers which sometimes compelled I. V. to read whole pages. It was unpleasant for him to have to admit that really a great deal of what had so enraptured him in Schelling was in the Church Fathers. He would surreptitiously take his wife's books and read them with enthusiasm, although he did not like to admit to having done so. Acquaintance with the Novospassky monk, Filaret,[12] conversations with the holy elder (*starets*), and the reading of various works of the Church Fathers delighted him and drew him to the side of piety. He would go to Fr. Filaret, but always as if under duress. It was evident that he wanted to go to him, but always felt some kind of constraint. Finally the death of Elder Filaret in 1842 confirmed him once and for all in the path of piety. Ivan Kireevsky had never worn a cross. His wife had asked him about this more than once, but I. V. would fall silent. At length, however, he said to her that he would wear a cross if it were sent to him by Fr. Filaret, whose intelligence and piety he already prized highly. Nat. Petr. went to Fr. Filaret and communicated this to him. The elder, crossing himself, took off his own cross and gave it to Nat. Petr., saying "May it work to his salvation." When Natal'ia Petrovna came home, I. V. met her and asked: "Well, what did Father Filaret say?" She took out the cross and gave it to I. V., who asked her: "What sort of a cross is this?" Nat. Petr. said that Fr. Filaret had taken it from his own person and said "Let it work to his salvation." I. V. fell on his knees and said "Well now I hope for the salvation of my soul, for it must be that if Father Filaret has taken off his own cross and sent it to me, God has clearly called me to salvation." From this moment, a decisive change (*povorot*) in I. V.'s thoughts and feelings was perceptible. After the death of Father Filaret, I. V., living near the Optina Monastery, was increasingly strengthened in his piety by conversations with Fathers Leonid and Makary and other elders. He read a great deal of patristic literature, talked frequently with the elders, and strengthened himself more and more for his future activity.

However true certain details of this account may be, the overall impression it conveys is to some degree misleading. To be sure, Kireevsky had not been a believer in the Orthodox Church since his youth, but almost everything we know about him testifies to the fact that he was never quite as "irreligious" (as opposed to "not Christian") as this account would have it. If we assume that the "Story of the Conversion of Ivan Vasil'evich" was a collaboration between two people who knew him as well as did Koshelëv and Natal'ia Petrovna, the mystery only deepens. Furthermore, whatever confessional value this document may have, it is not very helpful in the matter of relating Kireevsky's Orthodoxy to his Slavophilism. It was allegedly the death of Filaret which "confirmed [Ivan] once and for all in the path of piety." But all the elements of Kireevsky's mature world view were present in his "Answer to Khomiakov," written in 1839.

There are grounds for skepticism even in matters of detail. The likelihood, for example, of Kireevsky's trying to seduce his wife with Voltaire seems slight, although it would be foolish to rule out the possibility, since so much in their relationship remains obscure. On one occasion Kireevsky expressed a certain sympathy with the moral passion of Robespierre,[13] but he never showed anything but aversion for the writings of Voltaire, which, it will be recalled, his father used to buy up in Moscow and burn.

Nevertheless, there can be no doubt that Kireevsky's close relationship, first with his wife's confessor, Filaret, and then with the Optina elder, Makary, were both cause and effect of his changing views. Furthermore, given what we may call Kireevsky's religious sensibility, there is nothing unexpected in his taking refuge from the buffeting which the "world" had just administered in a new and close relationship with the Orthodox Church. Previously he had thought that religion was a vital part of human life, and even himself been "religious" in some wise, but as a letter to Koshelëv in the early thirties makes clear, he was at that time "incapable of belief." [14] At some point in the course of the thirties he found the capacity, or at any rate a powerful impulsion toward it.

Setting aside, for the moment, the complex part which Orthodoxy played in Kireevsky's Slavophilism, let us turn to the question of his relations with the two men whom K. D. Kavelin called the "first Slavophiles": Aleksei Stepanovich Khomiakov and Ivan's own brother, Peter Vasil'evich.[15] At least a nodding acquaintance had existed between Khomiakov and Ivan since the fall of 1826, when both men frequented the Venevitinov house in Moscow. We know, for example, that they were both present on October 12 of that year, when Pushkin read *Boris Godunov* aloud to a considerable gathering. Twelve days later, Khomiakov gave the dinner at which the birth of the Moscow *Messenger* was celebrated, and both Ivan and Peter were on hand.

Although conclusive evidence is unfortunately lacking, there has been general agreement among both biographers and intellectual historians of the period that the close relationship between the two men could not have begun earlier than 1831.[16] Some small evidence for a greater intimacy may perhaps be seen in the fact that Khomiakov contributed two poems to the second booklet of the *European*. Nevertheless, I have found no evidence that the two began to see very much of each other before early 1833; Khomiakov, in fact, did not spend much time in Moscow between 1826 and the spring of 1832. In April 1833, Kireevsky wrote to Iazykov that he was seeing Khomiakov "almost every day." [17] The invaluable Koshelëv has also left us an account of this period. "At the beginning of 1833," he wrote many years later,

I again saw a great deal of Khomiakov in Moscow. From that time on we spent our winters in Moscow, and we saw each other very frequently at his house, at mine, and especially at I. V. Kireevsky's. The latter was living at the *Krasnye Vorota* with his mother, A. P. Elagina, of whom we were all passionately fond, and whom we respected enormously. There took place endless conversations and arguments, beginning in the evening and ending at three, four or even five or six at night or in the morning. There was hammered out and developed that Orthodox-Russian way of thinking, whose soul and prime mover was Khomiakov. Many of us at the beginning were vehement Westerners, and Khomiakov, almost alone, insisted on the necessity of an indigenous development for each people, on the meaning of faith in man's spiritual and moral existence, and the superiority of our Church over the teachings of Catholicism and Protestantism.[18]

In his memoirs, Koshelëv included a portrait of Kireevsky, which, although curiously exaggerated and lacking in sympathy, does shed further light on the Kireevsky-Khomiakov relationship.

[Ivan Kireevsky] was clever and gifted, but had little originality or independence, and he was easily moved, now in one, now in another direction. He was (successively) a disciple of Locke, Spinoza, Kant, Schelling, and even Hegel. In his unbelief, he even went so far as to deny the necessity for the existence of God; subsequently, however, he became not merely Orthodox, but a proponent of the *Dobrotoliubie*,[19] a well-known work of Vasily the Great, compiled for the guidance of Russian monks. Between Khomiakov and Kireevsky there were the usual endless quarrels: at first Kireevsky found Khomiakov too churchy (*tserkoven*), that he did not prize European civilization highly enough, that he wanted to dress us in homespun and shoe us with bast sandals. Subsequently, Kireevsky reproached Khomiakov for unwarranted rationalism and insufficient feeling in matters of belief . . . They valued each other highly, respected each other profoundly, and loved each other passionately.[20]

Koshelëv here exaggerated Kireevsky's early uncertainties; in no meaningful sense was Ivan ever a "disciple" of Spinoza or Kant.

Nevertheless, it is true that Khomiakov was, like Peter Kireevsky, an extraordinarily consistent character, while Ivan Kireevsky was not. Khomiakov seems to have sprung from the earth, like one of Cadmus' soldiers, fully armed. "I knew Khomiakov for thirty-seven years," Koshelëv wrote late in his life, "and his fundamental convictions of 1823 had not altered in 1860." [21] These convictions were a deep devotion to the Orthodox Church and a Russian patriotism which, although strongly colored by belief in the autocracy, also contained from early on a definite hostility to the European Russia of Peter the Great. Khomiakov's dislike of St. Petersburg can allegedly be traced back to his eleventh year, when, visiting the imperial capital for the first time, he fully expected, in that heathen milieu, to be persecuted for his faith.[22] In part as a result of his participation in the Russo-Turkish War of 1828–1830, Khomiakov had a much greater feeling for the notion of "Slavdom," which was closely linked with Orthodoxy in his mind, than Ivan Kireevsky ever did.

Again in contrast with Kireevsky, Khomiakov appears never to have had the slightest sympathy with the ideas of the Decembrists, although he had enjoyed good personal relations with some of the conspirators.[23] He viewed the uprising itself as "absurd" and "infamous." Try as one will, one cannot discover a trace of those "liberal" impulses and ideas which can be observed in Kireevsky's *Weltanschauung* until well into the thirties, and which survived in the form of a strong, personal attraction toward many of the Westerners. None of them, it should be noted, were personally very fond of Khomiakov, although they respected him as the most formidable and single-minded of their antagonists.[24]

Kireevsky's aristocratic — or snobbish — fastidiousness was likewise alien to Khomiakov, who was as much a Tory democrat as any English country squire. Coming from very much the same kind of patriarchal background as Kireevsky, he was remarkably akin to him in the breadth of his personal culture — and may, in fact, have surpassed him in some sense, for Aleksei Stepanovich was interested in a variety of technological and scientific subjects about which Kireevsky could not have cared less.[25] And unlike his friend, Khomiakov moved easily and effectively in the larger world of Russian society. To illustrate Kireevsky's "commercial philosophy," Herzen told the following anecdote, observing that "there is no one in the world with whom I should so much like to transact business as with Kireevsky."

Ivan had a stud farm, from which horses were brought to Moscow, valued, and sold. On one occasion, a young officer came to buy a horse to which he had taken a fancy. The coachman, seeing this, raised the price. They haggled, the officer agreed on the price and went to Kireevsky. Taking the money, Kireevsky looked on his list and observed to the officer that the price of the horse was eight hundred rubles, not a thousand; the coachman had probably made a mistake. This so perplexed the cavalry officer that he asked permission to examine the horse again, and having done so, refused to buy it, saying: "A fine horse it must be for which the owner is ashamed to take money." [26]

No such story could be told on Khomiakov, who managed his estates with the energy and hard-headedness of Balzac's bourgeois.[27] E. N. Konshina, in her survey of the Kireevsky and Elagin Archive at the Lenin Library, declared that the family estates appear to have been run in a "primitive" fashion, the only sources of income being *obrok* (quitrent) and the sale of "raw materials" (*syr'ë*).[28] Khomiakov was, in a practical sense, far more at home in the nineteenth century than Ivan Kireevsky.

The other person who had an important influence on the evolution of Ivan's views in the course of the thirties was his brother Peter. Like Khomiakov, he seemed to his contemporaries to have come into the world completely formed; as Gershenzon put it, his character, personality, and ideas seemed to undergo no sort of evolution; their essence was merely ever more fully revealed.[29] However similar to Khomiakov in this one respect, in most ways his personality seems to have been a more extreme version of his brother's. Their contemporaries tended to think of them together. "The two Kireevsky brothers stand like melancholy shades at the dividing line of the national renaissance," Herzen wrote in his memoirs, and Khomiakov denied the possibility of writing a biography of *one* brother without the other.[30]

Peter lived wholly within the communal life of the Kireevsky-Elagin family, outdoing even his elder brother in this respect. He consciously chose never to marry. His mother, his brother — whose children he looked upon as his own — and a few close friends like the poet Iazykov were, excepting his folkloric and historical studies, all he lived for.[31] Ivan, beside him, seems frivolous and gregarious. Steeped to such a degree in patriarchal and familial relations, he early developed a quiet detestation of the Russia which he felt had been the handiwork of Peter the Great. Ivan's self-conscious "cultivation" and snobbery seem to have been wholly alien to him, and — perhaps alone among the Slavophiles — he had a genuine love of the common people. He was never happier, in fact, than when wandering from place to place, collecting songs. Although he participated in the salon life of Moscow for three decades, he did so, as Gershenzon observes, "mechanically," and the circles left no mark on him.

Peter's reaction to his trip to Germany was an even sharper hostility than Ivan's, although he traveled more and was, one feels, more open to experience than his brother. But he detested bourgeois, university Germany, comparing the gradual, almost imperceptible movement of the seasons in Germany to the German burghers themselves — stolid, lukewarm, uncaring. The Russians had great moral qualities — they were full of passionate life — but were, at the same time, "lazy" and inactive.[32] European energy had to be instilled into them; this was all, Peter felt, that Europe could really do for Russia. Ivan saw the need for European "energy," too — how could he not? In all probability this notion played a role in Ivan's decision to call his journal the *European*.

Despite his deep and lifelong attachment to his brother, Peter always felt to some degree inadequate and inferior beside him. He was very shy in company, a tortuously slow worker, and although he read seven languages, he never managed to speak French properly.[33] And mixed with Ivan's affection for Peter was, one cannot help feeling, something a bit patronizing.[34] In their youth, Peter often referred to Ivan acidly — if affectionately — as "Socrates." Along with their intellectual differences, these factors, too, may have played a part in the "passionate arguments" which, according to N. A. Elagin, took place between the two brothers in the early 1830's. These bitter disputes were, of course, about the value of old Russian culture and Russia's cultural relations with the West.[35] The closeness between the brothers was such, Elagin concluded, that one or the other had to give in, and it was Ivan who gradually did so. Alas, no written record of the course of their disagreements has survived, but Elagin may be considered, in such a family matter, a credible witness.[36]

Following his marriage, Ivan settled into the routine which was to endure, with little change, until nearly the end of his life. His rural base of operations was Dolbino, which fell to him in the division of property which took place in 1836. Peter received two estates, of which the more important was the so-called *Kireevskaia Sloboda*, near Orël, together with about 300 serfs. The senior Elagins lived at Utkino, in Belëv district, an estate which had come down to Avdot'ia Petrovna from the Iushkov family.

In Moscow, Ivan and his bride lived in a house of their own, "on the Ostozhenko, on the left, if you come from the Prechistensky Gates, near the Church of the Resurrection." In the words of the distinguished folklorist, F. I. Buslaev, a frequent visitor, the house was "of stone, two stories high, and old, with an iron outer door and iron bars on the first-floor windows, like a fortress.

Having survived the Moscow fire of 1812 in this condition, it stood in a shady, overgrown garden, without paths. On the street side, the garden was bounded only by a sturdy fence with a gate. . . ." The house was large and roomy, but scarcely luxurious. "The large room off the vestibule," in the words of Buslaev, "was both a drawing room for guests and a study for [Ivan]; the worn, uneven floor was full of chinks. For furniture there was only a dilapidated sofa against a wall, blank except for a window. Across the room at the other window was a great, padlocked country chest." For the rest, there was only a well-stocked oak bookcase, a large, square table, and "up to a half a dozen chairs and armchairs of various types." [37] Peter, who lived on the second floor when he was in Moscow, kept his collection of songs and folktales in the chest, including, he would inform visitors, the packet given him by Pushkin. It was in this austere and rather rural atmosphere that the Kireevskys did their Moscow entertaining in the thirties and forties.

In spite of the great happiness which his marriage brought him and the new regularity of his life, Ivan Kireevsky's literary output remained meager. Absorbed in family life, occupied with his estate, his views in flux, and the *European* still hanging over his head, Kireevsky wrote almost nothing, and his lack of productivity is scarcely surprising. In 1833, at the behest of his aunt, Anna Petrovna Sontag, he did produce a short piece on female writers for an almanac which the cultivated ladies of Odessa were putting out.[38] He saw their commendable enterprise not in isolation, but as part of the general spread of "enlightenment" then taking place in Russia. He dilated with considerable enthusiasm on the increased participation of women in Russian culture and on their changing role: instead of merely beguiling us with sweet phrases, they have now begun to think and even to have "opinions." We can even, he wrote, detect that melancholy and dissatisfaction which is the inevitable concomitant of culture. He concluded with graceful tributes to a number of lady poets and translators, including Princess Zinaida Volkonskaia, Caroline von Jaenisch[39] and Mme. Sontag. No names, however, were mentioned. Was he afraid, nearly two years after the demise of the *European*, that praise from him might be dangerous for lady litterateurs?

The second piece, dating from 1834, was a critical appreciation of the poetry of Iazykov.[40] It is very elegantly written, although perhaps a bit rhapsodic and lacking in concreteness. As had been the case with much of Kireevsky's previous writing on such poets as Pushkin, Del'vig, and Zhukovsky, his basic concern was to get at the poet's "world," the "character" of his poetry. "In defining the character of a poetry," he wrote, "we have defined all." [41] As always, he was very successful in this: the duality in Iazykov between sensualism and spirituality, the psalm and the drinking song, made him the ideal subject for such an effort. Again we see the importance of feeling for Kireevsky in the grasping of poetic — or indeed any other kind of — truth.[42] The highest kind of knowledge is achieved through empathy. The hostility to "abstract reason," which we find in Slavophilism, is in part a generalized, philosophical formulation of a deeply felt emotional attitude. Worth noting as well is the fact that in the Iazykov review, the role of the critic has undergone a certain shrinkage. There is no talk of the critic as the maker of an all-important public opinion; Kireevsky confined himself to observing that, in the presence of genius, the critic cannot be elucidator and explainer. His part is the more modest one of witness.

The Poems of Nikolai Iazykov had appeared in April 1833,[43] and Kireevsky's article, which was printed in the Moscow *Telegraph*, was prompted in part by what he felt to be the lack of critical attention to a most important book. The review, however, was unsigned. Even Iazykov did not know the identity of the author.

Kireevsky had fresh evidence in 1834 that the government had not forgotten the *European*. In the course of the year, he and a number of his friends, with Shevyrëv playing a particularly important role, decided to try another journal as a counterpoise to the "commercial" journalism of Grech and Polevoi.[44] Each of them put up a thousand rubles, and it was decided that the journal should be called the Moscow *Observer* (*Moskovskii Nabliudatel'*). In view of the unfortunate experience that Shevyrëv and Pogodin had undergone with the Moscow *Messenger*, and the disinclination of the others for the job, the editorship was given to an economist and statistician named Androsov, who had been peripherally involved in Moscow intellectual life since the days of the Raich circle.[45] On December 9, 1834, the word came down from Uvarov: the journal was to be allowed, with the provisos that the name of Ivan Kireevsky was not to appear on the masthead and that the aims of the journal were to be "purely literary, without the insertion of anything political," an obvious reference to the *European*.[46] The government was clearly not disposed to forgive and forget.

On the basis of the small information we possess, it is clear that the *European* marks the high-water mark of those elements in Kireevsky's personality and intellectual makeup which were outward and "forward" looking, which tended to accept the modern world and Russian society as they were. Not that Kireevsky did not hope for great changes and developments for Russian culture and society — he obviously did. But he "accepted" the society around him, in the sense that he believed that it was moving toward goals which were desirable, and he felt that he could contribute to the realization of these goals. His aspirations — the creation of a broadly educated, enlightened public opinion in Russia, the rapprochement with European culture, the acceptance of an age of "realism" — had a definite liberal cast. At the same time, however, there was nothing overtly political here — or so he had thought — and nothing to prevent him from working to these ends in the Russia of his day.

The suppression of the *European* was brutal enough evidence to the contrary. It now became clear that Nicholas' government regarded his program — and not without some justice — as an attack on itself. Might it be that the Russia of Nicholas I simply could not become part of this "new era"? Or that terrible violence and upheavals, of the sort that had already begun to take place in Europe, might be the path, for Russia, to the nineteenth century?

At this point, when the bureaucratic absolutism of Nicholas had just crushed the most important enterprise of his life and dimmed his hopes for a gradual rapprochement between Russia and Europe (branding him a subversive in the process), it is scarcely surprising that he began to give a more serious ear to a pair of gifted men who felt that no help would be forthcoming from Europe and who were, furthermore, essentially hostile to the intellectual, social — and political — developments which had taken place in Russia since Peter the Great. The world they exalted and subsequently mythologized (Peter alone perhaps still lived in it) was the patriarchal world of the Russian gentry, inimical to the claims of the centralized state, to the bureaucracy of St. Petersburg, to urban life, and to rationalism in general, whether political or intellectual, whether bourgeois or bureaucratic.

Revealed religion and the traditions of the church played an important role in almost all the aristocratic, antimodern ideologies of early nineteenth-century Europe, and Slavophilism was no exception. It is Walicki's opinion, in fact, that Kireevsky's "conversion" was simply the implicit recognition that religion and the church were necessary components of his evolving Slavophile ideology.[47] This rather bald explanation is inadequate, for Kireevsky's turning to the Orthodox Church must be seen in the whole complicated pattern of his life, or it makes no sense. Yet Walicki forces us to realize how intimately related Kireevsky's new religiosity was to the whole structure of his Slavophilism, as we will see in analyzing his later writings.

One may, of course, imagine a quite different response to a disaster like that which overtook Ivan Kireevsky in 1832, a response based on outrage and resulting in direct hostility to the sovereign and his government. Why did the suppression of the *European* not lead Kireevsky to adopt a more radical position? A brief comparison of Kireevsky with Alexander Herzen, whose radicalism was ultimately based on personal frustration, may have a certain utility in this connection.

Herzen and Kireevsky were both unhappy in Nicholas' Russia, and both created coherent ideological structures which were, to a greater or lesser degree, "oppositional." Why did Kireevsky derive his blueprint from an idealized version of the preindustrial past, rather than transmuting his frustration into an extreme form of libertarian protest, as did Herzen? [48] The root of the divergence, it seems to me, lies in family differences. Herzen's father and his three uncles present an appalling portrait gallery of aimlessness, cruelty, and, perhaps above all, waste. As Malia observes, "The salient trait of the family's mores in the generation of Herzen's father was that all the brothers sired their children out of wedlock by women who lived in total servitude to them." For the illegitimate Alexander Herzen, the first collision with the brutality of Russian life arose through his own anomalous position in his relations with his father.

The contrast with the Kireevsky-Elagin ménage could hardly be greater. The European gloss that their education provided the Iakovlév brothers only made them among the first "superfluous men," but Kireevsky's father, Vasily Ivanovich, was conscious of no conflict between his broad personal culture and the time-

honored, patriarchal gentry life he led. Ivan's family life was unusually close and warm — if not, at times, stifling. What could
be more natural than that Kireevsky should be, in his dissatisfaction with the present, backward-looking, and Herzen not?

Without being unduly psychoanalytic, one might observe that
for Kireevsky, it was quite natural that the tsar ought to be, in
the fullest sense, a father; Herzen, on the other hand, found
Nicholas only too like *his* father. While Kireevsky's upbringing
led him toward a patriarchal ideal to oppose to the present order
of things, Herzen tended to generalize his own rebellion against
his father. As Malia puts it, "In condemning the social order of
the old regime [Herzen] was first of all condemning his father's
family." [49] Kireevsky affirmed his family — but the end result of
this affirmation was also offensive to the government.

This comparison is not meant to revive the old saw to the effect
that all the Slavophiles had happy childhoods, while all the
Westerners had unhappy ones. Michael Bakunin, by all reports,
had an idyllic childhood; there are many roads to radicalism.
Nevertheless, one cannot help observing that the Kireevskys, Iury
Samarin, the Aksakovs, and Khomiakov came from much the
same kind of background and had, from the cradle, very strong
ties with a patriarchal past, the pre-Petrine, Muscovite past.

VIII. The "Elagin Salon" and the First Slavophile Writings

In the case of the romanticists the thinker is, so to speak, the starting point, and all his efforts are directed to discover, if possible, a world that will satisfy him.

— Karl Mannheim

The first fruit of Kireevsky's new way of looking at things was a brief essay entitled *In Answer to Khomiakov*.[1] It is redolent not only of Kireevsky's changing fortunes, but of changing times, that the *Answer* was not set forth in the pages of a journal, but was presented to a relatively small group of sympathetic listeners in the course of two of his mother's "evenings," early in 1839. What has been called the "Elagin Salon" — or, quite inaccurately, the Slavophile Salon — assumed, at this time, an extraordinary importance, not only for the emerging Slavophile constellation, but (somewhat later) for their rivals, the so-called "Westerners," as well.[2]

A "salon" had in fact existed in the big house near the *Krasnye Vorota* since the mid-twenties, at least in the sense that Avdot'ia Petrovna loved to entertain; she was beloved of a wide variety of interesting people, ranging in age from Zhukovsky to the contemporaries of the younger Elagin children. But as the 1830's wore on, the "Elagin Salon" — and other similar groupings — became increasingly central to the intellectual life of Moscow. Journals became fewer in number, for one thing, and editors more nervous. Ivan Kireevsky's fate — and, even more spectacularly, that of Peter Chaadaev — made an intimate circle seem a safer arena for the advancement of new and possibly controversial ideas than what remained of the public prints. Avdot'ia Petrovna's entertaining had always had an intellectual cast, but as the thirties waned, it became increasingly pronounced, and the "debate" between the Slavophiles and Westerners in the forties gave the evenings an added focus and intensity.

Almost all the intellectual luminaries of the period paid glowing tribute to Avdot'ia Petrovna's warmth, charm, and hospitality. "From the thirties right up until the new reign," Kavelin remembered, "Avdot'ia Petrovna's house and salon were among the most favored and frequented gathering places of Russian literary and scholarly people. All of intelligent, enlightened, and talented Moscow gathered there on Sundays. Any celebrity, Russian or foreign, would appear at the Elagin Salon upon his arrival in Moscow."[3] T. N. Granovsky wrote to A. E. Kromida in 1840: "What more can I tell you about my life in Moscow? Every Wednesday I go to the Kireevskys', a house where I enjoy myself a great deal. *Monsieur* Kireevsky is a most distinguished man in every way. The company is not numerous, about thirty at most, but they are the most cultivated and interesting people in Moscow. Each time something new is read. . . ."[4] P. I. Bartenev, editor of *Russkii arkhiv* (and subsequently publisher of *War and Peace*), spoke of the catalytic effect that Avdot'ia Petrovna had on any literary or intellectual gathering, with her "unfeigned sympathy toward people who are talented and alive, toward every noble undertaking."[5] Here, in Iazykov's "Republic of Liberty at the Red Gates"[6] (the poet was once crowned with flowers by his angelic hostess), in Kireevsky's new house and elsewhere the regime of symposia, readings, theatrical performances, arguments, and concerts continued undiminished, if not unchanged.

The changing personnel of the "evenings" bears witness not only to the passage of time and the succession of generations, but to Ivan Kireevsky's changing concerns, to the lessening of his interest in literature. Friends of his adolescence and youth, like Rozhalin and D. V. Venevitinov were dead; Titov had moved to Kiev. Kireevsky's correspondence with Pushkin ended with the *European*, and he apparently ceased writing to Baratynsky at about the time of his marriage. In May 1845, Peter Chaadaev wrote Kireevsky a wistful note: "I would so like to see you at my place nowadays, my dear Ivan Vasil'evich, to read the speeches of Peel and Russell with you, but since you will probably not be at my place, I am sending you the list *of debates* . . ." [7]

On the other hand, both Kireevsky brothers remained close to Iazykov, whose views had evolved in a direction similar to theirs, and to Koshelëv. The old relationship with Pogodin — on Kireevsky's side, a mélange of camaraderie, respect for his zeal and energy, and contempt for his crudity — remained. Gogol was a friend and read the first chapters of *Dead Souls* in the Elagin drawing room. There was no doubt, however, that Kireevsky's developing friendship with Khomiakov became for a time his most rewarding relationship, on the intellectual level, if not on the personal, and it is appropriate that the first written evidence of his "Slavophilism" is entitled *In Answer to Khomiakov*. In fact, the exchange between the two men, which took place over an unspecified number of evenings in early 1839, provides our first real glimpse of that working out of the Slavophile doctrine which had already been in progress for some time. [8] It is a great pity that the two men's opinions were not recorded in detail a year or two earlier, for that would have given us a far better sense of their evolution; Kireevsky's views, at any rate, were beginning to be quite defined by the winter of 1839. Both essays were subsequently circulated in manuscript and created considerable stir in Moscow literary and social circles. [9]

Two further points might be made about the general nature of these important discussions, which we first glimpse in 1839. The first has to do with the salon origins of Slavophilism: more specifically, its origin in *talk* and its present-mindedness. It is, of course, pointless to investigate the structure of belief and intuition which we see emerging here solely in terms of historical "accuracy." Kireevsky's Slavophilism, in particular, has almost nothing to do with the systematic investigation of the past, with archives, or anything of that nature. It originated in argument and talk, in relatively restricted groups of beleaguered intellectuals, whose feelings about their present position underlay a great deal of what was being said.

The second point is no less important, although it is more difficult to pin down. There was, in the late thirties, no "oppositional group," of the type of the so-called "Westerners," who began to develop a certain rudimentary coherence only later, largely in response to the emergence of a Slavophile "position." But the intellectual presence of one opponent can be felt in what we know of these proto-Slavophile discussions — particularly in the formulations of Khomiakov. I am referring, of course, to Peter Chaadaev.

Chaadaev's critique of the provinciality, backwardness, and spiritual emptiness of Russia's past and present was undoubtedly well known to both Khomiakov and Kireevsky, and it had been so for almost a decade. The sensational affair of the *Telescope* was only three years old, and it certainly made Chaadaev, in the salon world of Moscow, the leading critic of his country's history and culture — or its lack thereof. Unfortunately, we have no very precise way of knowing to what degree Khomiakov and Kireevsky together were hammering out what might be called "an answer to Chaadaev," but certainly his Byronic figure may be seen in the background of these 1839 evening discussions.

Khomiakov's essay, entitled *On the Old and New*, appeared, at certain points, to be directed against an opponent who was an uncritical admirer of pre-Petrine Russia.[10] This fact has been of some concern to students of Khomiakov; one historian has even

referred to Khomiakov's "curiously anti-Slavophil position" and
suggested that the piece "was intended to provoke a more positive, pro-Slavophil declaration in Kireevski and possibly others
in the audience." [11] Given Khomiakov's temperament, there could
be some truth in this notion. Nevertheless, in view of the fact
that there was really no such thing as "Slavophilism" in 1838–
1839 — and differences between individuals continued to exist,
even after the loose body of doctrine had taken on somewhat
more definite shape — there seems to be no reason to accept
Christoff's hypothesis. It merely appears that Kireevsky's views
on pre-Petrine Russia had crystallized into something like their
mature form in a way that Khomiakov's had not. But the author
of *On the Old and New* can certainly not be described as "anti-
Slavophile."

Khomiakov began by remarking that a thesis had been advanced that the quality of life in old Russia was better than it
is today, that there was "literacy in the villages, order in the
towns, justice in the courts, and contentment in men's lives."
Two "principles," foreign to the rest of the world, allegedly preserved and strengthened Russia in those days: "the power of a
government in harmony with the people, and freedom of the
Church, pure and enlightened." [12]

Khomiakov then addressed himself to these claims, seeming for
a moment to deny them outright. Literacy, order, justice — there
was ample evidence, some of which he cited, to show that these
qualities had often been lacking in old Russia. The "Stoglav"
Church Council of 1551 uncovered the most appalling abuses,
"a deathless monument of ignorance, crudity, and paganism." Bad
as the Romanov period was, things had been even worse before:
an endless procession of "illiteracy, injustice, brigandage, sedition . . . persecution, poverty, disorder, ignorance, and lewd-
ness." [13]

Having apparently taken his stand with the detractors of pre-

Petrine Russia, having given, perhaps he thought, a Chaadaev viewpoint, Khomiakov then turned around and showed that there was also ample evidence to support those who admired her civilization. How, he then asked, are we to evaluate all this contradictory evidence? What are we to believe? It is vital to answer this question properly, for on our response depends our evaluation of Russia today and our decision as to the direction in which she should develop.

In discussing the "first principles" of Russian history, Khomiakov laid stress on two aspects of the Russian state: the Varangian princely power and the "local veche (popular assembly)." The prince and his entourage (*druzhina*) were responsible for defense (and foreign relations in general), while the veche was responsible for dispensing justice, the maintenance of custom, and the "resolution of all questions of internal government." Christianity was of course of fundamental importance, but by itself it could not be decisive in cultural formation. This becomes clear when we see how the paganism of the classical world affected the Roman Catholic Church, bringing about the rationalist disintegration which led ultimately to the Reformation. Greece remained for a long time the hearth of the purest faith, but here, too, pagan culture eventually worked its mischief, and those who would keep their faith unsullied were finally forced to take refuge, one way or another, in the desert. Only when Greek Christianity was brought to Russia could a true Christian society be born, and even there the process took a long time, for Russia was a very wild and crude place at the time Christianity was introduced.

Furthermore, "Russia," in the true sense of the word, did not yet exist; there was merely a federation of small city-states, the most important of which — Kiev and Novgorod — were doomed to fall before the Mongols. But this seeming catastrophe was to result in a great good, for the Moscow state which arose after the period of Mongol domination showed an "all-Russian" (*obshche-russkii*) spirit. Novgorod could not stand against Moscow, for "the idea of the town had to give way to the idea of the state."[14]

Khomiakov saw the history of Russia between the Mongol period and the death of Peter the Great as the triumph and consolidation of the idea of the state — a necessary, if dreadful, process. The order, justice, and harmony of the patriarchal Russia of the past had to be sacrificed to unification: the old communal way of life was virtually annihilated. Khomiakov spoke of Peter I in this context with rare balance, almost with sympathy, a circumstance which is presumably among the reasons why certain historians have suspected Khomiakov's sincerity. In the first place, he regarded the horrors of Peter's reign as in large part necessary for the final triumph of the "state principle." Then, too, with the weakening of the old, communal ways, various groups had arisen — boyars, ecclesiastical dignitaries, townsmen — who had developed pretensions to wealth, power, and independence (as had similar groups in the West) and had "forgotten their Fatherland." Peter had been merciless with such individuals and groups, and Khomiakov, despite his abhorrence of Peter's means, despite the fact that Peter had never understood either love or personal freedom — Khomiakov here came close to justifying him. He was, of course, most unsympathetic to Peter's "Germanization" of Russia, but he did not seek to explore the connection between the consolidation of the idea of the state (of which he approved) and the penetration of the country by foreign influences (which he detested).

"All this having been said," concluded Khomiakov, "we have countless advantages over the West."[15] The earliest chapters of Russian history were not sullied by the blood and hostility of conquest (an important idea, both for the Slavophiles and the "Official Nationalists"). Despite the environment in which the

Russian church evolved, Khomiakov continued, it has never lost "the purity of its inward life." The simplicity of the pre-Mongol communal organization of society was very near to some kind of ultimate human truth, founded as it was on "the law of justice and mutual love." Our task is now to "move forward," he concluded resoundingly (if vaguely), basing ourselves on "our deep sense of the state" and on the old "patriarchal existence," which remains unknown to the West. Its sparks are still alive in Russian hearts, and its ancient principles "may, in fact must, be developed."

Certain of the weaknesses of Khomiakov's paper were immediately obvious to Kireevsky. For one thing, Khomiakov had been extraordinarily vague about the *present* condition of Russia. To Kireevsky, the question of whether old Russia was "better" than the Russia of his time was academic. He preferred, he said, to approach the matter in a more historical — and useful — way, by asking what the more fruitful course of action would be for those anxious to improve the quality of Russian life: to return to the old Russian ways or to develop the "Western elements" which are opposed to them. For, regardless of what we may feel, the fact of the matter is that Russian *reality* contains both elements — or, to put it another way, is "the struggle of two hostile principles." [16] We do not have the luxury of being able to choose which of these principles to "develop"; in fact we can only attempt to determine what "direction" to give to the complex aggregate which is contemporary Russian reality. And what, he asked, have we to hope — or fear — from future developments?

Having said this, Kireevsky turned, like Khomiakov, to the Russian past and to that of Europe as well. "Contemplating the basic principles of life," he wrote, "which form the forces of nationality in Russia and the West, we immediately discover one common element: Christianity." [17] What is the origin, then, of the multiform differences between Russian and Western culture? Kireevsky still, in 1839, found Guizot's triad to be valid. He still believed the bases of European culture to be the pagan classical world, the barbarian tribes which destroyed it, and Christianity. But in "The Nineteenth Century," he had referred to the third element as "the Christian religion"; in the *Answer* it has become "Roman Christianity." "This classical world of ancient paganism, which is not part of Russia's heritage," Kireevsky continued, is essentially the triumph of man's formal reason over everything inside and outside of it — pure, naked reason, based upon itself, recognizing nothing higher than or beyond itself, and manifesting itself in two particular aspects — that of formal abstractness and that of abstract sensuality. The effect of classicism upon European culture had to be of this same character." [18]

It was this influence of classical paganism, Kireevsky concluded, which infected the Church of Rome and led to its deviation (*uklonenie*) from Orthodoxy. Here we see "the same triumph of rationalism over tradition, of external rationality (*razumnost*') over inner, spiritual reason." [19] As a result of a syllogism based on the divine equality of the Father and Son, the dogma of the Trinity was perverted. Likewise the result of the victory of syllogistic rationalism over tradition was the substitution of the Pope for Christ as head of the Church; the Pope subsequently became a wielder of enormous temporal power and was alleged to be "infallible." And, continued Kireevsky with a rush, scholasticism, the Inquisition, and even Protestantism — all have developed out of Catholic rationalism!

Kireevsky displayed, in this essay, the most important quality of the ideologist or mythmaker — the ability to ignore historical or moral complexity and to pursue a single idea, or group of ideas, to the end. Khomiakov was not, in his essay, the ruthless simplifier that Kireevsky was in his. Khomiakov paid a wholly unnecessary tribute to the elusiveness and complexity of historical reality; Kireevsky ignored everything but the achievement of a large and simply coherent intellectual structure, and thereby gained enormously in polemical force.

The results of the rationalism which pagan Rome had loosed on the Western world were as stark and simple as could be, and Kireevsky was more than willing to provide a catalogue of the baneful results of this intellectual tyranny in contemporary Europe: "Strauss and the new philosophy in all its aspects, industrialism, the mainspring of social life, philanthropy, based on calculating self-interest, a system of upbringing (*vospitanie*) accelerated by exacerbated covetousness. Also Goethe, the crowning glory of modern poetry and a literary Talleyrand, who changes his ideal of beauty the way the latter changed governments, and Napoleon, and that hero of modern times, the ideal of soulless calculation, and the corporeal majority, that fruit of rationalist politics, and Louis Philippe, the end result of such hopes and such costly experiences." [20] What Kireevsky was attacking in this torrid denunciation was obviously that cluster of qualities which we associate with the rising entrepreneurial middle class: greed, low cunning, the dirty business of politics, "enrichissez-vous." He was attacking that coherent system of values which, in Marx's words, "left remaining no other nexus between man and man than naked self-interest, than callous 'cash payment'." [21] Significantly, he regarded Napoleon not as a Peter the Great on a European scale, not as the satanic consummator of the French Revolution, but as the apogee of soulless, bourgeois calculation.

On the heels of this abuse, Kireevsky confessed that not only did he value the "conveniences" which were the result of rationalism, but he even "still love[d]" the West, to which he belonged by virtue of his upbringing, habits, and tastes, as well as his "quarrelsome cast of mind." [22] At the same time, there could be no doubt that the quality of life in contemporary Europe was diseased and from the standpoint of its inhabitants, devoid of any genuine satisfaction: "All the lofty minds of Europe are lamenting the current conditions of moral apathy, the lack of conviction, the prevalence of egoism, and demand a new spiritual force, beyond reason. . . ." [23] In other words, he concluded, they are seeking belief and cannot find it in Western Christianity.

In order better to understand the pervasive power of rationalism in European culture, he continued, let us compare the "fundamental principles of social and private existence in the West" with those which existed — however imperfectly developed — in the Russia of an earlier day. Life in the West is founded on individualism: "every *individuum — within the sphere of his rights*, an autocratic (*samovlastnyi*), absolute person — a law unto himself." [24] At this point Kireevsky ended the first part of his presentation; the remainder of the evening, presumably, was given over to discussion, a discussion of which, sadly enough, we have no record.

The following Wednesday, Kireevsky recapitulated some of what he had said previously, stressing the corruption which pagan antiquity had breathed into "Western Christianity." The initial result in the intellectual realm, he said, of the infusion of rationalism into the body of the Church was scholastic philosophy. Purporting to reconcile faith and reason, scholasticism simply extinguished the former by means of the latter, in the form of syllogistic constructs. The employment of "reason" outside of the limits defined by scholastic theology was of course met by the Catholic Church with maledictions and persecution, but that fact, he said, should not obscure from us the predominantly rationalist method of scholasticism. Furthermore, the attempt of the Western church to "annihilate" reason, outside of the arbitrary limits of scholastic dogma, provoked a violent counterreaction, which has defined the character of contemporary Western culture (*prosveshchenie*). Eastern Christianity, on the other hand, knew neither the struggle between faith and reason nor the triumph of the latter over the former.

Turning to the social structure of old Russia, Kireevsky found a number of differences from the West, the most important being the organization of society into small "communities" (*miry*).[25] Private or social "originality" (in the sense of institutional creativity) was as little known in Russia as social "autocracy" (*samovlastie*). The individual and the community belonged to each other. "Landed property, the source of personal rights in the West, belonged, in Russia, to the society." Significantly, however, the sovereignty of the society was limited, for it could not "organize itself or invent new laws for itself," since it was indissolubly part of a whole network of similar societies, governed by uniform custom.

We are reminded here of what Max Weber said of the patriarchal ruler, and his words may be applied more generally to sovereignty in a patriarchal society: "A master who violated tradition without let or hindrance would thereby endanger the legitimacy of his own authority, which is based entirely on the sanctity of that tradition. As a matter of principle it is out of the question to create new laws," although in practice, of course, these norms are not immutable.[26] Clearly, the direction in which Kireevsky's picture of pre-Petrine Russia was tending was toward an idealized, patriarchal version of preindustrial society, similar to Weber's "patrimonial" variant of traditional domination.[27]

Kireevsky's idealized picture of the communal structure of medieval Russia is of the greatest interest. Here, for the first time, the Russian commune was presented both as a survival from the untainted past and as a basis — in a sense as yet unclear — for the future development of Russian society. The great Russian myth of the nineteenth century was born that winter night in Avdot'ia Petrovna Elagina's drawing room.

"The countless multitudes of these small communities," continued Kireevsky, "which made up Russia, were covered with a network of churches, monasteries, and dwelling places of solitary hermits, from which identical ideas of social and private relationships were constantly being diffused. Of necessity, these ideas (*poniatiia*), little by little, took on first the character of common conviction and then of custom, which took the place of law. . . ." [28] So strongly rooted were these ideas that even the history of the last two hundred years has not been able to eradicate them entirely, he maintained, and strong traces survive even into our own day.

In the West, on the other hand, truth and justice, rather than being embodied in and inseparable from a concrete way of life, are mere "terms." Outside of these intellectual constructions, all was — and is — arbitrary: the "autocracy" of the ruling class, the "liberty" of the ruled. Social rights, forces, and interests are "reconciled" either by brute force or by an artificial "sum of individual understandings." These seemingly opposed methods of rule were, according to Kireevsky, ultimately one and the same — at bottom there is no real difference between having more physical force than your neighbor and having more votes. The idea of the "social contract" was by no means the invention of recent theoreticians — it is the "ideal" toward which Western society has been moving for many long centuries.

It is true, Kireevsky admitted, that we do not as yet have any very clear idea of the extent of the Russian prince's power during the appanage period. Having conceded this important point, however, he nevertheless went on to state that the determination "of the general course of things" lay with the community (*mir*), and that in the rare instance when the prince exceeded his traditionally sanctioned authority — acting as judge and conducting foreign relations — he was "driven out by the people itself." [29] Thus he concluded, on the basis of his own vision, rather than any real historical evidence, that there could be no comparison made between the territorial princes of Russia and the "petty proprietors" of the West, who exploited society as if it were their property, or those "noble knights," who recognized no law but their own sword. There could be no "chivalry" (*rytsarstvo*) in Russia, because the Russian Church never lent its sanction to the oppression of the weak by the strong. The rule of the numerical majority was the natural response of the oppressed common people to the material force used against them by the aristocratic minority; the one followed dialectically from the other. Both are alien to Russia.

Like Western social forms, art and science in the West derived certain "temporary advantages," an illusory vitality, from the pagan spirit which animated them. Why this should have been so, Kireevsky did not say. But eventually it had been necessary for Western art to return to the pagan source for revitalization, and today Western art "abases itself before the abstract formulas of philosophy," and Western science has ended in atheism.

Necessarily, then, Kireevsky now viewed what he had previously thought of as Russian backwardness in a wholly new perspective. "Russia," he wrote, "has not been ablaze with works of art or scientific discovery, not having had time to develop independently in this regard and not having adopted an alien development, based on a false view and consequently inimical to her Christian spirit." [30] It is Russian Christianity alone which can provide the proper foundation for a culture. The translated works of the Eastern Fathers have been preserved in that network of monasteries which covers Russia, and those monasteries have been in "living, uninterruped contact" with the people.

All this said, continued Kireevsky, one cannot avoid asking how it was that Peter was able virtually to destroy this living culture. Or, if the work of destruction was begun before Peter, how was the Grand Duchy of Moscow to blame? What happened?

Interestingly enough, Kireevsky eschewed Khomiakov's quite tenable notion that the long struggle for unification, for the consolidation of the idea of the state, was responsible for the demise of patriarchal Russia. Rather than seeking the solution of this key problem in the warp and woof of history, he preferred a more "philosophical" or spiritual solution, some development in the world of the mind. He found it in the Church Council of 1551, which, he alleged, introduced rationalism and a party spirit into the Church.[31] From the work of the Council, according to Kireevsky, followed religious formalism and the Schism, "and hence *mestnichestvo*, the *oprichnina*, slavery, etc." Above all, of course, Peter!

In his surprisingly bitter concluding paragraphs, Kireevsky was no more able than Khomiakov to say precisely what remained from the old communal civilization or how it could be utilized in the building of a new Russia. "One cannot," he stated finally, "bring back the Russia of the past." On the other hand, one cannot destroy "what remains of the forms," for that would be to abandon the hope that "at some point Russia will return to that living spirit which her Church exudes." Kireevsky considered the only hope to be that "some Frenchman or other might understand the originality of our Christian doctrine as it is embodied in our Church and write a journal article about it, and that a German, believing him, might study our Church more deeply and demonstrate in lectures that in it is contained — completely unexpectedly — what is needed by European culture. Then we would undoubtedly believe the Frenchman and the German and ourselves recognize what we have."[32]

It is clear, when one looks at Kireevsky's article in its entirety, that the opposition between Russia and the West was not really the fundamental dichotomy which he was attempting to describe. Much more basic was the struggle between two "principles," or ways of thinking, from each of which springs completely different social forms as well as spiritual values. One of these he designated as "abstract reason" or "external rationality," while the opposed principle was a kind of "spiritual reason," which was inherent in Orthodox Christianity.

This dichotomy, significantly, was neither so explicit nor so central to Khomiakov's essay. Furthermore, Kireevsky, with the zeal of the convert, attributed a supreme importance to the values inherent in Orthodoxy, which distinguished his position from Khomiakov's. The latter, it will be recalled, did not think that Christianity was a "decisive" factor in the creation of Russian culture.

The "external rationality," against which Kireevsky inveighed, was alleged to give rise to violence and oppression, either naked or disguised by some formal democratic process. This was because it had nothing to do with a "concrete way of life," nothing to do with "tradition." Abstract reason is a lie, because it is based only on itself.

Much of Kireevsky's invective, when reduced to its essentials, is quite familiar. The belief that the ills of the modern world were largely brought on by rationalism, secularism, and the flouting of tradition was central to the expressed views of most of the important theoreticians of romantic conservatism in Europe. They were the spokesmen for an older social order increasingly threatened by new social forces and institutions. To the intellectual and political rationalism of the bourgeoisie and the "enlightened," rationalizing despots, men like Adam Müller, Friedrich Schlegel, and Franz Baader had opposed the irrational, the historically sanctioned, the communal, the aristocratic — in varying combinations. In its main lines, Kireevsky's Slavophilism is a Russian expression of these counterrevolutionary impulses.

In England and France, rationalism had been primarily the weapon of the ascendant bourgeoisie against an older society which had no real place for them or their values. In Russia, as in much of the rest of Europe, rationalism had made itself felt primarily as an instrument of the centralizing monarchy, turned against a sluggish and traditional body social. In Russia, particularly, the "bourgeoisie" hardly existed. The bearer of political and social rationalism, such as it was, had been the Romanov dynasty. This was what Kireevsky's hostility to Peter the Great really meant, and the government was not slow to see that the Slavophiles, for all their "Russianness," for all their religiosity and hostility to "Western" liberalism, were really an oppositional force.

Certain continuities in attitude can be observed between the "literary aristocrats" and Kireevsky in his new Slavophile incarnation. He, like Pushkin and Viazemsky before him, was opposed to the post-Petrine autocracy and its agents — the bureaucracy, the "new notables," and miserable creatures like Bulgarin. But the differences, too, are obvious. The "literary aristocrats" had no ideological structure, no mythology. Nor were their outspokenly aristocratic attitudes really characteristic of Kireevsky's Slavophilism — although he certainly believed that the gentry, or some portion of it, was the only hope for Russia. Kireevsky believed that the peasantry was the principle repository of what remained of the old, communal Russia, but he was far from thinking that the peasants themselves could give Russian culture the proper direction. That could only be done by people like himself.

Still, the fact that the aristocratic element in Slavophilism remained muted — almost implicit — is curious and not easy to explain. One never hears from Kireevsky, for instance, what role members of his own class played in the communal society of the past, with its sacred, inviolate traditions. When he spoke of the Russian past, Kireevsky almost always spoke of the peasant communes, the monasteries, or the fatherly prince with limited powers. And of course he was sharply critical of the "feudal" aristocracies of Western Europe. It may be that this rather obvious gap in the ideological structure was due to the fact that minutes?

the Russian gentry was not a real aristocracy, but a creation of the monarchy. Still, there is no mention of the old *boiarstvo* either, and when Kireevsky refers to people like himself, it is always in vague terms, such as a "thinking and independent" minority, which sound at least as much like an *intelligentsiia* as an aristocracy. Apollon Grigoriev and other critics of Slavophilism often mentioned its "old boyar" feeling — but the aristocratism was seldom, if ever, articulated.

The essential opposition of Slavophilism to the dynasty and its policies was what separated Kireevsky from men like Pogodin, Shevyrëv, and others, who were often referred to as "Official Nationalists." Although many of the latter were touched by the currents of political romanticism and irrationalism, they had no patriarchal nostalgia, tended to be suspicious of the gentry, and of course were enthusiastic supporters of the autocracy and the status quo. Pogodin, of course, often expressed a much simpler and more visceral dislike of Western liberalism than Kireevsky ever proclaimed, but his extreme and grotesque adulation of Peter the Great was an indication that he might well approve of violent change, provided it came from above. Nor did he indicate any particular nostalgia for the values that Peter might be supposed to have destroyed, for the values, in other words, that Kireevsky idealized and defended.

We may perhaps get a somewhat better sense of the emotional and historical roots of Kireevsky's revised world view by examining in some detail a brief, unfinished story called "Island," which he wrote a few months prior to his encounter with Khomiakov.[33] The scene was laid in the Greek islands. Off the coast of an isolated island lay a great mountain of rock, which for many years had served to warn vessels that they were approaching a particularly treacherous area of rocks and shoals. This barren and forbidding mountain, jutting out of the sea, had never been explored, serving only to warn the pilots of craft of all sizes that they had better change course and give the area a wide berth.

One day in the late sixteenth century, two monks in a small sailboat were caught in a storm and carried far off their course. The storm having abated, they saw to their terror that they were near the great pile of rock and were being carried rapidly toward it by the current. Just as they had abandoned all hope, their boat slipped into a small deep channel in the midst of the shoals and through this aperture they were able to maneuver to safety on the great rock itself.

They immediately set out to investigate the barren area on which they had come to rest, and to their amazement, they discovered that behind the great, gray walls of rock there was concealed something in the way of an island paradise, intersected by life-giving streams, and containing olive, lemon, orange, and peach trees and every variety of nature's abundance. It was a tropical garden, completely invisible from without and unknown to the entire outside world. They spent the night there and returned, the following morning, to the mainland and thence to their monastery.

Word of their discovery soon spread among the monks of Greece, and not long afterward a monastery was founded there. Many of the most pious and scholarly monks in Greece and Palestine chose to settle there, as did a certain number of families, who, "pursued by unbelievers [the Turks, of course], preferred to take refuge in eternal solitude than to exchange their Orthodox home for an alien, Latin land." An extraordinary spirituality developed in this sanctuary, and a "remarkably rich library" preserved the sacred books.

A most unusual form of life prevailed on that part of the island where the victims of Turkish persecution lived, apart from the monks. "Land was common, work cooperative, money did not circulate, luxury was unknown." Manual labor was combined with intellectual activity, and a spirit of justice and nobility pre-vailed in the communal assembly; "deep peace and purity" marked the home life of the inhabitants. Competition was dis-couraged, and the inhabitants were not involved in or troubled by the "superficial tinsel of European culture." [34]

While this small island community was leading its life, Europe continued on its fixed course, abandoned to its life of selfishness, every man concerned only about his own petty affairs.

But suddenly the order in the West gave way: the people were stirred up, passions ran high, thrones came tumbling down, blood flowed, the Church declined, the whole order of things was over-thrown, a new order emerged which in turn was destroyed, the executioner worked day and night, blood flowed in rivers, the people wept, passions knew no bounds, screams of ecstasy mingled with cries of despair and with the thunder of cannons and drums. The call to glory and victory resounded together with shrieks of bloodthirsty brutality, with the deep sighing of a deep love for humanity, with the laughter of debauchery and oblivion. All Europe trembled at the aroused people, all the kingdoms united against it in war, but could not overcome its concentrated force. What would become of en-lightened humanity? [35]

Were all these sacrifices, was all this blood "enlightened hu-manity's punishment for the lie in its enlightenment," for its selfishness, cruelty, and blasphemy? [36] The French Revolution was in full swing.

While these terrible alarms were taking place in Europe, the Paleologue family was bringing up its children on the island. A descendant, significantly, of the Greek imperial family, Paleologue had tried to serve the Porte, but had soon been forced to flee. His family life was a model of harmony, nobility, and tact, marred by no sort of controversy, until one of the rare visitors to the island from the outside world, from Greece, stimulated Paleo-logue's young son Alexander to an interest in his lost country. This interest soon developed into a passion.

Meanwhile, in Europe, the anarchic violence of the French Revolution had been tamed by Napoleon. Kireevsky gave an interesting, almost Dostoevskian description of him — without mentioning him by name — some of which runs as follows:

A man came, thoughtful and stubborn, contempt for human beings in his eyes, sickness and bile in his heart. He came alone, without a name, without wealth, without patronage, without friends, without secret conspiracies, without any visible support outside of his own will and cold calculation, and through calculation and will he brought the wheel of revolution to a stop . . . the people, saluting him, were still. And he put them in chains and drew them up before him in obedient ranks, and turned them smartly to the sound of a drum and led them far from their fatherland and commanded them to die in his name, at his whim, to enrich the least of his relatives. The people marched to the sound of his drum and died bravely at his whim, and as they lay dying, sent their children to take service with him, and blessed his name and there were ecstatic cries without end. And he was alone. An autocrat with no right to power . . . By what sorcery did he do his miracles? While others lived, he considered; while others lost themselves in revelry, he contemplated everything with a single end in view and considered; others relaxed after their labors, he laid his hand in his breast and considered. . . . Neither love, nor wine, nor poetry, nor friendly conversation, nor compassion, nor the lustre of greatness, not even glory — nothing distracted him. . . . His whole life was a single mathematical calculation, such that one mistake could annihilate the whole gigantic structure of his life.[37]

This portrait contains classic conservative features: Napoleon personifies the naked power of despotic rationalism, "calculation." Society is reduced to an army of automatons, to a militarized "mass society," to use the current term. Legitimate authority has been replaced by "power."

Meanwhile, back on the island, young Alexander Paleologue, as he approached his twenty-first birthday, grew increasingly restive. His desire to see Greece had developed into an obsession to visit the larger outside world of which his parents had told him and about which he had read in books. Nothing else now had any meaning for him. Finally, he received permission from his father and from the island assembly to leave the island and travel to Greece.

Upon his arrival, he found that all he had been told was true: the Greeks were enslaved — and far worse — had been degraded and spiritually destroyed by the barbarians who ruled them. Only the common people "were not completely ruined. In them the seeds of resurrection yet lived: their holy, deep attachment to belief. This feeling, for him who understood it, was rich in meaning: a veritable repository of incalculable strength, waiting to be awakened, an invincible strength, only covered with chains, buried in ignorance, forgotten by the indifferent foreign onlookers. . . ."

A trip around the country confirmed his initial impressions but also led him to believe that something was stirring among the people — notions of the restoration of true Christianity, together with revolt against the Turks. He went to Constantinople, to pay his respects to the Patriarch and then to set sail for the West. To his surprise the Patriarch was perfectly informed as to who he was and about his mission of exploration. He confirmed Alexander's impression of popular unrest, and added apropos of European life: "You see, all the ill stems from the fact that contemporary culture has developed under the influence of heresy. Hence the lie in it, and the lie has given rise to unbelief. What has happened? The truth and the mind have become enemies." [38] The Patriarch pinned his hopes, he said, on certain fellow Orthodox, who had a "great state, rich in hopes." Earlier, all had been heresy and degeneracy there too, but now the mist was lifting. Providence was sending them men who know the truth. And so, finally, Russia enters Kireevsky's tale. At the conclusion of their interview, the Patriarch gave him a passport and letters to European notables, and armed with these, Alexander took ship for Europe — for Italy.

The remainder of the fragment may be quickly summarized. On the boat, Alexander met a countess, whose aristocratic hauteur was played off against his simplicity and directness. After visiting Vienna (with the Congress just getting underway), Alexander fell in with a young German poet-painter who was also, not unexpectedly, something of a philosopher, and together they traveled to Italy. The purpose of this section was clearly to set up a confrontation between the representative of the old, communal Greek culture and a representative of what was best in the romanticism — and patheism — of contemporary Germany, but this interesting project was not realized, and the narrative comes to an end, virtually in mid-sentence.

"Island" is not very rewarding as fiction. Despite the passionate longing — even nostalgia — which underlay Kireevsky's portrayal of the island paradise (with its obvious relationship to Mt. Athos), it has the undeniable quality of an amateur stage set for the Garden of Eden. The dialogue is wooden and abstract throughout, especially when it is between members of the Paleologue family. And Kireevsky had the same problem with Alexander Paleologue, on a much lower level, that Dostoevsky had with Alyosha Karamazov. He was unable to dramatize his idea of goodness and truth, even with the chaos and bloodshed of Napoleonic Europe as a gigantic foil.

Nevertheless, the clumsy fictionalizing of "Island" is quite helpful in elucidating Kireevsky's feelings and ideas; it helps us to see how they are rooted in the concrete experience of real life. The heavy emphasis on the family life of the Paleologues gives us a renewed consciousness of the importance of his own family in his exaltation of communalism, with its serenity and tranquility. Furthermore, when Kireevsky recounts the horrors of the French

Revolution, his voice becomes shrill, almost hysterical. One feels a real fear of the aroused "people." The portrait of Napoleon, too, is revealing. He stands before us, summing up his age, a kind of cross between Fichte and Père Grandet, all will and "calculation." "Island" also reminds us again that no simple dichotomy between Russia and "the West" is possible in Kireevsky's variety of Slavophilism. Just as Greece lay debased and desecrated under the heel of the Turks, so Russia, thanks to Peter the Great and his successors, lay under the dominion of European "principles." Nicholas I was no closer to the patrimonial ideal of the sovereign than Peter had been — "immutable traditions" interested him only insofar as they promised dividends in the form of immediate political stability. The country was governed by a no less "rational" but far less competent version of the Prussian bureaucracy. The political police were ubiquitous, as Kireevsky had good reason to know. Political and cultural pressures — if not economic ones — were destroying the common interest between the Tsar and the gentry; 1825, of course, had been an important step along this path.

In other words, what drove Kireevsky to his attack on the political rationalism of the modern era was not primarily an abstract, intellectual perception of that evil as it was manifest in contemporary Europe, but a more concrete, immediate realization of what Russian society had become. Russia might appear, to the outsider, to be a more brutal, less developed version of Europe, but Kireevsky knew that Russia still contained within herself traces of the old, the communal. He knew this from his own experience, and he knew that on these traces the Russia of the future would have to be built.

Thus he used the idealized models of the *ancien régime* that Western European conservatives had formulated before him, although he was far from undiscriminating in his borrowing and synthesizing, as we shall see. The attack on Roman law, with its codifying, rationalizing, and abstracting spirit became an attack on the whole "Roman" element in Western European culture.[39] The traditional, the evolutionary, the communal, the unrationalized — these were the cultural (and economic) elements that European conservatives sought to preserve against the onrushing new civilization, whose triumph meant their destruction. These were the qualities which they abstracted from their way of life for its — and their — defense. Any direct, straightforward rallying to these values in the Russia of the 1830's and 1840's was bound to bring the defenders into conflict with the status quo: the activist Russian state and the bureaucracy. One cannot help feeling that this was at least part of the reason for the concentration on the Western European origins of the rationalist heresy. One must also remember that for generations, cultivated Russians had been "learning from the West." It was time, in Ivan Kireevsky's view, to reexamine just what Russians had been learning all this time.

Despite the success that the gentry enjoyed in its efforts to dismantle the Petrine state after 1730, the intellectual and social roots of Slavophilism go back to the palmiest days of the "dyarchy." The opposition between town and country in Russia began with the construction of St. Petersburg and extended well beyond the Slavophiles. The relatively straightforward detestation of Khomiakov and Peter Kireevsky for Peter's city was to give way to the demonologies of Dostoevsky and Andrei Belyi.

By the middle of the eighteenth century, a celebration of the Russian village had begun which was more than mere literary convention. This "ruralism," clearly observable in the poems of Sumarokov and M. M. Kheraskov, "had as its native sources the wish of significant portions of the gentry to be spared the supervision and demands of autocracy and the desire to escape the luxury, the expense, the loss in status brought about by life at court. The patriarchal village in which he was still unquestioned

master, where he was not at every step reminded of his relative
impotence vis-à-vis a powerful state — this was the place to which
many a Russian nobleman began to look with longing and
nostalgia." [40] A yearning for some kind of spiritual "wholeness,"
in opposition to the culture of St. Petersburg, is clearly evident
in eighteenth-century Russian Freemasonry, as Florovsky and
others have pointed out.[41]

Nevertheless, it was not until the relationship between the
absolutist state and the gentry had seriously deteriorated, not
until after December 14, 1825, that the cluster of attitudes, intuitions, prejudices, and insights could crystallize into a coherent
statement and structure. And it was not until representatives of
the Russian gentry had achieved a certain familiarity with the
tenets of romantic and counterrevolutionary thought that they had
the means to create the system of ideas which has come to be
known as Slavophilism.

IX. Slavophilism and
the Muscovite

*The best, the most thoughtful and cultured people
of the nineteenth century did not live in the
present, which was abhorrent to them; they lived
in the future, or in the past.*

— Nicolas Berdyaev

In looking back at the "Slavophile-Westerner debate" of the 1840's,
historians have tended, until fairly recently, to regard it as the
confrontation of two quite homogeneous groups, each of which
had a well-defined and mutually exclusive philosophical outlook
and program for Russia. This view owes a great deal to Herzen,
who in his memoirs juxtaposed the two groups for maximum
dramatic clarity, while suffusing the great debate in a delightful
nostalgia.

Although the story tells well that way, it should be pointed out
that such unity as the Westerners had came, in large part, as a
reaction to the formation of the Slavophile group. Like the
Mensheviks subsequently, the Westerners received their collective designation from their opponents; it was of course intended
as an abusive epithet, but they chose to wear it as a badge of
honor. In the latter part of the decade, without the Slavophile
enemy to hold them together, the Westerners split into two
groups, a left constellation, comprising Herzen, Ogarëv, and
Belinsky, and a more moderate group, headed by Botkin and
Granovsky.[1] As Malia observed of the Westerners, "In making
clear their differences with the enemy, they had also articulated
latent differences among themselves."[2] In addition to the above-
mentioned two groups, it should be obvious that Peter Chaadaev,

180

who has some claim on the title of "Westerner," was far removed from the world of French socialism and varieties of Hegelianism in which the other members of the "group" moved. And, had Belinsky not died in 1848, his fragile intellectual congruence with Herzen would very likely not have survived the latter's "Russian socialism," which owed so much to the Slavophiles.

That Herzen took Ivan Kireevsky's discovery — the peasant commune — and stood it on its head is well known. Herzen expressed his ambiguous attraction to Kireevsky and his ideas when he observed of him that "it was as though the truth had not disappeared altogether behind [his mysticism], but was hidden in fantastic outlines and monastic cassocks." [3] Beyond this, of course, are the common aristocratic lines which we have observed. The hostility of both Kireevsky and Herzen to industrialism and to the "bourgeoisie" was — insofar as either man really understood what was at issue — backward-looking and essentially nostalgic.

In his study of Ivan Kireevsky, Eberhard Müller attempted to carry this blurring process a step further by declaring that Kireevsky was not really a Slavophile, but occupied a "complicated position between the Slavophiles and the Westerners." [4] This assertion is based primarily on the fact that Kireevsky was on excellent terms with a number of the opposition, with Herzen and Granovsky in particular. Granovsky did not initially take to Ivan. "I have been rather frequently at the Kireevskys'," he wrote to Stankevich in November 1839.

Peter (the collector of Russian folksongs) is a very good fellow; to Ivan, the elder, I somehow do not respond. You cannot imagine what sort of philosophy these people have. Their chief position: the West has become rotten and nothing can now come from it. Russian history has been spoiled by Peter — we have been violently cut off from our indigenous historical foundations and are living at random. The only advantage of our contemporary life consists in the ability to dispassionately observe an alien history . . . All human wisdom is

contained in the writings of the holy fathers of the Greek church . . .
One need only study them: there is nothing to add; everything has
been said. They reproach Hegel for not valuing facts. Kireevsky says
these things in prose, Khomiakov in verse. It is sad that they are
attracting students: many of the best young men are gathering around
them and drinking in these fine ideas. Ivan Kireevsky is now seeking
a post as professor of philosophy.[5] He has many patrons, but memories
of the *European* are a hindrance. He is unquestionably a man with
talent and can have a strong influence on students . . . because he
is a fanatic and speaks gloriously.[6]

On January 4, 1840, however, we find Granovsky describing
the personal qualities of the Kireevskys in glowing terms. He
then went on to say that "the eldest brother, Ivan, has written a
superb article on reform of the popular schools (*narodnye
uchilishchi*) and has given it to the Count [Stroganov] by way of
a project. The realization of his ideas is impossible, but there is
much that is profound in them, and notwithstanding his simple
confusion, mysticism, and morbid patriotism, he has an unusual
understanding of the present moment of Russian history."[7]

The Kireevskys were frequently mentioned in Granovsky's correspondence during the winter and spring of 1840. Typical is a
letter of February 15 to Stankevich, in which Granovsky repeated that he feared Ivan Kireevsky's influence, but valued his
"nobility and independence of character" and his "warmth of
soul."[8] Particularly interesting is another letter to Stankevich,
written only three days later, apropos of an attack on Hegel
by Shevyrëv.[9] The burden of Shevyrëv's crude critique was that
the Hegelian system was a "godless" one. This accusation,
Granovsky indignantly remarked, was "tantamount to a denunciation." Fortunately, however, Hegel was well beyond the reach
of Nicholas' zealous agents — although his Russian disciples were
not. "Here again," continued Granovsky, "was revealed the
splendid character of Ivan Kireevsky. He does not like Hegel
and is in revolt against him, but he was even more indignant

about Shevyrëv's letter than I."[10] More interesting still is the passage that follows, which must be taken as showing that the *philosophical* aspects of Kireevsky's Slavophilism — the critique of "Western" philosophical rationalism which he elaborated in his last writings — was not yet clear and definite in his mind. "I even begin to think," wrote Granovsky, "that his mysticism is only a passing moment: he is now deeply involved with Hegel's logic and his *Religionsphilosophie.* He owns that this has afforded him the greatest pleasure after his long estrangement from philosophy and that Hegel is the greatest man of our era. That is a great concession for him."[11] When Khomiakov began inveighing against Hegel's politics, his *Preussentum,* and so forth, Kireevsky broke in, saying "that is all in his remarks, but not in his system."[12]

In June 1844, Granovsky went to spend a few days with Kireevsky at Dolbino. "We sat up every night until three o'clock and talked of many things," he wrote to his wife.[13] "He [Kireevsky] has almost decided to take the *Muscovite* and is glad that his journal will be at our disposal. He very well understands that it will be impossible for us to be regular colleagues on a journal to which he wishes to give a certain definite character. But to work with him will not be difficult. He has such a broad, noble nature that no sort of opinion can narrow it. But his friends! I. V.'s words about Herzen gladdened my heart. He valued him so highly and spoke of him with such respect and love that I almost wanted to say: 'yes, but he's a drunkard.' "[14]

Müller's principal piece of evidence, however, is a letter which Kireevsky wrote to Khomiakov in May 1844, likewise relating to Kireevsky's assumption of the editorship of the *Muscovite.* Kireevsky, as Granovsky's letter made clear, wanted the Westerners to feel that the journal was "at their disposal," although they were not to be "regular colleagues." Khomiakov's attitude was much harder on this question; at the end of a letter devoted to questions of the editorship, Kireevsky wrote: "One thing more. You write that our opponents are going to put out the *Galateia*.[15] Who in fact are these opponents? Can it be that you are referring to Granovsky and Co.? If so, are you not also mistaken in me? Perhaps you take me for a damned (*proklatyi*) Slavophile, and for this reason propose the *Muscovite* to me. As far as that is concerned, I must say that I share this Slavophile way of thinking only *in part*, but *another part of it I consider further from myself than the most eccentric opinions of Granovsky*."[16]

This statement would seem, on the face of it, good grounds for locating Kireevsky in some kind of middle position between the two camps. But it should not be forgotten that this rather heated declaration was made in a very specific context: that of the personal and journalistic relations which were to prevail in the larger and as yet not totally polarized group which included both Slavophiles and Westerners. Kireevsky was a friend of Granovsky and Herzen — Khomiakov was not. It is also true that Kireevsky loved much of Western culture in a way that Khomiakov did not. His reconsideration of Hegel, of however brief duration, certainly indicated that he had not as yet arrived at a firm and coherent view of Western philosophy. But the men themselves thought of two camps and no one doubted that Ivan Kireevsky was a Slavophile — except, perhaps, Kireevsky himself.

From an analytic standpoint, to concede — as Müller does here tacitly — that an intellectual position called "Slavophilism" existed, but to assert that Ivan Kireevsky was not part of it, is to involve oneself in great difficulties. Any analysis of Slavophilism must place the idea of the *mir* and the opposition between the abstract rationalism of the West and the integral Christian civilization of pre-Petrine Russia at the heart of the matter. Ivan Kireevsky played a primary — perhaps *the* primary — role in the utilization and elaboration of both these elements into a coherent structure. That he was hostile to the crude chauvinism of Pogodin and Shevyrëv, that he was fond of Herzen and Granovsky, even that he proclaimed in a moment of heat to be only "in part" a Slavophile — these facts are fundamentally beside the point. The most that can truly be said is that Kireevsky lacked Khomiakov's polemical self-confidence (together with his energy and vitality), that the evolution of his views was painful and at times uncertain, that he was bitterly sorry to see the polarization of the two groups that developed in the course of the 1840's and that he fought against it.

A more legitimate approach to the question would be to call into question the whole notion of "Slavophilism." Certain differences, not all of them merely of nuance, existed between Kireevsky, Khomiakov, Constantine Aksakov, and Iury Samarin in the 1840's. The later careers of Ivan Aksakov and Samarin bear witness to a sharp diminution in the hostility to the bureaucratic state which was so marked in certain of the writings of Kireevsky and Khomiakov, to the point where the term Slavophile is probably more misleading than useful.

But in the 1840's, Kireevsky's Christian communalism, together with his critique of Western rationalism, meant that in terms of the debate of the day he was a "Slavophile." On May 12, 1844, Herzen wrote in his diary that "a true rapprochement between their view and mine can never be, but there can be confidence and respect, such as in fact exists . . . between us and the Kireevskys." [17]

As Martin Malia has pointed out, the period 1840–1848 was, relatively speaking, the most liberal period of the reign of Nicholas I.[18] It is therefore scarcely surprising that the salon discussions and confrontations, characteristic of the previous decade, should have begun seeping into print in the years that followed. The *Annals of the Fatherland*, founded, significantly enough, in 1839, became the organ of the Westerners, while the Slavophiles turned to the *Muscovite*, edited until 1845 by Pogodin. The *Muscovite* had in fact been authorized by Nicholas as early as 1837, but was galvanized into publication only by the quickening of intellectual life which had become evident, both within the university and in Moscow society, by 1840.[19]

As has often been pointed out, neither journal was an entirely satisfactory vehicle for its "party." Malia has well described the *Annals* as a "commercial publication which printed cryptoradical literature only because it sold well with the public." [20] The Slavophiles were much slower to get into print than the Westerners, a circumstance due in part to their differences with Pogodin and to their low opinion of the *Muscovite* under his editorship. As Eberhard Müller has observed, the "polemic which the *Muscovite* carried on, often with a narrow-minded party spirit and at a low level . . . against the West, had conferred upon it a certain government odor and the obloquy of being no better than the official ideologues of the Bulgarin-Grech clique." [21] The correspondence of the Slavophiles is full of criticism of the *Muscovite*. Shortly before the question of Kireevsky's editorship was raised, Khomiakov wrote to Venevitinov that "the *Muscovite*, that sufficiently sad sign of our intellectual life, is in full decline . . . No one writes for it and no one is troubled about its support." [22] In January 1845, Gogol wrote to Iazykov that "the *Muscovite* has been appearing for four years now, and has not added a single shining star to the literary firmament. Only some antediluvian old men stick out their noses, then turn and flee." [23]

So matters stood when the proposal was made that Ivan Kireevsky become the editor of the *Muscovite*, which would then, in turn, become a real Slavophile journal. "It should be a glorious publication, if Kireevsky only proves capable of the work, to which he is, from long inactivity, unaccustomed," wrote Khomia-

kov to Venevitinov in the fall of 1844. "How strange it would be
if the former 'European' should be resurrected as the 'Muscovite'!
Would that not be a symbol of the inevitable path which our
education must travel, and does Kireevsky's conversion not minister to our hopes?" [24]

The initiative in the matter of editorial change seems to have
lain, as Müller has said, with Khomiakov, but behind the entire
effort lay the felt need of the Slavophile group to have an organ
of its own.[25] Pogodin's projected trip abroad provided an ideal
opportunity; Khomiakov wrote to Kireevsky at Dolbino in March
1844, proposing the change. After a moment of hesitation, Kireevsky professed himself interested, but typically enough, he remained in the country and left the most arduous negotiating with
Pogodin to his brother Peter and to Khomiakov.

Editor Pogodin had been much concerned with matters of
profit and loss; Kireevsky's worries were utterly different. His
initial response to Khomiakov's proposal was to suggest that
Khomiakov himself should take over the job — or perhaps
Shevyrëv, whose energy, at any rate, he had always admired.[26]
At the same time, he confessed that the job would be a real spur
to his own activity, since he had always needed some kind of
"external" and even "compelling" pressure to produce.

He was most concerned, of course, that the experience of 1832
not be repeated — for his own sake, for Pogodin's, and for the
journal's. He had to be sure of the government, and he wanted
some kind of "guarantee" that he would not become a "victim of
Bulgarin" for a second time; this he never received, for no
guarantees of that sort were to be had. In the same letter to
Khomiakov Kireevsky made a remark, significant for the light it
sheds on Kireevsky's attitude toward Pogodin and the previous
career of the *Muscovite*. "What could seem more loyal [in the
eyes of the censorship] than Pogodin and his *Muscovite*? So I
think, even though I have not read it." [27]

The *Muscovite's* excellent reputation in government circles notwithstanding, Kireevsky felt that he would have to make the most energetic advances to that quarter, if the enterprise were to have any chance of success — particularly in view of his confessed failure to defend himself in 1832. He pledged that he would write not only to Benckendorff but to Nicholas himself, since the Emperor had played such a direct and energetic part in ending the career of the *European*. We have, however, no evidence that these petitions were ever written, save for the fact that his editorship was in fact permitted. He also hoped that Count S. G. Stroganov, the cultivated curator of the Moscow educational district, might become the journal's patron and protector, and in this he appears to have succeeded.

Kireevsky also felt that he must at all costs have a free hand with the journal vis-à-vis Pogodin. As a journalist, he knew that Pogodin's solemn zealotry, together with his nonstop hankering after profits, would be a heavy burden indeed. He also knew that his desire to broaden the base of the magazine and to raise its tone must bring him into conflict with Pogodin, if the latter retained any voice in the management of the *Muscovite*. Its outright sale would have been, from Kireevsky's standpoint, the most desirable solution, but Pogodin could apparently not be persuaded. Despite Kireevsky's worries about his old comrade and about the government, he eventually agreed to take on the editorship de facto, with Pogodin remaining the owner and nominal editor.

At the end of January 1845, Kireevsky wrote to Zhukovsky, informing him of the resurrection of his journalist's career.[28] Like all his letters to the old poet, this one conveyed a sense of a son asking his father's blessing. He wrote that Pogodin had informed "the Minister" of the transferral of the editorship and that Stroganov, when consulted, had found the project "feasible." He then poured out his reasons for taking the risk that was involved. In the first place, there was the old need of external pressure to make him write. Interesting in this connection is the fact that already in 1842 Kireevsky had inquired of Viazemsky (then, *inter alia,* a censor in St. Petersburg) whether he might "write and take part in journals." [29] Viazemsky had been confident that he could go ahead, pointing to Polevoi and Nadezhdin, now active journalists again, despite their difficulties in the thirties. But Kireevsky produced nothing until he took over the *Muscovite.* He also confided to Zhukovsky that he simply liked journalism; furthermore, he was not as yet ready, he confessed, to embody his new views in anything more lengthy than a periodical article. A further reason — surprising and illuminating — was that the acceptance of the editorship would enable him "not to live in the country, which I have never been able to like, despite many years of trying." [30] Kireevsky could simply not get Moscow out of his system. A more important reason for his assumption of the editorial burdens, finally, related to the need of his friends for a literary organ and the stimulus which his editorship would provide for them.

"But over all this," he went on, "soars the thought, or, it may be, the dream, that the time has now come when the expression of my deepest convictions will be possible and not without value. It seems to me probable that in our time, when Western literature does not present anything in particular to dominate the intelligence, no particular principle which does not contain contradictions, no sort of conviction in which even its advocates believe — now, that is to say, the hour has come when our Orthodox principle of spiritual and intellectual life can find sympathy with our so-called educated public, which has hitherto lived in the belief in Western systems." [31]

Having remarked ominously that if this current enterprise did not succeed, it would be his last, Kireevsky went on to describe some of the highlights of the first issues. In addition to his own three-part article, there were poems by Iazykov, Avdot'ia Petrovna Elagina's translation of excerpts from the memoirs of the philosopher, Henrik Steffens, a sermon of Metropolitan Filaret, and a tale by Pogodin.[32] Kireevsky dilated on Zhukovsky's letter about his translation of the *Odyssey;* "it would be impossible not to print" a portion of it, he said, which may have been a tactful way of informing Zhukovsky that the whole letter would *not* be printed. Kireevsky felt that the translation itself was a great event in the development of Russian *narodnost'* into a "new, living view." Russians were in fact better able to understand the patriarchal Homer than were certain "old, clever peoples."

Kireevsky also raged against the censors for holding up their approval of his brother Peter's folksongs, a group of which was due to appear as soon as the censors passed them. The Petersburg censors, he wrote indignantly, "know only foreign songs," and believed that the folksongs of Russia could be kept from Russians. "Between Russian songs and the Russian people — the Petersburg censorship." [33]

In addition to fulfilling his editorial duties, Kireevsky contributed a long and important article to the *Muscovite* in 1845; it appeared serially in the three issues which he edited. Much of the tone of the piece and certain of the opinions there expressed cannot be fully understood without bearing in mind the growing tension between the Slavophiles and Westerners, which had come to a point of crisis just before Kireevsky took over the *Muscovite.* These developments are by and large well known, but they must be at least touched upon here. Particularly important is the complexity of the group relationships, the degree to which the Slavophiles were caught between Pogodin and Shevyrëv on the one hand and the well-disposed Westerners — Herzen and Granovsky — on the other.

In the course of the previous four years, the most bitter polemics had been between Belinsky and Shevyrëv in the *Annals* and the *Muscovite,* respectively.[34] Shevyrëv's harping on the fact that Belinsky knew no German, despite the fact that he was "drunk on German aesthetics," tended to promote bad feeling, as did his heavily ironic remarks about Belinsky's oscillating convictions. In 1842, Shevyrëv pressed the attack in his "View of the Contemporary Direction of Russian Literature," and Belinsky replied with his pamphlet, *The Pedant.* Belinsky and Constantine Aksakov also disagreed over whether Gogol's *Dead Souls* was a realistic indictment of contemporary Russia or a revival of the epic genre, a nineteenth-century *Iliad.*[35] Khomiakov refused to "meet" Belinsky, who retaliated by castigating the other Westerners, from St. Petersburg, for hobnobbing with the enemy. "I am a Jew by nature," he declared passionately, "and cannot sit at the same table with the Philistines." [36]

The culmination of this process of polarization came in late 1844, when Iazykov circulated a group of poems against the Westerners, individually and collectively.[37] Although Iazykov was not part of the Slavophile group and had in fact only recently returned from Western Europe, he was Khomiakov's brother-in-law, a dear friend of Kireevsky's, and at least a Slavophile fellow-traveler. In the overheated atmosphere of the time, his accusation of a "treasonous" lack of patriotism made a split inevitable. Herzen, in the *Annals,* compared Iazykov with the reactionary German playwright Kotzebue (who, it should be observed, had been in the pay of Metternich and was assassinated by a German student) and "the author of Vyzhigin." [38] Granovsky and Peter Kireevsky came to the brink of a duel, and social relations between the two groups were never really restored.

Khomiakov, if he did not actually egg Iazykov on, was not terribly upset about the break. Peter Kireevsky sided with

Iazykov, but the general family response was much more am-
bivalent. A clear indication of this is provided by a letter from
the twenty-year-old Elizaveta Elagina to her father. "Dear Papa,"
she wrote, "I am sending you the poems of Iazykov which have
produced so great an effect. Why does Iazykov write such
poems? Everyone is very angry at him, the more so as they have
been circulated everywhere . . . The Iazykovs, particularly Peter
Mikhailovich [Nicholas' brother], are just delighted by it all,
and Nicholas Mikhailovich is planning to write more to please
Khomiakov, who originally incited him to write." [39]

Relations — personal and intellectual — were of course far more
complex than this scenario of developing hostility would indicate.
Alone of the Westerners, Belinsky made no real ideological or
personal distinction between Shevyrëv and Pogodin, on the one
hand, and the Slavophiles on the other. His archetypal Slavophile,
drawn from a satire of Sollogub, was called "Ivan Vasil'evich,"
but was far more like Shevyrëv than Kireevsky. [40] Herzen, as Malia
has pointed out, was very drawn, not only to Ivan Kireevsky, but
to Constantine Aksakov and to Iury Samarin. [41] Granovsky, too,
had great respect for Aksakov and Samarin and the warmest
feelings for both Kireevskys, as we have seen, although he was at
somewhat more pains to distance himself from Slavophile ideas
and manners than was Herzen. Thus the forces making for a
clear division and an open break were Belinsky, both personally
and through his journalism, and Pogodin and Shevyrëv. The
Slavophiles considered the latter two really "not ours," in the
language of the day, but their close — if not harmonious —
relations were never broken off. Only Khomiakov, whom all the
Westerners disliked, appears to have played some small role
in the break, which really just "happened."

Ivan Kireevsky was undoubtedly the principal force for modera-
tion on the Slavophile side. He had hoped that both Herzen and
Granovsky would write for the *Muscovite*, although they were

not to be, it will be recalled, "regular colleagues." But his efforts to keep bridges up were in vain. Herzen adopted a wait-and-see attitude about publishing in the *Muscovite,* and Granovsky decided in early December 1844 that he could have no part of it.[42] In earlier and happier times, both men had published occasionally in the journal of the opposition. Then, about a week before Christmas, came the verses of Iazykov, and all was lost.

X. Russia and
the West in the
Post-Hegelian
Period

Kireevsky's "Survey of the Current State of Literature" was written during the last, critical months of polarization between the Slavophiles and Westerners. One senses in it an attempt to damp down the conflict, by isolating a proto-Belinsky on one extreme and a proto-Shevyrëv on the other, leaving a middle position where a real conversation about Russian and Western culture could continue. Kireevsky indulged in no shrill diatribes about the "rotten West," but at the same time he gently insisted that principles which underlay old Russian society were in an ultimate sense "the truth." [1]

Eberhard Müller is right to speak of the mood of disappointment which pervades the "Survey." [2] Its subject is "literature" in the broadest sense: philosophy, history, theology, political economy, and journalism all get more attention than fiction, poetry, or belles lettres. His focus obviously reflects not only his own changed preoccupations but also his view of the spirit of the time, for the basic preoccupations of enlightened Europe, he felt, were religious and social.[3] He had felt this also in 1832, but the "new era" which he had then seen just around the corner was still struggling to be born. Now the age of the "great poets" was past; gone was the purely literary passion and delight which they stirred in their readers. We read, he observed, much more than we used to, but "like a bureaucrat," without real empathy. What was to have been the age of realism had turned out to be merely an age of "journalism." Here Kireevsky echoed Shevyrëv.[4] But Kireevsky made of the notion of an age of journalism something far more serious and thoughtful than Shevyrëv's superficial, anti-Western sloganizing.

"Wherever we look," he wrote,

thought is universally subordinated to present contingencies, feeling is the servant of party interest, form is tricked out in accord with the demands of the moment. The novel has become statistics on mores, poetry has become "occasional" poems. History, which used to be the echo of the past, is trying instead to become mirror of the present or the proof of some social conviction or other . . . and philosophy, in the guise of the most abstract contemplation of eternal truths, is continually occupied with their relationship to the present moment. Even works of theology in the West are, for the most part, given birth by some subsidiary circumstance of external life.[5]

It is ironical, too, that Kireevsky's own writings are so illustrative of the tendencies of the "age of journalism." So much for that "turning to reality" about which Kireevsky had had such hopeful — albeit complex — feelings in the days of the *European*.

Significantly and accurately enough, Kireevsky believed, Europe's old interest in politics was giving way to a concern with "social questions," with "the inner life of society." But he found that Western thinkers, in their laudable desire to discover the "moral mainspring" which turns the wheels of society, were hamstrung by a lack of all real conviction. The result was a flood of "systems," each purporting to annihilate its predecessors, each in turn collapsing before it was fairly launched. Hence, in all the literature and thought of the West, "beginning with the newest philosophy of Schelling and ending with the long-forgotten system of the Saint-Simonians," Kireevsky found both a "positive" and a "negative" side. In the former — tantamount to self-criticism by Western society — there was often "much that is true." But what passed for the "positive" was simply a hopeless attempt to create "by force" or through abstract thought a fundamental conviction that was lacking. It was this basic lack of shared belief which accounted for the fact that "in our time there are so many talents and not a single true poet," for poets are created by "the force of inner (*vnutrennii*) thought," by a "living, integral view," by "supra-personal" conviction.[6] Artificial theories and intellectual constructs cannot help. This view was, of course, something of a commonplace critique of bourgeois civilization; on this point, conservative romantics and the Saint-Simonians could agree.

The eighteenth century, continued Kireevsky, may have been an era of unbelief, but its spokesmen believed passionately in their unbelief. The collapse of their cherished convictions was followed by despair and Byronism. Two "tendencies" resulted from this dismal situation. On the one hand, "thought, unsupported by higher spiritual aims," became the servant of base forms of egoism and sensualism; commercialism penetrated into every area of contemporary life, even the most sacred and intimate. The second and complementary tendency, according to Kireevsky, was that desperate thirst for belief, which has interacted so variously with the dominant mode of "European science."

German thought, predominantly philosophical still, was divided into a "historical-theological" tendency, which Kireevsky obviously considered the main stream, and a Francophile, "political" wing which he did not discuss. The new system of Schelling, he concluded, so long anticipated, has satisfied neither the philosophers nor the believers.[7] It has attracted little attention, while Hegelianism continues to grow more popular and, seemingly, more influential. Nevertheless, Schelling's "refutation of previous philosophies" (particularly that of Hegel) has been increasingly influential on a small circle of far-seeing men.[8] As one historian has shrewdly noted, Kireevsky's fundamental elitism survived all changes in his opinions.[9] He continued to look for the intimations of the future in gifted individuals and small groups.

As far as the Hegelians themselves were concerned, Kireevsky found it noteworthy that they were presently able to agree only on method, in some vague sense, and on mode of expression. Hegel and some of his followers, he thought, had ended in a kind of "aristocratism" — but now the Hegelians are developing both an extreme democratic position and one of a "fanatical absolutism" — from the same "principles." From the religious point of view, both the most antique, primitive Protestantism and the extremes of godlessness can be derived from Hegel. Hence the enormous confusion, particularly outside of Germany, as to what Hegelians think and what Hegelianism "is." To buttress this point, Kireevsky cited a number of the master's most eminent disciples: Erdmann, Rosenkranz, Michelet, Werder, and others, but he concluded that Hegel remains the only real Hegelian.[10] Kireevsky also mentioned sympathetically two men whom he regarded as direct opponents of Hegel: Johann Friedrich Herbart and Friedrich Adolf Trendelenburg. As Müller has shown, Trendelenburg and Schelling — whatever their other differences — shared a hostility to "pure thought" and were more than once bracketed in German post-Hegelian polemics as proponents of a kind of empiricism.[11] Herbart's thought was in many respects consciously antithetical to the whole development of German idealism: he rejected dialectical logic and returned to do battle with Kant, accepting the "thing in itself" as unknowable and attacking the transcendental dialectic as the source of Fichte's "Ego" and ultimately the development of idealism which followed.[12] But in the case of Trendelenburg, too, Kireevsky found that his "destructive force" — his attack on the citadel of idealism — was far more impressive than his creative powers.

The disintegration of Hegelianism was a congenial topic, and Kireevsky rightly placed it at the center of the intellectual scene in Germany. His feel for the process and his knowledge of what was actually going on was impressive. Nevertheless, despite — or perhaps because of — Germany's philosophical bankruptcy, Kireevsky thought that the obvious thirst for belief among the country's best minds would soon bring about something in the nature of a spiritual revolution. Here, as elsewhere, it is plain that despite Kireevsky's dislike of Germany's soulless *Bürgertum,* he continued to find that country's intellectual and spiritual life fascinating and of major import for the future.[13]

Turning to theology, Kireevsky first provided a brief historical résumé, beginning at the turn of the century, when German Lutheranism (he did not even mention Catholic theology) was little more than a mélange of French "popular rationalism" with "the formulas of the German schools." The only countervailing tendency was Pietism, then limited to a "small circle."

The fall of Napoleon changed this situation drastically: a wave of patriotic exultation swept Europe, kindling the most roseate hopes for the future and, more specifically, producing two strong theological currents. The first was strongly antirational, hostile to philosophy, and close to Pietism. The second defended reason, "and sometimes bordered on pure rationalism." Developing dialectically out of all this hurly-burly, out of the collision between the two dominant theological currents, out of the attacks on both by the "pure rationalists" (presumably Strauss and his followers), came the impulse for a new and more searching study of Holy Writ, as well as "the necessity for a firm definition of the boundaries between reason and belief." Among the many representatives of "philosophical theology," Kireevsky singled out Schleiermacher and Karl Daub.[14]

The more conservative, Pietistic wing of Lutheranism, the followers of the Augsburg Confession, Kireevsky noted, were having "little success." The state protection which had worked to their advantage for so long now seemed morally and intellectually disabling, but even more important was the fact that the Augsburg Confession was founded, in Kireevsky's words, "on the right of personal interpretation," which its adherents now seemed to deny. From Kireevsky's point of view, of course, the fault was not in the current rigidity of the state confessionalism, but in the essence of Protestant individualism which underlay the Augsburg Confession.

Kireevsky closed out Germany with some brief remarks on the most important (antiliberal) theologians of the post-Schleiermacher period: Julius Müller, Ernst Wilhelm Hengstenberg, F. A. Tholuck, August Neander, K. A. Nitzsch, Friedrich Lücke, and Johann Beck. He had particularly sympathy for Beck, the admirer of Kierkegaard, whose emphasis on Biblical studies must have appealed to him.[15] Despite the cursoriness of his remarks, it is clear that his knowledge of Protestant theology and its current representatives in Germany was considerable.

The question posed by intellectual developments in France and England was fundamentally that of the industrial revolution and the response of society to it. Kireevsky noted aphoristically that while in Germany, every problem of life became "science," in France, "every scientific and literary problem turns into a problem of life."[16] The novels of Eugène Sue had their principal impact on society, rather than on literature; Balzac, Kireevsky claimed, was "almost forgotten," because the society he described in his novels perished in 1830. Such "German" problems as the relationship between philosophy and belief, or that between religion and the state — as revealed, for instance, by the Cologne Episcopal dispute[17] — simply do not exist in France, where empiricism and the natural sciences hold sway. There, "the essential question of the present moment consists in the reconciliation of religion and society"; it was in the resolution of this important question, Kireevsky felt, that France might make her contributions to "the general development of the culture of humanity."

"Will a new science be born," Kireevsky asked rhetorically, "the science of *social life*," corresponding to that "*science of the wealth of nations*," which developed in England at the end of the last century? [18] It is too early to say, he concluded, too early to conclude that France will redeem her promises, but it will be very interesting to see how the new "movement" in France will affect matters of political economy. "Questions of competition and monopoly, about the relationship between the surplus production of luxury goods and the prosperity of the people, of the low price of manufactured goods and the poverty of the laborer (*rabotnik*), of the wealth of the state and the wealth of the capitalists, of the value of labor and the value of manufactured goods, of the development of luxury and the misery of poverty, of physical violence and intellectual anarchy, of the moral health of a people and its industrial culture (*obrazovannost'*)" [19] — all these questions, Kireevsky felt, were posed in such a way as to directly oppose the conclusions of "political economy," by which he meant, of course, the laissez-faire economics of Adam Smith and David Ricardo. No sound solutions have been thus far achieved for these problems: those which have been suggested are "too immature," "too one-sided," and dominated by a "party spirit." But solutions there must be.

It seems probable that the "one-sided" and unsound solutions to which Kireevsky referred were various currents of French socialism. Although he was not much interested in the phenomenon per se (or claimed not to be — witness his offhand dismissal of the "long-forgotten" system of the Saint-Simonians), it is scarcely surprising that he should have been intrigued with the nascent "science of social life" which seemed to be taking shape in France.[20] The juxtaposition of "political" and "social" was common to conservative and radical critics of rationalized, bourgeois society. For both, the political economy of Adam Smith and the new industrial order so intimately related to it were hostile entities. Certainly, Kireevsky's language is remarkably similar to that of the *Doctrine de Saint-Simon.* Russia had been spared these things — in the purely economic sphere — but for how long? The contrast between Kireevsky's relatively optimistic remarks about industrialism and the new civilization which was to accompany it, in the pages of the *European,* and his remarks on the same subject here are striking, and further indicative of the changes which his views had undergone.[21]

Intellectual developments in France, Kireevsky observed, were part of the total evolution of French culture, not simply the result of the poverty of the lower orders there. This could be seen with reference to England, where poverty was even worse; the dominant intellectual currents across the channel, however, were very different.

The difference between Kireevsky's and Khomiakov's attitude toward England is striking.[22] Khomiakov was vividly aware of a patriarchal, Tory England to which he felt a certain attachment.[23] Kireevsky, on the other hand, seems to have regarded England as the bearer of political liberalism and the worst excesses of industrialism, a country where the cynical play of "interests" and parties was all-powerful. Here indeed was the center of the spider's web.

Seeing in England only triumphant Whiggery, Kireevsky completely failed to grasp the mood of crisis which gripped England in the late 1830's and early 1840's — he made no mention in the "Survey" of Poor Law agitation or Chartism or the Anti-Corn-Law League. Certainly the two figures that he seized upon as representative of English thought — Thomas Carlyle and Benjamin Disraeli — are central to the period, but his view was a rather unfocused one. The two men, he wrote, "are completely opposite in their tendencies, thoughts, parties, goals, and views." [24] They were united only by a common conviction that "the hour has come when the insular separatism of England is beginning to yield to the generality of continental culture and to fuse with it into one sympathetic whole." [25] In the case of Carlyle, Kireevsky was clearly referring to the German inspiration of his ideas and the Germanisms of his language. Disraeli's contribution to the dissolution of England's "insular separatism" is hard to find. What Kireevsky seems to have meant is that Disraeli and his "Young England" friends were in the process of destroying historically conditioned English "Toryism," diminishing the historical uniqueness of England in the process.[26] This was scarcely a program to commend itself to a person of Kireevsky's convictions.

Kireevsky had read *Coningsby: or, The New Generation,* which appeared in 1844. One might have expected that he would have regarded "Young England" with some sympathy, particularly in view of his concern to find the straws of a new social and religious order in the wind. There could have been, in fact, no other reason for mentioning the group at all. There was much in the program of Young England to attract him: the hostility to commercialism, the notion of an alliance between a renewed Tory aristocracy and the common people against Whiggery and pauperism, the stress on the vital role of religion and the Church. Kireevsky did not, however, take Young England very seriously, viewing it basically as a kind of Tory "extremism" which threatened the party and the country. If he sensed real common ground between his hopes and aspirations and those of Disraeli, he did not succeed in communicating it to his readers. He even remarked that since Disraeli is a Jew, he "therefore has particular views of his own which do not permit us to rely fully upon the truth of the younger generation's convictions, as he depicts them." Kireevsky was by and large quite right in his view that Young England was not to be taken very seriously, although he was right for the wrong reasons. And he seems to have been unaware of the deep unrest in England, which was the essential backdrop for the "movement's" emergence and lent it larger significance. It would have been interesting, too, to have had his evaluation of those Tory radicals, Richard Oastler and Michael Sadler, whose views had certain striking points of contact with his own.[27] But Kireevsky was much farther away from England than from Germany, and not only geographically.

Carlyle's thought, according to Kireevsky, partook of a "dreamy German indefiniteness." For the rest, Carlyle, he judged, "is not haunted by the old order of things, is not opposed to new movement; he values both, he loves both, esteeming in both an organic fullness of life. Himself belonging to the party of progress, by the very development of its fundamental principle he annihilates the exclusive striving for novelty." [28] Kireevsky's language here has the vagueness which is often indicative of a lack of hard information. Furthermore, if there was ever a man who was "haunted by the old order of things," it was Carlyle. The conclusion is inescapable that Kireevsky's knowledge of the author of *Past and Present* was sketchy indeed.[29]

Having apologized for the brevity of his whirlwind tour, Kireevsky proceeded to draw some general conclusions about European culture as a whole. He began with the premise that the great voyage of national self-discovery upon which the individual cultures of Europe had embarked at the end of the eighteenth century was over. The Age of Herder was past. The deeper the excavators of the *Volksgeist* had dug, he argued, the clearer it became that the bases of European culture were not national. European culture had to be regarded as a single great entity; the national differences which he had just enumerated were presumably to be regarded merely as variants and subvariants. The recognition of a greater European culture was accompanied by three other developments: (1) the various literary genres were

tending to fuse into "one indefinite form"; (2) the boundaries
between "sciences" were tending to fade and blur; they were
increasingly closely related to their "general center" — philosophy; (3) philosophy, in its turn, was seeking a principle by virtue
of which it could fuse with "belief" into a "single speculative
(*umozritel'nyi*) unity." [30]

In our time, he continued, the inadequacy of European culture has been more and more strikingly revealed, for *"the distinctive character of Western culture in all its aspects and as a
whole [is] a fundamental striving toward personal and self-
contained (samobytnyi) rationalism in thought, in life, in society,
and in the motivating forces and forms of human life."* [31] Now
the insufficiency of this rationalism has been recognized; the
realization of this fact developed dialectically from the conviction,
held until very recently, that contemporary European culture
was the very highest manifestation of human development. Obviously, this was just the disintegration of Hegelianism — the most
extreme development of Western rationalism — writ large for all
of Western culture.

The final development of the rational principle has now produced a thirst for belief, but a return to the "religion" which en-
gendered rationalism in the first place is not possible. A new
principle must be found — without one, European culture cannot live again. The last great European poet was Goethe, who
finally abandoned poetry altogether for "the tasks of industry."
In its important respects, the situation now is identical, he found
with the Saint-Simonians, to that which existed at the end of
the Ancient World. Greco-Roman culture had developed to the
point of self-contradiction; then, as now, a "new principle" was
necessary, one which *"had been preserved by other tribes which
had not hitherto had world-historical significance."* [32] The future
of Europe — in every area of life and culture — depends upon
Europe's future relationship to "the principal of life, thought and

culture which lies at the base of the Orthodox-Slavonic world." [33]

When we consider the various literatures of Western Europe, continued Kireevsky, we find that all of them differ from Russian literature in one crucial respect. In Russia, one can find traces of an immense variety of alien national literatures: German, French, English, Italian, Polish, Swedish, and so on. Despite the falsity of the fundamental principle upon which all of the national cultures in the West are based, there is a certain organic unity between the historical existence of each individual people and its literature. Even when one nation submitted to the cultural tutelage of another, it did so temporarily and for reasons which related to its own national needs: "the foreign, for them, is not a contradiction of their individuality, but only a step upward on the stair" [34] — an "organic" stair, to be sure, leading to the realization of their national genius.

Among Russia's Western neighbors, Kireevsky wrote, only one nation did not exhibit this organic relationship between the people's historical existence and the national culture — Poland. Contemporary Russia was ("thank God," Kireevsky exclaimed) utterly unlike medieval Poland, but it had to be admitted that "with respect to literature" Russia exhibited that same "abstract artificiality," those "same rootless flowers, plucked from alien fields," so characteristic of earlier Polish culture. Great writers like Derzhavin, Karamzin, Zhukovsky, Pushkin, and Gogol notwithstanding, there is "no doubt that a manifest difference exists between our literary culture and the fundamental elements of our intellectual life, which developed in our ancient history and are now preserved in our so-called uneducated people." [35]

Two answers are generally given, he wrote, to the question of how our literature can escape from the painful situation in which it finds itself. "Some think that the most complete assimilation of foreign culture can, with time, refashion (*peresozdat'*) the whole Russian man, as it has refashioned certain productive and non-

productive litterateurs, and that the totality of our culture will
subsequently come to agree with the character of our literature." [36] This, of course, is Kireevsky's nutshell paraphrase of the
argument of the Westerners, and of course its "falseness is . . .
evident." It is impossible to annihilate the "fundamental convictions of a people" by means of "literary ideas," and even if such
a thing were possible it would be highly undesirable, for the
West has no real alternative to offer Russia. An example of what
happens when "European principles" are transferred to a "new
people" may be seen in the United States of America; Kireevsky
found the results of this experiment scarcely encouraging. The
total lack of high culture in that unhappy country, the soulless
egoism, the grotesque materialism, the rampant rationalism and
legalism — the results were only too clear.[37] The devastating
rationalism of modern life had advanced even farther in the
United States than in England, the source of its "culture."

The second of the two most frequently proposed remedies for
the derivative character of Russian culture was, according to Kireevsky, equally one-sided, but far less popular and a good deal
more logical. It was, quite simply, to obliterate all traces of Western influence and return to the "forms of our antiquity." This
Shevyrëvian program was more "logical" than the Westerner position, since it recognized the superiority of old Russian culture
to that of the West, but it was quite impossible to bring off. It
would require a miracle; it would be to raise the dead.

Since to return to the past is out of the question (and even if
it were possible, it would cut Russia off from the culture of all
humanity, Kireevsky remarked in a curiously Hegelian way),
what must we then do? Since Russians can never unlearn, never
divest themselves of what has become part of them — even if it
be wrong or false — the "path to true *narodnost'* " must lie
through and beyond European culture. To deny it altogether
simply means "spiritual provincialism." Kireevsky then formu-

lated his alternative to Shevyrëv's purely negative view of the
West in language which surely justified Gogol's complaint that
the "Survey" was too "abstract." [38] "If European culture is in fact
false," he wrote, "if it really contradicts the principle of true culture, then that principle which is true must not leave that contradiction in the mind of man. On the contrary, it must take [the
contradiction] into itself, evaluate it, set boundaries to it, and
having thus established its own superiority, it must reveal [to
the contradiction] its own true sense. The presumed falseness of
this culture in no wise rules out the possibility of its submission
to the truth." [39]

Having formulated these positions, Kireevsky then condemned
the dispute as to whether Russia or the West was superior as
one of the "most useless, most empty questions that ever any
thinking man, in his idleness, might dream up." [40] In the context
of the debate of the 1840's, this was conciliatory language indeed,
and very different from that to which the readers of the *Muscovite* were accustomed. But Kireevsky was far from declaring his
neutrality, in any sense, between the old Russian "principle" and
the Western "principle." Since our principle is "true," he went on
to say, whatever is good in the life of the West is an expression
of it. Furthermore, he continued, "if the proponents of European
culture wished to raise themselves from an instinctive passion for
this or the other form, for this or the other negative truth, to the
real principle of the intellectual life of man and nations, which
alone gives sense and truth to all external forms and particular
truths, they would without doubt have to recognize that Western
culture does not present that high, central, dominating principle." [41] To *introduce* Western forms from without, even if they
contain something "real" (*sushchestvennyi*), can only be destructive.

After deploring at considerable length the frivolous, effeminate
nonentities who merely ape the fashionable glitter of Western

culture (and upon whom his arguments were of course wasted), Kireevsky turned to the concept of "culture" (*obrazovannost'*) which he had been employing and drew an important distinction.[42] Throughout all history, he claimed, there had actually been two kinds of culture. The first, and spiritually primary, type he defined as "the internal ordering (*ustroenie*) of the soul by the power of truth manifest in it"; this kind of culture is "dependent on that principle to which the individual submits himself." Here there is no "changing development, but only direct recognition, preservation, and diffusion of the human spirit into subordinate spheres." It alone has "essential meaning," for it "defines the internal order of a people and the direction of their external existence, the character of their private, family, and social relations. It is the mainspring of their thought, the dominant tone of the movement of their soul, the cause of their conscious preference and their unconscious passion, the basis of *mores* and custom, the sense of their history." [43]

Kireevsky defined the second type of culture as "the formal development of reason and external cognition." The product of centuries of evolution, it lends "fullness and content" to the first "type" of culture, but it is dependent on it for "sense" and "meaning." An essential characteristic of the "second culture," as Kireevsky defined it, was that, like an artist's technique, it was morally and spiritually neutral. Due to its "lack of character," to its "logical-technical" essence, it could survive the destruction or disintegration of that higher type of culture based upon the "fundamental principle" of a people. In periods of cultural decline or decay — as, for example, the periods which followed the deaths of Hegel and Aristotle — the second culture becomes "the sole support of speculative thought." [44]

These two cultures had been, according to Kireevsky, generally confused. Thus, the fact that progress had undeniably been made in certain sciences led the men of the eighteenth century (Kireevsky mentioned Lessing and Condorcet) to their belief in the perfectibility of the human race. Even more fundamental to the growth of this belief, however, was the proposition that "the living understanding of the soul, that inner ordering of man" could be "artificially" produced, "mechanically" achieved by the "development of logical formulas alone." The achievement of these things was promised by "logical reason, torn away from the other sources of knowledge": only now, having entirely realized its potential, has it come to recognize its own incompleteness and its need for a higher principle.

The situation in which Western culture found itself also had implications for the relations of that culture with the bases of Russian culture. Russia and the West, Kireevsky concluded, needed each other. In 1832, it had been the radical break in the intellectual development of Europe which took place in the mid-eighteenth century which was to have made possible the appropriation of subsequent European culture by Russia. Now Kireevsky saw the exhaustion of Western culture as having created a situation where the Russian principle could provide the basis for a new stage in human history, while "European culture, the ripe fruit of the development of humanity, torn from the old tree, must serve as nourishment for a new life, a new stimulus to the development of our intellectual life." [45] The love of European culture and the love of Russian culture are thus really only one love. And, although Kireevsky did not quite say so, European culture clearly represented, in his scheme, the lower-level "logical-technical" culture, while Russian culture was that higher, "essential" culture, whose essence was the ordering of the soul.

Having thus dealt with the larger philosophical questions, Kireevsky turned to Russian literature, which, since it existed fundamentally as a reflection of foreign literature, had the same journalistic character. It was either this journalistic character of the times or limitations of space, presumably, which led him to confine his remarks on Russian literature to a discussion of the periodical press. He took up the subject with the obvious relish of an inveterate reader of journals. Flashes of his old (one is tempted to say "pre-Slavophile") wit are apparent in his discussion of the *Library for Reading*. This bulky journal, Kireevsky found, could be characterized only by its total lack of character. Completely innocent of tendency, it "praises today what it damned yesterday." It constantly passed judgment on every conceivable development in literature on the basis of some "law" or other, but one always feels, Kireevsky wrote elegantly, that the judgment and its object are like two people who have just had a hurried and inconclusive encounter and are unlikely to recognize each other the next time that they meet. The editor of the *Library*, Osip Senkovsky, was a talented popularizer and a man of the broadest cultivation and great shrewdness.[46] The *Library's* reviews were almost invariably clever and left the public — and even the author of the book under review — helpless with laughter, but for the most part they were neither serious nor useful for Russian literature.

The *Beacon* (*Maiak*) and the *Annals of the Fatherland* were of an utterly different character. They had tendency with a vengeance. The *Annals* (the principal organ of the Westerners, it will be recalled) "tries to guess at and then to assimilate that view of things which, it believes, is the latest expression of European culture." [47] Thus, although its opinions change constantly, it remains faithful to its task of "reflecting the most fashionable thought, the very latest feeling from Western literature."

The *Beacon*, on the other hand, damns all Western culture out of hand, although it only takes up those aspects of it which seem particularly "harmful or immoral." It is not necessary to read both of these journals, since the *Beacon* is simply the *Annals* stood on its head. Kireevsky did not — at least so he maintained — juxtapose these two journals simply for the sake of the annoyance which both were sure to feel, but to demonstrate that one-sidedness which was so deeply rooted in Russian intellectual life. Nicholas Riasanovsky called the *Beacon* "fantastically reaction-ary, obscurantist, and nationalist," and in fact it seems to have been completely beyond the pale, virtually ignored by all seri-ous members of the intellectual community, of whatever ideologi-cal persuasion.[48] The real opposition, of course, would have been between the *Muscovite* (under its previous management) and the *Annals*. This comparison, however, would obviously have been awkward, since the *Muscovite* was now striving for modera-tion and the middle ground. When Kireevsky wrote that "the very polemic between them serves to bind them indissolubly to-gether and constitutes, so to speak, the necessary condition of their intellectual activity," he made sense only if Slavophiles and Westerners are substituted for the *Beacon* and the *Annals*.[49]

Kireevsky went on to accuse the latter journal of not only an enslavement to the novelty and fashion of the West, but of ig-norance of the totality of Western culture and the inability to distinguish what was really new. The Westerners, that is to say, clung to Hegel, without realizing the desuetude into which "Hegelianism" had now fallen, without realizing that Schelling had given Hegel the coup de grace, without realizing the crisis in which Western culture now found itself. The result was that their discussions of Russia and the West lacked, among other things, context and intelligibility. Certain conclusions, for exam-ple, which had emerged in the West as the result of a given nation's search for *narodnost'*, had been cited by the *Annals* to deny the *narodnost'* of Russia. The situation, Kireevsky felt, was similar to that which had prevailed "in the old days when the Germans had denied their *narodnost'* because it was not like that of the French." Because certain false literary idols in the West had been pulled down, the *Annals* had felt it incumbent upon them to "diminish the literary reputations of Derzhavin, Karam-

zin, Zhukovsky, Baratynsky, Iazykov, Khomiakov, and to exalt
I. Turgenev and F. [*sic*] Maikov in their place." [50]

The *Northern Bee* — Bulgarin's journal — Kireevsky found
more "political" than literary. In its unpolitical parts, he remarked
with delicate distaste, the *Bee* "expresses just that striving for
morality, good order, and decorum which the *Annals* displays
for European culture." The *Bee* "tells us everything which pleases
it, denounces everything not to its liking with the utmost zeal,
but not, perhaps, always justly. We have some grounds for thinking that it is not always just." [51]

Of the other journals of the day, Kireevsky found the *Literary
Gazette* now totally devoid of interest. For Pushkin's old journal,
the *Contemporary*, now edited by P. N. Pletnëv, he had high
praise. In fact, the *Contemporary* was an honorable relic of the
time of Pushkin; its devotion to a purely aesthetic truth and its
refusal to take any part in literary polemics had reduced its subscribers to a pitiful handful, and it was soon to become a very
different journal under Nekrasov and Panaev. The *Finnish Messenger* (*Finnskii vestnik*) Kireevsky saw as a healthy sign of rapprochement between Scandinavian and Russian literature.

The dominance of the journal, Kireevsky concluded, was part
and parcel of the dominance of received opinion, of fragments of
Western culture. His concern, more than ever before, was with
the totality and essence of cultures; this, perhaps, was why he
did not discuss individual writers — Gogol or Lermontov — in
the "Survey" itself. Gogol and Zhukovsky, he remarked elsewhere,
pointed the way to the future development of Russian *narodnost'*,
but he rested his deepest hopes on

an important change which has already begun in one little corner
of our literature, a change which is still scarcely perceptible, a change
which is expressed not so much in literary productions as it is
revealed in the condition of our culture as a whole. It promises to
transform the character of our imitative submission into the distinctive

development of the internal principles of our own life. The reader will have guessed, of course, that I am speaking of that Slavo-Christian direction, which has been the recipient, on the one hand, of what may be an exaggerated partiality, but on the other, has been visited by strange, desperate attacks, sneers, and slander. But in any case, it is worthy of attention as an event which in all probability will not occupy the lowest place in the destiny of our culture.[52]

Given Kireevsky's involvement with the "Slavo-Christian direction," his conclusion was curiously diffident. Was it merely the desire not to stir up strife?

The focus of the "Survey" was on sociology and what might be called cultural history, but Kireevsky did touch on literature, more narrowly conceived, elsewhere in the *Muscovite*. Particularly interesting in this connection are the several pages he wrote to introduce a series of book reviews.[53] One recalls in reading these rather rambling pages how strongly Kireevsky's literary taste was formed by Pushkin and his contemporaries; the feeling of nostalgia for the "Golden Age" is even stronger in his obituary for Baratynsky.[54] Kireevsky was of course some years younger than they; his philosophical (and subsequently social) interests always separated him from them to some degree, but from the vantage point of what is generally regarded as his own "time" — the social and polemical 1840's — he looked back on these men who had been content to be literary artists with a rather poignant admiration, even with a feeling of identification. Kireevsky might almost have been speaking of himself when he wrote, "born for an intimate circle of family and friends, unusually sensitive to the sympathy of people who were close to him, Baratynsky expressed himself freely and profoundly in quiet, friendly conversations, thus at times assuaging his need to address himself to the public." [55]

How different from the gaiety and creative vitality of Pushkin and his friends was the literary world which met his gaze in 1845!

Or, one is entitled to ask, was the deterioration really as great as he seems to have felt? Was not a large part of the gloom with which he regarded the contemporary scene and his nostalgia for the "Golden Age" a question of temperament? Nostalgia was, after all, a vital element in his personality. When he wrote the "Survey," Kireevsky was thirty-nine, but Herzen, who knew Kireevsky only in the 1840's, described his face as "prematurely aged." The impression is confirmed by much of what he wrote in the *Muscovite*.

It will not do to exaggerate either the gloom or the nostalgia, however. The "Survey," after all, ended on a note of hope, however ambiguous, and when Kireevsky turned specifically to Russian literature, one senses real anticipation. "Will this new year, 1845, also be a new year for our literature?" he began the book review. Will it bestow upon our literature some lofty, mighty work of genius, to raise its flagging spirit . . . ?" [56] The reader is given leave to hope, since although Russia has as yet no "literature," she has produced a certain number of great literary works, and even now there are men of great gifts on the scene, although they were somehow burdened, he felt, with a strange lethargy and were only fitfully productive. Only as Russian culture as a whole becomes properly oriented, he recapitulated, only as it becomes an organic totality, can even talented individuals produce the long-awaited *literature*.

This brought Kireevsky to the question of Russia's *narodnost'*, which he dealt with here from a literary point of view. He found the fables of the seventy-seven-year-old Krylov (who had recently died) notable even more for the "beauty" of their *narodnost'* than for their "literary merit"; that was his "talent." His Russianness had attracted Russians even at a time when the word "foreign" had been synonymous with "beautiful" or "clever." Krylov's own literary influence was limited, but that which he gave us in his fables, Gogol has expressed "for our time and in a broader sphere."

Hitherto our literary culture has been separate from "the life of our people. But, reading Gogol, we understand the possibility of their unity." Why, Kireevsky asked, is Gogol "*narodnyi*"? Not because he writes about Russia, nor because he is read by the "people," [57] but because "in the depths of his soul are concealed certain sounds, because particular colors flash in his words, certain forms live in his imagination, forms which are unique to the Russian people — that unspoiled, profound people, which has not yet lost its personality in the imitation of foreigners." [58]

It is obvious from this passage that when Kireevsky spoke of *narodnost'* in literature, he did not mean a quality which could be linked directly to literary distinction, at least on the level of an individual work. Nor did the term seem to refer specifically to the Orthodox "principle" of old Russia — surely any people could produce a writer who was "*narodnyi*" in the sense that Gogol was. To this Kireevsky might have answered that every people had some kind of *narodnost'* or *Volkstümlichkeit*, but that Russia's contained a truth which was greater than itself. That Kireevsky did not "define" *narodnost'* should not surprise us. "When a thought is clear for one's reason," he had written to Khomiakov in 1840, "or accessible to the word, it is still powerless [to act upon] the soul and will. Only when it develops to the point of inexpressibility has it arrived at maturity." [59]

Diplomatically enough, Kireevsky had words of praise, in the *Muscovite*, both for Granovsky's lectures on Russian history[60] and for Shevyrëv's lectures on old Russian literature, occasions of triumph for their respective parties.[61] To Shevyrëv's lectures, a more recent event, Kireevsky devoted a short and highly appreciative article.[62] One might disagree with this or that opinion, he observed, but the result of Professor Shevyrëv's massive research was an event of "European significance" and a great act of historical self-discovery.[63] Historically speaking, Kireevsky's judgment has stood the test of time. Shevyrëv's lectures, in their expanded book form, are one of the great landmarks in the study of old Russian literature, despite a certain one-sidedness in matters such as "foreign influence." [64] Kireevsky, it should be noted, concurred with Shevyrëv as to the "autocthonous" development of old Russian literature. In the materials assembled by Shevyrëv, Kireevsky found "clearly expressed the profound significance of ancient Russian culture (*prosveshchenie*), which is assumed by the freely chosen influence of the Christian faith on our people, unfettered by the pagan culture of Greece and Rome, unconquered by other tribes." [65]

The response to the resurrected *Muscovite* and Kireevsky's three-stage article varied — as one would expect — along party lines. The Slavophiles were much cheered by the fact that they now had their literary outlet. "Our situation," Khomiakov wrote to Samarin, "has been clarified in many respects. We have at once been *recognized* (by the police, the *Annals of the Fatherland,* the *Library for Reading*), and not been exiled. This is an enormous and undisputed advantage: our hands have been untied for any cautious action." [66] Pogodin wrote in his diary that "the first number is splendid. It will go, if they [presumably the government] don't crush it. Dined at the Aksakovs, with Khomiakov, Sverbeev, etc. Praise for the *Muscovite*, and I am sincerely overjoyed." [67] In a letter to Venevitinov, Khomiakov was positively exultant. "What a first number of the *Muscovite* — put out, as you know, by the new editor — and what a *Survey of Foreign Literature!* This is something to brag about." Even Granovsky, that "known enemy of our opinions," Khomiakov continued, had nothing but the highest praise for it. Granovsky's response, it should be noted, was typical of his fair-mindedness; as usual, Khomiakov was surprised. The censor had been less kind than the liberal historian, however; Khomiakov was vexed that the "glorious lines of Pavlova" [68] had not been passed. The final one read: "and there is an answer to every question" — a notion which must have seemed to the censor to exude a vague impiety.

Herzen and Belinsky were less enthusiastic about the journal as a whole. In an *Annals* article entitled "The *Muscovite* and the Universe," Herzen mocked the editor's portentousness — employing a rather heavy hand himself.[69] "While the solar system," he began, "foreseeing nothing, peacefully continues its monotonous round, and the peoples of the West, drawn since the time of Thales into the paths of error . . . pursue their various affairs, a decisive event is being prepared in secret. The editor of the *Muscovite* has informed the public that next year it will subscribe to foreign journals, get hold of the *most important* books, that it will have new collaborators, who will not only participate but also 'take action.'" [70]

After making appropriate fun of the idea of a "new *Muscovite*" with ambitions to "save" Europe, Herzen complained that he already missed the old *Muscovite*. He dwelt nostalgically on the impatience with which he had always awaited the December issue in mid-February. One always knew that it would contain something to "lighten the heart" — and sure enough! A fragment from Pogodin's travel diary! Those energetic phrases. It seemed to be autumn again, and one was celebrating *Fasching* with him. Well, said Herzen — so be it. Good-bye *"Muscovite-père,"* hello *"Muscovite-fils."*

Herzen greeted Iazykov's poetry with a special venom: "The embittered poet does not confine himself to abstractions, but points with an indignant finger to *persons* (in his complete works, addresses may be appended)." [71] To the "Survey," by contrast, Herzen was relatively kind. "The talent of the author will surprise no one," he wrote. "We would have recognized his article without a signature by its noble language, by its poetic cast; there is, of course, nothing comparable in all the rest of the *Muscovite*. To agree with it, however, is impossible . . . After a lively, en-

ergetic account of the current state of mind in Europe, after a
picture sketched with a resolute and talented brush, in places terribly true, in places too redolent of personal opinion — a poor,
strange conclusion, which follows from nothing!" [72] What is the
"idea," Herzen inquired, which Russia has for Europe? What
evidence do we have that Europe is interested in Russia? "The
strongest influence which the Slavic world has on Europe,"
Herzen observed, "consists in the dispatching of regiments." [73]

Herzen applauded Kireevsky's remarks about the new emphasis
on social thought and social problems in Europe. "Slavism," on the
other hand, he found to be a "fashion, which will soon be boring;
imported from Europe and grafted on to our mores, it contains
nothing inherently national." [74] Herzen had a point. If Slavophilism was a stage in the history of Russian thought, it was also, as
Father George Florovsky noted, a stage in Russian "Europeanism"
as well.[75] To Herzen, it was an "abstract, bookish, literary phenomenon," which would soon "dry up." But here Herzen was correct only as far as the "pure" Slavophilism of the 1840's was concerned. After suffering through the Revolution of 1848 in Paris
Herzen was to develop his own variety of "slavism," which would
owe much to that "bookish" movement of Kireevsky and Khomiakov.

Belinsky, also writing in the *Annals*,[76] took much the same line
as Herzen, although his focus was more narrowly on the literary
and journalistic questions raised by Kireevsky. He too rejected
the idea that the *Muscovite* had really changed; in his discussion
of the "sameness" of the contributors, he did not mention that
Herzen and Granovsky had been asked to contribute, but had
refused. Kireevsky's "Survey," however, made considerable impression on him. "Despite the false foundations and arbitrary
conclusions of this article," he wrote, "much that is said in it about
the current condition of Europe is sensible, true, and intelligent,
and is said with such a knowledge of the facts, with such talent,

and with such a sense of integrity . . . as we have never encountered in the works of our so-called slavophiles." [77]

This said, the cavilling began. Belinsky was still in the dark, he
said, about the "strange and indefinite" doctrine of Slavophilism.
What was it? He was, of course, infuriated about the bracketing
of the *Annals* and the *Beacon* and may be said to have won the
argument. He could not, however, help adding that "it is another
thing to collate the *Beacon* with the *Muscovite*. Anyone who had
the temerity to undertake such a task might draw conclusions
which would at any rate be amusing." [78] As for himself, he found
them identical in spirit and "direction."

Belinsky also denied that the *Annals* (and here he was most
obviously defending himself) had ever belittled the literary
achievement or historical importance of Derzhavin, Karamzin,
Baratynsky, Zhukovsky, and so forth. Who is it, he cried, who says
we have no literature? As far as Iazykov and Khomiakov were
concerned, however, Belinsky refused to admit that "attacking"
them was like attacking Derzhavin or Zhukovsky. Zhukovsky and
Khomiakov — the very idea! And here posterity has seen the
matter his way. Belinsky closed in a cloud of bitter reproaches
about Kireevsky's unwillingness to render justice to his opponents
and their point of view.

It is worth observing, in conclusion, that both Westerners were
impressed by Kireevsky's description of the ills of Western Europe, although their agreement was unfortunately couched in the
most general literary terms. Both men rejected Kireevsky's religious, national — and, strictly speaking, "reactionary" — aspirations, although Herzen's rejection was to be a most complex one.
While it would be utterly unjust to call Kireevsky a "Pan-Slav,"
the notion of Orthodox, communal Russia "saving" the rationalist
West was protean indeed, and the writings of Kireevsky as well
as those of Shevyrëv on the "rotten" West must be considered a
historical stage in the development of a Pan-Slav movement.

Unfortunately for the Slavophile group, Ivan Kireevsky's tour of duty as the editor of the *Muscovite* was brief. The nexus of reasons why he renounced the editorship in May, after only three issues had appeared, was a complicated one, but at the heart of it was his old inability to get on with Pogodin, who unfortunately remained in Russia during this period. The account by Barsukov, Pogodin's biographer, stresses Kireevsky's incapacity as editor: there was trouble with the typesetters; Kireevsky was ignorant of the procedures relating to censorship; the printing press was troublesome.[79]

Things got off on the wrong foot, when many of the new subscribers (including, unfortunately, Zhukovsky) failed to receive the first issue, due to confusion in the office. Kireevsky was very angry, and Pogodin confessed himself at fault. When the typesetters complained to Pogodin that Kireevsky continued to make corrections after the presses had begun to roll, Pogodin took their side. Kireevsky was increasingly irritated at Pogodin's interference, but continued to turn to him for advice. It is impossible not to sympathize with the practical Pogodin in these moments. Kireevsky was obviously at once hopelessly maladroit and maddeningly superior. At the same time, Pogodin was confiding to his diary that Kireevsky, in his article, "is saying what I said long ago, but he never wants to read my things." [80] Pogodin complained that Kireevsky wanted him to be Prince Albert while Kireevsky got to be Victoria — an accurate enough description of the situation, but Pogodin was far from wishing to retire to his "Coburg estate" and collect rents. On May 5, Kireevsky renounced the editorship, alleging illness as the reason. Of his family and friends, only Natal'ia Petrovna, who was worried about his health, and his brother, who had been having his own troubles with Pogodin, supported him.[81]

The irritation and regret with which the Slavophiles and their sympathizers greeted his decision not to carry on is evident in

Sergei Aksakov's letter to Gogol. "Kireevsky has given up the journal for many good reasons," he wrote. "In the first place, Kireevsky was not created by God to be the editor of a journal. He is so hopeless in real life that, for all his intelligence, he is worse than any kind of fool. In the second place, nothing. In the third place, Kireevsky has made himself sick with his absurd way of life. These three reasons are sufficient." [82] To which Khomiakov added: "His work was all at night, and to banish sleep, he used the strongest tea." [83] The abrupt change from his former life of leisure affected his health.

Kireevsky left the material for the fourth issue and retired to Dolbino, where he remained until the fall of 1846. Khomiakov hated to abandon the idea of a journal and tried to persuade Pogodin to turn the *Muscovite* over to Constantine Aksakov, to the "younger generation." To a generation which doesn't even know the alphabet, Pogodin responded indignantly. He saw clearly enough what Khomiakov was up to. "Friends are really worse than enemies," he wrote bitterly in his diary on May 30.[84] He eventually resumed his editorial duties, and again nobody read the *Muscovite*.

XI. Withdrawal
Again

The middle and latter 1840's were a cruel and sad time for the Kireevskys and Elagins, a period marked by the almost constant presence of death. From the correspondence of both the family and outside observers, one has the impression of an ongoing process of mourning for the dead, mixed with anxious premonitions about the living. Ivan Kireevsky, having just abandoned public life again, seems to have been particularly afflicted, but perhaps it is merely that we see him rather more clearly in the letters and memoirs of the period than the shadowy Peter, whose ties were so few and whose life was always so inward. Avdot'ia Petrovna Elagina, more than either of her elder sons, continued to take an active part in society and interest herself in the outside world. Ivan Kireevsky's response, particularly in the dreadful year of 1846, was withdrawal — and illness.

A mood of resigned nostalgia and a clear sense of advancing age had already been evident in Kireevsky's obituary for Baratynsky and in his correspondence of the mid-forties. Following the termination of his career on the *Muscovite*, his "illness," and retirement to Dolbino, the blows really began to fall. Young Dmitri Valuev, whose brother later became Minister of the Interior under Alexander II, died of tuberculosis in November 1845. A close friend of the young Elagins, he had lived for several years in the house at the Red Gates, and his death at the age of twenty-five was a great shock to the whole family.[1] Then, on December 3, Alexander Turgenev died in Moscow. He had been Zhukovsky's friend almost from childhood and Ivan Kireevsky's Paris correspondent for both the *European* and the *Muscovite*.

The next few months were the worst. Early in 1846, Aleksei Andreevich Elagin died of a stroke. He seems to have faded out of Ivan Kireevsky's life almost completely after Ivan's marriage, and of course his own marriage with Avdot'ia Petrovna had not been entirely happy. Nevertheless, his death could not but affect the whole family deeply. A few months later, Kireesvky buried his little daughter, Ekaterina, and at the end of the year his dear friend, Iazykov.[2] "This year," he wrote to his brother Peter, "I have been through the most agonizing time, coupled with almost uninterrupted misfortunes, to the point that when I bore my poor Katiusha into the church it was in fact almost easy, by comparison with other feelings." [3] This same period in Kireevsky's life was marked — not surprisingly — by a dramatic increase in the frequency of the "illnesses" which are such a salient feature of his biography. According to Khomiakov, he was sick in December 1845 and off and on throughout 1846.[4] In the spring of 1847, he was consumed by a raging fever and for a few days in May his life was despaired of.[5] The fever was generally attributed to the effect of Iazykov's death on his nerves and constitution.

Kireevsky's state of mind, as well as his health, remained problematical in 1847. At some point in the early part of the year, V. P. Botkin, one of the Westerners, wrote to Annenkov apropos of the progress of S. M. Solov'ev's historical studies. "Solov'ev [he wrote] has so immersed himself in the chronicles and old charters (*gramoty*) that he has mastered their language, which he speaks and writes freely. For a joke, he has been carrying on a correspondence in it with Aksakov. At one social gathering, Aksakov was reading one of the *epistles* which Solov'ev had written to him. Suddenly, Ivan Kireevsky, who was there, rose up in indignation that anyone should have the temerity to use the language in which our Sacred Books are written for a humorous letter. It so upset him that he was taken sick (*sdelalsia bolen*)." [6]

Meanwhile, all was not well with the Slavophile group. Partly as a result of the loss of what had promised to be "their" journal, partly as a result of a lack of personal contact with the Westerners, the ties which had become quite close in the earlier part of the decade weakened in 1846 and 1847. Furthermore, Kireevsky, at any rate, began to feel a pervasive dissatisfaction with the "group," and their inability, in particular, to agree on a precise definition of certain key terms. This was the subject of an interesting open letter "to Moscow Friends," which he wrote in the spring of 1847.[7] As a rather melancholy coda to the great debate of the forties, it is worth examining in some detail.

On March 28, began Kireevsky, he had taken himself all the way across Moscow to dine with Pogodin, in honor of the seven hundredth anniversary of the city. He did so, he said, because there a group of friends were gathering, who — despite their "heterogeneous relations" with one another[8] — shared a love of Moscow which had been important in the intellectual formation of each of them and thus constituted a real bond of sympathy. Kireevsky "expected much from this day," he said, specifically the frank recognition of the differences which existed between them and an attempt to resolve them into a "fuller, more living, more life-giving" sympathy.

The occasion, however, had been a disappointment. Kireevsky had sat in silence, suffering "from those monotonous repetitions of certain phrases, common to all, but understood differently by everyone, from the fact that every thought was unfinished, from those endless, burning arguments, at once dry, scholarly, clever, and empty." [9] The indefinite sympathy between them had failed, in other words, to evolve into anything more than avid discussion. It had not become "a common enterprise of thought and life." When he, Kireevsky, had tried to turn the discussion into this channel, the evening had disintegrated and the company dispersed. Some of those present even denied that there *were* differences between them, or that such differences might have suprapersonal significance. The "Slavic-Christian direction," in other words, was failing to grow and develop.

Confronted by such wrongheadedness, Kireevsky had decided, he said, to set down on paper some of these difficult questions. "In the first place," he said, "we call ourselves Slavs, but everyone understands this word in a different sense." Some of his friends saw in *slavianizm*[10] merely a matter of language and nationality, others defined it as something opposed to "Europeanism," others thought it an aspiration to *narodnost'*, or to orthodoxy. Everyone thought his definition the correct one — but the vital question as to whether there was some common, unifying principle underlying this diversity had not been broached.

Narodnost', continued Kireevsky, is another of these terms for which no clear definition has been achieved. Some relate it to the *"simple people,"* others to the *"idea* of the national particularity," reflected in Russian history, still others to the "traces of the ecclesiastical order which have persisted in the life and customs of our people, etc., etc., etc." [11] The aspiration toward *narodnost'* is our salvation — and Europe's — but merely to emulate the "simple people" is to court an even lower level of consciousness than we now possess. *Narodnost'* is certainly not the "ideas and tastes of the people" *tout court*.

Kireevsky was quick to add, however, that the other definitions of the term presented comparable difficulties. One might perhaps have expected something in the nature of a *mea culpa* from Kireevsky, since he himself had used the term many a time, without advancing its precision much beyond the "ineffable" quality of Russian folksongs. Nor had matters of precise definition appeared to worry him in the past — quite the reverse, in fact.[12]

We will never know, he said, whether agreement on these matters is possible unless we sit down and really try to thrash them out. Kireevsky pleaded with his friends to make this effort, to write down their thoughts and exchange them. It was important to him, he said, for "sympathy with you comprises, so to speak, half of my moral life." [13]

But it was not merely over the proper definition of *narodnost'* or *slavianizm* that Kireevsky differed with his comrades in these years. Probably in part as a result of the complex state in which he found himself, of his feeling that he was old, ill, and in some sense defeated, we see a new spirit of timidity and illiberality in him, which seems to have become more pronounced as his ties with his old friends loosened. Riasanovsky exaggerates only slightly when he speaks of "paralysis," [14] and the two most striking manifestations of it were his attitude toward the emancipation of the serfs and his terrified repudiation of free speech during the revolutions of 1848 in Europe.

There is no published pronouncement by Kireevsky on the question of serfdom before the latter 1840's. This is not altogether surprising, since it was only in that period that his friends began to concern themselves seriously with the matter. It was precisely in 1847 that Koshelëv and Cherkassky made their first public pronouncements on the peasant question. It should nevertheless be pointed out that Kireevsky was simply not very interested in the physical facts of rural life as his peasants, in particular, experienced it. His letters — with the exception of a few near the end of his life — contain none of the details about crops, weather, and the state of the peasants which were usually staples of conversation and correspondence for men of his class. When he talked about the *narod*, he was invariably thinking about philos-

ophy or literature. Unlike Khomiakov, he could by no stretch of
the imagination be considered a "reforming landlord," [15] in the
English sense of the term, and, unlike his brother Peter, he always preferred Moscow to the country. Although he often fled
to Dolbino for one reason or another, he knew and feared his
vegetable response to country life.

Slavophilism, as a loose body of intuitions, myths, and dogma,
offered no practical assistance in the matter of peasant emancipation. To be sure, Kireevsky and all his like-minded friends regarded the enserfing of the peasantry as part of the corrosive
process which had virtually destroyed the old Russian communal
structure; that it was an evil, none of them denied. Slavophilism,
however, could provide no "answers" as to how this evil might
be eliminated. As an articulation of patriarchal, preindustrial
hostility to rationalism, it could simply not give birth to an action
program for a socioeconomic problem of such magnitude.

Nevertheless, Ivan Kireevsky was the only important slavophile
who was not an advocate of emancipation as soon as a practical,
moderate program could be worked out. He was even isolated
within the family.[16] Before taking up his arguments in some
detail, one perhaps ought to recall the fear of the aroused masses
that was so evident in *Island*. Khomiakov, Samarin, and the
Aksakovs were of course no less "opposed" to revolution than
he. But for Kireevsky, in the 1840's, the fear of change — *any*
change, as he later stressed — outweighed the evil and the danger
of continuing with the present system. However dreadful serfdom might be, it was something one knew, and it had a certain
stability. As he wrote to Koshelëv in 1851: "Hence my one wish
at present is that they leave us in the situation in which we find
ourselves — be it good or ill — just let them not trouble us with
changes." [17] One should of course add that Kireevsky said more
than once that when Orthodox principles had replaced German
formalism and rationalism as the animating spirit of Russian

society, it would be possible to realize such reforms — or, perhaps, they would realize themselves. Nevertheless, to accept this
protestation at face value, as Eberhard Müller does, is a serious
misreading of Kireevsky's psychology.[18]

Let us examine a letter of Kireevsky to Mar'ia Vasil'evna, for
his apprehensions are best rendered by his own words. "You
write, my dear sister," he began, "that you have long been
haunted by the thought of the emancipation of the peasants,
that you pray to God that He may grant that you realize this
sweet dream, that you think that we too will sympathize with
your wish in this case and you ask our counsel as to how *actually
to implement* your intentions." [19] Kireevsky's negative view of the
whole business was thus clear from the start: his sister was
"haunted" by a "sweet dream."

It was impossible, however, to discuss her affairs in isolation,
he observed, since everyone was now talking about emancipation.
He mentioned Koshelëv and Khomiakov, two of the strongest
proponents of the abolition of serfdom among the Slavophiles,
but went on to add that he did not share their views. Serfdom,
of course, could not continue "forever." It would have to be
eliminated, but only "after other reforms have been achieved in
the State: legality in the courts (*zakonnost' sudov*), the in-
violability of the private person from the arbitrariness of officials."
Such an "all-embracing change" at the present time would only
lead to "disturbances, general disorder, the rapid development of
immorality; may Heaven forfend that our fatherland be placed
in such a position!" [20]

The manumitted peasant, in other words, would be left to the
tender mercies of the Russian bureaucracy. The landlord has,
Kireevsky maintained, some stake in the welfare of his peasants,
and even the "very worst landlord" has more conscience than the
official. Then, too, the landlord has, "more or less, a sentiment of
honor which impedes him in the abuse of his power." The pres-

sure of his peers was another factor which had led the landlord to steadily improve the situation of his peasants, a process which has been going on, Kireevsky stated, for as long as he could remember. To persuade his sister of the evils visited upon the peasant who had become the plaything of the bureaucrats, he pointed to the "state peasants," whose woes, he implied, were far worse than those of the landlords' peasants, a judgment with which few historians nowadays would concur.[21]

This all had to do, of course, with emancipation in the large; there was nothing to prevent a private individual from manumitting his or her peasants if he or she were so inclined. But Kireevsky suggested in a rather unpleasant way that Mar'ia Vasil'evna should seriously examine her motives: was she sacrificing the real economic and social welfare of her peasants to some kind of pharasaical self-love? Or to a desire for "praise"?

At least one of the arguments which Kireevsky advanced against his sister's scheme almost certainly had some validity. The peasants were to be manumitted, with land, for 100,000 rubles. The richer peasants, he pointed out, desired the manumission, but the large majority would find even the advantageous terms which she offered economically very difficult — or so, he alleged, the peasants had told him. Nevertheless, so generous were the terms that Mar'ia Vasil'evna was offering that the peasants feared that other landowners, tempted by the prospect, would besiege her with better offers; the peasants allegedly feared that they might fall into bad hands, instead of living with her *"in the bosom of Christ,"* as Kireevsky put it.

The bureaucratic threat to Kireevskaia's peasants resulted from the government's intention to eliminate the "free farmer" (*vol'nyi* or *svobodnyi khlebopashets*) category — that of serfs freed (with land) by private agreement with the landlord — which had existed since 1803.[22] With the decree of July 15, 1848, the freed serf received the confusing appellation of "state peasant settled on his own land," and Kireevsky was not slow to point out the financial disadvantage that this status would entail for his sister's peasants, who payed an *obrok* (quitrent) of only four silver rubles — well below average for the 1840's. But worst of all was the fact that the state peasants were casually at the mercy of drunken clerks and petty bureaucratic despots, surrounded by usurers, prey for the tavern keeper.

If she could not be dissuaded from the idea of manumission, Kireevsky concluded, it could be done after her death, but if she chose this course, she should make sure that the peasants did not get wind of her plans — for fear of giving rise to "harmful thoughts" among them. Kireevsky felt so intensely about all this that he persuaded Peter to add a postscript endorsing what he said; Koshelëv, too, was in agreement. Neither man, of course, supported Ivan in the larger matter of ending serfdom altogether.

We find the issue of serfdom coming up repeatedly in Kireevsky's correspondence with Koshelëv between the late forties and his death in 1856. In an impassioned letter of February 20, 1851, for instance, he repeated the objections which he had raised in the letter to his sister, adding an attack on "inventories" — documents which defined the size of peasant holdings and fixed the amount of dues to be paid for them.[23] However inoffensive to the seignorial power of the Russian landlord the inventories were in actual fact, any attempt to enforce them would have meant bureaucratic intervention in the affairs of the landlord on some scale — a policy which anyone touched with Slavophile opinions might be expected to oppose.[24]

In another letter to Koshelëv, written several months later, Kireevsky referred to the question of "economic reform" as "the central question of our time."[25] He asked a number of technical questions about Koshelëv's projected freeing of his own serfs: how much land were they to be given, how would the funding work? But he had not had a change of heart, for he added gloomily that "there is no doubt that the emancipated peasants will not only be ruined but debauched as well in a very short time, with the help of the taverns, clerks, etc., etc." Kireevsky, like his father, was no friend of the publican! "Then who will ensure that your woods will not be cut down, your fields trampled, your wheat carried off in the sheaf, your horses stolen from the pasture, etc., etc.? It may be possible for a tax-farmer like you [an unkind remark] to be constantly dealing with the police station (*zemskii sud*), but for landowners in general, it would mean making the constable into the real proprietor — which would mean ruining oneself and one's peasants completely." [26] When every landlord in the district has manumitted his peasants, Kireevsky concluded, fifty constables will be insufficient to handle the resulting litigation between the landlords and their erstwhile serfs.

This passage makes perfectly clear what should have been clear enough anyway: Kireevsky's opposition to emancipation "now" had its roots in concrete economic apprehensions which were widespread among the Russian gentry. This is not of course to imply that he was not perfectly sincere in his hopes for the great change in Russian society that the elimination of Western rationalism would bring. He once mentioned ten or fifteen years as a possible time span for the change, but it is hard to believe that he really expected such momentous developments in so brief a period.

L. A. Perovsky, the Minister of the Interior, reported to Nicholas in 1845 that many Russian landowners had begun to realize that hired labor might be more profitable for them than *barshchina* (corvée). "But," he went on, "they dread the resulting changes [resulting, that is, from emancipation] which every sensible person, knowing the common people and the mind of the common people and their inclinations, ought to dread." [27] That dread was shared by Ivan Kireevsky. In the last months of his life he wrote again to Koshelëv that an emancipation "now" would only do "enormous harm." [28]

Kireevsky greeted the European revolutions in 1848, as did most of the Slavophiles, with a mixture of hope and dread.[29] The hope was that if the Austro-Hungarian Empire fell to pieces or were destroyed, its Slavic components might rally to Russia in some way or actually come under Russian hegemony. This prospect, clearly, could be conceived of in purely political terms, or in a way which would later be called Pan-Slav, depending on one's attitude towards the Slavic peoples of the Balkans. Kireevsky, concerned far less than Khomiakov about Russia's Slavic brethren, let alone foreign policy, put it this way in a letter of April 20, 1848, to Pogodin: "Austria is collapsing. The Slavic states are beginning to crystallize. The whole great problem of the world consists in what sort of direction these states take: German, Polish, or true Slavic. It is not merely the fate of Russia that is at stake, but the fate of all Europe." [30] And Kireevsky urged Pogodin to stop writing about "trifles" and use the *Muscovite* ("which is read . . . in Prague") to good purpose. Kireevsky, it is clear, was thinking of the Orthodox-Slavic principle, rather than of Russian "hegemony" in any political sense. Might not the revolutions in Europe be a bloody — but important — step toward the destruction of rationalism?

Kireevsky's primary reaction to the events of 1848, however, was fear — as is dramatically revealed by another letter to Pogodin, written at about the same time.[31] Pogodin had produced one of his frequent blasts against the *Annals of the Fatherland*, which the censor had refused to pass, and the indignant Pogodin conceived the idea of an address to the throne in protest.[32] One would have thought that Kireevsky's response would have mixed approval and indifference. Instead, we find him writting anxiously to Pogodin that he was "frightened both for you and for the enterprise." He urged Pogodin to consider whether, "given the present incoherent upheavals in the West, *this is the time* to give us *addresses* about literature. The constraints of censorship are, of course, harmful, not only to culture, but even to the Government, since they weaken minds for no reason at all. These considerations, however, are all as nothing, compared with the important questions of the moment, whose correct resolution we must expect from the Government. It is no great misfortune if our literature is killed off for two or three years. It will come to life again." [33] To launch an address of the kind that Pogodin was considering, Kireevsky went on, would be to sow distrust between the government and men of letters just at that time when the former desperately needed the support of all "well-wishers." If necessary, all "secondary interests" should be sacrificed to save Russia from chaos and "unnecessary war." We must wish, he went on, "only that the government should not involve us in war out of some caprice or out of friendship for some Swedish king or . . . [word missing in the text] that it should not set out to crush our Slavs together with the Germans, that it should *not arouse the people with false rumors of freedom and not introduce any sort of new legislation until the situation in the West has quieted down and cleared up*, that it should not, for instance, make inventories of landowners' estates, which practice stirs up minds with vain speculation." [34]

Here is a melancholy spectacle indeed: Kireevsky accusing Pogodin of a boldness in effect subversive; Kireevsky calling literature a "secondary interest" and virtually advocating that it be "killed off for two or three years." On the basis of this rather pathetic letter, no one can doubt that Kireevsky's fear of "revolution" or even mere disorder was very great indeed, setting wholly at naught his dislike of Nicholas' government. In this moment of crisis — and not really a very grave crisis for Russia — Ivan Kireevsky sounded like nothing more than another confused and terrified landowner.

It is clear, furthermore, that whatever divine spark Kireevsky believed the Russian peasant still bore in his bosom, it was insufficient to save him from the temptations of the tavern, the wiles of the bureaucrat, or the contagion of revolutionary disorder. The salvation of Russia, as Kireevsky later said in so many words, would have to come from his own class, the landed gentry. They would have to realize the insufficiencies of Western rationalism and themselves return to the patriarchal values of old Russia. The peasantry might provide a kind of storehouse, where the residuum of these values might be found, but no important changes were to be expected from that quarter. Meanwhile, they were a kind of powder keg, which could not be defused by an emancipation or by "Western" reforms such as inventories, but only by a gradual realization on the part of the gentry elite — the only creative social force in Russia — of what religious and social truth in fact was.

"I am profoundly sympathetic to Slavophilism in its love for the people's ways," Apollon Grigor'ev once wrote, "and for the people's highest blessing, religion, but I hate that ancient boyar direction with its pride just as profoundly." [35]

None of the other Slavophiles were so fearful and pessimistic as Kireevsky, none were so convinced that the necessary prelude to *any* improvement in Russia's situation had to be the root and branch change for which he was waiting. There was, consequently, little to absorb him in the present, save his very real fears and chimerical hopes. With death stalking his family and friends, and chaos in Europe, it is small wonder that he turned, in this period, to the study of the Eastern Church Fathers, seeking there to discover, clarify, and elaborate the theological content of the

Orthodox "principle" from which the salvation of both Russia and the West had to come.

Small wonder, too, that Kireevsky's friends were worried about him. In the spring of 1848, he left Dolbino and came to Moscow; Avdot'ia Petrovna urged Pogodin and Gogol to visit him and see that he was not lonely.[36] At about the same time, Khomiakov wrote to A. N. Popov: "I am sorry to see in any one of our spiritual friends anything at all like the spiritual condition of I. V. Kireevsky." [37]

XII. The Optina Monastery and Mystical Theology

As the Slavophile circle and Kireevsky's other friends increasingly ceased to satisfy him, either intellectually or personally, he began to develop new personal ties and new projects, which had little to do with salons and journals. The most important intellectual influence in Kireevsky's life, from the latter 1840's on, was the "Elder" (*Starets*) Makary, of the Optina Monastery. Kireevsky's new field of activity became the study, translation, and publication of the writings of the Eastern Church Fathers. These new interests were accompanied by quite distinct personality changes. The Kireevskys became more solitary, more withdrawn, more self-absorbed. This development can be partially explained by the lack of a social arena and focus for Ivan Vasil'evich's intellectual activity; the Optina Monastery was a very different place from his mother's drawing room, and Makary was a very different kind of collaborator from Khomiakov. But there is more to the change than this. Kireevsky's intellectual labors, in the last decade of his life, were increasingly accompanied by feelings of gloom, guilt, and personal inadequacy. Kireevsky turned, in this period, to the great treasure house of Eastern spirituality for intellectual guidance and personal solace. But his quest brought him more pain than joy.

Makary's predecessor as the Kireevskys' spiritual mentor, it will be recalled, was Filaret, a monk from the Novospassky Monastery. He had died in 1842, and Kireevsky had apparently "sat up entire nights" with the dying man.[1] According to the "Confession of Ivan Vasil'evich," [2] Kireevsky's first serious encounter with Eastern patristic literature came through the dual agency of his wife and Filaret. Indirect confirmation of this can be had from Kireevsky's letter to Makary in 1852, in which he refers to his first reading of Isaac the Syrian "sixteen years ago." [3] How much patristic literature he had read before the mid-forties we unfortunately have no way of knowing.

We are likewise in the dark as to how the connection between the Kireevskys and the Optina Monastery actually came about.[4] Perhaps they were drawn there by the growing renown of Father Leonid, the first of the three famous Optina "elders." [5] The elders (*startsy*) were monks who conceived their ministry to be the spiritual direction of the laity, as well as younger monks, and they almost always possessed a certain personal charisma.[6] Or it may have been that Kireevsky was already intrigued by the figure of Paisy Velichkovsky, the great eighteenth-century renewer of Russian spiritual life, many of whose students and followers were at Optina.[7] In any case, the monastery was only forty versts from Dolbino, and at some point in the early forties the Kireevskys made the trip.

Whatever the early history of the relationship, the year 1846 saw the first fruits of the collaboration between Kireevsky and Makary in the translation and publication of the literature of Orthodox spirituality. This process consisted in part in the emendation and publication of Paisy's own translations, many of which had been brought to the library at Optina. Appropriately enough, a biography of Paisy was the first book to appear; it was followed in the course of the next decade by various works of Isaac the Syrian, the sixth-century mystic Barsanuthios, Mark the Anchorite, Simeon the New Theologian, Maximus the Confessor,

Theodore Studite, Thallasios, Gregory of Sinai, and others.[8] In addition to Makary and Kireevsky, Shevyrëv and Professor F. A. Golubinsky of the Moscow Theological Academy took some part in the work; they were joined, in the fifties, by other lay and ecclesiastical figures, among them T. S. Filippov, one of the "young editors" of the *Muscovite*, a group which included the playwright Ostrovsky and the critic-poet Appollon Grigor'ev. Metropolitan Filaret, long a champion of religious literature and instruction in the vernacular, was a powerful patron of the project. Kireevsky's correspondence with Makary attests to his keen interest in the work, down to the most minute details of textual criticism.

This interest, however, was by no means confined to the publication or republication of the Eastern Fathers, although the idea of making this spiritual treasure available obviously appealed to the cultural missionary, the "enlightener," in Kireevsky. He also read zealously for his own salvation not only all the patristic literature he could get his hands on, but the writings of Russian spirituality as well: Nil Sorsky, Paisy Velichkovsky, and Tikhon of Voronezh. He also read up quite extensively on church history. In a single letter to Koshelëv, for instance, we find him mentioning or briefly discussing books by Innokenty Borisov, Neander, J. H. von Mosheim, and a number of other writer.[9]

No doubt these new activities flowed, in a sense, quite naturally from one of the central tenets of Slavophilism: that God's truth was to be found in the uncorrupted doctrines and spiritual life of the Eastern church. Khomiakov and Koshelëv, and to a lesser extent most of the other Slavophiles, shared his interest — up to a point. But Kireevsky's greater pessimism about the present undoubtedly further stimulated his interest in the past; in the course of the forties, it became quite clear that the great turning point in the history of Russia for which he was hoping was still some years away at best.

The events of the year 1848 brought Kireevsky no satisfaction. True, there had been no lasting revolutionary "success," but neither had the upheavals in central Europe led to any positive development as far as the "Slavic-Christian direction" was concerned. And while Europe continued along its perverse path, Russian intellectual life was in the doldrums. P. V. Annenkov, who arrived back in Russia from Paris in the fall of 1848, wrote of the following winter that "the situation in Petersburg seems extraordinary: the government's fear of revolution, the terror within brought on by the fear itself, persecution of the press, the buildup of the police, the suspiciousness . . . The reign of terror has reached even the provinces . . . denunciations proliferate." [10] With the discovery of the Petrashevsky "circle" the following winter, the rigors of the censorship increased yet further and Uvarov departed from the Ministry of Education, under suspicion of liberalism. Small wonder that Peter Kireevsky found the intellectual life of Moscow in the spring of 1850 to be characterized by a sort of "torpor," which resulted in no one's doing or saying anything interesting. "Even Khomiakov and Aksakov," he reported to his half-sister, "are now playing cards." [11] Together with Kireevsky's personal sorrows of the period 1845–1847 and his difficulties with his friends, the milieu in Russia undoubtedly helped propel him out of the Russian present into the Orthodox past.

Furthermore, it may not be out of place at this point to make some general observations about the appeal of Orthodoxy to the corporate sensibility of romanticism. It was not only Russians or other Slavs who felt this attraction; Franz Baader's view of the Orthodox Church was very close to that of Kireevsky and Khomiakov. In Berdyaev's phrase, "a great deal of it might stand over the signature of Khomyakov." [12]

One important difference between the Eastern and Western churches which is obviously germane is the latter's relative "rationalism" — in its structure, in ecclesiastical practice, and in theology. One should not make the mistake of thinking that Kireevsky simply and arbitrarily read a preconceived ideological dislike of "abstract reason" into his discussion of the two churches. The fact is that his ideological predisposition enabled him to see certain very real differences between the Roman Catholic and Orthodox churches, although he was far from magisterial or even fair in his discussion of these differences, here exaggerating, there passing over important distinctions.

There is, for example, a legal, contractual aspect to the relationship between God and man in Roman Catholicism which is much less pronounced in the Orthodox Church; it may be more or less directly traced to the influence of Roman law on Latin Christianity. In the words of Ernst Benz, "In the East, the Apostle Paul's teaching on justification has never been alloted a decisive significance, but with Augustine, the teaching on justification is already the basis of his conception of the relationship of man to God and of his view of sin, guilt, and mercy. Tertullian subsequently introduced a series of fundamental legal concepts into theology. Western theology has remained faithful to these fundamental tenets (*Grundlinie*)." [13] There is a perceptible tendency in Catholicism to say that man has certain "legal" obligations to God. When he sins he violates the law and must come to the Church, where the gravity of the sin is determined and a penance is assigned. The ultimate development of this idea was that one may atone for one's sins by paying a "fine" to the Church. By comparison, the lack of these "legal" relationships in the Orthodox Church is striking. Benz, exaggerating a bit, says that in the West, sin is "a violation of the law"; in the East it is "a wound in the soul." [14]

The structure of the Western Church is likewise penetrated by what Benz calls the "*Rechtsidee*." [15] Christ, it is alleged, gave "full power" to Peter and his successors; the bishop confers on the priest the "right" to forgive sins when he ordains him. Behind the temporal power of the Papacy may be seen the shadow of the Roman emperors; the institution of the Papacy took shape in the vacuum left by the collapse of Roman power. In the East, the Church never became a legal entity. It was never, as Kireevsky pointed out, incorporated into a feudal structure.[16] It was, in fact, only with Khomiakov that the Eastern church came to define itself more sharply than in such general terms as the community of the faithful or the "body of Christ." [17]

The comparative vagueness of the Eastern Church's definition of itself brings us to a further, related point: the attitude of the Orthodox Church toward dogma and theology in general. Here again we find it to be less "rationalist" than Roman Catholicism. As Vladimir Lossky has put it, "The eastern tradition has never made a sharp distinction between mysticism and theology; between personal experience of the divine mysteries and the dogma affirmed by the Church." [18] And again, "We must live the dogma expressing a revealed truth, which appears to us as an unfathomable mystery, in such a fashion that instead of assimilating the mystery to our mode of understanding, we should, on the contrary, look for a profound change, an inner transformation of spirit, enabling us to experience it mystically." [19] Excess of "knowledge" is a great barrier to union with God. The best way to approach Him is negatively, "apophatically," which Lossky defined as meaning "above all an attitude of mind which refuses to form concepts about God. Such an attitude utterly excludes all abstract and purely intellectual theology which would adapt the mysteries of the wisdom of God to human ways of thought . . . there is no theology apart from experience." [20] What is necessary are not "rational notions," but "images or ideas intended to guide us and to fit our faculties for the contemplation of that which transcends all understanding," to paraphrase Gregory of Nyssa.[21]

Thus Kireevsky's romantic hatred of "abstract reason" was

sensitive to important elements within the Orthodox tradition
and eventually helped it to define itself. For Kireevsky, papal
"tyranny" was in the last analysis the tyranny of abstract reason,
one part of the totality, over the rest. Kireevsky's respect for the
traditional, the historical, and the "empirical" was brought to
bear against the Roman spirit of Roman Catholicism — and
Protestantism, its dialectical companion.

The living embodiment, for Kireevsky, of the tradition of
Orthodox mystical theology, came to be Father Makary, the
second of the three great "elders" of the Optina Monastery. The
veneration which all of Kireevsky's extant letters to Makary reveal gradually evolved into a quite striking and almost unhealthy
spiritual-psychological dependence. There is a real pathos in
certain late letters, where Kireevsky writes almost desperately
of his inability to give up chess or smoking and implores Makary's
prayers and spiritual assistance.[22] When he produced his article,
"On the Character of the Culture of Europe and Its Relationship
to the Culture of Russia," for the Slavophile *Moscow Miscellany*
in 1852, it was Makary whom he consulted about it, not Khomiakov — to the latter's annoyance.[23]

We can only guess as to the precise nature of Makary's attractive power — spiritual and otherwise — for Kireevsky. Nevertheless, the none-too-substantial biographical information which
we have on Makary is at least suggestive.[24] The elder, whose
worldly name was Ivanov, was the offspring of a prosperous
gentry family of Orël province. He was small, frail, suffered from
a stammer, and was apparently quite ugly in some way which
did not diminish his "attractiveness." He loved flowers and music
(and had in fact played the violin), was a great reader, and before his entry into Holy Orders had been much interested in
philosophy. He slept, according to one historian, only four hours
a night.[25] "His whitewashed hut," in the words of a visitor to
Optina, "consists of three . . . cells with an ante-room each.

The entrance is a small wooden porch painted the same dark red as the roof slates, but the wood is almost hidden with vine." [26] The cell where he lived "has two small windows, one looking south, the other east; its large, low stove, like a huge chest, is built of bricks and faced with tile. The room smells of dried apples and incense." The visitor who came there, like Kireevsky, for spiritual guidance, found the cell "decorated with shelves loaded with books; one saw there works in various languages, as well as patristic literature. Philosophy had its place, and the Latin and Greek dictionaries were not omitted." [27] That such a man should have been congenial to Kireevsky is scarcely surprising; when one further recalls that this man was the contemporary incarnation of the Orthodox spiritual tradition, it seems wholly natural that Kireevsky should have regarded Makary as his "spiritual father." Still the degree of personal ascendancy which Makary had over him is not wholly explained by the religious dimension — perhaps the early death of his real father may have added to the intensity of his feelings. Certainly the loneliness and isolation of the last decade of his life must have been a factor. Cut off from the present, Kireevsky found in Makary the spiritual wisdom of the past.

In part because of Kireevsky's enthusiasm for the more mystical writers of the Orthodox canon — Isaac the Syrian, Simeon the New Theologian, Maximus the Confessor, Gregory Palamas — the statement has frequently been made that he himself was a "mystic." His romantic longing for "wholeness," his melancholy, his unworldliness, the sense of being born out of time which he often conveyed to people — all these things helped the impression along. To some observers, his very presence exuded a kind of spirituality. The sort of impression which he made on people in the last ten years of his life is well conveyed by the testimony of a young literary man, T. I. Filippov, who first met Kireevsky in 1850. "On that occasion," he wrote, having arrived at Shevyrëv's earlier than usual and found that he had not yet risen from his after-dinner nap, the members of the "Young Muscovite" [28] met in his living room an elderly (*pozhiloi*) man whom they did not know; by his appearance they initially took him for some provincial, newly arrived in Moscow. A conversation ensued, in which the stranger surprised them first by the fineness of his speech and then by the astonishing depth of his thought and the breadth of his knowledge. The mystery was solved with the arrival of Shevyrëv. The supposed provincial was none other than I. V. Kireevsky. The impression which he made on the members of the circle was very strong. He somehow did not fit into an ordinary mold. In his whole being and by his every word he somehow introduced the warmth and charm of a spiritual atmosphere. [29]

Herzen was given to dilating on Kireevsky's "myticism," but of course in his mouth the word had no very precise meaning. Herzen also alleged that Kireevsky once related the following anecdote to him:

I once stood at a shrine and gazed at a wonder-working icon of the Mother of God, thinking of the childlike faith of the people praying before it; some women and infirm old men knelt, crossing themselves and bowing down to the earth. With ardent hope I gazed at the holy features, and little by little the secret of their marvelous power began to grow clear to me. Yes, this was not simply a painted board . . . for whole ages it had absorbed these streams of passionate aspiration, the prayers of the afflicted and unhappy; it must have been filled with the power which emanates from it, is reflected from it, upon the believing. It had become a living organism, a meeting place between the Creator and men. Thinking of this, I looked once more at the old men, at the women and children prostrate in the dust, and at the holy icon — then I myself saw the features of the Mother of God suffused with life, she looked with love and mercy at these simple folk . . . and I sank on my knees and meekly prayed to her. [30]

Among the most serious proponents of Kireevsky's "mysticism" was the distinguished historian, M. O. Gershenzon. By "mysticism," however, Gershenzon, too, seems only to have meant Kireevsky's quest for "wholeness," the reintegration of all the powers of the soul: the unification of mind and feeling, as Gershenzon put it, with the "moral kernel." [31] This, however, is not mysticism. V. V. Zenkovsky was somewhat more circumspect in his claims. "Kireevsky," he wrote, "actually lived not only by religious thought but also by religious feeling. His whole personality and spiritual world were shot through with the rays of religious consciousness. His was a genuine and profound religious experience, and in giving it meaning he drew very close to the immense spiritual wealth that was opened to him in the Optina Cloister." [32]

Eberhard Müller has disagreed with the proponents of Kireevsky's "mysticism," in my opinion quite rightly. "In fact," he stated tartly, "we find in Kireevsky's case no evidence of a genuine mystical experience." [33] Müller accepts Masaryk's firm statement that not only was Kireevsky not a mystic, but in fact he "was never able to rid himself completely of the sting of doubt." [34] This assertion is really no more than surmise, but the sense of melancholy struggle which Kireevsky's correspondence with Makary exudes, the strong feeling of guilt and insufficiency which is so striking in it, would seem evidence of a kind that a "sting of doubt" might be there. Perhaps Kireevsky was so drawn to Makary in part because here was a man, temperamentally much like himself, who really had what Kireevsky was still painfully seeking. As far as Herzen's anecdote is concerned, Müller remarks tellingly that "the difference between Kireevsky's attitude and the piety of the simple people whom he described is clear at once: they pray naively to a wonder-working image of the Mother of God, which derives its power from itself, that is, from the real, present Mother of God, according to the orthodox teaching on icons. For Kireevsky, however, above all an outside observer, she comes alive only through an inverse intellectual auxiliary construction: the icon itself has no inherent reality; it draws its power, its meaning, only from the prayers of the simple believers." [35]

To call Kireevsky, in his religious search, "a typical intellectual" is to introduce a note of imprecision into the discussion, but Müller is on firm ground when he cites a letter of 1851 to Koshelëv to demonstrate Kireevsky's "basic uncertainty" as to the "intimate sense" and "methodology" of the Fathers.[36] Koshelëv had already read Vasily the Great, John Chrysostom, and Tikhon of Voronezh — where, he wanted to know, should he go from there? "You ask me," Kireevsky replied,

whom you should read first and whom later, and I have to tell you that this simple question has been difficult for me. In order that this reading be of real use, it must be in conformity with the particular nature of each person. In my case, before I had mastered what was fundamental and general, I grasped at the more lofty, proper only to him who has been tried and perfected, and I confess to you that by this arrogance I paralyzed my forces, nurturing in myself precisely that dividedness, the elimination of which is the principal goal of spiritual introspection (*umozrenie*). To close a breach in a building which is already built is more difficult than to build a new one. Therefore, dear friend, it is not for me to give you advice; on the contrary, you must support me with your sympathy, or rather with that reciprocity of sympathy which redoubles one's forces.[37]

To the impressionable Filippov, Kireevsky himself conveyed a sense of the *starets*. How well he knew that he was no such thing is fully revealed in the letter to Koshelëv: "To close a breach in a building which is already built is more difficult than to build a new one." One is tempted to employ that sentence as an epigraph not merely for Kireevsky's difficulties with the method of the Eastern Fathers, but for the last decade of his life as a whole, so well does it express his growing sense of failure and helplessness. Having confessed his own inadequacies candidly to his oldest friend, Kireevsky closed by advising Koshelëv to find an elder himself.

How Kireevsky's increasing preoccupation with church history and mystical theology meshed with his long-held views on Russia and the West may be seen most fully in "On the Character of the Culture of Europe and Its Relationship to the Culture of Russia." [38] This article appeared in 1852, and from the first few pages it is clear that there is no sharp break with the past. Kireevsky, as Florovsky observed, was a man "of one theme, if not of one thought." [39]

One finds in the new article a more developed treatment of the influence of Rome — its rationalism, legalism, and internationalism — on Western culture, and a rather sketchy account of how modern philosophy developed from scholasticism through Descartes to Hegel and Schelling. There is also a fuller discussion of the integral Christian civilization of old Russia; in relation to it, Kireevsky dwelt at greater length on the historical development of both the Eastern and the Western churches. Nevertheless, the viewpoint and focus are fundamentally the same as in the "Answer to Khomiakov" back in 1839. "European Culture," despite its heavily historical structure, was intended to minister to the needs and aspirations of Russian society of the time. The only hint of Kireevsky's own religious search was perhaps to be found in the increased stress on *integrality* of knowledge and the proper condition of the soul. And this preoccupation was not merely personal for Kireevsky.

In the introduction, Kireevsky began by repeating what he had written seven years previously in the *Muscovite*: European rationalism has fully realized its pernicious essence and is now in process of disintegration. In 1852, however, Kireevsky omitted what he had written earlier about the two "types of culture" and the role which Russia might play in the reinvigoration of Europe. Since "intellectual Europe" cannot return to its prerationalist past, its thinkers have perforce been left to their own inadequate, individualistic devices. They all became Columbuses, Kireevsky wrote,[40] "they embarked on voyages of discovery within their own minds, seeking new Americas amid the vast oceans of impossible expectations, individual assumptions, and strict syllogisms." [41]

Kireevsky, as we know, considered ancient Rome the seedbed of Western rationalism: "It left its imprint on the basic structure of society, on the laws, the language, the mores and customs, the early arts and learning of Europe." He believed that the fundamental quality of Roman civilization was "the preference for mere cerebration, rather than the inner essence of things."

This is clearly to be seen in Roman public and family life, where natural and moral human relationships were ruthlessly distorted in the name of logic, according to the literal interpretation of a law, cast in a certain form by pure chance. We find the same characteristic in Roman poetry, which was concerned with perfecting forms of foreign inspiration. The language of the Romans, too, bears the same stamp, for its grammatical constructions are so rigid and artificial that they stifle all natural freedom and spontaneity of emotion. We see the same thing when we look at the famous Roman laws, with their amazing logical perfection of form and an equally amazing lack of essential justice. Roman religion, which concentrated on the formal aspect of rites until their mystical significance was almost forgotten, presents the same picture of a formal sequence of ideas achieved at the expense of all living meaning. [42]

The typical Roman, as described by Kireevsky, sounds remarkably like Napoleon (that incarnation of soulless calculation), as he appeared in *Island*. Kireevsky certainly did not discover his Roman citizen after a deep study of Roman history and society. Rome, for Kireevsky, was an earlier incarnation of contemporary Europe. Rome was where

external activity was so highly esteemed and so little attention was paid to its inner meaning, where pride was held to be a virtue, where each man was guided in his actions solely by his own logical convictions, where each person consequently regarded himself as being not merely distinct but different from his fellow men and could conceive of no relationships with them, save those which could be logically deduced from the external circumstances of life. For this reason, the Roman was hardly aware of any possible bond between people but the bond of mutual interest, or of any unity but party unity . . . He did not love the smoke of his fatherland; even the smoke of a Greek hearth had greater attraction for him. What he loved in his country was his party's interests, and, even more, the fact that it flattered his pride to be a Roman. But he was virtually impervious to spontaneous human feelings. He regarded his compatriots much as great Rome regarded the cities which surrounded it. Equally ready for alliance or war, he chose the one or the other on the basis of self-interest, being ever sensible to the dictates of that passion which is generally uppermost in arid, logical, and self-seeking minds — the desire to dominate, which occupied the same place in the soul of the Roman that the blind love of glory held in the soul of the sympathetic Greek.[43]

Roman legal formalism was infused into the body of Western society even as the Roman Empire itself was being destroyed. Kireevsky found its influence everywhere — most obviously, of course, in law and legal relationships. Not so with Russia.

Whereas Roman and Western jurisprudence drew abstract logical conclusions from every legal form, saying: *"The form is the very law,"* and tried to link all forms into a coherent system, each part of which follows logically from the whole, with the whole itself constituting not merely a reasonable text but *reason itself expressed in writing,* customary law in Russia, springing as it did from daily life, knew nothing of abstract logic. In Russia, laws were not formulated in advance by certain learned jurists, they were not ponderously and eloquently discussed at some legislative assembly, and they did not subsequently fall like an avalanche upon an astounded citizenry, destroying some already long-established order of things. A law in Russia was not composed, but usually written down on paper only after it had itself taken shape in the people's understanding and gradually, impelled by the necessity of things, became a part of popular mores and life. Logical progress in the law can exist only where the community (*obshchestvennost'*) itself rests on artificial conditions and where, consequently, the *opinion* of some or all may and must govern the development of the social order. But where the community has been founded on a fundamental unanimity of views, the solidarity of mores, the sanctity of tradition, the stronghold of customary relationships cannot be violated without destroying the very fabric of social life.[44]

The distinction between "opinion" and "conviction" is crucial to Kireevsky's idea of the truly organic society. Kireevsky sounded a particularly Burkean note when he wrote that

Opinion and conviction are two wholly different mainsprings of two entirely different kinds of social order. Opinion differs from conviction not only in that the former is more transitory while the latter is more lasting. The former results from logical reasoning; the latter is the end result of whole lives. In a political sense, however, they have yet a further distinction: conviction is a spontaneous awareness of the sum total of human relationships; opinion is an exaggerated inclination toward those social interests which happen to coincide with the interests of some one party, whereby its egotistical exclusiveness takes on the deceptive appearance of a desire for the common weal.[45]

"Opinion," then, was clearly related to a society based on the formal concordance of "interests," to a society embodying the idea of "progress," where today's opinion succeeds yesterday's through some kind of formal democratic process or through an upheaval of some sort — it was all the same. Although its outlines are a bit fuzzy, the idea of society here under attack is obviously that of the French eighteenth century — of the theoreticians of the "social contract" in particular. But their social theory, for Kireevsky, was merely a late stage in the long journey which began in Rome.

How closely Kireevsky's thought is here related to that of other spokesmen for a preindustrial social order may be seen in his words on the subject of "property." The abstract, contractual idea of property, associated primarily with the ascendant bourgeoisie, was anathema to such feudal spokesmen as Adam Müller or Friedrich Schlegel, who regarded property (in land) as a cluster of concrete, historically derived *relationships*.[46] Both exalted common law and detested Roman law. In Kireevsky's case, however, what was basically a critique of one class by another was subsumed under the rubric of a struggle between two opposed civilizations. "The entire edifice of the Western social order," he wrote, "may be said to rest on the development of the personal right of ownership, so that personality itself — in juridical terms — is no more than an expression of this right." This was Hegel's view, although Kireevsky does not say so;[47] here again the arch-priest of rationalism expressed the essence of the tendency most fully. In the West, continued Kireevsky, one *owned* land; in Russia, the land stood in a complex relationship to the commune and to the landlord. Insofar as the land "belonged" to the commune, it was given to its members because "they were able to cultivate" it. This "right of use" was also important to Schlegel. The landlord's "rights" to the land also depended on a relationship — to the state. Unfortunately, Kireevsky did not discuss the current status of the landlord's relation to the state.

In the spiritual-intellectual realm, the result of the permeation of Western Christianity by Roman rationalism was scholasticism, which Kireevsky characterized as "nothing other than the aspiration for a scientific (*naukoobraznyi*) theology . . . It was the task of scholasticism not only to combine theological concepts into a reasonable system, but also to give them a rational-metaphysical foundation."[48] The most important "instruments" in the creation of scholasticism were the logic of Aristotle[49] and the writings of St. Augustine, the most "Latin" of the Fathers. Kireevsky's verdict on the "abstract arguments of the nominalists and the realists" and "the strange debates about the Eucharist" was wholly negative.

This endless, tiresome game of concepts over a period of seven hundred years, this useless kaleidoscope of abstract categories revolving constantly before the mind's eye, was bound to produce a general blindness to those living convictions which lie above the sphere of reason and logic, convictions to which man does not attain by syllogisms. On the contrary, the attempt to found them on syllogistic conclusions only distorts their truth, when it does not destroy it completely.

A living, integral understanding of inner, spiritual life and a living, unprejudiced contemplation of external nature were alike hounded out of the charmed circle of Western thought.[50]

Nor, of course, was the baneful influence of scholasticism confined to theology. Although "modern" philosophy seemed to repudiate scholasticism root and branch, it retained, according to Kireevsky, scholasticism's rational-syllogistic essence. Descartes did not regard an "inner, direct" conviction of his own existence as "proof," but was forced to resort to a syllogism! This being so, "it is scarcely surprising that his pupil and successor . . . , the famous Spinoza, was able to forge so skillfully and densely his rational conclusions about the first cause, about the ultimate order and structure of the entire universe, that through this compact and continuous network of theorems and syllogisms he could discern no trace of the Living Creator in all creation, nor perceive the inner freedom of man." [51] Kireevsky was somewhat better disposed toward Leibniz. He condemned him as well for trafficking in "abstract concepts," but found that the Leibnizian "Preestablished Harmony" had a certain poetry, which helped to compensate for its one-sidedness. He justified what at first glance might seem a frivolous observation by remarking that "when aesthetic or moral merit is united to logical merit, the mind itself, through this uniting of forces, returns — more or less — to its primal wholeness, and hence approaches the truth." [52]

Kireevsky seems to have regarded Hume's skepticism as a key stage in the development of Western one-sidedness. Kant's assertion that the truths of religion were not susceptible of "proof" was, he said, "perhaps but one step from the truth," although "the Western world was then not yet ripe for it." Fichte and Schelling each developed "one abstract aspect" of Kant's system. The former "proved, through a remarkable chain of syllogisms, that the whole external world is but a fleeting phantom of the imagination, and all that in fact exists is the self-developing *ego*." [53] Schelling, according to Kireevsky's précis, held that the world has real existence, but "the spirit of the world is none other than this human *ego*, which develops in the life of the universe, only to recognize itself in man." [54] This, of course, is early Schelling. Hegel then carried the laws of logical thinking to their "ultimate conclusion," enabling Schelling to reveal for all time their insufficiency. Thus, from a philosophical point of view, did thinking Europe arrive at its present impasse.

One of the few "Western" thinkers that Kireevsky found at all appealing was Blaise Pascal.[55] He was rather vague about why he approved of Pascal, but he certainly sympathized with the Jansenist struggle against the Jesuits and the tribulations and persecution to which the movement was subject. Kireevsky was warmly appreciative of what one historian has called Pascal's "repudiation of scholastic theology and the incursion of human reason into the domain of faith." [56] One may surmise, too, that Pascal's belief in feeling as an essential precursor of faith and his definition of true reason as a function of the total self must have appealed to Kireevsky.

While "Roman theology" was developing into scholasticism, a very different process was going on in the East, where writers and theologians "were not lured into the one-sidedness of syllogistic constructions, but continued to maintain that fullness and wholeness of vision which is the distinguishing mark of Christian philosophy (*liubomudrie*)." It must not be forgotten, Kireevsky stressed, that during the Middle Ages, "all contemporary culture was concentrated in Byzantium," while — virtually until the fourteenth century — the West knew only "a narrow circle of Latin writers." The theologians of the Greek East knew

Aristotle, of course — and knew him far more fully than the Western writers of the time — but they preferred Plato. This was not because they accepted his "pagan concepts," but because Plato's mode of thought "came closer to engaging the integral faculties of the mind and because his speculative thinking was distinguished by great warmth and harmony." [57]

Kireevsky displayed considerable missionary zeal on behalf of the Eastern Fathers who lived and wrote after the tenth century. Although he mentioned no names, we may assume that he was thinking primarily of Gregory Palamas, Gregory of Sinai, and other representatives of the controversial Hesychast movement. Theirs, he maintained,

was a directly and purely Christian philosophy — profound, living, elevating the mind from ratiocinating mechanism to lofty, morally free introspection, a philosophy which even a nonbeliever might well find instructive in the remarkable wealth, depth, and delicacy of its psychological observations. Despite all its merits (I am speaking here only of its intellectual merits, setting aside its theological significance), this philosophy was so little accessible to the rationalistic inclinations of the West that not only has it never been appreciated by Western thinkers, but, even more surprising, it has remained to this day almost totally unknown to them . . . in practically none of the theologians of the West do we perceive living traces of that influence which the writings of the Eastern Church would certainly have left on them, had they known them even half so well as they knew the ancient pagan writers. Perhaps the only exception is Thomas-à-Kempis — or Gerson — if the book ascribed to him is really his and not, as some think, a translation from the Greek, slightly altered in accordance with Latin ideas.[58]

Nothing new in the way of doctrine could be expected from the later Fathers, of course, for it is only in the West that "novelty" and progress have a value of their own. Even the early Greek Fathers have not been properly understood in the West, Kireevsky maintained, for Western scholars approached the Greeks with minds already formed by their Roman teachers.

Perhaps even more fundamental than the theological, conceptual differences which separated the Eastern and Western churches was the difference in the *method* of their search for the truth.

For, striving for truth through introspection (*umozrenie*), the Eastern thinkers are concerned above all with the proper inner condition of the thinking spirit, while the Westerners are more interested in the external linking of concepts. Eastern thinkers, that they may achieve the complete truth, seek the inner wholeness of the intellect, that concentration, so to speak, of the mind's forces, in which all the faculties of the spirit are fused into one living and exalted unity. Western philosophers, on the other hand, assume that the full truth may be achieved by the disparate forces of the mind, acting automatically (*samodvizhno*) and in isolation. They use one faculty to understand the moral and another to grasp the aesthetic; yet a third they employ for the useful; they attempt to understand the true through abstract reason. No one faculty knows what the others are doing until the action has been completed.[59]

Thus rationalism affected not only culture and society, but the most vital resources of the human personality itself. The totality of the soul was fragmented into various "faculties"; to the lost unity of society, Kireevsky added the lost unity of the individual.

Kireevsky's discussion of old Russian culture is largely a fuller restatement of his previous views. It is interesting, however, that he adopted Pogodin's thesis (in the modified form for which his brother Peter had polemicized)[60] that the achievement of the national state in the West had been by conquest, or through a violent struggle between the oppressors and oppressed, whereas in Russia, the formation of society and state had been an organic and natural process, which was no more than the realization in a larger arena of Russian moral principles. Thus both internally and externally Russia was harmony, while the West was despotism and discord. This, surely, is one of the most breathtaking generalizations of Kireevsky's Slavophilism.

Kireevsky, as we have seen, had an extraordinary feeling for the family and fully realized its importance in his general view of things. He did not fail to observe that it had degenerated terribly in the West. "Particularly in countries where women of quality were educated outside the family, there was a marvelous, bewitching development of social refinement, which was accompanied by the moral decay of the upper class, in which we find the first seeds of what was subsequently to become the notorious doctrine of the complete emancipation of women." [61] Kireevsky had never truly espoused that "notorious doctrine," but the view which he expressed in "European Culture" was very different from his pre-Slavophile opinions as set forth, above all, in his 1833 article on lady writers.[62] And what, one wonders, did his mother think of his harsh condemnation of the arid and artificial pleasures of the salon? [63] No wonder Kireevsky's friends did not come to his house as they had in the past.

In accounting for the loss of vitality in the spirit and social institutions of old Russia, in attempting to "explain" Peter the Great, Kireevsky was once more cautious and tentative. But his approach to an explanation was very different from what it had been in 1839. Then he had found the source of weakness and decline in the Church itself, in the *Stoglav* council. By implication, at any rate, the Old Believers represented the purity of the old way. But Kireevsky's increasing idealization of the Orthodox Church made this explanation rather awkward.[64] In "European Culture," it was the formalism, which manifested itself in the Old Believer movement, which was to blame. In the sixteenth century, "certain distortions, which had crept into the books of divine service, and certain peculiarities in Church ritual persisted among the people, despite the fact that constant contact with the East should have revealed to them the differences with the other churches." [65]

Finally, Kireevsky reaffirmed that the rebuilding of Russian culture out of "our own pure materials" depends not on the people, but on the gentry. This rebuilding

can be carried out when that class of our people which is not wholly occupied with the acquisition of the material means of life and whose function in the structure of society is largely to shape social consciousness — when this class, I say, which is still saturated with Western ideas, finally becomes fully convinced of the one-sidedness of European culture, when it feels more keenly the need for new intellectual principles, when, in a reasonable desire for the whole truth, it turns to the pure source of the ancient Orthodox faith of its people, and with a responsive heart harkens after the still clear echoes of its fatherland's Holy faith in the ancient, indigenous life of Russia.[66]

XIII. The Search for Wholeness

Kireevsky's "European Culture" was printed in the first number of the *Moscow Miscellany*, which appeared on April 21, 1852. On June 1, Adjutant-general N. N. Annenkov wrote to Shirinsky-Shikhmatov, the Minister of Education (who had already noticed the "pernicious almanac"), directing his attention particularly to Kireevsky's article, Ivan Aksakov's "A Few Words about Gogol," and Constantine Aksakov's "On the Old Slavic Way of Life in General and the Russian in Particular." [1] The government "Committee of April 2, 1848" [2] criticized Constantine Aksakov for stressing "democratic" residua in the Russian past (like the veche, the popular assembly) and paying insufficient attention to the growth of the "autocratic principle," which, the Committee maintained, had wholly superseded "popular government" after the Mongol period. Aksakov's errors were particularly dangerous, since the *Miscellany* was intended for a wide audience of non-historians, among whom there were bound to be "frivolous" people who would interpret any ambiguity in a "harmful" sense. [3] Shirinsky-Shikhmatov in fact denied that the veche had been of any importance whatsoever in old Russia, except in Novgorod and Pskov, where its introduction had doubtless been an unfortunate result of trade relations with the Germans. [4]

The Main Administration of the Censorship criticized Kireev-

sky's article for much the same reason; his hostility to the autocracy did not escape them. "It is not known [ran the report]
what Kireevsky means by the integrality (*integralnost'*) of Orthodox Russia. One thing, however, is clear: that in his apparently
right-thinking article he does not render the justice which is due
to the immortal contribution of the Great Reformer of Russia
and his imperial successors, who spared neither labor nor effort
to the end of making Western civilization ours, the only means
by which the power and glory of our Fatherland might have
been raised to its contemporary splendor." [5] After some delibera-
tion, the Committee of April 2 decided to recommend to the
Ministry of Education that the republication of Aksakov's article
be forbidden, and that both he and Prince L'vov, the responsible
censor, should be reprimanded. In addition, the remaining three ·
numbers of the *Moscow Miscellany* should be subjected to a
special censorship.[6]

With this pronouncement, the role of the committee came to
an end, but the difficulties of the *Miscellany*, unfortunately, did
not. After a complicated series of arguments and discussions with
the Third Section, the Ministry of Education finally declared on
March 3, 1853, that the *Miscellany* should be suppressed entirely
and that Ivan Aksakov should be forbidden to serve as the editor
of any publication whatsoever. The Aksakov brothers, Ivan
Kireevsky, and Prince Cherkassky were to receive "the most
severe reprimand, for wishing to spread ridiculous and harmful
ideas." They were also to be required in the future to submit
their manuscripts prior to publication to the Main Administration
of the Censorship. Shirinsky-Shikhmatov had even considered de-
priving them of all access to the printed word, but decided
against this more extreme measure. At the suggestion of Count
Orlov, Benckendorff's successor, the four were placed under
police surveillance for an indefinite period.[7]

"European Culture" pleased the other Slavophiles almost as

little as it pleased Shirinsky-Shikhmatov. In May of 1852, Ivan Aksakov wrote to Ivan Turgenev that "if you have read the *Miscellany,* you may have been embarrassed by Kireevsky's article. You should know that neither Constantine nor I nor Khomiakov would have put our signatures to this article. In the second number of the *Miscellany* there will be a supplement to the article by Khomiakov." [8] In a letter to his father, written a few days after the first number had appeared, Aksakov confided that "Kireevsky's article has annoyed a great many people. Granovsky, whom I have seen, told me that although he disagrees most emphatically with Kireevsky, he nevertheless finds the article excellent in many ways, splendidly set forth, etc. I was very glad to hear Granovsky's opinion, because some people have insisted that it is impossible even to reply to Kireevsky's article, that it is in the government spirit, etc., and thus casts a rather bad light on the *Miscellany.*" [9] Even Pogodin accused Kireevsky of seeing only "the better side of Russia" and the worst side of the West.[10] Khomiakov, who of all the Slavophiles was the most concerned to air his disagreement with Kireevsky publicly, was not able to do so. His "supplement" was rejected by the censor, together with the entire second number of the *Miscellany,* and was published only much later.

This is not the place to attempt a full-dress discussion of Khomiakov's "On the Occasion of I. V. Kireevsky's Article," but the similarities and differences between the two men's historical treatment of Russian and "Western" development are illuminating and should be taken up briefly. In their 1839 exchange, Kireevsky had revealed himself to be more ideologically daring, more powerful in the greater sweep and simplicity of his polemical statement. It was in fact Khomiakov's relative sobriety in "On the Old and New," his willingness at least to confront some of the darker side of medieval Russian history which has led certain observers and historians to conclude that the article was a polemical device to goad Kireevsky into a more "positive" response to old Russian history and culture. It is significant that Khomiakov's 1852 reply to Kireevsky had much in common with what he had written thirteen years before. Khomiakov clearly believed that Kireevsky, in "European Culture," had gone "too far," both in his hostility to Western culture and (to a much greater extent) in his idealization of old Russia.

In his basic analytical distinctions and categories, Khomiakov scarcely differed from Kireevsky. He too saw Roman rationalism as the great destructive force which lay behind the whole development of Western culture, and his own analysis of the Roman influence on the nations of the West was entirely in the spirit of Kireevsky. Yet the vehemence of feeling which characterized "European Culture" was absent from Khomiakov's piece, and he even ventured a kind of appreciation of the achievements of Western culture which might have come from Kireevsky's pen in the forties. We, wrote Khomiakov, do not belong to this self-condemned world,

and this we may say even while rendering a wholly justified tribute of amazement to its great historical, artistic, and scientific manifestations, whether they be Hildebrand and Gottfried, or Luther and Gustavus Adolphus, or the creator of the Sistine Madonna, or the builder of the Cologne Cathedral, or Kant, or Hegel, the consummators of rationalist philosophy. Honest if blind, acting out of love . . . elevated by that moral grandeur which they retained despite the incompleteness of the law to which they had subjected themselves, or mighty with an intellectual power, despite the falsity of the basis of their thinking: all of them . . . in part involuntary victims of the historical process, may, for their great exploits, hear from us a word of honest respect, unsullied by condemnation or reproach.[11]

May God grant to us — who know the path — their power, he concluded.

It was only when he turned to Russia that Khomiakov clearly differed with his colleague: he accused Kireevsky, in no uncertain terms, of a radical idealization of ancient Russia. To Kireevsky's statement that "Christian doctrine developed in purity and wholeness throughout the social and private life of ancient Russia," Khomiakov replied that no nation on earth deserved such praise, particularly not one whose princes had so shamefully pillaged and slaughtered enemies and allies alike.[12] He went on to stress Russia's cultural debt to Byzantium and pointed out that Kireevsky's sharp distinction between Rome and Byzantium was untenable. Particularly in the realm of law and jurisprudence, and even in "social institutions," Byzantium had been strongly marked by the Roman spirit. Byzantium could not *be* the Christian society, but it could — and did — preserve Christian doctrine in all its purity and fullness for Russia.

Khomiakov was a good deal more critical about the extent to which ancient Russia had actually embodied the unsullied truth of Eastern Christianity than Kireevsky; he had been so in 1839 and was still in 1852. And, as he had in "On the Old and the New," he related the failings of ancient Russia to the vast dislocations brought on by the necessary unification of the nation. Unlike Kireevsky, Khomiakov viewed the fatal "formalism" which had begun to be manifest in the late Middle Ages as stemming not only from the "masses," but also — and perhaps primarily — from the princes and their entourage, the *druzhina*. Largely of foreign origin (Khomiakov stressed), they performed a heroic and necessary task, as the bearer of the "principle of the state," but at the same time they inevitably did much damage to the old communal spirit of the Slavs, which was indissolubly bound up with a spirit of particularism and "local egotism," which had to perish. Khomiakov regarded the boyar class (and presumably the territorial princes as well) as both the lineal and spiritual heirs of the Scandinavian princes and their servitors; he contemplated them with mingled admiration and abhorrence. While achieving their task at such cost, they introduced a spirit of

aristocratic individualism into Russia, which manifested itself —
for example — in *mestnichestvo,** which Khomiakov found to be
not unlike Western feudalism.[13]

The effect of Khomiakov's remarks was to soften somewhat the
typological distinction between Russia and the West — or rather
to blur the distinction on the historical level, while accepting the
dichotomy between rationalism and "wholeness" on the spiritual
plane. For, although Russia had suffered — and continued to do
so — from "dividedness," it was not the result of an underlying
spiritual falseness, as in the West, but merely a contingent fact
of history, thus making it — Khomiakov felt — easier to overcome.

The necessary unification of the country was not, however, the
only source of that formalism which both men believed to be a
crucial weakness of Russian culture. While Kireevsky located the
source of this malaise in the very fullness and wholeness of Russian communal life (a situation in which the letter might the
more easily be mistaken for the spirit), Khomiakov saw its source
in the *imperfect* Christianization of Russia. The mass of the
people was never really able to distinguish the letter from the
spirit; the schism was being prepared even before the Christianization of Russia had fairly gotten underway.[14]

Khomiakov fully endorsed Kireevsky's view that the Russian
Church had never involved itself in politics, towering, as it did,
high above the state. Nevertheless, he could not forbear pointing
out the enormously important role it had played in the unification
of the country around the Grand Duchy of Moscow and the
creation of the Russian state. The two statements are laid out
side by side, but not reconciled.

Khomiakov's view of the course of Russian history thus continued to pay a much greater tribute to historical complexity
than did Kireevsky's. For Khomiakov, Russian history had been

* The Muscovite system of state appointments, based on a hierarchical
ranking of boyar families and individual members of a given family.

the battleground of two principles, neither of which was wholly good or wholly bad. There was, however, a bit more to the story. Khomiakov, while stressing the idea of "wholeness" of the spirit and subscribing completely to Kireevsky's indictment of Roman rationalism, obviously felt that his friend had swung too far in what might be called an irrationalist direction — at least by implication. "Logical reason," according to Khomiakov, when properly integrated and subordinated to a higher and more complete kind of knowledge (*soznanie*), was an essential part of any culture — and it had been sadly lacking, he felt, in ancient Russia.[15] This was particularly apparent in the case of the Schism, for the schismatics were clearly unable to perceive the "logical" difference between Orthodox teaching and the ritual in which the teaching was embodied. The Russian ritual had gradually changed, while the future schismatics stubbornly clung to it.

Finally, Khomiakov endorsed the conclusion to which Kireevsky had come in 1845 — and would again accept in 1856 — that Russia needed the "logical-technical" culture of the West, to use Kireevsky's own term. If Russia could fuse the living faith of her past to this culture, a new civilization might be created in which the West could play a part.

As we have seen, there is a certain hostility to the state — at any rate, in its modern, rationalized, activist form — in Kireevsky's thought. Indeed, in speaking of old Russia, Kireevsky more than once contrasted the "state," or the sovereign power of the prince, with the communal society, for the benefit of which the prince exercized his limited powers of judging and conducting foreign relations. By contrast, the Russian state, from Peter the Great to the present, had far exceeded this limited patriarchal function and had continually acted directly upon society in a highly destructive fashion.

An antipathy for the modern state, combined with deep sympathy for a traditional, communal "society," had distinctly radical implications. This fact would become clear to everyone some years later, with the development of Russian Populism into a "movement," but elements within the Russian government realized it full well in Kireevsky's time. Herzen was only the first of those "frivolous" people who were to seize upon the "ambiguities" of Slavophilism and interpret them in a "harmful" sense.

Kireevsky himself, however, never pushed this line of reasoning beyond his very general discussion of old Russian institutions. Practically speaking, it is hard to believe that his feelings of personal and ideological hostility toward the Russian state were not at least partially held in check by his dependence on that state as a bulwark of "order" against possible peasant disturbances. Certainly Kireevsky's 1848 letter to Pogodin about Pogodin's projected protest against the censorship leads one so to believe.[16]

Kireevsky's attitude toward the state and its relations both to the Church and "society" is clarified to some degree by his correspondence in the fall of 1853 with Koshelëv.[17] At issue between the two men was the question of the separation of church and state, as posed by the Swiss theologian and literary critic Alexandre Vinet, in his *Essai sur la manifestation des convictions religieuses et sur la séparation de l'église et de l'état.*[18]

Vinet's writings were well known to the Slavophiles.[19] Khomiakov considered him a man of the greatest purity and was much interested by his observations on the subject of Catholic and Protestant differences.[20] The Swiss pastor was most noted, however, for his hostility to the state church and ultimately for his advocacy of the separation of church and state, a position at which he gradually arrived in the course of the turbulent conflicts between the state churches of Switzerland and the Methodist movement in the 1820's.

Vinet was a strong Protestant individualist and a cautious but determined political liberal. For him, the individual conscience overshadowed all else in the drama of man's salvation. He had no very developed theory of the state, regarding it as a purely temporal organization to provide for the material necessities of men who must live together on earth. As his biographer has written, "The most important task for the state was merely to protect and maintain the social ethic; it might never, however, intrude into the domain of conscience, or even try to determine or influence religious convictions, even with the object of acting as the defender of the faith." [21]

Kireevsky was not greatly attracted to Vinet. The latter's abstract way of putting things, making "rules" about "*the* Church" and "*the* State," offended Kireevsky's inclination for the concrete and historical. And further, he inquired ironically of Koshelëv, did Vinet suppose that the church and state could exist not only independently of one another, but "without any sort of connection between them? Is this his thought? But *what sort of church and what sort of state must* act this way? And what is this *must*? What sort of *law* will they be fulfilling in so acting: the law of the church, or the law of the state? And what sort of church and state, acting with such a principle of direction? Or does the word *must* not refer to any special law of any particular church or any known state or to any known philosophical idea of the state, but is merely the postulating of those ideas which Vinet has drawn up for himself as to the best arrangement for the Protestant Church and an ideal state?" [22]

Thus mockingly did Kireevsky indict Vinet for his lack of discrimination, for his lack of system, for his lack of historical precision. Vinet was not an "organic" thinker, nor was he particularly sensitive to historical evolution and tradition. Vinet himself, Kireevsky felt, had come to realize these shortcomings by the end of the book, for by that time he was no longer speaking of every conceivable variety of conviction — Moslem, Jewish, or pagan — and of some abstract state, but conceding tacitly that his demand for the separation of the two powers could relate *"merely and solely to the Protestant confessions."* [23] Even here, Kireevsky noted, the historical evolution and practice of Protestant sects in their relations with the state differed to such a marked degree that subsuming them under one general law was a matter of the greatest difficulty. Central, of course, was the question whether their relations with the state were governed by dogma or merely by historical practice.

Kireevsky was most annoyed at Vinet's suggestion that the "fusion" of church and state under Constantine the Great was at the root of the current problem. "In other words," he observed sarcastically, "the Holy Spirit, soon after apostolic times, left the Church and is returning to her only in the sermons of Vinet. Or perhaps the Holy Spirit has not left the Church, but while dwelling in her has been confused and is now being set right by Vinet." [24] The principal value of Vinet's book for the Orthodox reader, Kireevsky concluded, will be as a demonstration of Western confusion and the enmeshing of the Church in politics.

For Kireevsky, however, the heart of the matter was that he believed that "a state wholly without relation (*bezotnositel'noe*) to the Church is just as impossible as a philosophy wholly without relation to the teaching of faith." [25] Koshelëv had mentioned the United States, which Vinet had long thought of as a possible model in this regard, but Kireevsky was not impressed. "This is not a state," he wrote, "but a coincidental linking of several heterogeneous groups, constantly ready to fall to pieces." [26] In any case, the only reason that the American state has not taken control of religion is that there are so many "religions." "Unity in way of thinking cannot but demand unity in form of action." [27] A certain *belief* demands and produces certain mores, a specific kind of family and social relations, a definite state structure. The contrast with the "mechanistic" thinking of Vinet could not be clearer.

Kireevsky expanded on the organic connection between church, state and society in his next letter to Koshelëv:

The Church, you say, is not an organization of society, for the social element is secondary in it. Primary in it is man, that is, the person. In the state everything is society; in the Church everything is man. But if for the Church there is nothing but man, if it embraces him fully, how can this be done without defining the character of his relations to society? It is impossible for a society of Moslems or Jews to have the same mores as a Christian society. Or for a society of Quakers to have the same mores as a society of Latins. If the Lutherans, the Latins, the Calvinists, and the Anglicans each built their lives completely in accord with their convictions, would it not then be impossible for each society not to have its own particular mores and customs, corresponding to the particularity of its convictions? [28]

The state, as a terrestrial organization of society, must serve the Church, also a social organization, but oriented toward "eternal life." The state must be permeated by the Church, which for Kireevsky was synonymous with the "convictions" of society. In the sixteenth century, he claimed, "all the states of Europe were thus bound to their peoples, all of whom were of one faith." Of ancient Russia this was particularly true, and "even now," he wrote, "no one is entitled to look upon Russia as other than an Orthodox state." [29]

This bald statement is hard to reconcile with the totality of Kireevsky's views on ancient and modern Russian society, as expressed in all the journalism of his Slavophile period. The country was in the hands of a bureaucracy of whom Kireevsky had the lowest opinion, whose members he had described as motivated by a crass and egotistical self-interest. The gentry were still almost entirely under the sway of foreign, "Western," rationalist ideas, and among the common people were preserved only "traces" of the old Orthodox community. One can see how Russian society might still be called "Orthodox," albeit in a less comprehensive, sociological sense than was generally intended by Kireevsky when he employed the term. But the Russian *state?* By unabashedly calling it "Orthodox," Kireevsky appeared to deny the radical break between ancient and modern Russia which had been an article of faith with him since at least 1839. Russia was still, it now seemed, an "organic" unity — with that unity, at most, somewhat impaired. "Of course [Kireevsky wrote to Koshelëv] with both your and my idea of the state, one must assume the possibility of an overturn of things in which a crude, egotistical force will come to dominate the reason and convictions of the people." [30] What was the state of Nicholas I, if not such a force?

The radical (in the most general sense of the word) and critical force of Kireevsky's Slavophile thought had been in his confronting the Russia of his day with an idealized tableau of a communal, premodern society, thus revealing to his contemporaries the values which they had lost — or were in danger of losing — through the adoption of "Western" rationalism. But in the last decade of his life, Kireevsky was ever less willing to criticize the status quo in Russia, laying increased stress in his writings on the pernicious historical development of the West. Significantly enough, in Kireevsky's journalism of the forties and fifties, there was less and less criticism of Peter the Great. The active role of the state in the virtual destruction of old Russian culture was ignored; instead Kireevsky talked mostly about the formalism of the peasantry.

Kireevsky's last years were not happy. His writing continued to come hard, and the heavy cloud of grim piety seemed to enclose him ever more closely. His family life appears to have been definitely affected — and here, as in so many other areas of his life, the period 1846–1847 seems to have been a crucial time. Natal'ia Petrovna Kireevskaia's letters to Makary give us some insight into these domestic difficulties, although the picture is far from complete. "My heart is very heavy," she wrote to him on September 20, 1846. "Something sad is oppressing me." [31] This vague complaint was several times repeated. Then, a few months later, she wrote: "Ivan Vasil'evich's health is fair [this was only a few months before his desperate illness of May 1847], but he seems to be hiding some secret sorrow in his heart." [32] On January 24, 1847, however, she came right out with what was bothering her.

I am often, very often [she wrote to Makary] — yes, and right now — really depressed. There is something not firm in our relationship. At times things go along all right, but even then there is something forced. Sometimes, however — as just now — there is suddenly coldness, inattention, and, what is more, a kind of unpleasantness that has no place in love . . . My heart — truly — is loaded with grief, and I don't know what to do. Should I be colder with him, or — but I really don't know — perhaps he will take the coldness for some caprice and distance himself still more. It would be easier for me if I loved him less.

Everything is in disorder, both at the stable and in the house; we are spending more than our income, and no care is taken about anything. If, in a friendly, tender way, I propose something or remind him of something, he merely falls silent, but if I speak in a normal, conversational tone, then he is angry and caustic and there is unpleasantness again.[33]

There is no real trace of family problems in Kireevsky's own correspondence of the latter forties. In the course of the fifties, however, there began to be brief references — mostly in letters to Makary — to domestic "problems" and "disorder." In 1855, Kireevsky wrote to Makary, asking him to pray "to the Merciful God that everything in our family should be peaceful, harmonious, loving, and happy. We have nothing, thank God, which could be called unhappiness or trouble, but there are certain spider webs, spun by a sort of gloom over the vague nuances of our emotional life, which have little by little developed into whole tissues, estranging people and making it difficult for them to face things." [34] One may legitimately infer from this tortuous passage that Kireevsky's frequently irritable remoteness from both his family and the events of the daily round continued to plague the household. So much of Kireevsky's intellectual concern centered on the problem of breaking through the constructions of the mind to reality itself — how ironical, then, to find these "spider webs" beclouding his most intimate personal relations. "Wholeness," in life as well as in philosophy, seems to have remained an "intellectual" ideal, which Kireevsky could only understand the way he understood philosophy and intellectual systems in general. "Wholeness" and the "reintegration of the soul," perhaps, could only be fully comprehended by those who were already whole — from within, that is. Since Kireevsky was not "within," these ideals simply tortured him, by underlining, in every area of his life, how inadequate he was. It was easier, no doubt, to build an altogether new building. We can imagine him looking back, as he must have, at his own Dolbino childhood, idealizing the regime when Vasily Ivanovich was master, and feeling the deterioration in the quality of life.

Kireevsky's eldest son, Vasily (born in 1836), gave his father a good deal of anxiety. In 1849, Vasily was enrolled — through the good offices of Zhukovsky — in the St. Petersburg Lyceum. [35] In order to gain admittance, however, he had to undergo an intensive period of cramming in Grozdov's private preparatory school, which, according to his father, was so difficult that "my heart bleeds for him constantly." As Kireevsky wrote to Zhukovsky, "Vasia was not born a businesslike chap, but an artist. By nature he is inclined to lose himself in his thoughts, to the point that even in his childhood he would forget whether he had eaten. I made a great mistake in his upbringing, for not then having thought to send him to public schools, I taught him to understand the lesson, rather than to grind until he had it by heart, which is what grinding demands. Thus he now finds himself in a position where he must engage in a steady, minute-to-minute struggle with himself, constantly destroying in himself the need to really think and understand, in order not to lose the minute which has been earmarked for cramming." [36] Vasia, however, seems to have found it hard to break the habit of thinking about what he read, and he continued to lose time and get bad marks (*durnye bally*), while other, less capable students met the requirement without any particular effort. Such, at any rate, was his father's diagnosis of his academic difficulties.

Kireevsky had chosen the Lyceum for his son not only for its inherent quality, but also for the advantages which it conferred on its graduates in the area of state service, advantages which he himself never enjoyed.[37] It seems clear that Kireevsky hoped to overcome — insofar as possible — for his son the disabilities resulting from his own equivocal relations with the government. At any rate, if Vasily should want a government career, if he should want to be "useful," he should have the opportunity. Again, indirectly we see Ivan Kireevsky's growing fear that his own life had not been "useful."

Kireevsky stayed away from Dolbino entirely between 1851 and 1855, almost certainly because of the dispiriting effect which country life had on him, particularly in the melancholy state in which he now found himself almost constantly. Even in Moscow, however, Kireevsky's social life was now much less extensive than it had been, although in the correspondence and memoir literature of the period one still reads occasionally that Khomiakov or Apollon Grigor'ev had read his poems one evening "at Kireevsky's." Kireevsky's published diary for the years 1852–1854 makes gloomy reading.[38] It confirms that he spent a good deal of time working on the various editions of the Church Fathers, but it also reveals long days with apparently little or no occupation, and nothing of note to jot down but the daily church service. He seems to have brooded endlessly and indulged his constant feelings of guilt and inadequacy. On August 15, 1853, he wrote: "The disorder of my external life: economic affairs, domestic situation, my studies, the children's upbringing — all of this proceeds from the disorder of my inner forces." [39] And then, on October 3, 1853, at greater length:

If I can always remember that it is Almighty God who is continually surrounding me with all the events of my life, that what is to me empty, melancholy, and bad is the very best thing for that condition in which I have set my soul. If I wish to depart from that condition by some way not in accord with the will of God, I can only end in a still worse state; what is necessary is firmly, invincibly, immovably, with adamantine resolution, to set myself bounds, not only in my actions, but in my most imperceptible wishes — fearing like fire, like dishonor, the smallest deviltry in the most fleeting daydream. Lord! Give me strength and let me always wish to be true, in all the windings of my mind and heart . . . My life now, that is, the real side of my earthly life, is the life of my children . . . as far as real deeds are concerned, I am baffled as to how to act; then one thing distracts me from another and life goes by in inactivity.[40]

This is the diary of an unhappy man, who believed that an unremitting and iron discipline was required to control the depravity in his heart. In his old age, Kireevsky's attitude toward the salvation of his soul seems to have become far more Calvinist than "romantic," recalling his father's dour piety. Small wonder that an old friend like Odoevsky, upon spending an evening with him, should have felt that Kireevsky's whole bearing was in some vague way a criticism or reproach.[41]

Kireevsky, like many of the Slavophiles, considered the Crimean War to be "a war between Russia and Europe," a war between two hostile principles, which might inaugurate a new era of human civilization, "based on a renaissance of the Slavic tribes, under the banner of Orthodox Christianity." [42] In a letter to Makary written in April 1854, Kireevsky observed — with the slightly triumphant air of one who finds confirmation of a long-held view — that "the Bishop of Paris said openly in his speech that the war was not against the Turks, but against the schismatic church, as they call our holy, Orthodox Church. In fact, this is rather like the last days, as they were prophesied in the Apocalypse." [43] In June 1854, his enthusiasm for the war was undiminished. He upbraided A. V. Venevitinov, a Petersburger, for the bad spirit in the capital: while everyone in Moscow, he wrote, "is in despair at the news of our concessions," in St. Petersburg, "it is said, they do not hide their fear of the war and are seeking peace." [44] But things developed — as they had in 1848 — in the most disappointing fashion, and Kireevsky came to realize that the great moment was not yet at hand. At the end of 1855, in another letter to Venevitinov — this time about the death of the latter's brother-in-law — Kireevsky called it "this accursed war." [45]

"My literary activities," Kireevsky wrote to Koshelëv in the fall of 1852,

have been limited to a certain amount of reading. I read little that is new, preferring the old, perhaps because I myself am getting old. I have not, however, lost the inclination to write, *when it becomes possible to do so*, a course of philosophy, in which, I think, there will be many new truths — new, that is, because of human forgetfulness. It is a pity, a great pity, that Western folly now hampers our thought too — now, that is to say, when it would appear that the time has come for Russia to say its word in philosophy, to show them, the heretics, that the truth of science is to be found only in the truth of Orthodoxy. Incidentally, it is also true that one may leave these anxieties about the fate of human reason to a Master who knows to whom his business is to be entrusted, and when.[46]

The "course of philosophy" was a long-cherished project, probably dating from the period when he hoped to achieve the chair in philosophy at Moscow University; certainly it was much on his mind in 1847, after his withdrawal from the *Muscovite*.[47] At best, however, Kireevsky's projects were realized only in a small way. According to Khomiakov, Kireevsky's last article, rather cumbersomely entitled "On the Necessity and Possibility of New Principles in Philosophy," was to have been the beginning of the larger work over which he had mulled for so long.[48] The published portion, Khomiakov wrote, "contains a critique of the historical development of philosophy, while the following part was to be a systematic working out of the new principles. Such was the intention of the author; such were our hopes." [49] Khomiakov's words were written soon after Kireevsky's death in June 1856 of cholera.

"On the Necessity and Possibility" appeared in the Slavophile periodical *Russian Colloquy* (*Russkaia beseda*), edited by Koshelëv and Ivan Aksakov, with the active collaboration of Kireevsky's friend, T. I. Filippov. The struggle with the government for permission to put out a journal was once more a long and weary one.[50] Koshelëv and Khomiakov took the lead; Kireevsky had almost no part in the tedious and frustrating round of petitions, letters, and visits to state functionaries. He did write one letter to A. S. Norov, the new Minister of Culture. In an interview with Khomiakov about the journal, Norov mentioned having received a letter from Kireevsky, "and just imagine! He asked permission, and at the same time declared that he had no intention of changing either his views, his behavior, or his way of expressing himself." To which Khomiakov, with considerable presence of mind, replied that "of course Kireevsky was speaking in jest. He must know you, know that Your Excellency realizes that a man does not change his convictions like his shirt." [51] Only after many months of enervating and degrading effort did the first number of the *Russian Colloquy* appear, toward the end of 1856.

Kireevsky's starting point, in "On the Necessity and Possibility," was the cul-de-sac in which Western philosophy now found itself. Western rationalism, Kireevsky had long maintained, had reached the end of its centuries of development, thus posing the question: where does European culture go from here? As was really the case with all his Slavophile writings, the structure of the essay was basically an extended comparison of the Eastern and Western "principles."

That Kireevsky never continued "On the Necessity and Possibility," that he never wove the principles of old Russian culture and the "integral way of thinking" into a "positive philosophy" is not to be explained merely by the fact of his death or by his chronic inability to see a project through to the end. Kireevsky was in fact unable to get beyond the purely historical comparison which he developed from 1839 until his death. On the basis of his journalism, and more particularly of his correspondence, it is fair to conclude that he was simply unable to show *how* his idealized picture of the past might be made fruitful for the present, or how the "method" of the Eastern Fathers might be applied to the philosophical needs of his day.

"On the Necessity and Possibility" is particularly notable, however, in that Kireevsky discussed more fully than he had in 1852 his notion of the proper, "integrated" condition of the soul and the relationship between man's reason and the totality of his spiritual being. Before examining what he said on this subject, however, let us look at some of the lesser points of interest in Kireevsky's last essay, a few modifications and elaborations of that single canvas upon which he had been engaged since the 1830's.

The "West," for one thing, was now conceived in a less monolithic and grimly historicist fashion than it had been in 1852.

Kireevsky several times permitted himself to ask "what if?," the most interesting instance being the possibility that France might have developed a "positive philosophy" in the seventeenth century; had this happened, the baneful and acid skepticism of the Age of Reason might have been avoided. "The principles," he wrote, "of this potential French philosophy were contained in what there was in common between the convictions of the Port-Royal school and certain opinions of Fénelon . . . both strove to develop the inner life, and sought in its depths the living bond between faith and reason, beyond the sphere of the external linking of concepts. Port-Royal and Fénelon received this orientation from the same source, from that part of Christian philosophy (*liubomudrie*) which they found in the ancient Church Fathers, and which was free from the teachings of Rome." [52]

From Sainte-Beuve's *Port-Royal,* Kireevsky had apparently passed to Pascal's *Pensées,* which he found had

not only revealed a new foundation for the moral order of the world, for the understanding of the living relationship between Divine Providence and human freedom, but also contained profound suggestions in the direction of a different way of thinking, differing equally from the Roman-scholastic and the rational-philosophical. If these sparks from his ideas had united into a common consciousness with those which had inspired Fénelon, when, in defense of Guyon, he collected the teachings of the Holy Fathers on the inner life, then from the combined flame there would surely have sprung a new, original philosophy which might have saved France from unbelief and its consequences. [53]

But the Jesuits destroyed Port-Royal, and with its members perished the "vigorous, life-giving orientation of their thought." The great message of Pascal was drowned out by the "raucous laughter of Voltaire."

What would have been the effect on Western culture of the

development of a "positive philosophy" in seventeenth-century France? Might the world have been spared the ultimate development of abstract reason by Fichte, Schelling, and Hegel? What would have been the relationship between the "positive philosophy" in France and Orthodoxy? But Kireevsky did not speculate further.

Following his discussion of Pascal, Kireevsky turned once more to the philosophy of Aristotle, attempting to define more satisfactorily his relation to that Greek culture which Kireevsky continued to admire. The two principal components of Greek culture — "tangible," mythological belief and the penchant for abstract reasoning — could be reconciled, Kireevsky found, only in "the contemplation of the beautiful." But as Greek "reasoning" developed, the power of Greek mythology to compel belief weakened (here we can see definite traces of Schelling's ideas about mythology). Philosophy — and it is the philosophy of Aristotle which Kireevsky had in mind — "was born in and grew out of Greek concepts, but in its maturity it became the legacy of all mankind as the separate fruit of reason, rounding out and ripening and eventually parting from its natural root." [54]

Philosophy thus grew out of the totality of Greek culture, essentially as its negation. In destroying the pagan mythology of the Greeks, philosophy performed a useful, if negative, service. Nevertheless, in so doing, Aristotle's system "broke the wholeness of man's intellectual self-consciousness and transferred the root of man's inner convictions from the moral and aesthetic sense into the abstract consciousness of deliberative reason." [55] The deliberative coolness and measure of Aristotelianism was deeply offensive to Kireevsky: it seemed to him entirely of a piece with the calculating self-interest of modern political economy. "By undermining all convictions which existed above the level of rationalist logic, it destroyed all convictions capable of elevating man above his personal interests. The animating spirit of morality declined.

The mainsprings of inner autonomy weakened. Man became the obedient tool of surrounding circumstances, the deliberating but passive object of external forces — intelligent matter obedient to the power of earthly motives: personal advantage and fear." [56] Aristotle's ideal — in practice — was a "reasonable mediocrity"; it produced "intelligent spectators," but "insignificant men of action." [57]

Despite this highly destructive side of Aristotelian philosophy, Christianity did not attempt to destroy it, "but accepted it and transformed it in accordance with its own higher philosophy." Kireevsky developed this idea in the section that followed, and it is a reasonable guess that Khomiakov's strictures may have played some role in what was, for Kireevsky, at least a shift in emphasis. "Plato and Aristotle," he wrote, "could only be of use to Christian culture as great students of reason; they could not endanger it so long as Christian truth occupied the summit of man's culture." And, he added, "the growth of rational knowledge, of course, does not offer salvation, but it guards against false knowledge." [58] In fact, Kireevsky now stressed, it was the *ignorance* of the West which permitted the spirit of Roman rationalism to do such damage.

In 1856, Kireevsky reverted to his earlier stress on the view that the destinies of Russia and the West were intertwined, for, he wrote, "the fate of all mankind is in a state of living and sympathetic reciprocity, not always noticeable, but real just the same. The defection of Rome deprived the West of the purity of Christian teaching, and at the same time halted the development of the culture of society in the East. What should have been accomplished through the combined efforts of East and West was now beyond the power of the East alone, which was thus condemned merely to preserve Divine truth in its purity and holiness, without being able to embody it in the external culture of nations." [59]

It is important to see as precisely as possible what Kireevsky

meant by the phenomenon of "industrialism," which he so resoundingly denounced in "On the Necessity and Possibility." On
the metaphysical level, industrialism was intimately related to
both rationalism and materialism. It was the characteristic mode
of activity for man in a world deprived of all transcendent significance, where "the reality of being survived only in his physical
person." It was the result of man's reason having separated itself
from the totality of his being and from God. It was "abstract
reason" unshackled, operating without let or hindrance in the
arena of this world. The further the process of secularization advanced, the greater was man's egoistic lust for gain, for the material goods of this world, for power. "Industry," Kireevsky noted
bitterly, "rules the world, without faith or poetry. In our time it
unites and divides people, it determines one's fatherland, it
delineates classes, it lies at the basis of the state structure, it moves
nations, it declares war and makes peace, it alters mores, gives a
direction to science and determines the character of culture. Men
bow down before it and erect temples to it. It is the real deity in
which people sincerely believe and to which they submit." [60] Industry was the apotheosis of rationalism in action, and Kireevsky
was increasingly pessimistic about how soon this false god might
be dethroned. He found it probable "that we are seeing only the
beginning of the unlimited domination of industry and of the
recent phase of philosophy. Proceeding hand in hand, they have
yet to run the full course of the modern development of European
life." [61]

It was in his last essay that Kireevsky discussed his idea of
"wholeness" — in terms of the individual human soul — most
fully. Together with his communal picture of old Russian culture,
which he developed first, this "integrality" was at the very center
of Kireevsky's world view. This being so, it has been much discussed — by historians of Slavophilism, by students of "Russian
philosophy," by Kireevsky's biographers. It has been described

and sometimes analyzed from the standpoint of sociology, philosophy, and the history of religion. It has been viewed as Kireevsky's own brilliant insight, and it has been seen as merely a piece of typically "romantic" doctrine, the analogue of Kireevsky's exaltation of the communal and prerational on the social level.

According to Kireevsky's analysis, the dreadful situation of the Western "thinker" was that, in order even to attempt to achieve religious faith, he had to repudiate the entire culture which surrounded him. This sad fact, of course, was the result of centuries of rationalist evolution in Western religion and culture. In what Kireevsky usually called "Orthodox thinking," on the other hand, faith did not dispose of, arrange, or even govern reason (although Kireevsky occasionally slipped into that usage). In "Orthodox thinking," the attempt was made "to elevate reason itself above its usual level," to restore it to its proper place in the harmony of the soul. In Kireevsky's own words,

the first condition for such an elevation of reason is that man should strive to gather into one indivisible whole all his separate forces, which in his ordinary condition are in a state of disunity and contradiction; that he should not consider his abstract logical capacity as the only organ for the comprehension of truth; that he should not consider the voice of ecstatic feeling, uncoordinated with the other forces of the spirit, as an infallible guide to truth; that he should not consider the inspiration of an isolated aesthetic sense, independent of other concepts, as the true guide to the comprehension of the higher order of the universe; that he should not consider even the overmastering love of his heart, separate from the other demands of the spirit, as an infallible guide to the attainment of the supreme good; but that he should constantly seek in the depths of his soul that inner root of understanding where all the separate forces fuse into one living and whole vision of the mind.[62]

When a man's thought process is in accord with a soul thus ordered, its "strivings" should blend into "a single, harmonious sound."

Although the "love of the heart" is but one of the forces of the soul, Kireevsky — with Pascal and, for that matter, Isaac the Syrian — laid particular stress on it. "As long as [the Orthodox believer] believes with his heart," he wrote, "logical reason is harmless to him." No thinking can be "separated from the memory of the inner wholeness of the mind, of that focal point of self-consciousness which is the locus of supreme truth, and where not abstract reason alone, but the sum total of man's intellectual and spiritual forces sets one general seal of authenticity on the thought which confronts reason—just as on Mt. Athos each monastery bears only one part of the seal which, when all its parts are put together at the meeting of the monastic representatives, constitutes the one legal seal of Athos." [63]

One possible interpretation of Kireevsky's idea of "wholeness" is, in the words of Henry Lanz, simply that "the spiritual influences which tended to determine the philosophical aspect of Slavophilism seem to lie in the direction of the Orthodox theological tradition . . . Slavophilism is not a patriotic perversion of German idealism, not even a reaction against modern European rationalism. It is simply and solely a modern continuation of a religious tradition which has been dominating Russian life since the time of Saint Vladimir, and which was temporarily driven into the underworld by the violent reforms of Peter the Great and his successors." [64] This, of course, is much the way Kireevsky himself saw the matter. To buttress this contention, Lanz cited from Isaac the Syrian, and particularly from the correspondence of Maximus the Confessor, concluding that "reason, according to Maximus, is merely the organ of knowledge, whereas the organ of wisdom is the whole soul." [65]

In spite of Lanz's bald and obvious overstatement, his view should not be dismissed out of hand, as Walicki has done.[66] Kireevsky's division of the soul into parts has a strong Christian theological resonance, and in fact the idea can be traced back to

Plato, if not even further into the Greek past. This kind of division of the soul was central to what a Swedish scholar has called the "theological anthropology" of Maximus the Confessor. Man, as Maximus saw him, "is not only composed of body and soul but also of different and distinct 'parts' and powers or faculties of the soul, which in fallen man are contradictory to one another, and in the Christian are thus to be restored to their unity and order." [67] More broadly speaking, no modern student of Slavophilism should fail to take account of the fact that one aspect of the thought of Kireevsky and Khomiakov was the conscious attempt of Orthodox Christians to reestablish living contact with the spiritual sources of their faith, which had become progressively less accessible since the seventeenth century.

Nevertheless, although Lanz may very well be correct about the theological origins of Kireevsky's division of the soul into parts, he misses the social and intellectual context and derivation of Kireevsky's thought completely. He is altogether wrong in denying that Kireevsky developed his ideas in opposition to European rationalism, or that Slavophilism has anything to do with German idealism. Kireevsky did, of course, ultimately reject all the idealist systems, but every aspect of his thought was colored by his rejected first love. And, incidentally, at the end of his life he could still write: "I believe that German philosophy, in combination with that development which it underwent in Schelling's late system, could serve us as the most convenient point of departure on our way from borrowed systems to an independent philosophy, corresponding to the basic principles of ancient Russian culture and capable of subjecting the divided culture of the West to the integrated consciousness of believing reason." [68] And although one may find that Kireevsky and Khomiakov do represent a kind of theological continuity with Paisy Velichkovsky and certain currents of Orthodox theology, the new elements in their thought are more significant than the old. The heavy stress on the collective and the communal relates not to the Orthodox tradition, but primarily, as Walicki has said, to German counterrevolutionary and antirationalist ideology.

Michael Gershenzon's approach could hardly be more different from that of Lanz. Gershenzon tended to interpret "wholeness" in such a way as to minimize the theological, even the religious element, while continuing to insist, curiously enough, that Kireevsky was a "mystic." He ended his essay by relating Kireevsky's ideas about the structure of the soul rather vaguely to later psychological studies of the unconscious.[69] He was nevertheless right to minimize the importance of the "national" aspect of Kireevsky's analysis and to stress the importance of "feeling" in Kireevsky's intellectual formation, the pietistic milieu in which he grew up, the significance of his remarkably close family relations. It is clear that Kireevsky's idea of "wholeness" is related to the intimacy of the world of his family and childhood and a nostalgia for it. One should not, however, lose sight of the fact that the "religiosity" of Kireevsky's last years was far from a mere extension of the "world of feeling" that Gershenzon writes about, a slide from romantic sentimentalism into Christianity. Gershenzon neglects the dour, grim side of Kireevsky, his feelings of duty, failure, and general insufficiency, which accompanied the most specifically "religious" period of his life.

Eberhard Müller has criticized Gershenzon for ignoring Kireevsky's *intentions*. "Wholeness," Müller feels, has a distinct, theological meaning, which must not be lost sight of; Kireevsky was seeking a "higher knowledge," not attempting to recover elements from the unconscious.[70] Müller is of course quite right; when Kireevsky exalted "the heart," he was thinking in terms of Pascal, rather than any kind of "emotionalism" or sentimentalism. But Kireevsky was not Pascal, nor was he a Desert Father. His search for wholeness took place against a backdrop of what he considered the arid and rampant rationalism of his era. And it was by contrast with his experience of "community" — childhood at Dolbino, family life, the intimate circle of friends — that he came to define what rationalism was and meant. One cannot fully understand Kireevsky's thirst for wholeness merely by examining the philosophy books and theological treatises which he read. Kireevsky's hatred of abstract reason originated not in books, but in experience. A man's "intentions" are not always identical with his deepest feelings and impulses.

Andrzej Walicki regards Kireevsky's "integralism" as part and parcel of a sweeping critique of revolutionary rationalism, almost all the elements of which were taken from German romantic and counterrevolutionary thought. Both Walicki and Müller have stressed the similarities between Kireevsky's "integralism" (a term which Müller does not use) and that of Friedrich Schlegel.[71] What Kireevsky called "the union of all the forces of the soul" seems to have been essentially what Schlegel meant by *"die Einheit des Bewusstseyns."* [72]

Walicki has found — in my view quite correctly — that the "convergence" between Kireevsky's views and those of certain German conservatives were due, above all, not to questions of "influence" — although such influences undoubtedly exist — but to similarities in the history and social structure of Russia and Germany.[73] Both countries were visited with an "enlightened despotism," a bureaucratic "revolution from above." Both were economically "backward," relative to England and France; hence, according to Walicki, thinkers in both Russia and Germany were able to analyze developments in the more "progressive" parts of Europe, while remaining vividly aware of the "living elements in the precapitalist social structure."

If one is concerned with Slavophilism as a social movement of primarily Russian significance, Walicki's approach is the most fruitful one to pursue. Nevertheless, it sometimes suffers from a certain schematism — particularly when applied not to the movement, but to the human individuals who composed it. This is probably inevitable in any analysis which is so dependent on the construction of a model or "ideal type." Due to his dependence on the "ideal type," for instance, Walicki is likely to miss the importance of the influence of theology at a certain juncture of Kireevsky's life. In terms of the "ideal type," such an influence is of secondary importance at best. But in terms of the biography of Kireevsky it is important. The man, the idiosyncratic human individual, rooted in a complex, concrete, dense historical tissue, tends to elude Walicki's analysis. The events of a man's life — the suppression of a magazine, a marriage, the death of a child or father — all have an effect, often a profound one, on the development of a man's intellect or his political views; they may mean the accentuation or the distortion of some basic impulse; they give form to the "idea." Intellectual biography, that is to say, is inseparable from biography — in the broadest, deepest sense of the word. Slavophilism is only the thoughts and actions of individual men, however broad the perspective in which it is viewed.

Kireevsky's biography, when all is said and done, is obviously far from a triumphant or even a happy story. This is not only because the last years of his life were shrouded in a gloom which remains, finally, only partly intelligible. His career as a literary critic, his career as a publicist, his career as a philosopher — none of them ever really came off. Even his attempts at fiction tended to remain unfinished. His life was a series of beginnings, full of brillance and promise, but only beginnings after all. Nothing was ever really completed; there was no harvest. And each time he found it more difficult to begin again.

Part of Kireevsky's failure to realize his gifts in the major way that he ought to have may be laid at the door of the Russia of Nicholas I. Kireevsky's life and career might conceivably have been very different had the *European* not been so summarily suppressed. Fundamentally, however, that is to suggest that Kireevsky's life would have been different if the Russia in which he lived had been different, which is not a very illuminating remark.

Certainly the Russian government can not be held entirely responsible for what Kireevsky did not do. Other men of his generation — Herzen, Khomiakov, Belinsky, to name only three — managed to achieve more in the teeth of adversity than did Kireevsky. He was more fragile, sensitive, and easily discouraged than they, more prone to passivity and withdrawal. He lacked will and — in a sense — courage. All three of his contemporaries threw themselves into life in a way (and their ways were very different) that he never could.

Kireevsky's life expresses — with a kind of vivid hopelessness — many of the dilemmas which we find in his work. He was too much of a modern *intelligent* to be able to live happily on the land. His vision of communal social life remained a childhood memory, fed by his own very different experiences of romantic collectivism, or *Gemeinschaft,* among his contemporaries. But these experiences nourished him less and less as his life passed. The Russian peasant was never more for him than a theoretical construction, a stylized figure from a religious pageant. Of the actual men and women who lived on his estate we hear almost nothing — except that they are better off, for the time being, under serfdom. In any event, the Russian peasant, wholly occupied with the grinding struggle for survival, could not possibly have provided an audience for Kireevsky; only in his stubborn refusal to accept technological innovation, perhaps, did he reveal his own hostility to the "new" and to the West.

Roughly the same situation would appear to pertain in the matter of Kireevsky's religious and philosophical views. He had a vision of "integrality," of a human personality untouched by rationalist disintegration, but he was never able to escape from his "Western" way of thinking and perceiving. His study of the

Eastern Fathers provided him only with the vague outlines of a
spirituality which consistently eluded him on the existential level,
which he never understood from within. It may even be that a
more ordinary kind of Christian belief proved beyond him; certainly it was not the firm foundation which enabled him to live
out his days in serenity.

Finally, Kireevsky's Slavophilism remained an ideology man-
qué, for he was never able really to articulate a social role for
himself or for his peers. The gentry as a whole did not perceive
the threat of "Western rationalism," and Kireevsky and his friends
remained isolated "enlighteners," conservative *intelligenty* without an audience. In the West, ideological structures similar to
Slavophilism appealed more directly to the aristocracy, for even
in the nineteenth century these aristocracies were more cohesive
and self-conscious than the Russian gentry, which had originated,
after all, as the creature of the state. Iury Samarin, for instance,
in an essay on Tocqueville, wrote that

> Tocqueville, Montalembert, Riehl,[74] and others, in defending the
> liberty of life and tradition, preferred to address themselves to the
> aristocracy, because, in the annals of Western European history, it
> is the aristocracy above all which has realized a *vital toryism* . . .
> We, by contrast — we address ourselves to the simple people, but
> for the same reason which makes them sympathize with the aris-
> tocracy. That is to say because *with us,* the people has preserved in
> itself the gift of self-sacrifice, the freedom of moral inspiration and
> the respect for tradition. In Russia, the sole shelter of toryism is the
> black hut of the peasant. In our administration, in our university
> lecture halls, blows the dessicating wind of whiggery.[75]

Samarin's toryism, of course, like that of Kireevsky or Khomiakov,
was a merely contemplative relationship with the common people.
None of them were really able to *use* what the peasant had preserved, any more than were the Populists, who radicalized
Slavophilism but were eventually defeated by the same difficulty.

All of them — tories and revolutionaries alike — were eventually forced into elitist positions. There is no question that Slavophiles of Samarin's generation were willing to "accept" the state and all its works (however they hoped to change it) in a way that Kireevsky was not. They grew tired, that is, of merely "addressing the simple people." And even Kireevsky wanted his son to have the option of being "useful" if he so desired, an indication of the degree to which he judged himself to have been merely a voice crying in the wilderness.

Even if Kireevsky was, by his own standards, a failure, he was an important failure for Russian history and culture. Slavophilism was the form in which a cluster of Romantic ideas and anti-modernist impulses were first articulated in Russia, and their influence was deep and pervasive. A whole broad current of Orthodox theology developed from the thinking of Kireevsky and — more directly — Khomiakov; much of contemporary Orthodox writing — and not all of it Russian — centers on the Catholic-Orthodox differences which Kireevsky and Khomiakov first formulated.[76] Russian philosophy, too, has been deeply marked by Slavophile antirationalism. Solov'ev, Berdiaev, Shestov — they and many less significant figures were influenced by (and did battle with) Kireevsky's "integral knowledge." In the area of literature, the most famous figure who was deeply marked by Slavophilism was Fëdor Dostoevsky, whose attitudes toward human reason, the Russian peasant, and the Orthodox Church were all partly formed by the Slavophiles, as well as by their vulgar epigones, the Pan-Slavs. The reason for this continuing influence lies deeper than the genius of individual Slavophile thinkers. The resistance of the Russian society and government to "modernization," industrialization, and social rationalization was to continue up to 1917 and even beyond. The Slavophiles were in the field first, however, and it is only to be expected that others who

wished to combat the enemies that the Slavophiles opposed
would have recourse to some of the weapons which they had
forged.

Perhaps the most important influence of Kireevsky's Slavophilism — and certainly the most obvious — was on Alexander Herzen, and through him on the formation of Russian Populism.
When Herzen first formulated his "Russian Socialism," he did so
by seizing upon a number of the central aspects of Slavophilism
and giving them a consequent and left interpretation. It was the
Slavophiles who first focused attention upon the Russian peasant
and his way of life as providing the key to necessary changes in
Russian life, who first saw his collectivism as an antidote to the
corrosive individualism of the nineteenth century. It was Kireevsky and his friends who conceived of the Russian state as an
alien, oppressive, and "non-Russian" entity, imposed from outside
onto the organic life of the people. It was the Slavophiles who
developed the idea that Russia had a unique destiny, a special
path to the modern world based on communal social institutions
which did not exist in Western Europe. All of these ideas were
transformed by Herzen and his successors and in a somewhat
altered form provided many of the essential tenets of Populism,
particularly in its more naive and romantic manifestations.[77]

The reassertion of the corporate and communal in the social
thought of nineteenth-century Europe came first from the Right,
not from the Left; Herzen's relationship to the Slavophiles in this
respect is typical. The communal ideal which Kireevsky opposed
to the society of his day was destined to have a long and turbulent career, both in Russia and throughout the modern world. The
longing for "community" in industrialized societies is perhaps
even stronger today than in Kireevsky's time; it has certainly
transcended its origins in the European class conflicts of the late
eighteenth century. Even in the Soviet Union today, Slavophilism
and vaguely Slavophile ideas seem to retain an attractive power

for intellectuals. "Old Russia," a student is reported to have said recently, "the *real* old Russia, was outlawed for decades. It was obscured and almost destroyed by an attempt to fit our background and history into Marxist-Leninist slogans. So we grew up nearly rootless in our own country, almost like immigrants." [78] Thus the contemporary Soviet state is regarded much as the Slavophiles regarded the state of Peter I and Nicholas I, while in Western Europe and the United States, "community" has obsessed an entire student generation.

Perhaps the most striking analogues to Russian Slavophilism — and of the most obvious interest to sociologists — are to be found in various non-European cultures which have come in contact with the dynamic and expansive "West" in the last century or so. In various African countries, in China and elsewhere, both traditionalist and radical intellectuals have developed arguments "against the West" remarkably similar to those of Slavophilism.[79] Here we see repeated both the reaffirmation of the traditional culture and a pervasive hostility to the "dehumanizing" social and economic ways of the industrial, bureaucratic West. Whether these protests are more than just a *cri de coeur* remains one of the great questions of our time.

Ivan Kireevsky was certainly not a historian, but he was more keenly aware than any Russian of his day of the great problems which the industrial revolution and the growth of the bureaucratic state were in the process of presenting to nineteenth-century Europeans. These problems received their classic formulations in the writings of the leading sociologists of the late nineteenth and early twentieth centuries — Tönnies, Durckheim, Marx, and Weber. Nor have these problems yet been "solved." In the eyes of many, bureaucracy, political rationalism, and technology still need to be tamed.

Kireevsky's mature writings also relate to the moment in the intellectual history of Europe when Hegelian "rationalism" ceased to satisfy the most searching and thoughtful men of the age. This is one of the most fundamental points made by Eberhard Müller in his extremely erudite book on Kireevsky, and it is one of his differences with Andrzej Walicki, who tends to see Kireevsky in terms of the "classic" European conservatism — largely German — which was so brilliantly anatomized by Karl Mannheim.

There is, however, no fundamental contradiction here. Without engaging in the sort of reductionism that Eberhard Müller and others rightly deplore, one can say that Schelling's attack on what he considered to be Hegel's rationalism is a further development of Adam Müller's and Friedrich Schlegel's criticism of the political and social theory of the Enlightenment. This is not to say that Schelling's philosophy has merely political or social significance. It is to say that a man's philosophy cannot be considered *in vacuo* or solely in relation to other philosophies. Schelling's — and Kireevsky's — search for a kind of Christian empiricism belongs to a specific moment in the history of European society, as well as to a specific moment in the history of European philosophy.

The increasing predominance of Kireevsky's religious preoccupations in the last decade of his life is closely related to changes in the emphasis of his Slavophilism. To an ever greater degree, Kireevsky focused on the deleterious effects of rationalism on the human individual, rather than on "society" — although it should be stressed that this was merely a change in emphasis.

Together with this development, however, we find another and much less fruitful tendency. Kireevsky continued to hope — until the end of his life — that the old Orthodox and communal "principles" of Russia might somehow become the basis for a new civilization. To this extent, he obviously considered that the Russian state and society of his day were part of the "bad" world of modern rationalism. Increasingly, however, the critical force of

Slavophilism ceased to be turned against Russia, and the dichotomy between "rationalism" and "Orthodoxy" inevitably took on a more nationalist tinge. The Russian autocracy was obviously a classic example of the kind of political structure against which Kireevsky's Slavophilism was directed — indeed, an aversion to the autocracy was at the very root of Slavophilism. To exempt Russian institutions from criticism was to move in the direction of an ordinary and vulgar nationalism. This, of course, was one direction in which Slavophilism moved after the death of Kireevsky and Khomiakov.

The reasons for this evolution lie deep in Kireevsky's character and personality, as well as in the events of his life, not least in the timidity and fear with which he regarded the political and social events of the period after he abandoned the *Muscovite*. He was never, of course, a rebel. When the *European* was suppressed, he embodied his criticism of the society of his day in a brilliant and deeply felt idealization of the past. He had no real love for, or understanding of, the "common people" — not for the Russian peasant, let alone the European artisan or factory worker. In the 1840's and 1850's, his fear of revolution in Europe and of peasant insurrection at home grew apace. While he moved from his veiled "social criticism" toward a neo-Romantic religious speculation, he increasingly — in practice — endorsed "things as they were" in Russia. The Russian state — the state of Benckendorff and Nicholas — was now an "Orthodox state." That is why one is tempted to regard the religiosity of Kireevsky's last years — all grim and joyless as it seems to have been — as both a neurotic symptom and the usual companion of a deep fear of social change.

Any straightforward equation must be resisted. And yet, Kireevsky's pathetic dependence on Makary and his retreat from "the world" cannot be explained solely in religious or intellectua' terms. At the end of his life, Kireevsky was obviously prey to overmastering sense of guilt and failure. He was desperately afraid of God's judgment, feeling himself corrupt and unclean in the deepest recesses of his being. Nothing now remained of the optimism with which he had set out on his odyssey in the twenties. Slowly and inexorably it had been drained from his life. Long before his death, he was living, as he put it, only for his children.

Epilogue

In 1856, just after he had observed the solemnities of Lent, Kireevsky set off from Dolbino for St. Petersburg to be with his son, Vasily, while the young man took his final examination at the Lyceum. He spent several days in Moscow on the way, where he saw his mother and brother for what turned out to be the last time.[1] On June 10, Kireevsky contracted cholera in St. Petersburg. The development of the disease was extremely rapid, and, according to Pogodin's biographer, "of a terrible force."[2] On the eve of his departure from Peter's city, he had gone for a stroll on the Nevsky Prospekt and stopped to greet some acquaintance. The weather was warm, he contracted a chill, and "within a few hours he was no more." He died "in the arms of" his son and his Petersburg friends, Venevitinov and Count Komarovsky, to whom he had dedicated "On the Character of European Culture" four years previously. Pogodin set down a few characteristically pompous words of "evaluation" in his diary but then added, simply, "I do not remember when I last wept so bitterly."[3] "What a strange destiny was that of I. V. Kireevsky [Khomiakov wrote to Kireevsky's oldest friend, Koshelëv]. First he was stymied by the censor and the imperial power, and now by death. Our generation has undergone a particularly severe ordeal, as if to test our patience and constancy. Our ranks are thinning; for each of us, life is turning into memory." [4]

Kireevsky was buried at the Optina Monastery. On his grave were written some words from the Wisdom of Solomon: "I loved wisdom and sought her out from my youth . . . Nevertheless, when I perceived that I could not otherwise obtain her, except God should give her me, I prayed unto the Lord and sought him with my whole heart." Peter Kireevsky did not long survive his brother. During the summer he had a "bilious attack" and died in October apparently of jaundice. It was generally said that he died of grief; it is certainly true that his will to live died with his brother, beside whom he was buried at Optina.

Notes
Bibliography
Index

Notes

Introduction

1. See, in particular, the essays by Karl Mannheim, collected in *Essays on Sociology and Social Psychology* (Oxford, 1953) and *Essays on the Sociology of Knowledge* (New York, 1952).

2. This relationship was recognized shortly after Kireevsky's death by the perceptive Russian critic, Apollon Grigor'ev. See his letter to Dostoevsky, pulished in the journal *Epokha*, 1864, no. 6, and reprinted in his *Sochineniia*, I (St. Petersburg, 1876), 632–643.

3. This point is clearly brought out in both Martin Malia, *Alexander Herzen and the Birth of Russian Socialism* (Cambridge, 1961), and Eberhard Müller, *Russischer Intellekt in europäischer Krise: Ivan V. Kireevskij* (Cologne, 1966).

I. Family and Childhood

1. *Russkii arkhiv*, 1877, no. 8, p. 482. The *votchina* was an inherited estate. The *pomestie*, like the Western European benefice, was granted on condition of service.

2. *Stol'nik:* by the seventeenth century, simply a high court rank, just below the *boiarin*. It is a fact of more than metaphorical significance that the Kireevsky family's opposition to the innovations of Peter the Great seems to have been immediate.

3. See Tolycheva, "Rasskazy i anekdoty," *Russkii arkhiv*, 1877, no. 7, pp. 361–368.

4. According to Liaskovsky, this second Kireevsky estate was

"situated on the Little Dry Orlits [Orlik?] River, three versts from its mouth in Orlik. On the left bank, sloping to the south, stands a small country house in the heavy shade of surrounding trees. To the east, on the town side, stretches the great Naugorskaia Road . . . Further up the river, two versts to the west, is the village of Dmitrovskoe-Istomino" (*Brat'ia Kireevskie, zhizn' i trudy ikh* [St. Petersburg, 1899], p. 55).

5. See the account in Tolycheva, "Rasskazy."

6. K. D. Kavelin, *Sobranie sochinenii,* III (St. Petersburg, 1899), 1117.

7. Alexander Peterson, "Cherty starinnogo dvorianskogo byta," *Russkii arkhiv,* 1877, no. 8, pp. 481–482. Peterson was Avdot'ia Petrovna [Iushkova] Elagina's illegitimate half-brother.

8. Alexandre Koyré, "La Jeunesse d'Ivan Kireevski," in *Etudes sur l'histoire de la pensée philosophique en Russie* (Paris, 1950), p. 2.

9. M. O. Gershenzon, *Obrazy proshlogo* (Moscow, 1912), p. 89.

10. N. Koliupanov, *Biografiia Kosheleva* (Moscow, 1889), vol. I, bk. 2, p. 68, quoted in Koyré, *Etudes,* p. 3.

11. "Materialy dlia biografii I. V. Kireevskogo," *Polnoe sobranie sochinenii I. V. Kireevskogo,* ed. M. O. Gershenzon (Moscow, 1911), I, 3.

12. Peterson, "Cherty," p. 480. This tradition survived Vasily Ivanovich. There was schooling for the Kireevsky-Elagin serfs in the 1820's, if not later. See G. N. Parilova and A. D. Soimonov, "P. V. Kireevskii i sobrannye im pesni," *Literaturnoe nasledstvo,* 79 (1968), 46–47.

13. P. I. Bartenev, "Ivan Vasil'evich Kireevskii," *Russkii arkhiv,* 1894, no. 7, p. 332.

14. Peterson, "Cherty," p. 480.

15. *Ibid.,* pp. 479–480. Ivan Ivanovich Khemnitser (1745–1784) was, along with Krylov, the most notable Russian writer of humorous fables.

16. Koyré, *Etudes,* p. 1.

17. Peterson, "Cherty," p. 481.

18. Koyré, *Etudes,* pp. 3–4.

19. Carl v. Seidlitz, *Wasily Andrejewitsch Joukoffsky* (Mitau, 1870), p. 11.

20. Portions of Zhukovsky's voluminous correspondence with

Avdot'ia Petrovna may be found in: *Utkinskii sbornik,* ed. A. E. Gruzinsky (Moscow, 1904); *Russkaia starina,* Jan.–Oct. 1883; S. A. Rachinsky, ed., *Tatevskii sbornik* (St. Petersburg, 1899); V. A. Zhukovskii, edition of the magazine "Russkii bibliofil" (St. Petersburg, [1913?]). See also Parilova and Soimonov, "P. V. Kireevskii," *Literaturnoe nasledstvo,* 79 (1968), esp. 10–17.

21. Koyré, *Etudes,* p. 4.

22. Koliupanov, *Biografiia,* vol. I, bk. 2, p. 3.

23. Kavelin, *Sobranie sochinenii,* III, 1125–1126.

24. Marcelle Ehrhard, *Joukovski et le préromantisme russe* (Paris, 1938), pp. 13–14.

25. Gershenzon, *Obrazy,* p. 89.

26. In a letter of April 5, 1818, Mar'ia Andreevna Moier, Avdot'ia Petrovna's cousin, sent her a ring containing a lock of Dar'ia Vasil'evna's hair; she referred to the dead girl as "our common daughter" (*Utkinskii sbornik,* p. 205).

27. Koliupanov, *Biografiia,* vol. I, bk. 2, pp. 9–10.

28. Gershenzon, *Obrazy,* p. 92. Gershenzon had access to a certain number of unpublished letters of Avdot'ia Petrovna and "more than 200" unpublished letters of Peter Kireevsky. Presumably these are the source of his extremely interesting account of the supernatural "events" in the life of the Kireevsky family.

29. *Ibid.,* pp. 93–94.

30. An excellent account of the whole affair may be found in Ehrhard, *Joukovski,* pp. 141–162.

31. *Ibid.,* p. 142.

32. The ten-year-old Avdot'ia Petrovna, writing to Zhukovsky, then a student in Moscow, was in the habit of referring to him as the "Jupiter of my heart" (Seidlitz, *Joukoffsky,* p. 18).

33. *Utkinskii sbornik,* p. 263.

34. "Vasilii Andreevich Zhukovskii v ego pismakh," *Russkaia starina,* 37 (Jan. 1883), 197–199.

35. The "Dolbino Poems" are in most editions of his poetry. See, for example, Krasnov, ed., *Polnoe sobranie sochinenii* (Moscow and St. Petersburg, 1909), pp. 104–120.

36. See, for example, Gershenzon, *Istoricheskie zapiski* (Moscow, 1910), p. 11. Koyré agrees, but stresses the intellectual debt, a more dubious proposition than Gershenzon's contention that Zhukovsky was

the creator of the "world of feeling" in which Ivan grew up (Koyré, *Etudes,* p. 4). Nevertheless, Ivan is supposed to have "wept with joy" when Zhukovsky sent him his portrait in 1815. Cf. Parilova and Soimonov, "P. V. Kireevskii," p. 14.

37. Ehrhard, *Joukovski,* pp. 293–304.

38. See, for example, Zhukovsky's letter to Avdot'ia Petrovna, Feb. 7/19, 1824, in V. A. *Zhukovskii,* "Russkii bibliofil," pp. 100–103.

39. See his letter of Nov. 1815, in *Utkinskii sbornik,* pp. 18–20.

40. Liaskovsky, *Brat'ia Kireevskie,* p. 1.

41. *Russkaia starina,* 38 (April 1883), 99.

42. *Ibid.,* 37 (March 1883), 674. Sokovnin was from a good gentry family and had been a friend of Zhukovsky and the Turgenev brothers from their student days in Moscow.

43. *Utkinskii sbornik,* pp. 164–170; *Russkaia starina,* 39 (Aug. 1883), 229–235.

44. *Russkaia starina,* 39 (Aug. 1883), 229.

45. Gershenzon, *Obrazy,* pp. 92–93.

46. Quoted in A. A. Saburov, "Dekabrist G. S. Baten'kov," in B. P. Koz'min, ed., *Pis'ma G. S. Baten'kova, I. I. Pushchina i E. G. Tollia* (Moscow, 1936), p. 21. See also N. P. Barsukov, *Zhizn' i trudy M. P. Pogodina,* VIII (St. Petersburg, 1894), 487.

47. On Elagin, see esp. Koyré, *Etudes,* p. 5, and "Materialy dlia biografii I. V. Kireevskogo," pp. 5–6; also G. S. Baten'kov's letter to Peter Kireevsky in *Russkie propilei,* 2 (1916), 51.

48. Quoted in Parilova and Soimonov, "P. V. Kireevskii," p. 17. The "Undine" referred to is probably that of Friedrich de la Motte Fouqué, a writer of the most impeccable romantic credentials. "Lalla Rookh," by Thomas Moore, is a series of oriental tales in verse, connected by a prose narrative. The Sismondi is almost certainly his *De la literature du Midi de l'Europe* (4 vols., Paris, 1813). The Karamzin is of course his famous *Istoriia gosudarstva Rossiiskogo,* all but the final volume of which had appeared by 1824. The concerto is probably by Ferdinand Ries, a second-rate student of Beethoven, but the reference might be to another member of this large and prolific musical family.

49. *Russkaia starina,* 39 (Sept. 1883), 533–541.

50. "Materialy dlia biografii I. V. Kireevskogo," p. 5.

51. *Ibid.,* pp. 4–5.

52. Rachinsky, *Tatevskii sbornik,* pp. 72–73.

II. The Lovers of Wisdom

1. Bartenev, "Avdot'ia Petrovna Elagina," *Russkii arkhiv*, 1887, no. 8, p. 491.

2. On Herzen and the University of Moscow, see Malia, *Herzen*, chap. 4, esp. pp. 57–59. On the university itself at this time, see also D. M. Shchepkin, "Moskovskii universitet v polovine dvadtsatykh godov," *Vestnik Evropy*, 4 (1903), 226–261.

3. D. S. Mirsky, *A History of Russian Literature* (New York, 1960), p. 67. In the bosom of the Elagin family, Merzliakov's classicism was already much criticized in the mid-twenties. Cf. Parilova and Soimonov, "P. V. Kireevskii," p. 19. For a balanced view of Merzliakov's poetry and criticism, see Koliupanov, *Biografiia*, vol. I, bk. 1, pp. 463–470.

4. Alexander Herzen, *Byloe i dumy* (Moscow, 1962), I, 119.

5. On Tsvetaev, see M. N. Tikhomirov, ed., *Istoriia Moskovskogo universiteta* (Moscow, 1955), I, 174–175.

6. On the general subject of Schelling's influence in Russia, see Wsewolod Setschkareff, *Schellings Einfluss in der russischen Literatur der 20er und 30er Jahre des XIX Jahrhunderts* (Berlin, 1939); P. N. Sakulin, *Iz istorii russkogo idealizma. Kniaz' V. F. Odoevskii* (Moscow, 1913); Alexandre Koyré, *La Philosophie et le problème national en Russie au début du XIX siècle* (Paris, 1929). Shorter and particularly valuable are chap. 5, "Schelling and Idealism," in Malia, *Herzen*, and G. V. Florovsky, *Puti russkogo bogosloviia* (Paris, 1937), pp. 237–253.

7. *Sobranie sochineniia I. V. Kireevskogo*, I, 6. See also Koliupanov, *Biografiia*, vol. I, bk. 2, p. 9.

8. Koyré, *La Philosophie*, p. 128.

9. *Ibid.*, pp. 126–136.

10. See, for instance, Kuno Fischer, *Geschichte der neueren Philosophie*, VI (Heidelberg, 1872), 197–200.

11. Schelling, *Ages of the World*, ed. Frederick Bolman (New York, 1942), p. 14.

12. Wilhelm Windelband, *A History of Philosophy*, trans. J. Tufts, II (New York, 1958), 607. One may trace this idea back to Herder's idea that the making of poetry is an "imitation" of God's creation. See his "Über Bild, Dichtung und Fabel," *Sämmtliche Werke*, XV (Berlin, 1888), 526.

13. V. A. Zhukovskii, "Russkii bibliofil," pp. 102–103.

14. See Karl Mannheim, "The History of the Concept of the State as an Organism," in *Essays on Sociology and Social Psychology.*

15. See Setschkareff's discussion of the problem in *Schellings Einfluss,* p. 204.

16. Koyré, *La Philosophie,* esp. pp. 9–32, and Herbert Bowman, *Vissarion Belinski, 1811–1848* (Cambridge, 1954), pp. 15–31. Also Aleksandr Pypin, *Obshchestvennoe dvizhenie v Rossii pri Aleksandre I* (St. Petersburg, 1900).

17. See "Turgot, Baron l'Aulne" in Frank Manuel, *The Prophets of Paris* (Cambridge, Mass., 1962), esp. pp. 26–33.

18. Malia, *Herzen,* pp. 440–441.

19. Mannheim, *Essays on Sociology and Social Psychology,* p. 172.

20. The best short account of the *Obshchestvo liubomudriia* is in Koyré, *La Philosophie,* pp. 37–45, and passim. See also Sakulin, *Iz istorii,* pp. 103–176.

21. Alexander Ivanovich Koshelëv, *Zapiski* (Berlin, 1884), p. 7.

22. Kireevsky, *Sobranie sochinenii,* II, 225.

23. Koshelëv, *Zapiski,* p. 8.

24. *Ibid.,* pp. 8–9.

25. *Ibid.*

26. V. A. Zhukovskii, "Russkii bibliofil," pp. 94–95.

27. *Evgeny Onegin,* VII, 46, quoted in Koyré, *La Philosophie,* p. 34.

28. Koyré, *La Philosophie,* p. 33.

29. M. A. Dmitriev, "Vospominaniia o S. E. Raiche, *Moskovskie vedomosti,* 1855, No. 141, quoted in M. Aronson and S. Reiser, *Literaturnye kruzhki i salony* (Leningrad, 1929), p. 124.

30. S. E. Raich, "Avtobiografiia," *Russkii bibliofil,* 1913, no. 8, pp. 28–30, quoted in Aronson and Reiser, *Literaturnye kruzhki,* p. 123.

31. Barsukov, *Zhizn' Pogodina,* I, 212, quoted in Sakulin, *Iz istorii,* p. 103.

32. By far the best account of the complicated relations between the Raich circle and the *Obshchestvo liubomudriia* is given in Aronson's and Reiser's exemplary work, pp. 265–271.

33. Koyré, *La Philosophie,* p. 37.

34. Koshelëv, *Zapiski,* p. 12.

35. Sakulin, *Iz istorii,* p. 132.

36. Carl Schmitt, *Politische Romantik* (Leipzig, 1925).

37. Malia, *Herzen*, p. 93. See also Peter Scheibert, *Von Bakunin zu Lenin* (Leiden, 1956), pp. 77–78.
38. Koyré, *La Philosophie*, p. 36.
39. *Ibid.*, p. 39.
40. Koshelëv, *Zapiski*, p. 13.
41. *Ibid.*, p. 12, quoted in Koyré, *La Philosophie*, p. 38.
42. Koshelëv, *Zapiski*, p. 12.
43. *Ibid.*, p. 15, quoted in Koyré, *La Philosophie*, p. 38.
44. Müller, *Russischer Intellekt*, p. 5; see also *Russkaia starina*, 40 (1883), 88. For several of Avdot'ia Petrovna's letters on Baten'kov's behalf, see *Russkie propilei*, 2 (1916), 31–32. For a general account of the Elagin family's efforts on Baten'kov's behalf, see Koz'min, *Pis'ma Baten'kova, Pushchina i Tollia*, pp. 36–42.
45. For Avdot'ia Petrovna's letters on behalf of the Iakushkin and Fonvizin families, see *Izvestiia AN SSSR*, otdelenie lituratury i iazyka, 1961, vol. XX, issue 2, p. 144. The author, A. D. Soimonov, has done excellent work on Peter Kireevsky, but exaggerates the "leftness" of the family.
46. *Ibid.*
47. *Literaturnoe nasledstvo*, 58 (1952), 212, 220, quoted in Müller, *Russischer Intellekt*, p. 5.
48. *Izvestiia AN SSSR*, p. 147.
49. Kireevsky, *Sobranie sochinenii*, I, 10.
50. *Ibid.*, p. 11.
51. Gershenzon, *Obrazy*, p. 93.
52. M. Lemke, *Nikolaevskie zhandarmy i literatura* (St. Petersburg, 1909), pp. 67–68.

III. The Literary Aristocracy

1. On Bulgarin's feud with Pushkin and Viazemsky, see, *inter alia*, Sidney Monas, "Šiškov, Bulgarin and the Russian Censorship," in *Harvard Slavic Studies*, 4 (Cambridge, 1957); also his *The Third Section* (Cambridge, 1961), esp. chap. 5; also Gunther Wytrzens, *Pjotr Andreevič Vjazemskij* (Vienna, 1961), passim. See also Barsukov, *Zhizn' Pogodina*, vol. III, chap. 29, for a sample of the polemics of 1830.
2. Evgen'ev–Maksimov, Mordovchenko, Iampol'sky, eds., *Ocherki po istorii russkoi zhurnalistiki i kritiki*, I (Leningrad, 1950), 389.

3. Quoted in Waclaw Lednicki, ed., *Adam Mickiewicz in World Literature* (Berkeley and Los Angeles, 1956), p. 73.

4. Wytrzens, *Vjazemskij*, pp. 115 and 116.

5. See in particular Viazemsky's "O dukhe partii; o literaturnoi aristokratii" in *Polnoe sobranie sochinenii*, II (St. Petersburg, 1879), 156–163.

6. Wytrzens, *Vjazemskij*, p. 115.

7. For an interesting memoir on Pletnëv, see David Magarshack, ed., *Turgenev's Literary Reminiscences* (New York, 1958), pp. 105–116.

8. Karamzin can scarcely be left out entirely, in view of the importance of Arzamas to the subsequent "aristocratic direction." Viazemsky, in "O dukhe partii," p. 157, refers to Karamzin and Dmitriev as "founders of the new school."

9. Viazemsky, "O dukhe partii," p. 156.

10. *Ibid.*, p. 161.

11. Mirsky, *History of Russian Literature*, p. 117.

12. Evgen'ev-Maksimov et al., *Ocherki po istorii russkoi zhurnalistiki*, p. 391.

13. Pushkin, "Opyt otrazheniia nekotorykh neliteraturnykh obvinenii," *Polnoe sobranie sochinenii*, VII (Moscow, 1958), pp. 207–208.

14. Quoted in Monas, *Third Section*, p. 216. It is worth noting that the principal Decembrist journalists, Küchelbecker, Ryleev, and Bestuzhev, all had close ties to the "Poets' Party."

15. Quoted in N. Riasanovsky, *Nicholas I and Official Nationality in Russia* (Berkeley and Los Angeles, 1961), p. 104.

16. Wytrzens, *Vjazemskij*, p. 116. See also D. S. Mirsky, *Pushkin* (New York, 1963), p. 122.

17. On Kireevsky's relations with Polevoi, see N. L. Brodsky, *Literaturnye salony i kruzhki* (Moscow, 1930), pp. 151–154.

18. B. Tomashevsky, *Pushkin*, I (Moscow and Leningrad, 1956), 625.

19. Kireevsky, *Sobranie sochinenii*, II, 26.

20. "These gentlemen, Kireevsky, Somov, and Prince Viazemsky," wrote Polevoi in the first number of the Moscow *Telegraph* for 1930, "talk incessantly of good tone, of the preservation of decency, while at the same time they rail as hard as the others" (quoted in Wytrzens, *Vjazemskij*, p. 112). See also Ksenofont Polevoi's remarks, quoted in Barsukov, *Zhizn' Pogodina*, III, 53–54.

21. See chap. V.

22. "Pis'ma Pogodina k Shevyrëvu," *Russkii arkhiv,* 1882, no. 6, p. 191.

23. D. S. Mirsky, *Pushkin* (New York, 1963), p. 237.

24. Mirsky, *History of Russian Literature,* p. 171.

25. Kireevsky, *Sobranie sochinenii,* II, 17.

26. Ehrhard, *Jouvkovski,* pp. 174–213, passim.

27. A. I. Komarov, "Moskovskii vestnik," in *Ocherki po istorii russkoi zhurnalistiki,* pp. 300–301. Mr. Komarov's essay must be used with caution, as he is embarrassed by Pushkin's association with the "idealist position" of the *Messenger.*

28. On Pushkin's return and interview with Nicholas, see Monas, *Third Section,* pp. 203–204.

29. Komarov, "Moskovskii Vestnik," p. 300.

30. See *Izvestiia AN SSSR,* p. 145.

31. *Ibid.*

32. Barsukov, *Zhizn' Pogodina,* II, 47–48.

33. Monas, *Third Section,* p. 208.

34. Komarov, "Moskovskii Vestnik," p. 301.

35. Quoted in Monas, *Third Section,* pp. 208–209.

36. See, for instance, Pushkin's review of Kireevsky's "Survey of Russian Literature in 1829" in *Polnoe sobranie sochinenii,* VII (1958), 108.

37. As Müller has pointed out; see *Russischer Intellekt,* p. 80.

38. Kireevsky, *Sobranie sochinenii,* II, 1.

39. *Ibid.,* p. 4.

40. *Ibid.,* p. 5.

41. *Ibid.,* p. 6.

42. *Ibid.,* p. 11.

43. *Ibid.,* pp. 10–11.

44. *Ibid.,* p. 8.

45. *Ibid.,* p. 12.

46. *Ibid.*

47. Pushkin, *Polnoe sobranie sochinenii,* VII, 108.

48. *Literaturnoe nasledstvo,* 58 (1952), 108.

49. Tomashevsky, *Pushkin,* I, 639–640.

50. Quoted in Bowman, *Belinski,* p. 20.

51. See his letter to Koshelëv, Oct. 1, 1828, *Sobranie sochinenii,* I, 12.

52. Müller notes that Kireevsky used the word *slovesnost'* in his title (as distinguished from *literatura* in the narrower sense), widening his rubric to include works like Karamzin's *History* (Müller, *Russischer Intellekt,* p. 58.)

53. The Russian "almanacs" were annuals containing miscellaneous prose, poetry, and articles of general interest. The most illustrious almanac of the period was Del'vig's *Northern Flowers* (*Severnye tsvety*).

54. Kireevsky, *Sobranie sochinenii,* II, 14.

55. *Ibid.,* p. 17.

56. N. S. Artsybashev's attack is the principal such piece.

57. Ivan is here referring to Polevoi, who found no system or "organic development" in Karamzin's primarily political narrative. One might have expected Kireevsky to show somewhat more sympathy for this view. See Barsukov, *Zhizn' Pogodina,* II, 334–338, and Müller, *Russischer Intellekt,* p. 8. A good summary of Polevoi's article is contained in S. Vesin, *Ocherki istorii russkoi zhurnalistiki* (St. Petersburg, 1881), pp. 48–52.

58. Kireevsky, *Sobranie sochinenii,* II, 23.

59. Mirsky, *Pushkin,* pp. 115–116.

60. Kireevsky, *Sobranie sochinenii,* II, 27.

61. Bowman, *Belinski,* p. 16.

62. See René Wellek, *A History of Modern Criticism,* vol. II: *The Romantic Age* (New Haven, 1955), on Jean Paul, the Schlegels, and Schiller, esp. pp. 11–14 and 102–103.

63. In the autumn of 1830, Pushkin undertook a long article on his critics, most of which remained unpublished. In it he wrote: "young Kireevsky, in his full and eloquent survey of our literature, used this recherché expression in speaking of Del'vig. His antique muse is sometimes clothed in the sheepskin jacket of modern melancholy. A laughable expression of course. Why not simply say: sometimes, in the poems of Del'vig, the melancholy of modern poetry is evoked? Our journalists, about whom Mr. Kireevsky has spoken rather impolitely, rejoiced, seized this sheepskin jacket, tore it to pieces, and they have been flaunting it now for a whole year, to amuse their public." See Pushkin, "Oproverzhenie na kritiki," *Polnoe sobranie sochinenii,* VII, 178–179.

64. Kireevsky, *Sobranie sochinenii,* II, 35.

65. *Ibid.,* p. 38.

66. A good many writers, Koyré and Walicki among them, have linked Kireevsky and Tocqueville, implying that they had something of a common vision of Russia and America in relation to Europe. See Eberhard Müller's sensible remarks on this doubtful proposition (*Russischer Intellekt*, p. 117).

67. See their exchange of letters in *Ostaf'evskii arkhiv kniazei Viazemskikh*, III (St. Petersburg, 1899), 202–203, 208.

68. Pushkin, *Polnoe sobranie sochinenii*, VII, 118–119.

69. Tomashevsky, *Pushkin*, II, 140–141.

70. Kireevsky, *Sobranie sochinenii*, I, 17.

71. *Ibid.*, I, 49. See also *Ostaf'evskii arkhiv* (notes to the third volume, published separately in 1908, p. 564). Kireevsky was in Germany when Bulgarin's blast appeared. He received it with equanimity, almost with satisfaction, but thought it would be "degrading" to reply. See *sobranie sochinenii*, I, 30.

72. Lemke, *Nikolaevskie zhandarmy i literatura* (St. Petersburg, 1909), p. 270. Lemke believes that Bulgarin's campaign against Zhukovsky resulted in a certain imperial coldness toward the poet in 1830. Zhukovsky wrote to Nicholas on March 30 of that year, complaining of Bulgarin, and observing that "Bulgarin would proclaim it from the housetops, if only Kireevsky would write me some kind of liberal letter which would become known to the government" (Lemke, *Nikolaevskie zhandarmy*, p. 274).

73. Lemke, *Nikolaevskie zhandarmy*, pp. 271–273.

74. Koyré, *La Philosophie*, pp. 166–167.

75. Andrzej Walicki, *W kręgu konserwatywnej utopii* (Warsaw, 1964), p. 100.

76. See N. Riasanovsky, *Russia and the West in the Teaching of the Slavophiles* (Cambridge, 1952), pp. 78–82, and his *Nicholas I*, pp. 105–115. Riasanovsky describes these differences, which remain, in his accounts, mere differences in opinion.

77. Walicki, *W kręgu*, pp. 100–101.

78. Kireevsky, *Sobranie sochinenii*, I, 11.

79. *Ibid.*, II, 148–149.

80. One such quarrel is described in Barsukov, *Zhizn' Pogodina*, II, 189–190. See also "Pis'ma Pogodina k Shevyrëvu," *Russkii arkhiv*, 1882, no. 5, p. 79.

81. See Richard Pipes' *Karamzin's Memoir on Ancient and Modern Russia* (Cambridge, 1959), and Hans Rogger's essay on the Russian

"right" in Hans Rogger and Eugen Weber, eds., *The European Right* (Berkeley and Los Angeles, 1966), pp. 447–453.

82. Barsukov, *Zhizn' Pogodina*, II, 234–264. See also Müller, *Russischer Intellekt*, pp. 6–8. A good summary of Artsybashev's article and a sample of the ensuing polemic is contained in Vesin, *Ocherki*, pp. 29–43.

83. Barsukov, *Zhizn' Pogodina*, II, 250.

84. See Kireevsky's letter to Pogodin, ca. Nov. 1, 1827, in *Literaturnoe nasledstvo*, 16/18 (1934), 695. In 1829, the fortunes of the *Messenger* were at such a low ebb that Pogodin considered turning it over to Kireevsky, Baratynsky, and Iazykov.

85. Barsukov, *Zhizn' Pogodina*, II, 189.

86. *Ibid.*, p. 403, cited in Müller, *Russischer Intellekt*, p. 7.

87. Kireevsky, *Sobranie sochinenii*, II, 216.

88. *Ibid.*, p. 217. In a letter which reached Kireevsky while he was in St. Petersburg, Pogodin accused him of having been overcome by a "fear of praising the plebeians and a longing to please the aristocrats," as well as revealing a "boundless self-love." See Barsukov, *Zhizn' Pogodina*, III, 57ff, quoted in Müller, *Russischer Intellekt*, p. 10. The fact that Kireevsky even "praised" Polevoi was, in Pogodin's view, the last straw. "How he piles it on," he confided bitterly to his diary on Jan. 1, 1830 (Barsukov, *Zhizn' Pogodina*, III, 55).

89. Pogodin, like Bulgarin, believed in a "democratic" monarchy. See Riasanovsky, *Nicholas I*, p. 143.

90. Lednicki, "Mickiewicz's Stay in Russia," in W. Lednicki, ed., *Mickiewicz in World Literature*, p. 33. See also Gleb Struve, "Mickiewicz in Russia," *Slavonic and East European Review*, 26 (1947–48), 126–145.

91. According to Gleb Struve, Kireevsky's poem "was first published in Latin characters in the notes to the 1872 French edition of Mickiewicz's works, and then, in 1874, in *Russkii arkhiv*." Cf. Struve, "Mickiewicz in Russian Translations," in Lednicki, *Michiewicz in World Literature*, p. 149. The poem is also reprinted in Gershenzon's 1911 edition of Kireevsky's *Sobranie sochinenii*, II, 210.

92. A. E. Gruzinsky, ed., *Utkinskii sbornik*, pp. 48–49.

93. In a typical laconic diary entry, Pogodin noted on August 23 that Kireevsky was "probably in love" (Barsukov, *Zhizn' Pogodina*, II, 309).

94. *Utkinskii sbornik*, p. 50.

95. Kireevsky also intended to spend considerable time in Paris. Pogodin wrote to Shevyrëv on Oct. 20, 1829, that Ivan was to be the *Messenger's* Paris correspondent ("Pis'ma Pogodina k Shevyrëvu," *Russkii arkhiv*, 1882, no. 5, p. 117).

IV. Germany

1. For further information on Russian students in Germany, see D. Tschijewskij, "Hegel in Russland," in *Hegel bei den Slawen* (Bad Homburg, 1961), passim, and Scheibert, *Von Bakunin zu Lenin*, esp. pp. 79–92.
2. Kireevsky, *Sobranie sochinenii*, I, 14–15.
3. Kireevsky, *Sobranie sochinenii*, I, 16.
4. Gruzinsky, *Utkinskii sbornik*, p. 51. The journal appears to have been largely the work of the younger Elagin children; whether it contained articles or poems by Ivan or Peter is not clear.
5. Kireevsky, *Sobranie sochinenii*, I, 17.
6. Nikolai Matveevich Rozhalin (1805–1833) was a close friend of Ivan and Peter from the early 1820's. He was one of the "Young Men of the Archives" and collaborated with Pogodin on the Moscow *Messenger*. He translated *Das Leiden des jungen Werthers* (Moscow, 1829), and then went to Germany as the tutor of General Kaisarov's children. Avdot'ia Petrovna provided him with considerable financial assistance, and he left the Kaisarov family to hear lectures at the University of Munich. He contracted tuberculosis and, after a stay in Rome, returned to Moscow, where he died early in 1833. Selections from his correspondence may be found in *Russkii arkhiv*, 1906, no. 2, pp. 221–259, and *ibid.*, 1909, no. 8, pp. 563–606.
7. Kireevsky, *Sobranie sochinenii*, I, 18.
8. *Ibid.*
9. See *Literaturnoe nasledstvo*, 58 (1952), 258, for an eyewitness account of the two evenings.
10. Kireevsky, *Sobranie sochinenii*, I, pp. 19–20.
11. The "bearcub" was Peter Kireevsky. Zhukovsky's letter is in *Utkinskii sbornik*, pp. 49–50. The greater part—although one very interesting conversation about Natal'ia Arbeneva is deleted — appears in Kireevsky's *Sobranie sochinenii*, I, 20–21.
12. Kireevsky, *Sobranie sochinenii*, I, 26. In *Russkii arkhiv*, 1907, no. 1, pp. 56–108, Ivan's letters from Munich are printed in a more

complete form, with many helpful notes by Bartenev, the editor of the journal. In his edition, Gershenzon has left out a good deal of interesting material of a personal nature.

13. Kireevsky, *Sobranie sochinenii,* I, 27. On Gans, see Hans Günther Reissner's biography, *Eduard Gans* (Tübingen, 1965). This volume is only moderately useful for the student of Gans's Hegelianism, however. By contrast with the unpopular historians, Gans drew about 1,500 students in the winter of 1830–1831 (Reissner, *Gans,* p. 132). See also Scheibert, *Von Bakunin zu Lenin,* pp. 21–23, for Gans's impact on visiting Russian students.

14. Kireevsky, *Sobranie Sochinenii,* I, 33, quoted in Müller, *Russischer Intellekt,* p. 15.

15. Kireevsky, *Sobranie sochinenii,* I, 34.

16. *Ibid.,* p. 27.

17. *Ibid.,* p. 28.

18. Eleven chapters of Barth's *Die protestantische Theologie im 19. Jahrhundert* (Zurich, 1946), have been translated into English as *Protestant Thought: From Rousseau to Ritschl* (New York, 1959), which includes his brilliant chapter on Schleiermacher. There is a good, brief introduction to Schleiermacher in Franz Schnabel, *Deutsche Geschichte im neunzehnten Jahrhundert* (Freiburg, 1965), V, 143–147. For a different, and much less critical view of Schleiermacher, see Paul Tillich, *Perspectives on Nineteenth and Twentieth Century Protestant Theology* (New York, 1967), pp. 90–114.

19. Kireevsky, *Sobranie sochinenii,* I, 32.

20. See the conclusion of his essay on Schleiermacher in *Protestant Thought.*

21. Kireevsky, *Sobranie sochinenii,* I, 34.

22. *Ibid.,* p. 35.

23. *Ibid.,* p. 36. The German passages may be translated as follows: "The professor would like to know [the date] in advance, since other people will also be invited"; and, "Yes indeed! You may well be right, but your opinion relates rather to Schelling's than to Hegel's system."

24. *Ibid.,* pp. 28–29.

25. *Ibid.*

26. *Ibid.,* p. 48.

27. For similar complaints by Peter (who was, however, a good

deal more charitable than Ivan), see his letters in *Russkii arkhiv,* 1905, no. 5, pp. 113–174, passim.

28. *Ibid.,* p. 136.

29. On Bakunin in Germany, see *Michael Bakunins Sozial-politischer Briefwechsel mit Alexander Iw. Herzen und Ogarjow* (Stuttgart, 1895), p. 5; on Khomiakov, see his *Sobranie sochinenii,* VIII, 9, quoted in Janet Vaillant, "Encountering the West: The Ideological Responses of Aleksei S. Khomiakov and Leopold S. Senghor" (Ph.D. diss. Harvard, 1969), p. 35.

30. Kireevsky, *Sobranie sochinenii,* I, 25. Kireevsky may be referring, *inter alia,* to Constantine Nevolin, a graduate of the Moscow Theological Academy, and subsequently a professor at the University of Kiev.

31. *Ibid.,* p. 28.

32. "Pëtr Vasil'evich Kireevskii: Ego pis'ma," *Russkii arkhiv,* 1905, no. 5, pp. 129, 132.

33. Koyré, *Etudes,* p. 9.

34. See, for example, the July letter in *Sobranie sochinenii,* I, 46–48.

35. *Ibid.,* p. 42. Several months earlier, Avdot'ia Petrovna wrote to Shevyrëv that "having seen Ivan off, nothing remained to me either within or without my soul. My whole life now consists in these blessed little messengers, the receiving and dispatching of which are the only interesting times in my life" (Barsukov, *Zhizn' Pogodina,* III, 60).

36. Kireevsky, *Sobranie sochinenii,* I, 43.

37. *Ibid.,* p. 48.

38. *Russkii arkhiv,* 1905, no. 5, pp. 142–143.

39. *Ibid.,* pp. 137–143. Sobolevsky, Peter reported, would sometimes "meow like a cat, for over us lives Boissère, renowned for his works on Gothic architecture, and the loud meowing must be audible to him, which drives Rozhalin to distraction. At first he was able to stop his noise with a bottle of wine, but eventually even that did not help, and Sobolevsky, by threatening to begin crying, has achieved unlimited power over him."

40. *Russkii arkhiv,* 1909, no. 7, pp. 482–484.

41. *Ibid.,* p. 491.

42. Kireevsky, *Sobranie sochinenii,* I, 50–51.

43. Bulgarin published, in #94 of the *Northern Bee,* a letter about

the suspicious number of young Russians "in foreign parts," giving French journalists "information about Russia." This rather clumsy and vague accusation of subversive activity was rebutted by Shevyrëv in the October 3, 1830, *Literary Gazette*. When Kireevsky wrote to Sobolevsky in Turin to say that he was returning to Russia, he added a postscript: "Do not think that the cause of my return is the swinishness of Bulgarin" (*Russkii arkhiv*, 1909, no. 7, p. 492).

44. See his letter in *Russkaia starina*, 115 (August 1903), 452–454.

45. See his letter of July, *Sobranie sochinenii*, I, 49.

46. *Ibid.*, p. 47.

47. *Ibid.*, pp. 41–42.

48. See Kireevsky's letters, *Sobranie sochinenii*, I, 43–53, passim.

49. Roderick E. McGrew, *Russia and the Cholera, 1823–1832* (Madison and Milwaukee, 1965), pp. 43, 76.

50. In a letter written in October, the word "plague" (*chuma*) is used to refer to the epidemic. See Kireevsky's *Sobranie sochinenii*, I, 55.

51. "Pis'ma Pogodina k Shevyrëvu," *Russkii arkhiv*, 1882, no. 6, p. 178.

52. Koyré, *Etudes*, pp. 8–9.

53. Walicki, *W kręgu*, pp. 101–102.

54. Müller, *Russischer Intellekt*, p. 16.

55. Kireevsky, *Sobranie sochinenii*, I, 48. On June 29, Ivan wrote to his family that he doubted whether it was worthwhile sending a copy of Schelling's lectures to Moscow, "since the mountain has brought forth a mouse. In sum, it appears that, over against the past of his system, there is not much new" (*ibid.*, p. 46).

V. *The European*

1. Herzen, *Byloe i dumy*, I, 476.

2. Malia, *Herzen*, pp. 168–172.

3. Bowman, *Belinski*, p. 82. See also Belinsky's letter to Ivanov (August 7, 1837). Belinsky justifies "acquiescence" to the external world by a "doctrine of withdrawal into the self, in safe seclusion from vulgar actuality" (Bowman, *Belinski*, p. 94).

4. Quoted in E. H. Carr, *Michael Bakunin* (New York, 1961), p. 69.

5. "Pis'ma Pogodina k Shevyrëvu," *Russkii arkhiv*, 1882, no. 3, p. 184, quoted in Müller, *Russischer Intellekt*, p. 16.

6. *Russkaia starina*, 118 (1904), 205, quoted in Müller, *Russischer Intellekt*, p. 16.

7. Nevertheless, Kireevsky did write a prose farce (with N. M. Iazykov) at this time, called *The Princess of Babylon*, and several other rather frivolous pieces, which were performed by members of the family. See Kireevsky, *Sobranie sochinenii*, I, 59.

8. On Del'vig's death and the demise of the *Literary Gazette*, see N. L. Stepanov, "Literaturnaia gazeta," in Evgen'ev-Maksimov et al., *Ocherki po istorii russkoi zhurnalistiki*, I, esp. 386–387.

9. In a letter to Zhukovsky on October 6, 1831, Kireevsky wrote that if Pushkin decided to put out a journal himself the *European* would be unnecessary. See Kireevsky, *Sobranie sochinenii*, II, 224–225.

10. Barsukov, *Zhizn' Pogodina*, III, 367. Oddly enough, another *European* was coming into existence at almost precisely the same time: that of the Saint-Simonian, Philippe-Joseph-Benjamin Buchez. There seems to be no connection between his journal and Kireevsky's. See H. J. Hunt, *Le Socialisme et le romantisme en France* (Oxford, 1935), pp. 83–93.

11. A. I. Turgenev, *Khronika russkogo. Dnevniki (1825–26)* (Moscow and Leningrad, 1964), p. 468.

12. Kireevsky had only gradually abandoned the idea of going abroad again.

13. Kireevsky, *Sobranie sochinenii*, II, 224–225.

14. On October 26, Kireevsky wrote to Shevyrëv, informing him of the birth of the *European*. "The chief goal," he said, "will consist in subscribing to *almost all* the foreign literary journals and choosing from them what is most interesting, and thus bringing about a rapprochement between our literature and foreign literature" (*Golos minuvshogo*, July 1914, p. 221).

15. Rachinsky, *Tatevskii sbornik*, pp. 21–22. Rachinsky gives 52 letters from Baratynsky, all between 1829 and 1833. Of these, 28 are reprinted in E. A. Boratynsky, *Stikhotvoreniia. Poemy. Proza. Pis'ma* (Moscow, 1951).

16. Other hoped-for contributors included Zhukovsky, Baratynsky, Iazykov, Khomiakov, Odoevsky, Viazemsky, Shevyrëv, and Peter Kireevsky. Even Pogodin was not excluded.

17. One of Pushkin's literary pseudonyms.

18. Pushkin, *Polnoe sobranie sochinenii*, XIV (1941), 238. It would appear that Kireevsky was quite friendly with Pushkin at this time, for Kireevsky was one of the dozen or so who attended Pushkin's bachelor dinner. See P. I. Bartenev, *Rasskazy o Pushkine* (Moscow, 1925), p. 53.

19. See Iazykov's correspondence with his friend, Komovsky, in St. Petersburg: "Iz neizdannoi perepiski N. M. Iazykova," *Literaturnoe nasledstvo*, 19–21 (1935), 33–142. See also Müller, *Russischer Intellekt*, pp. 151–152.

20. See Pushkin's letter in J. Thomas Shaw, trans. and ed., *The Letters of Alexander Pushkin* (Bloomington and Philadelphia, 1963), II, 534–535.

21. *Literaturnoe nasledstvo*, 58 (1952), 106–107.

22. *Utkinskii sbornik*, p. 54.

23. *Zven'ia*, IX (1951), 251.

24. Müller, *Russischer Intellekt*, p. 152.

25. *Utkinskii sbornik*, p. 54.

26. *Russkaia starina*, 118 (1904), 216.

27. Arnold Hauser, *The Social History of Art* (New York, 1958), IV, 4. George Lichtheim, in *The Origins of Socialism*, views 1830 in much the same way. He also notes the closeness of the romantic Left of 1830 to the conservative, romantic critics of the revolution, noting that the former "reacted to the new social environment in a manner determined by modes of thought proper to a pre-industrial culture. In particular, that generation showed an inclination to identify the critique of capitalism as a system of production with the rejection of industrialism as such. There was also a good deal of confusion over the role of science and in particular a tendency to dismiss economic reasoning as 'abstract,' by comparison with the greater concreteness of historical or literary perception. Lastly, the industrial revolution and the French Revolution were conflated into a single phenomenon: a challenge to what was sometimes described as a Christian social order." See *The Origins of Socialism* (New York and Washington, 1969), p. 5.

28. Quoted in E. T. Hobsbawm, *The Age of Revolution* (New York, 1964), p. 317.

29. Quoted in René Wellek, *A History of Modern Criticism*, vol. III: *The Age of Transition* (New Haven, 1965), p. 196.

30. See Eberhard Müller, *Russischer Intellekt*, passim.

31. Herzen, *Polnoe sobranie sochinenii i pisem*, ed. M. K. Lemke, III (Petrograd, 1919), 148.

32. Only the first half was published in 1831. The entire article is in the *Sobranie sochinenii*, I, 85–108.

33. As Müller puts it, ". . . he formulates his diagnosis of the times not only in his own contributions, but indirectly in the *European* as a whole . . . through a lens, the viewpoint and horizon of which were of truly European scope" (*Russischer Intellekt*, p. 174).

34. Kireevsky, *Sobranie sochinenii*, I, 90.

35. *Ibid.*, p. 91.

36. *Ibid.*, p. 92.

37. *Ibid.*

38. *Ibid.*, pp. 93–94.

39. Kireevsky, *Sobranie sochinenii*, I, 94. Eberhard Müller (*Russischer Intellekt*, pp. 209–210) suggests that Kireevsky's stress on religion as a "social" phenomenon was inspired by Saint-Simonian ideas on the subject. This is very likely indeed, although Kireevsky's words make one think of Herder as well. While Ivan never wrote anything much about Saint-Simon, his brother Peter produced an interesting article on Saint-Simon's life and doctrine at about this time; unfortunately only the first few pages have survived (see *Literaturnoe nasledstvo*, 79 [1968], 33–38). One should also remember that the question of religion and "society" was generally "in the air" at this time — one need only mention Lamennais, for instance. It is thus risky to attempt to locate the "source" of Kireevsky's ideas too precisely.

40. *Ibid.*, pp. 95–96.

41. Koyré, *La Philosophie*, p. 177.

42. Kireevsky, *Sobranie sochinenii*, I, 103.

43. See above, pp. 69–70.

44. Kireevsky, *Sobranie sochinenii*, I, 103.

45. *Ibid.*, p. 104.

46. *Ibid.*, pp. 107–108.

47. Walicki, *W kręgu*, p. 101.

48. N. Golitsyn, "Chaadaev i E. A. Sverbeeva," *Vestnik Evropy*, bks. I–IV (Petersburg, 1918), pp. 233–250. See also M. K. Azadovsky, ed., *Pis'ma P. V. Kireevskogo k N. M. Iazykovu* (Moscow-Leningrad, 1935), pp. 15–16.

49. Koyré, *La Philosophie*, pp. 192–193.

50. Müller, *Russischer Intellekt,* pp. 120–129.

51. Kireevsky, *Sobranie sochinenii,* I, 107.

52. Walicki, *W kręgu,* p. 105. Miliukov had already made essentially the same point. See his *Glavnyia techeniia russkoi istoricheskoi mysli* (Moscow, 1898), pp. 373–374.

53. Walicki, *W kręgu,* p. 106.

54. Kireevsky, *Sobranie sochinenii,* II, 41.

55. Müller gives several examples of the emendations and deletions of texts in *Russischer Intellekt,* pp. 153–154.

56. *Heinrich Heines Sämtliche Werke,* VI (Leipzig, 1912), 57–58, quoted in Müller, *Russischer Intellekt,* p. 156.

57. Müller's descriptive summary of the contents of the first two booklets of the *European* is exemplary (Müller, *Russischer Intellekt,* pp. 152–174).

58. Müller, *Russischer Intellekt,* p. 160.

59. Quoted in Hobsbawm, *Age of Revolution,* p. 163.

60. Walicki, *W kręgu,* p. 105.

61. Kireevsky, *Sobranie sochinenii,* II, 58–61.

62. *Ibid.,* pp. 164–179.

63. Karl Löwith, *From Hegel to Nietzsche* (New York, Chicago, San Francisco, 1964), p. 116.

64. Quoted in Paul C. Hayner, *Reason and Existence: Schelling's Philosophy of History* (Leiden, 1967), pp. 125–126.

65. Kireevsky, *Sobranie sochinenii,* I, 46.

66. Löwith, *From Hegel to Nietzsche,* pp. 115–121.

67. For an explicitly political interpretation of Stahl's attack on Hegel, see Herbert Marcuse, *Reason and Revolution* (Boston, 1960), pp. 360–373.

VI. Suppression

1. As Kireevsky's friend M. A. Maksimovich put it, "Kireevsky was deeply stricken by this failure in the area of journalistic activity; he looked upon it as the best way to be useful to his country, prepared himself for it, as for life's most sacred enterprise, and this activity was supported by the friendly collaboration of people whose esteem and approval he prized more highly than the glitter of success; this activity was suddenly broken off, just as it was getting under way" (quoted in Barsukov, *Zhizn' Pogodina,* IV, 9).

2. Gershenzon, *Istoricheskie zapiski*, pp. 6–7.

3. *Letters of Alexander Pushkin*, II, 545–546. Pushkin refers to "The War of the Mice and the Frogs" as "Stepanida the Mouse," after one of the characters.

4. Lemke, *Nikolaevskie zhandarmy*, p. 73.

5. *Ibid.*, p. 73.

6. *Ibid.*, p. 68.

7. *Ibid.*

8. *Ibid.*, pp. 68–69.

9. *Ibid.*, p. 69.

10. *Ibid.*, pp. 70–71.

11. Monas, *Third Section*, p. 153.

12. *Letters of Alexander Pushkin*, II, 553.

13. Liaskovsky, *Brat'ia Kireevskie*, p. 39.

14. Lemke, *Nikolaevskie zhandarmy*, p. 73.

15. *Ibid.*

16. *Literaturnoe nasledstvo*, 19–20 (1935), 70.

17. For the sequence of events, on the government side, see Barsukov, *Zhizn' Pogodina*, IV, 7.

18. *Ibid.*, pp. 10–11.

19. *Ibid.*, p. 10.

20. Liaskovsky, *Brat'ia Kireevskie*, p. 40.

21. Lemke, *Nikolaevskie zhandarmy*, pp. 75–76.

22. *Ibid.*, p. 75.

23. Liaskovsky, *Brat'ia Kireevskie*, pp. 38–39.

24. A. V. Nikitenko, *Dnevnik v trëkh tomakh*, I (Leningrad, 1955), 114. The remark also appears in Barsukov, *Zhizn' Pogodina*, IV, 9. All sorts of rumors were afoot in Moscow about Ivan's fate. Pogodin, for example, wrote in his diary on February 15: "They have suppressed the *European*. Kireevsky is in the fortress and Aksakov is in the guardhouse . . ." (Barsukov, *Zhizn' Pogodina*, IV, 7).

25. *Letters of Alexander Pushkin*, II, 547.

26. Rachinsky, *Tatevskii sbornik*, pp. 40–41.

27. See Viazemsky's letters to his wife in *Zven'ia*, IX (1951), esp. 251, 284, 286–287, 307–308, 320, 407. See also Viazemsky's letter to I. I. Dmitriev on the subject of "political" journals in Russia, in Barsukov, *Zhizn' Pogodina*, IV, 10.

28. Barsukov, *Zhizn' Pogodina*, IV, 8. See also "Pis'ma Pogodina k Shevyrëvu," *Russkii arkhiv*, 1882, no. 6, p. 196.

29. Gofman, M. L. "K zapreshcheniiu 'Evropeitsa' " (On the suppression of the "European") *Blagonamerennyi,* no. 1 (1926), pp. 143–146.

30. *Zven'ia,* IX, 320.

31. *Letters of Alexander Pushkin,* II, 553.

32. Gruzinsky, *Utkinskii sbornik,* p. 56.

33. *Ibid.*

34. The "Mémoire" is reprinted in M. O. Gershenzon, ed., *Sochineniia i pis'ma P. Ia. Chaadaeva* (Moscow, 1913), I, 335–341.

35. *Oeuvres choisies de Pierre Tchadaief, publiées pour la première fois par le p. Gagarin, de la Compagnie de Jésus* (Paris, 1862).

36. Quoted in *Sochineniia i pis'ma P. Ia. Chaadaeva,* I, 431.

37. *Sobranie sochinenii,* II, 232.

38. *Sochineniia i pis'ma P. Ia. Chaadaeva,* I, 335.

39. *Ibid.,* p. 338.

40. Lemke, *Nikolaevskie zhandarmy,* p. 76.

41. Koshelëv discusses Kireevsky's attitude — his fear of radicalism or "precipitate" action — and appears to be talking about the early thirties. See his "Moi vospominaniia ob A. S. Khomiakove," *Russkii arkhiv,* 1879, No. 11, p. 267.

42. Koyré, *La Philosophie,* p. 192.

VII. The "Conversion" of Ivan Kireevsky

1. Gruzinsky, *Utkinskii sbornik,* p. 55.

2. See above, chap. III.

3. *Utkinskii sbornik,* p. 56.

4. *Ibid.,* p. 50.

5. M. Gershenzon, *Obrazy,* p. 113. See also Kireevsky's jubilant letter to his stepfather in his *Sobranie sochinenii,* II, 228. In the mid-1840's, Natal'ia Petrovna suddenly began to worry about her husband's "rank." She pestered Pogodin and others to help Kireevsky's promotion along. Pogodin's biographer noted pompously — but accurately enough — that "self-love was alien to his soul, but not to that of his wife" (see Barsukov, *Zhizn' Pogodina,* V, 12).

6. *Utkinskii sbornik,* pp. 63–64. The property division was traumatic for everybody concerned. It apparently underlined Aleksei Aleksandrovich Elagin's financial dependence on his wife, and terrible quarrels ensued. Avdot'ia Petrovna took refuge with Peter and seriously con-

templated leaving her husband. See the family letters in Gershenzon, ed., *Russkie propilei*, I (Moscow, 1915), 161–164.

7. *Russkii arkhiv*, 1886, No. 3, p. 335.

8. A. V. Stankevich, *T. N. Granovskii i ego perepiska* (Moscow, 1897), II, 184.

9. Printed in the *Sobranie sochinenii*, I, 285–286.

10. *Ibid.*, p. 285.

11. Victor Cousin was a very popular lecturer at the University of Paris and probably the most successful popularizer of various systems of German idealism. He was much read in Russia, but among those who had drunk from the fountainhead, like Kireevsky, he was little esteemed. See Koyré, *La Philosophie*, p. 132.

12. Filaret had been for some time Natal'ia Petrovna's confessor.

13. *Sobranie sochinenii*, II, 225, cited in E. Müller, *Russischer Intellekt*, p. 154.

14. *Sobranie sochinenii*, II, 226.

15. Kavelin, *Sobranie Sochinenii*, III, 1120.

16. Peter K. Christoff, *An Introduction to Nineteenth-Century Russian Slavophilism*, Vol. I: *A. S. Xomjakov* (The Hague, 1961), pp. 41–42; P. Miliukov, *Glavnyia techeniia*, p. 310.

17. Azadovsky, ed. *Pis'ma P. V. Kireevskogo k N. M. Iazykovu* (Moscow and Leningrad, 1935), p. 36.

18. "Vospominaniia ob A. S. Khomiakove," *Russkii arkhiv*, 1879, no. 11, p. 266.

19. The *Dobrotoliubie* (or *Philokalia* in the Greek original) is a spiritual manual of writings by the Eastern Church Fathers, including the famous "Jesus Prayer." It was compiled by Macarius of Corinth (1731–1805) and Nicodemus of the Holy Mountain (1748?– 1809) and published in 1782. Paisy Velichkovsky translated it into Slavonic a few years later, and in this form it played an important role in the rebirth of monastic spirituality in nineteenth-century Russia. The first Russian translation (1894) was the work of Bishop Theophan the Recluse; an English version (*Writings from the Philokalia on Prayer of the Heart*, trans. Kadloubovsky and Palmer, London [1951– 52]), appeared in 1951.

20. Koshelëv, *Zapiski*, p. 73.

21. "Vospominaniia ob A. S. Khomiakove," quoted in Riasanovsky, *Russia and the West*, p. 39.

22. *Ibid.*, p. 39.

23. A. Gratieux, A. S. Khomiakov et le mouvement Slavophile (Paris, 1939), I, 15.

24. See, for instance, Herzen, Byloe i dumy, I, 464–465.

25. Riasanovsky, Russia and the West, pp. 37–38.

26. Byloe i dumy, I, 474.

27. The seamy side of Khomiakov's relations with his peasants is well documented in V. I. Semevsky, Krestianskii vopros v Rossii (St. Petersburg, 1888), II, 398–401.

28. Zapiski Otdela rukopisei biblioteki SSSR im. Lenina, issue 15, 1953, p. 40.

29. Gershenzon, Obrazy, p. 94.

30. Herzen, Byloe i dumy, I, 466. Khomiakov cited by N. A. Elagin in Kireevsky, Sobranie sochinenii, I, 61.

31. His devotion to Iazykov was such that he spent over a year with him in Western Europe, when Iazykov, for reasons of health, had to take the waters at Marienbad and elsewhere in the late 1830's. Peter seems to have been a combination of traveling companion, male nurse, and general morale-builder. See Gershenzon, Obrazy, p. 114.

32. "Pëtr Vasil'evich Kireevskii: Ego pis'ma," Russkii arkhiv, 1905, No. 5, p. 129.

33. Gershenzon, Obrazy, p. 102.

34. See Ivan's letter (April 5/17, 1830) to his parents, Sobranie sochinenii, I, 39.

35. Ibid., p. 62.

36. Traces of an earlier stage of these disagreements may be seen in Kireevsky's sharp words for "Peter the Great's detractors" in "The Nineteenth Century."

37. F. I. Buslaev, "Moi vospominaniia," Vestnik Evropy, Oct. 1891, p. 637.

38. Kireevsky, Sobranie sochinenii, II, 65–75.

39. Princess Volkonskaia had been a notable figure in the salon life of the 1820's, but had by this time settled in Italy, where Rozhalin and Shevyrëv, among others, had spent a great deal of time with her. It was for one of her soirées that Kireevsky wrote Tsaritsyn Night. On this phase of her career, see N. Belozerskaia, "Kniaginia Zinaida Aleksandrovna Volkonskaia," Istoricheskii vestnik, 68 (1897), 131–164. Caroline von Jaenisch is better known as Karolina Pavlovna. She was, at the time, the author of a volume of translations entitled

Das Nordlicht, Proben der neueren russischen Literatur (Dresden and Leipzig, 1833) and an old family friend. Cf. the excerpts from Mar'ia Vasil'evna Kireevskaia's diary in the 1820's, in *Literaturnoe nasledstvo,* 79 (1968), 23.

40. "O stikhotvoreniakh g. Iazykova," *Sobranie sochinenii,* II, 76–86.

41. *Ibid.,* p. 86.

42. "He who has not understood thought by feeling has not understood it," Kireevsky wrote to Koshelëv in 1828 (*Sobranie sochinenii,* I, 14). See also Gershenzon, *Istoricheskie zapiski,* pp. 10–14.

43. See Ivan's and Peter's congratulatory letters to Iazykov on the occasion, *Pis'ma P. V. Kireevskogo k Iazykovu,* pp. 35–37.

44. On the founding of the Moscow *Observer,* see, *inter alia,* Evgen'ev-Maksimov et al., *Ocherki po istorii russkoi zhurnalistiki,* I, 370–373; Koliupanov, *Biografiia,* II, 62; Gershenzon, *Istoricheskie zapiski,* p. 7.

45. Koliupanov, *Biografiia,* II, 62.

46. *Ocherki po istorii russkoi zhurnalistiki,* p. 372.

47. Walicki, *W kręgu,* p. 107.

48. This I take to be Malia's fundamental conclusion. See, in particular, chap. 6 of his *Herzen.*

49. *Ibid.,* p. 13.

VIII. The "Elagin Salon" and the First Slavophile Writings

1. Kireevsky, *Sobranie sochinenii,* I, 109–120.

2. A good introduction may be found in Aronson and Reiser, *Literaturnye kruzhki,* pp. 158–161, 277–278, as well as in their excellent bibliography.

3. Kavelin, *Sobranie sochinenii,* III, 1120–1121, quoted in Aronson and Reiser, *Literaturnye kruzhki,* p. 158.

4. Stankevich, *Granovskii,* II, 184.

5. Bartenev, "Avdot'ia Petrovna Elagina," quoted in Aronson and Reiser, *Literaturnye kruzhki,* p. 159.

6. *Ibid.*

7. *Sochineniia i pis'ma P. Ia. Chaadaeva,* I, 259.

8. Kireevsky, *Sobranie sochinenii,* I, 63.

9. S. S. Dmitriev, "Slavianofily i slavianofil'stvo," *Istorik-marksist*, 89 (1941), 87.

10. A. S. Khomiakov, *Sochineniia*, III (Moscow, 1900), 11–29.

11. Christoff, *A. S. Xomjakov*, p. 53. See also N. A. Elagin's notes (Kireevsky, *Sobranie sochinenii*, I, 63), upon which Christoff bases his speculations.

12. Khomiakov, *Sochineniia*, III, 11.

13. *Ibid.*, p. 13.

14. *Ibid.*, p. 25.

15. *Ibid.*, p. 28.

16. Kireevskii, *Sobranie sochinenii*, I, 110.

17. *Ibid.*, p. 111.

18. *Ibid.*

19. Kireevsky, *Sobranie sochinenii*, I, 112. The following summer, Kireevsky wrote to Khomiakov that the development of "abstract reason" in men and nations had been accompanied by a decline in will and feeling. "My thought is this," he wrote, "that logical sense (*soznanie*), which translates the deed into the word, life into a formula, does not grasp the object fully, and annihilates its action on the soul." We mistake the blueprint of the house for the structure itself, he went on; living as we do under the yoke of logic, we ought at least to recognize that it is not the "summit of knowledge" (*Sobranie sochinenii*, I, 67).

20. *Ibid.*

21. Marx, *The Communist Manifesto*, in Arthur Mendel, ed., *Essential Works of Marxism* (New York, 1961), p. 15.

22. Kireevsky, *Sobranie sochinenii*, I, 112.

23. *Ibid.*, p. 113.

24. *Ibid.*

25. *Ibid.*, p. 115.

26. Max Weber, *Staatssoziologie* (Berlin, 1956), p. 101, quoted in Reinhard Bendix, *Max Weber* (Garden City, 1962), p. 331.

27. For a general discussion of "patrimonialism" and its relation to feudalism, the other major mode of "traditional domination," see Weber, *Wirtschaft und Gesellschaft* (Tübingen, 1925), II, 679–752.

28. Kireevsky, *Sobranie sochinenii*, I, 115.

29. *Ibid.*, p. 116.

30. *Ibid.*, p. 118.

31. The Council of 1551 has generally been regarded as marking a long step forward in the domination of the Russian Church by the state. This is presumably why Kireevsky assigned it so central a role in the destruction of old Russian culture. The "party spirit" which he mentions would seem to be a reference to the struggle between the proponents and opponents of monastic landholding. Kireevsky was very vague as to precisely what the baneful effects of the Council were; he is obviously groping. For a general discussion of what went on at the Council, see A. V. Kartashëv, *Ocherki po istorii russkoi tserkvi* (Paris, 1959), 433–440.

32. Kireevsky, *Sobranie sochinenii*, I, 120.

33. Kireevsky, *Sobranie sochinenii*, II, 172–209.

34. *Ibid.*, p. 177.

35. *Ibid.*, p. 178.

36. The French legitimist Bonald, too, thought of the French Revolution as God's punishment of Europe's secular and individualist heresies. See Robert Nisbet, *The Sociological Tradition* (New York, 1966), p. 13.

37. Kireevsky, *Sobranie sochinenii*, II, 182–183.

38. *Ibid.*, p. 197.

39. Roman law had been for centuries a target of various nationalisms and protonationalisms. At the time of the Reformation, Roman and canon law were vigorously attacked by German humanists like Ulrich von Hutten and by the spiritual radicals of the period, such as the remarkable "Revolutionary of the Upper Rhine," who believed that Roman and canon law had initiated the distinction between "Mine" and "Thine" (Norman Cohn, *The Pursuit of the Millennium* [New York, 1961], pp. 114–123). Although the thrust of most of the hostility toward Roman law at this period was against its internationalism, one can see definite traces of the idea that it was destructive of local liberties which had evolved in a kind of common law texture. It was this aspect of Roman law which the theoreticians of political romanticism seized upon in their defense of the *ancien régime* against the political and economic rationalism of absolutism and liberalism. See, for example, Reinhold Aris, "Das Verhältnis von Staat und Recht und der Begriff des Rechts" in his *Staatslehre Adam Müllers in ihrem Verhältnis zur deutschen Romantik* (Tübingen, 1929).

40. Hans Rogger, *National Consciousness in Eighteenth Century Russia* (Cambridge, 1960), p. 129.

41. See, for example, Florovsky, *Puti russkogo bogosloviia*, p. 116.

IX. *Slavophilism and the* Muscovite

1. See Malia, *Herzen*, pp. 328–334.

2. *Ibid.*, p. 330.

3. Herzen, *Byloe i dumy*, II, 467.

4. Eberhard Müller, *Russischer Intellekt*, p. 223.

5. The philosophy chair at the University of Moscow — which meant, at the time, only logic — was vacant for several years around 1839–40. Kireevsky coveted the position and prepared a paper on the teaching of logic for Count S. G. Stroganov, the Curator of the Moscow Educational District. But memories of the *European* and official distrust apparently prevented his getting the position (cf. Kireevsky, *Sobranie sochinenii*, I, 68). Liaskovsky (*Brat'ia Kireevskie*, p. 62) claimed that Count Stroganov always favored the Westerners, and this was the reason Kireevsky failed to get the post. In view of Kireevsky's high opinion of Stroganov, this seems unlikely. The official reason for turning him down was his lack of an academic degree. Kireevsky was instead made an "honorary inspector" (*pochëtnyi smotritel'*) of the Belëv district school, a duty which he took with great seriousness. Kireevsky's "Zapiska o napravlenii i metodakh pervonachal'nogo obrazovaniia naroda v Rossii" is printed as an appendix in Müller, *Russischer Intellekt*, pp. 485–496.

6. Stankevich, *Granovskii*, II, 369–370.

7. *Ibid.*, pp. 415–416.

8. *Ibid.*, p. 381.

9. See Shevyrëv's "Izvlechenie iz pisem . . . k G. ministru narodnogo prosveshcheniia" in the *Zhurnal ministerstva narodnogo prosveshcheniia*, 1840, no. 1. There is an account of the incident in A. G. Dement'ev, *Ocherki po istorii russkoi zhurnalistiki 1840–1850 gg.* (Moscow-Leningrad, 1951), p. 197, but this bellicose and tendentious book should be used with the greatest caution.

10. *Granovskii*, II, 385.

11. *Ibid.*, p. 385.

12. *Ibid.*

13. *Ibid.,* p. 259.

14. *Ibid.,* quoted in Müller, *Russischer Intellekt,* p. 224.

15. The *Galateia* belonged to S. E. Raich, who had been the moving spirit in one of the first "circles" of the 1820's. It was one of the many journals that the "Westerners" tried to purchase, since buying an existing journal made fewer difficulties from the government point of view. They were also interested in Glinka's *Russian Messenger* and Senkovsky's *Library for Reading.* On their attempts to establish a journal of their own, see Barsukov, *Zhizn' Pogodina,* VII, 439–442.

16. Kireevsky, *Sobranie sochinenii,* II, 233, quoted in Müller, *Russischer Intellekt,* pp. 221–222.

17. Herzen, *Polnoe sobranie sochinenii,* III, 327.

18. Malia, *Herzen,* p. 280.

19. *Ibid.,* p. 281. The founding of the *Muscovite* is discussed in greater detail in Dement'ev, *Ocherki,* pp. 185–187. His account is interesting, despite the presence of such incredible assertions as that the *Muscovite* began publishing in 1841 to counteract the growing revolutionary struggle of the peasantry against serfdom.

20. Malia, *Herzen,* p. 280. See also V. I. Kuleshov, *Otechestvennye zapiski i literatura 40-kh godov XIX v.* (Moscow, 1958), passim.

21. Müller, *Russischer Intellekt,* p. 217.

22. Quoted in Christoff, *A. S. Xomjakov,* p. 65.

23. See Gogol's letter to Iazykov (January 2, 1845), quoted in Dement'ev, *Ocherki,* p. 191.

24. Quoted in Christoff, *A. S. Xomjakov,* p. 76, and in Müller, *Russischer Intellekt,* p. 221.

25. See Müller's excellent account of the whole transfer process in *Russischer Intellekt,* pp. 217–233, passim.

26. Kireevsky, *Sobranie sochinenii,* II, 230–232.

27. *Ibid.,* p. 231, quoted in Müller, *Russischer Intellekt,* p. 220.

28. Kireevsky, *Sobranie sochinenii,* II, 234–238.

29. *Ibid.,* p. 235.

30. *Ibid.,* p. 236.

31. *Ibid.* At the beginning and the end of the first number of Kireevsky's *Muscovite* were verses from Zhukovsky, rejoicing at Kireevsky's having become a "Muscovite" and urging him not to polemicize with other journals. Cf. Barsukov, *Zhizn' Pogodina,* VIII, 4.

32. Henrik Steffens (1774–1845) stood close to Schelling; his autobiography, *Was ich Erlebte,* appeared in 10 vols. (Breslau, 1840–

1845). Avdot'ia Petrovna Elagina translated excerpts from vols. III–V, and Kireevsky wrote a brief introduction.

33. Kireevsky, *Sobranie sochinenii,* II, 238.

34. See Kuleshov, *Otechestvennye zapiski,* and Dement'ev *Ocherki,* passim. Bowman's *Belinski* also contains some information.

35. On the disagreement between Belinsky and Aksakov, as well as Gogol's response to Aksakov's brochure (entitled "A Few Words about Gogol's Poem, 'Chichikov's Travels' or 'Dead Souls'"), see Edward Chmielewski, *Tribune of the Slavophiles: Konstantin Aksakov* (Gainesville, Fla., 1962), pp. 17–19.

36. Quoted in Christoff, *A. S. Xomjakov,* p. 75.

37. "To Those Who Are Not Ours" was first published in *Russkii archiv,* 1879, no. 3, pp. 399–400. It has been reprinted in N. M. Iazykov, *Polnoe sobranie stikhotvorenii* (Moscow-Leningrad, 1964), pp. 394–395. The Westerners were "readers of dark books" who wanted to "ruin us."

38. Herzen, *Polnoe sobranie sochinenii,* 469.

39. Quoted in Parilova and Soimonov, "P. V. Kireevskii," pp. 59–60.

40. Belinsky's "Tarantas" appeared in no. 6 of the *Annals* for 1845. It is reprinted in his *Polnoe sobranie sochinenii,* IX (Moscow, 1955), 75–117. See also Kuleshov's fair-minded discussion in *Otechestvennye zapiski,* pp. 203–205.

41. Malia, *Herzen,* pp. 299–300. "What a splendid, strong personality is Ivan Kireevsky," wrote Herzen in his diary. "So much has been killed in him and so much, at the same time, developed. He has been cut down the way an oak might be cut down . . . He is being consumed. The struggle continues in the depths of his being and saps him. He alone atones for the whole Slavophile party" (Barsukov, *Zhizn' Pogodina,* VII, 105).

42. Granovsky was particularly bitter about "intrigues" among conservative Moscow professors to achieve the rejection of his thesis. Rightly or wrongly, he also saw the hand of Pogodin and Shevyrëv in his failure to get permission to put out a journal. See Herzen's diary for Nov. 1845, *Polnoe sobranie sochinenii,* III, 358–361.

X. Russia and the West in the Post-Hegelian Period

1. The popular concept of the "rotten West" derived more from the writings of Shevyrëv than from those of the Slavophiles. The best

discussion of this aspect of Shevyrëv's thought — and in particular of how he was influenced by Philarète Chasles and Franz Baader — is still Peter Struve's "S. P. Shevyrëv i zapadnyia vnusheniia i istochniki teorii-aforizma o 'gnilom,' ili 'gniushchem' Zapade," *Zapiski Russkogo Nauchnogo Instituta v Belgrade*, issue 17, 1940. According to Struve, Shevyrëv never actually used the term "rotten West," but it rendered his meaning precisely.

2. Eberhard Müller, *Russischer Intellekt*, p. 235.

3. Eberhard Müller has shown that portions of Kireevsky's analysis of the West and its crisis were quite similar to some German journalism of the period on the same subject (*Russischer Intellekt*, pp. 239–242).

4. Kuleshov, *Otechestvennye zapiski*, pp. 200–201.

5. Kireevsky, *Sobranie sochinenii*, I, 122–123.

6. *Ibid.*, pp. 125–126.

7. Kireevsky included a discussion of Schelling's late "philosophy of mythology" in the *Muscovite*. Entitled "A Speech of Schelling" (*Sobranie sochinenii*, II, 92–103), it was made up largely of extracts from journals, his own lecture notes from the early 1830's, and perhaps some lecture notes from a considerably later period, brought to him by a person or persons unknown (perhaps Michael Katkov). Schelling's preoccupation with the *living* and *historical* as necessary bases for a Christian philosophy brought him to mythology, which he saw as a kind of naive, "natural" religion, which was subsequently to be liberated and purified by revelation — which, however, remained rooted in the "fact," in the reality of mythology. Kireevsky reported these developments, which he had obviously followed with interest, objectively enough, but without involvement or any particular enthusiasm.

8. Schelling's attack on Hegel remained, for Kireevsky, the great attack on the stronghold of Western rationalism. Schelling never produced the "positive" philosophy that Kireevsky was seeking, however, and always remained, for his Russian "student," an essentially negative force. Schelling may be said to have "influenced" Kireevsky with respect to the latter's quest for "living" knowledge, and the German philosopher helped Kireevsky to find the words to express his dislike of rationalism and "pure thought," which were always unable to grasp concrete historical reality. This was his major contribution to Kireevsky's Slavophilism.

9. Müller, *Russischer Intellekt*, p. 244.

10. Karl Werder was the teacher, friend, and mentor of a number of the Russians who came to Berlin. On his relations with the Russians, see, in particular, Dmitrij Tschijewskij, *Hegel bei den Slawen*, pp. 175–177 and passim.

11. Müller, *Russischer Intellekt*, pp. 269–274.

12. Herbart's relationship to Idealism is well treated in Windelband, *A History of Philosophy*, 572, 583–586, and passim.

13. A. I. Koshelëv made a trip to Europe in the early 1850's, and upon his return Kireevsky wrote him and inquired eagerly: "What new impression did Germany make on you? Any lively impression you might have would be valuable news for me, shut in as I am by the snows of Belëv . . ." (Kireevsky, *Sobranie sochinenii*, II, 252).

14. In his *Die protestantische Theologie im 19. Jahrhundert*, Karl Barth discussed Daub in his chapter on Marheineke.

15. On Beck, see Barth, *Protestantische Theologie*, pp. 562–569.

16. Kireevsky, *Sobranie sochinenii*, I, 137.

17. On this complex controversy, see Schnabel, *Deutsche Geschichte*, III, 138–205. In English, there is Heinrich Treitschke's *History of Germany in the Nineteenth Century* (London, 1915–1919); the Cologne dispute is discussed in vol. VI, chap. 10.

18. Kireevsky, *Sobranie sochinenii*, I, 138, quoted in Müller, *Russischer Intellekt*, p. 248.

19. Kireevsky, *Sobranie sochinenii*, I, 138, quoted in Müller, *Russischer Intellekt*, pp. 248–249.

20. It is very likely that Kireevsky, as Eberhard Müller has suggested, came upon the notion of a "science of social life" in Lorenz von Stein's *Der Sozialismus und Communismus im heutigen Frankreich*, which A. I. Turgenev discussed in the *Muscovite* while Kireevsky was editor; his remarks on Stein are reprinted in A. I. Turgenev, *Khronika russkogo* (Moscow-Leningrad, 1964), p. 244. Müller, however, goes on to claim that since Kireevsky expected the new science of society to be worked out in France, it is clear that the "context" of his thought is not "German-romantic Conservatism." This rather gnomic remark appears to be a glancing criticism of Andrzej Walicki's discussion of Slavophilism. It should be sufficient to point out that conservative romantics were often attracted to certain currents of "Utopian socialism," which, in the case of the Saint-Simonians, was strongly influenced by conservative thinkers. "Society"

was a common preoccupation of conservatives and socialists as against "liberal individualism." See Müller's "Zwischen Liberalismus und utopischem Sozialismus," *Jahrbücher für Geschichte Osteuropas,* Dec. 1965, esp. pp. 514–516.

21. See chap. V.

22. For Khomiakov on England, see Riasanovsky, *Russia and the West,* pp. 100–105.

23. "In the English character," wrote Khomiakov approvingly, "there is a deep and highly justified disbelief in human reason. In this respect an Englishman reminds one of a Russian. Rationalism does not enter into his character" (Khomiakov, *Sochineniia,* I, 135, quoted in Riasanovsky, *Russia and the West,* p. 102).

24. Kireevsky, *Sobranie sochinenii,* I, 140.

25. *Ibid.*

26. Robert Blake has an excellent chapter on "Young England" in his biography of Disraeli. His account is revealing of Disraeli's complex opportunism, but shows, as well, the deeper importance of the episode. See Robert Blake, *Disraeli* (New York, 1967), pp. 167–220. Background on the social unrest in England at the time may be had in Asa Briggs, *The Age of Improvement* (New York, 1959), pp. 286–343.

27. On Oastler, see Cecil Driver, *Tory Radical* (New York, 1946), which also contains material on Sadler and the Ten Hours Movement. Both men are also discussed, passim, in E. P. Thompson, *The Making of the English Working Class* (New York, 1963).

28. Kireevsky, *Sobranie sochinenii,* I, 140.

29. Müller has shown that Kireevsky's remarks on Carlyle owe a good deal to Philarète Chasles's review of *Past and Present* in the *Revue des deux mondes* (*Russischer Intellekt,* p. 252).

30. Kireevsky, *Sobranie sochinenii,* I, 142.

31. *Ibid.,* pp. 142–143.

32. *Ibid.,* p. 144.

33. *Ibid.*

34. *Ibid.,* p. 146.

35. *Ibid.,* pp. 149–150.

36. *Ibid.,* p. 152.

37. Certain points in Kireevsky's denunciation of the United States — particularly the commercialism found there and the separation between law and "probity" — may owe something to Hegel (see *The*

332   *Notes to Pages 207–215*

Philosophy of History [New York, 1900], pp. 85–86). Dostoevsky's view of America (as given, for example, in *The Brothers Karamazov*) is remarkably similar to Kireevsky's. Cf. the interesting analysis in Ia. E. Golosovker, *Dostoevskii i Kant* (Moscow, 1963), pp. 27–30.

38. Quoted in Barsukov, *Zhizn' Pogodina*, VIII, 7.

39. Kireevsky, *Sobranie sochinenii*, I, 156.

40. *Ibid.*, p. 157.

41. *Ibid.*

42. It is hard to discern the precise difference, in Kireevsky's writings, between *obrazovannost'* and *prosveshchenie*. Most often, however, Kireevsky used the former term when he wished to invoke the "organic" totality of a culture; *prosveshchenie* usually referred to "culture" in the narrower sense of poetry, music, art, journalism, etc.

43. Kireevsky, *Sobranie sochinenii*, I, 159.

44. *Ibid.*, p. 160.

45. *Ibid.*, p. 162.

46. On Senkovsky, see, *inter alia*, Riasanovsky, *Nicholas I*, pp. 65–70, and V. Kaverin's biography, *Baron Brambeus* (Moscow, 1966).

47. Kireevsky, *Sobranie sochinenii*, I, 165.

48. Riasanovsky, *Nicholas I*, p. 76. It should be pointed out, however, that on one occasion at least, Pogodin and Shevyrëv reprinted a crude denunciation of Belinsky from the *Beacon* (cf. Dement'ev, *Ocherki*, p. 203).

49. Kireevsky, *Sobranie sochinenii*, I, 166.

50. *Ibid.*, p. 168.

51. *Ibid.*, p. 169.

52. *Ibid.*, p. 173.

53. Kireevsky, *Sobranie sochinenii*, II, 119–127.

54. *Ibid.*, pp. 87–89.

55. *Ibid.*, p. 89.

56. *Ibid.*, p. 119.

57. "Our people, thank God, still live on Slavonic literature, and the few who have been enlightened by *civic* (*grazhdanskii*) literacy continue to educate themselves by means of Vyzhigin, Orlov and Paul de Kock . . ." (*ibid.*, p. 122).

58. *Ibid.*

59. Kireevsky, *Sobranie sochinenii*, I, 67.

60. Kireevsky had been at Dolbino while Granovsky was delivering his "brilliant" lectures.

61. On Granovsky's lectures and the social and intellectual repercussions, see Malia, *Herzen*, pp. 297–298, and Christoff, *A. S. Xomjakov*, p. 74.

62. Kireevsky, *Sobranie sochinenii*, II, 109–114.

63. *Ibid.*, p. 111.

64. *Istoriia russkoi slovesnosti*, 4 vols. (St. Petersburg, 1858–1860). N. K. Gudzy is very critical of Shevyrëv's "romantic, reactionary notions" and "sentimental idealization of the past." He goes on to say, however, that Shevyrëv's course, "what with its wealth of material and the serious erudition of its author, who was well informed as to all the results of previous research, represented an extraordinary accomplishment at the time when it appeared and served as a profound inspiration to subsequent investigators." See N. K. Gudzy, *History of Early Russian Literature* (New York, 1949), pp. 14–15.

65. Kireevsky, *Sobranie sochinenii*, II, 173.

66. Quoted in Barsukov, *Zhizn' Pogodina*, VIII, 16.

67. *Ibid.*, pp. 5–6.

68. *Ibid.*, p. 6.

69. " 'Moskvitianin' i vselennaia" appeared in the February number of the *Annals;* it is reprinted in Herzen's *Polnoe sobranie sochinenii*, III, 465–470.

70. *Ibid.*, p. 465.

71. *Ibid.*, pp. 467–468.

72. *Ibid.*, pp. 468–469.

73. *Ibid.*, p. 469.

74. *Ibid.*, pp. 469–470.

75. Florovsky, *Puti russkogo bogosloviia*, p. 253.

76. His "Literaturnye i zhurnal'nye zametki" appeared in the *Annals*, no. 5 (1845) and has been reprinted in his *Polnoe sobranie sochinenii*, IX, 66–74.

77. *Ibid.*, p. 68.

78. *Ibid.*, p. 69.

79. Barsukov, *Zhizn' Pogodina*, VIII, 22–28.

80. *Ibid.*, p. 25.

81. Peter Kireevsky published, in the third and last issue of his brother's *Muscovite*, an attack on Pogodin's article, "Za russkuiu

starinu." The gist of Kireevsky's unfinished piece in the *Muscovite* was that Pogodin had so stressed the "calling" of the Varangian princes (as opposed to the principle of "conquest" which underlay medieval history in the West), that the essential peaceful nature of the Russian people had been perverted into a kind of passivity and indifference. Pogodin, as usual, took criticism very ill. His diary for the period contains little notes ("To Kireevsky . . . argued until two o'clock") which indicate a series of boring and unpleasant evenings for poor Peter. See Barsukov, *Zhizn' Pogodina*, VIII, 126–138.

82. *Ibid.*, p. 28.

83. *Ibid.*, pp. 28–29. See also "Iz pisem Iazykova k bratu," *Russkaia starina*, 113 (March 1903), 533.

84. Barsukov, *Zhizn' Pogodina*, VIII, 31.

XI. *Withdrawal Again*

1. On Valuev, see N. V. Golitsyn, ed., *Dnevnik Elizavety Ivanovny Popovoi* (St. Petersburg, 1911), esp. pp. ix–xiii.

2. See Kireevsky's touching letters to his mother and brother in his *Sobranie sochinenii*, I, 72–74.

3. Barsukov, *Zhizn' Pogodina*, VIII, 487.

4. *Russkii arkhiv*, 1879, no. 11, p. 322.

5. *Dnevnik Popovoi*, pp. 64–68. See also Natal'ia Petrovna's letters to Makary in Sergei Chetverikov, *Optina Pustyn'* (Paris, [1926]), pp. 148–156.

6. Barsukov, *Zhizn' Pogodina*, IX, 117.

7. Contained in Kireevsky's *Sobranie sochinenii*, II, 245–248.

8. *Ibid.*, p. 245.

9. *Ibid.*, pp. 245–246.

10. *Slavianizm* corresponds roughly to Slavophilism, a word which Kireevsky never used. As employed here, *slavianizm* would appear to include Pogodin, showing how vague all such terminology was in the 1840's.

11. Kireevsky, *Sobranie sochinenii*, II, 247.

12. See Kireevsky's letter to Khomiakov (1840), where he wrote, *inter alia*, "only when a thought has developed to [the point of] inexpressability has it achieved maturity" (*Sobranie sochinenii*, I, 67).

13. Kireevsky, *Sobranie sochinenii*, II, 248.

14. Riasanovsky, *Russia and the West*, p. 44.

15. For a description of how the Kireevsky estate was run, see E. N. Konshina's survey of the Kireevsky-Elagin archive in *Zapiski Otdela rukopisei biblioteki SSSR im. Lenina*, issue 15, 1953, p. 40.

16. It may be of some significance that a manuscript copy of Radishchev's *Journey from St. Petersburg to Moscow*, dating from the 1820's, was carefully preserved in the Elagin family papers. See *Izvestiia AN SSR*, otdelenie literatury i iazyka, 1961, Vol. XX, issue 2, p. 145.

17. Kireevsky, *Sobranie sochinenii*, II, 253.

18. Eberhard Müller, *Russischer Intellekt*, pp. 475–484.

19. Kireevsky, *Sobranie sochinenii*, II, 241–242.

20. *Ibid.*

21. The standard work on the state peasants is of course N. M. Druzhinin's massive *Gosudarstvennye krest'iane*, 2 vols. (Moscow and Leningrad, 1946–1958). A convenient discussion of some of the principal subcategories of state peasant and a general assessment of their economic situation may be found in Jerome Blum's *Lord and Peasant in Russia from the Ninth to the Nineteenth Centuries* (Princeton, 1961), pp. 465–503. See also Olga Crisp, "The State Peasants under Nicholas I," *Slavic and East European Review*, 37 (1958–59), 387–412.

22. On the *ukaz* of 1803, see V. I. Semevsky, *Krestianskii vopros v Rossii* (St. Petersburg, 1888), I, 252–283; on the new arrangements which put freed serfs under the Ministry of State Domain, see *ibid.*, II, 232–235.

23. Kireevsky, *Sobranie sochinenii*, II, 252–253.

24. In 1846, "inventories" were introduced into Poland, and in the following year into Kiev, Volhynia, and Podolia. In the West, the inventories were part of a deliberate policy of russification. However, all the inventories (which were in fact drawn up by the landlord or his estate manager) could achieve was a stabilization of the existing situation; they were scarcely a step toward real reform.

25. Kireevsky, *Sobranie sochinenii*, II, 234.

26. *Ibid.*, p. 255.

27. Quoted in Blum, *Lord and Peasant*, p. 574.

28. Kireevsky, *Sobranie sochinenii*, II, 286.

29. On the Slavophile response in general, see A. S. Nifontow, *Russland im Jahre 1848* (Berlin, 1954), pp. 168–175.

30. Quoted in Barsukov, *Zhizn' Pogodina*, IX, 262.

31. Kireevsky, *Sobranie sochinenii*, II, 248–249.
32. A lengthy account of the whole affair can be found in Barsukov, *Zhizn' Pogodina*, IX, 289–302.
33. Kireevsky, *Sobranie sochinenii*, II, 249.
34. *Ibid.*, quoted in Riasanovsky, *Russia and the West*, p. 45.
35. Apollon Grigoryev, *My Literary and Moral Wanderings* (New York, 1962), p. 154.
36. Barsukov, *Zhizn' Pogodina*, X, 11.
37. *Ibid.*

XII. The Optina Monastery and Mystical Theology

1. Kireevsky, *Sobranie sochinenii*, I, 63.
2. See above, chap. VII.
3. Kireevsky, *Sobranie sochinenii*, II, 260.
4. On Optina and its history, see, in particular, Chetverikov, *Optina Pustyn'*.
5. On Father Leonid, see Igor Smolitsch, *Leben und Lehre der Starzen*, 2nd ed. (Cologne and Olten, 1952), pp. 127–131, and Ivan Tschetverikow, "La vie spirituelle dans l'Orthodoxie," in Seraphim, *L'Eglise Orthodoxe* (Paris, 1952), pp. 213–216.
6. Igor Smolitsch found the institution of the "elder" nearly as old as the Church; the expression *Pater spiritualis* was already employed in the fourth century. In Russia, Nil Sorsky was the first elder, according to Smolitsch, but there was not another one that we have any information about until Paisy Velichkovsky, in the late eighteenth century. Cf. Smolitsch, *Leben und Lehre*, pp. 131–139.
7. Paisy Velichkovsky, according to a recent historian, was the "son of a Kiev priest and of a Jewish-Christian mother. Ran away from the studies with their 'pagan mythology' and, after many difficulties and wanderings from one to the other community (1739–46), eventually reached Mt. Athos. Professed there and ordained (1758), he soon became a spiritual leader. He collected, copied and retranslated (sometimes literally) the writings of the ascetic and mystical fathers. His labour was the heavier, as he had no full knowledge of Greek or Syriac, and had to deal with defective Slavonic manuscripts. He had to move to Moldavia (1763), and after more peregrinations with his disciples became Superior of Niamets (1779), and after the

Russian occupation of Yassy (1790) was made Archimandrite by the Archbishop of Poltava. . . . He fostered a school of translators: over 200 manuscripts of the Niamets Monastery were their work . . . The followers of Paisy brought back to Russia the almost forgotten writings of the desert fathers and the Byzantine ascetics, and helped the revival of contemplative monasticism" (Nadejda Gorodetzky, *St. Tikhon Zadonsky* [London, 1951], pp. 215–216).

8. Among the works published — and in many cases translated or corrected — in Kireevsky's time were: *The Life and Works of the Moldavian Starets Paisii Velichkovskii* (1st ed. 1847, 2nd ed. 1848); *Gleanings for Spiritual Refreshment* (translations from the Fathers by Paisy Velichkovsky, 1849); Nil Sorsky, *Conferences on Monastic Life* (1849); Barsanuthios and John, *Introduction to the Spiritual Life* (1851); *Twelve Sermons* of Simeon the New Theologian (1852); Isaac the Syrian, *Spiritual-Ascetic Sermons* (1854); Abbot Dorotheos, *Instructions and Letters* (1856); Mark the Anchorite, *Moral-Ascetic Sermons* (1858); *The Ladder of St. John Climacus*, in several editions. See *Russian Letters of Direction 1834–1860: Macarius, Starets of Optino*, ed. Iulia de Beausobre (Westminster, 1944), pp. 20–21.

9. Kireevsky, *Sobranie sochinenii*, II, 256–258.

10. P. V. Annenkov, *The Extraordinary Decade*, ed. A. Mendel (Ann Arbor, 1968), p. 239.

11. Quoted in Parilova and Soimonov, "P. V. Kireevskii," p. 66.

12. Nicolas Berdyaev, *The Russian Idea* (Boston, 1962), p. 54. See also Ernst Benz, *Die abendländische Sendung der Östlich-orthodoxen Kirche* (Mainz, 1950).

13. Ernst Benz, *Geist und Leben der Ostkirche* (Hamburg, 1957), p. 43. Khomiakov cited Tertullian specifically in this connection. See his "Po povodu stat'i I. V. Kireevskogo," *Sochineniia* I, 205.

14. *Ibid.*, p. 47.

15. *Ibid.*, pp. 41–44.

16. Kireevsky and other Slavophiles, it should hardly be necessary to say, wildly idealized the "unpolitical" character of both the Byzantine and Russian churches. "Without any suspicion of paradox, a distinguished historian has written, "the religious history of Byzantium could be represented as a conflict between the Church and the State, a conflict from which the Church emerged unquestionably the victor" (Henri Grégoire, "The Byzantine Church," in N. H. Baynes and H. St. L. B. Moss, eds., *Byzantium* [Oxford, 1961], p. 130).

Grégoire's observation might also be applied to the Russian Church — with the conclusion, however, reversed.

17. Friedrich Heiler, *Urkirche und Ostkirche* (Munich, 1937), p. 213.

18. Vladimir Lossky, *The Mystical Theology of the Eastern Church* (London, 1957), p. 8.

19. *Ibid.,* p. 8.

20. *Ibid.,* pp. 38–39.

21. *Ibid.,* p. 40.

22. Kireevsky, *Sobranie sochinenii,* II, 282–283; Chetverikov, *Optina Pustyn'*, pp. 126–128.

23. Peter Christoff, *A. S. Xomjakov,* p. 102.

24. On Makary, see Smolitsch, *Leben und Lehre,* pp. 143–150; Chetverikov, *Optina Pustyn',* pp. 44–54; Seraphim, *L'Eglise Orthodoxe,* pp. 217–220.

25. Seraphim, *L'Eglise Orthodoxe,* p. 219.

26. Beausobre, *Russian Letters of Direction,* p. 16.

27. Seraphim, *L'Eglise Orthodoxe,* p. 218.

28. The *molodaia redaktsiia* was a group of young men who contributed to the *Muscovite* and participated in the editorial process in the course of the first four years of the 1850's. The most illustrious of these litterateurs were Apollon Grigor'ev, E. N. Edel'son, A. F. Pisemsky, and of course, A. N. Ostrovsky.

29. Barsukov, *Zhizn' Pogodina,* XI, 97–98.

30. Herzen, *Byloe i dumy,* I, 467.

31. Gershenzon, *Istoricheskie zapiski,* pp. 14–25.

32. V. V. Zenkovsky, *A History of Russian Philosophy* (New York and London, 1953), I, 213.

33. Müller, *Russischer Intellekt,* p. 407.

34. T. G. Masaryk, *The Spirit of Russia* (London and New York, 1955), I, 249, quoted in Müller, *Russischer Intellekt,* p. 407.

35. Müller, *Russischer Intellekt,* p. 407.

36. See Kireevsky's letter (1854) to Makary, in which he confesses with deep feeling how blind he is in understanding the "spiritual sense" of what the Fathers wrote (Chetverikov, *Optina Pustyn',* pp. 131–133). There is curiously little substance in Kireevsky's letters to Makary about the works which they were together engaged in translating and publishing. Kireevsky largely confined himself to rather timid suggestions about the translation of certain terms in the

texts. One of his concerns was to avoid terminology in any way suggestive of the language of "Western" philosophical speculation (Chetverikov, *Optina Pustyn'*, pp. 115–117).

37. Kireevsky, *Sobranie sochinenii*, II, 256–257. Eberhard Müller has perceptively observed that Koshelëv was probably the most spontaneous, least "theoretical" nature of all the Slavophile circle. Kireevsky had always been his teacher, and written to him with perhaps a shade of condescension, but the letter quoted above shows how little real use Kireevsky now found his "intellect" (in the Western sense!) to be. Perhaps Koshelëv's naiveté and directness might turn out to be greater gifts. Cf. Müller, *Russischer Intellekt*, p. 403.

38. Kireevsky, *Sobranie sochinenii*, I, 174–222. There is an English translation in Marc Raeff, ed., *Russian Intellectual History: An Anthology* (New York, Chicago, Burlingame, Harcourt, Brace & World, 1966), pp. 174–207.

39. George Florovsky, *Puti russkogo bogosloviia*, p. 258.

40. The "Columbus" reference is almost certainly a gibe at Odoevsky, who referred admiringly to Schelling as a "Columbus" in the preface to *Russian Nights*.

41. Kireevsky, *Sobranie sochinenii*, I, 180.

42. *Ibid.*, pp. 186–187.

43. *Ibid.*, p. 187.

44. *Ibid.*, pp. 207–208.

45. *Ibid.*, p. 208.

46. On Müller, see, in particular, "Das Verhältnis von Staat und Recht und der Begriff des Rechts" in Reinhold Aris, *Die Staatslehre Adam Müllers in ihrem Verhältnis zur deutschen Romantik;* on Schlegel, see Annette Kuhn, *Die Staats- und Gesellschaftslehre Friedrich Schlegels* (Munich, 1959), pp. 18–23.

47. "The personality came into existence chiefly through property (*im Eigentum*)," Hegel wrote in his *Lectures on the Philosophy of History*, Cf. *Vorlesungen über die Philosophie der Geschichte* (Stuttgart, 1928), p. 362, quoted in Kuhn, *Friedrich Schlegel*, p. 20.

48. Kireevsky, *Sobranie sochinenii*, I, 194.

49. Once Kireevsky had decided to locate the source of Western corruption not simply in classical antiquity, but specifically in Rome, the figure of Aristotle was bound to become a problem. Kireevsky did not wish to link pagan Greek culture to that of Rome because of the former's strong influence on the Eastern Fathers and on

Byzantine culture in general. Aristotle, however, almost had to be a villain, not only because of his importance to scholasticism, but because his name was virtually synonymous with "logic." Hence Kireevsky hedged on the innate value of his philosophy (although ranking him below Plato) and implied that the Aristotle of scholasticism was not only incomplete, but one-sided, thanks to the West's Arab intermediaries.

50. Kireevsky, *Sobranie sochinenii*, I, 195.

51. *Ibid.*, 196.

52. Kireevsky, *Sobranie sochinenii*, I, 197. The "Preestablished Harmony," briefly and vulgarly, was the device by which Leibniz regulated the relations between the monads, from the highest — God — to the lowest and most passive. Although the content of each monad was the same, they were completely independent of each other and had no reciprocal interaction. How, then, to account for what seems to us causality? Due to the fact that each monad contains the whole universe as a representation within itself, they harmonize with each other completely at every moment, and thus an appearance of interaction results. Cf. Bertrand Russell, *A Critical Exposition of the Philosophy of Leibniz* (London, 1937), esp. pp. 136–138.

53. Kireevsky, *Sobranie sochinenii*, I, 197.

54. *Ibid.*

55. See Kireevsky's "Sochineniia Paskalia, izdannyia Kuzenem," which originally appeared in the *Muscovite* in 1845 and is reprinted in the *Sobranie sochinenii*, II, 104–108.

56. Emile Cailliet, *Pascal: The Emergence of Genius* (New York, 1961), p. 119.

57. Kireevsky, *Sobranie sochinenii*, I, 199.

58. *Ibid.*, pp. 199–200. It might well be argued, incidentally, that Kireevsky's virtual identification of Orthodoxy with the Desert Fathers — to say nothing of Palamas and the Hesychasts — was nothing if not one-sided. Henri Grégoire has written of Palamas: "Thanks to him, his Church, which prided itself on its fidelity to the tradition of the ancient Fathers and the seven Councils — that tradition which it opposed to the sacrilegious novelties of the West — created in a fevered atmosphere an entirely new transcendent theology, a disordered mysticism full of unfamiliar formulas which its author himself presented as a divine revelation." Cf. Baynes and Moss, *Byzantium*, p. 116.

59. Kireevsky, *Sobranie sochinenii*, I, 201.
60. See note 81, chap. X.
61. Kireevsky, *Sobranie sochinenii*, I, 213.
62. "O russkikh pisatel'nitsakh," *Sobranie sochinenii*, II, 65–75.
63. *Sobranie sochinenii*, I, 213.
64. Walicki, *W kręgu*, p. 116.
65. Kireevsky, *Sobranie sochinenii*, I, 219.
66. *Ibid.*, pp. 220–221.

XIII. The Search for Wholeness

1. Mikhail Lemke, *Ocherki po istorii russkoi tsenzury* (St. Petersburg, 1904), pp. 284–285.
2. A secret, standing comittee, with Count D. P. Buturlin as chairman, which reported directly to Nicholas concerning "subversion." Dubbelt was for years the Third Section's representative.
3. Lemke, *Ocherki*, p. 285.
4. Barsukov, *Zhizn' Pogodina*, XII, 118.
5. *Ibid.*, p. 114.
6. Lemke, *Ocherki*, p. 285. On Kireevsky's personal experience with the censor, see "I. V. Kireevskii i tsenzura 'Moskovskago sbornika' 1852 g.," *Russkii arkhiv*, 1897, no. 10, pp. 287–291.
7. Lemke, *Ocherki*, p. 286.
8. Barsukov, *Zhizn' Pogodina*, XII, 113–114, quoted in Müller, *Russischer Intellekt*, p. 34.
9. *Ibid.*, p. 115, quoted in Müller, *Russischer Intellekt*, p. 33.
10. *Ibid.*, p. 123.
11. Khomiakov, *Sochineniia*, I, 211–212.
12. *Ibid.*, pp. 213–214.
13. *Ibid.*, pp. 221–226.
14. *Ibid.*, p. 233.
15. *Ibid.*, pp. 254–255.
16. Kireevsky, *Sobranie sochinenii*, II, 248–249; see also above, chap. XI.
17. Kireevsky's side of the correspondence is to be found in his *Sobranie sochinenii*, II, 264–280. A letter from Koshelëv is to be found in Koliupanov, *Biografiia*, II, App., 85–94.
18. Published in Paris in 1842. See also Müller, *Russischer Intellekt*, p. 467.

19. *Russischer Intellekt,* p. 467.

20. See his *Sochineniia,* II, 109–111.

21. Otto Erich Strasser, *Alexandre Vinet* (Erlenbach-Zurich, 1946), pp. 114–115.

22. Kireevsky, *Sobranie sochinenii,* II, 264–265.

23. *Ibid.,* p. 267.

24. *Ibid.,* p. 268.

25. *Ibid.,* p. 269.

26. *Ibid.*

27. *Ibid.*

28. *Ibid.,* p. 276. At one point, Koshelëv's "unorganic" way of thinking about these matters drew a sharp response from Kireevsky. "For you," he wrote, "the principal foundation of the state, the cause of whatever tendency or form it has — in a word, its *soul* — is *public opinion,* or the *opinion of the majority.* For me, the soul of the state is the *dominant belief of the whole people.*" *Ibid.,* p. 278.

29. *Ibid.,* p. 277.

30. *Ibid.,* pp. 278–279.

31. Chetverikov, *Optina Pustyn',* p. 144.

32. *Ibid.,* pp. 145–146.

33. *Ibid.,* pp. 152–153.

34. *Ibid.,* pp. 136–137.

35. See Kireevsky's letter to Zhukovsky, *Sobranie sochinenii,* II, 249–252, and Müller, *Russischer Intellekt,* pp. 32–33.

36. *Russkii arkhiv,* 1909, no. 4, p. 600.

37. Müller, *Russischer Intellekt,* pp. 32–33.

38. "Das Tagebuch Ivan Vasil'evič Kireevskijs, 1852–1854," *Jahrbücher für Geschichte Osteuropas,* 14 (June 1966), 167–194.

39. *Ibid.,* p. 177.

40. *Ibid.,* p. 184, quoted in Müller, *Russischer Intellekt,* pp. 36–37.

41. See Kireevsky's letter to Odoevsky, *Russkaia starina,* 118 (1904), 217.

42. "Tagebuch," p. 185.

43. Chetverikov, *Optina Pustyn',* pp. 124–125, quoted in Müller, *Russischer Intellekt,* pp. 39–40.

44. Kireevsky, *Sobranie sochinenii,* II, 282, quoted Müller, *Russischer Intellekt,* p. 39.

45. Kireevsky, *Sobranie sochinenii,* II, 289.

46. *Ibid.*, I, 74.

47. Barsukov, *Zhizn' Pogodina*, X, 9.

48. It is contained in his *Sobranie sochinenii*, I, 223–264. There is an English translation in J. M. Edie, J. P. Scanlan, and M.-B. Zeldin, *Russian Philosophy* (Chicago, Quadrangle Books, 1965), I, 171–213.

49. Quoted in Barsukov, *Zhizn' Pogodina*, XV, 156.

50. On the founding of *Russkaia beseda*, see Barsukov, *Zhizn' Pogodina*, XIV, 290–352, passim: Koliupanov, *Biografiia*, II, esp. 235–240. For the journal's later history see Michael Petrovich, *The Emergence of Russian Panslavism* (New York, 1956), pp. 111–114, and Dement'ev, *Ocherki*, pp. 362–397.

51. Quoted in Barsukov, *Zhizn' Pogodina*, XIV, 326.

52. Kireevsky, *Sobranie sochinenii*, I, 230–231.

53. *Ibid.*, p. 231.

54. *Ibid.*, p. 235.

55. *Ibid.*, p. 237.

56. *Ibid.*, p. 238.

57. These remarks are reminiscent of one aspect of Sören Kierkegaard's description of the times. See, in particular, *The Present Age* (New York, 1962), esp. pp. 33–69. One of the profound differences between the two men's analyses was that Kierkegaard did not seek salvation in collective or communal forms of life. Nevertheless, their contemporaneity is apparent.

58. Kireevsky, *Sobranie sochinenii*, I, 239–240.

59. *Ibid.*, p. 241.

60. *Ibid.*, p. 246.

61. *Ibid.*

62. *Ibid.*, p. 249.

63. *Ibid.*, p. 252.

64. Henry Lanz, "The Philosophy of Ivan Kireyevsky," *The Slavonic Review*, IV (1926), 604.

65. *Ibid.*, p. 603.

66. Andrzej Walicki, *W kręgu*, pp. 122–123.

67. Lars Thunberg, *Microcosm and Mediator: The Theological Anthropology of Maximus the Confessor*, Acta Seminarii Upsaliensis (Lund, 1965), p. 179. See also Maximus' *The Four Centuries on Charity*, trans. P. Sherwood (Westminster, Md., 1955). Zenkovsky

also stresses Kireevsky's closeness to patristic thought here. See his *History of Russian Philosophy* (New York and London, 1953), I, 214–219.

68. Kireevsky, *Sobranie sochinenii,* I, 264.
69. Gershenzon, *Istoricheskie zapiski,* esp. pp. 36–40.
70. Müller, *Russischer Intellekt,* p. 429.
71. Walicki, *W kręgu,* p. 124, and Müller, *Russischer Intellekt,* pp. 448–449. Müller quite correctly stresses the greater role of sin, properly speaking, in Schlegel's conception, which brings him closer to the theological tradition than Kireevsky, who almost always spoke of "rationalism" rather than sin.
72. Walicki, *W kręgu,* p. 123.
73. *Ibid.,* pp. 132–134.
74. Wilhelm Heinrich Riehl (1823–1897): German neo-Kantian. For Riehl as a "Western Slavophile," see Iu. F. Samarin, *Sochineniia,* I (Moscow, 1877), 401–402, and Walicki, *W kręgu,* pp. 184, 206.
75. Samarin, *Sochineniia,* I, 195–196, quoted in A. Gratieux, *A. S. Khomiakov et le mouvement Slavophile,* II, 3. I am obliged to Mrs. Janet Vaillant for making me aware of this quotation; it appears in her "Encountering the West: The Ideological Responses of Aleksei S. Khomiakov and Leopold S. Senghor" (Ph.D. diss. Harvard, 1969).
76. Ernst Benz's *Geist und Leben der Ostkirche* and Vladimir Lossky's *Mystical Theology of the Eastern Church* both reveal a Slavophile spirit and interpretive bias.
77. See my review-article in *Kritika,* VII (Fall 1970), 11–29, For an illuminating discussion of both the Slavophile and "Western" elements in Herzen's "Russian Socialism," see Walicki, *W kręgu,* pp. 468–482.
78. *Message from Moscow by an Observer* (New York, Knopf, 1969), pp. 230–231. The anonymous "Observer" goes so far as to say that "most people who yearn for radical changes in the present system are Slavophiles by inclination." See also Andrei Amalrik, *Will the Soviet Union Survive until 1984?* (New York and Evanston, 1970), pp. 11–12 and passim.
79. Leopold Senghor in Senegal and Liang Sou-ming in pre-Communist China may serve as examples. Cf. Vaillant, "Encountering the West," passim, and Jerome Grieder, *Hu Shih and the Chinese Renaissance,* (Cambridge, 1970), esp. pp. 135–145.

Epilogue

1. Barsukov, *Zhizn' Pogodina*, XIV, 573.
2. *Ibid.*, p. 574.
3. *Ibid.*, p. 575.
4. *Ibid.*, p. 579.

Bibliography

Works by Kireevsky

Polnoe sobranie sochinenii Ivan Vasil'evich Kireevskogo (Complete works of Ivan Vasil'evich Kireevsky). Ed. A. I. Koshelëv. 2 vols. Moscow, 1861.

Polnoe sobranie sochinenii I. V. Kireevskogo. Ed. M. O. Gershenzon. 2 vols. Moscow, 1911. This is the edition I have used unless otherwise specified.

There are several differences between the two editions. Gershenzon included 39 letters, culled from various books, periodicals, and private persons, which are not in the Koshelëv edition. Also missing from the Koshelëv edition is the brief obituary for Baratynsky, which first appeared in the *Biblioteka dlia vospitaniia* (Library for nurture) in 1845 and is reprinted by Gershenzon. On the other hand, Gershenzon chose to omit the excerpts from Henrik Steffens' autobiography (translated by Avdot'ia Petrovna Elagina), which Koshelëv had included. Gershenzon retained only the brief preface by Kireevsky.

Zapiska o napravlenii i metodakh pervonachalnogo obrazovaniia naroda v Rossii (A note on the direction and methods of popular primary education in Russia) has been published by Eberhard Müller as an appendix to his *Russischer Intellekt in europäischer Krise* (Cologne, 1966), pp. 485–496. The *Zapiska,* in a fairly brief compass, gives Kireevsky's ideas as to how the common people should be educated in a situation where the corrupt product of Western culture is so easily accessible. Kireevsky's views are relatively sophisticated and far from totally obscurantist, but he shows himself to be fully

347

aware of the dangers of educating people beyond their station. He strongly advocated the teaching of Slavonic in the schools, since everything written in it is "useful" and nothing is "harmful." The *Zapiska* was written some time in 1839; the original is in the Manuscript Division of the Lenin Library.

Das Tagebuch Ivan Vasil'evič Kireevskijs, 1852–1854 has been translated, also by Eberhard Müller, and published in *Jahrbücher für Geschichte Osteuropas*, 14 (June 1966), 167–194. The original is in the Central State Archive for Literature and Art (TsGALI) in Moscow, together with a typewritten copy by Gershenzon.

Published letters. What appears to be a reasonably complete listing of Kireevsky's published correspondence may be found in K. D. Muratova, *Istoriia russkoi literatury XIX veka: bibliograficheskii ukazatel'* (History of Russian literature in the nineteenth century: Bibliographical index) (Moscow-Leningrad, 1962), p. 367. Muratova's work does not, however, inform the reader that the bulk of the letters published over the years in *Russkii arkhiv* were collected, edited, and published by M. N. Gershenzon in his 1911 edition of Kireevsky's works. Muratova also fails to inform the reader of the 26 letters from Kireevsky to Father Makary which were published in S. Chetverikov, *Optina Pustyn'* (Optina Monastery) (Paris, [1926]). Chetverikov's selection overlaps somewhat with Gershenzon's selection for the 1911 edition and also with another group of letters published in *Russkii arkhiv* (Russian archive) (1912, no. 4, pp. 584–596). It should also be pointed out that the letters which were published in the 1911 edition of Kireevsky's works have been edited — in some cases fairly extensively — by M. O. Gershenzon. In general, he did an exemplary job, sacrificing nothing of importance as far as Kireevsky's thought was concerned. The reader who is interested in Kireevsky from a more biographical standpoint, however, is advised to consult the somewhat fuller versions of the letters published in *Russkii arkhiv*, often with helpful notes by its editor, Peter Bartenev.

Among the more significant letters published elsewhere than in Kireevsky's collected works are the following, most of which have been cited in this volume:

Two letters to Koshelëv of the early 1850's may be found in "Pis'ma I. V. Kireevskogo k A. I. Koshelëvu," *Russkii arkhiv*, 1909, no. 5, pp. 99, 104.

An important letter to S. P. Shevyrëv, having to do with the founding of the *European,* may be found in *Golos minuvshogo* (Voice of the past), no. 7 (July, 1914), pp. 220–224.

Two important letters to Zhukovsky (1832) are to be found in *Blagonamerennyi* (Loyal), no. 1 (1926), pp. 143–146; another letter to Zhukovsky, written from Berlin in March 1830, may be found in "Pis'ma k V. A. Zhukovskomu raznikh lits," *Russkaia starina* (Russian antiquity), 115 (Aug. 1903), 452–454. Another letter to Zhukovsky dating from late 1849 or early 1850 may be found in *Russkii arkhiv,* 1909, no. 4, p. 600.

Two letters from Kireevsky to Prince Vladimir Odoevsky are contained in "Iz perepiska kniazia V. F. Odoevskogo," *Russkaia starina,* 118 (April 1904), 215–217.

Two letters to Alexander Pushkin may be found in the latter's *Polnoe sobranie sochinenii,* XIV (1941), 238 (dated Oct. 1831), and XV (1948), 19–20 (dated March–April 1832).

Two letters to A. M. Iazykov, one of which is dated June 26, 1851, are in *Russkaia starina,* 39 (Sept. 1883), 633–634. Three others from 1852 are in *Russkii arkhiv,* 1897, no. 10, pp. 290–291.

An early letter to A. A. Elagin is to be found in "Pis'ma brat'ev Kireevskikh," *Russkii arkhiv,* 1894, no. 10, pp. 208–210. This letter is misdated 1823; it seems to have been written in May 1825.

Finally, a good many letters and fragments of letters from Kireevsky's hand have been published by N. P. Barsukov in his enormous *Zhizn' i trudy M. P. Pogodina* (St. Petersburg, 1888–1910), 22 vols., passim. Vol. 22 contains an index.

Books and Articles

P. V. Annenkov i ego druz'ia (P. V. Annenkov and his friends). St. Petersburg, 1892. Contains a considerable body of correspondence, with a number of references to Kireevsky.

Annenkov, P. V. *Literaturnye vospominaniia.* Introd. and notes by Boris Eikhenbaum. Leningrad, 1928. Valuable background. There is also an English edition, edited by Arthur Mendel, under the title *The Extraordinary Decade* (Ann Arbor, University of Michigan Press, 1968).

Aris, Reinhold. *Die Staatslehre Adam Müllers in ihrem Verhältnis zur deutschen Romantik.* Tübingen, 1929.

Aronson, M., and S. Reiser. *Literaturnye kruzhki i salony* (Literary circles and salons). Leningrad, 1929.

Atkin, E. G. "Villemain and French Classicism." In *Studies by Members of the Department of Romance Languages*. Madison, University of Wisconsin, 1924. Pp. 126–151.

Bakunin, Michael. *Sozial-politischer Briefwechsel mit Alexander Iw. Herzen und Ogarjow*. Stuttgart, 1895.

Balandin, A. I., and P. D. Ukhov. "Sud'ba pesen, sobrannykh P. V. Kireevskim" (The fate of the songs collected by P. V. Kireevsky). *Literaturnoe nasledstvo* (Literary heritage), 79 (1968), 79–120.

Barsukov, N. P. *Zhizn' i trudy M. P. Pogodina* (The life and works of M. P. Pogodin). 22 vols. St. Petersburg, 1888–1910.

Bartenev, P. I. "Avdot'ia Petrovna Elagina." *Russkii arkhiv*, 1877, no. 8, pp. 483–495.

——— "Ivan Vasil'evich Kireevskii." *Russkii arkhiv*, 1894, no. 7, pp. 325–343.

——— *Rasskazy o Pushkine* (Stories about Pushkin). Moscow, 1925.

Barth, Karl. *Die protestantische Theologie im 19. Jahrhundert*. Zurich, 1946. Eleven chapters have been translated into English as *Protestant Thought: From Rousseau to Ritschl* by Brian Cozens (New York, Harper & Bros., 1959).

Baynes, N. H., and H. St. L. B. Moss, eds. *Byzantium: An Introduction to East Roman Civilization*. Oxford, Clarendon Press, 1961. An anthology of a remarkably high quality and a particularly valuable corrective to the Slavophile view of the Eastern Church.

Beausobre, Isabel, ed. *Russian Letters of Direction 1834–1860: Macarius, Starets of Optino*. Westminster, 1944. A selection of Makary's correspondence with his spiritual children, abridged from the edition published by the Optina Monastery in 1880. There is some interesting information about Makary and an excellent description of the skeet and church.

Belinsky, V. *Polnoe sobranie sochinenii*. 13 vols. Moscow, 1953–1959.

Belozerskaia, N. "Kniaginia Zinaida Aleksandrovna Volkonskaia." *Istoricheskii vestnik*, 68 (1897), 131–164.

Bendix, Reinhard. *Max Weber: An Intellectual Portrait*. Garden City, Doubleday & Co., 1962.

Benz, E. *Die abendländische Sendung der Östlich-orthodoxen Kirche*. Mainz, 1950.

——— *Geist und Leben der Ostkirche*. Hamburg, 1957.

Berdiaev, Nikolai. *Aleksei Stepanovich Khomiakov.* Moscow, 1912.

――― *The Russian Idea.* Boston, 1962.

Berlin, Isaiah. "A Marvellous Decade: 1838–1848." *Encounter,* June 1955, pp. 27–39; November 1955, pp. 21–29; December 1955, pp. 22–43; May 1956, pp. 20–34.

Blake, Robert. *Disraeli.* New York, St. Martin's, 1967.

Blum, Jerome. *Lord and Peasant in Russia from the Ninth to the Nineteenth Centuries.* Princeton, Princeton University Press, 1961.

Bochkarev, V. N. "Iz istorii obshchestvennykh nastroenii v Rossii serediny XIX v" (From the history of the social mood in Russia in the middle of the nineteenth century). *Institut istorii RANION, Uchenye zapiski,* XV (Moscow, 1929), 460–472.

――― "Iz istorii pomeshchich'ego khoziaistva v Rossii srediny XIX veka" (From the history of manorial economic affairs in Russia in the mid-nineteenth century). *Institut istorii RANION, Uchenye zapiski,* IV (Moscow, 1929), 206–217. Both of Bochkarev's articles are based on family correspondence from the Elagin archive.

Bowman, Herbert. *Vissarion Belinski, 1811–1848: A Study in the Origins of Social Criticism in Russia.* Cambridge, Harvard University Press, 1954.

Briggs, Asa. *The Age of Improvement.* New York, David McKay, 1959.

Brodsky, N. L. *Literaturnye salony i kruzhki.* (Literary salons and circles) Moscow-Leningrad, 1930.

――― *Rannie slavianofily* (Early Slavophiles). Moscow, 1910.

Brunetière, Ferdinand. *Evolution de la critique.* Paris, 1890.

Buslaev, F. I. "Moi vospominaniia." *Vestnik Evropy,* Oct. 1891, pp. 612–648.

Cailliet, Emile. *Pascal: The Emergence of Genius.* New York, Harper & Row, 1961.

Carr, E. H. *Michael Bakunin.* New York, Random House, 1961.

Chaadaev, Peter. *Sochineniia i pis'ma* (Writings and letters), ed. M. O. Gershenzon. 2 vols. Moscow, 1913.

Chetverikov, Sergei. *Optina Pustyn'.* Paris, [1926].

Chmielewski, Edward. *Tribune of the Slavophiles: Konstantin Aksakov.* Gainesville, University of Florida Press, 1962.

Christoff, Peter. *An Introduction to Nineteenth-Century Russian Slavophilism. Vol. I: A. S. Xomjakov.* The Hague, 1961.

Crisp, Olga. "The State Peasants under Nicholas I." *Slavic and East European Review,* 37 (1958–1959), 387–412.

Darsky, D. S. "A. S. Pushkin i zhurnal 'Evropeets' " (A. S. Pushkin and the journal the "European"). *Knizhnye novosti* (Book news), 1937, no. 2, pp. 38–39.

Dement'ev, A. G. *Ocherki po istorii russkoi zhurnalistiki 1840–1850 gg.* (Essays on the history of Russian journalism, 1840–1850). Moscow-Leningrad, 1951. The essays on Slavophile journalism are often useful, but the book is highly unreliable as far as anything pertaining to interpretation is concerned.

Dmitriev, S. S. "Slavianofily i slavianofil'stvo" (Slavophiles and Slavophilism). *Istorik-marksist,* vol. 89 (1941), no. 1, pp. 85–97.

Doctrine Saint-Simonienne. Paris, 1854. Important for the ideas of the Saint-Simonians.

Dorn, N. *Kireevskii: Opyt kharakteristiki ucheniia i lichnosti* (Kireevsky: An attempt at a characterization of his doctrine and personality). Paris, 1938. A hostile and not very interesting treatment.

Driver, Cecil. *Tory Radical: The Life of Richard Oastler.* New York, Oxford University Press, 1946. Interesting for comparative purposes.

Droz, Jacques. *Le Romantisme allemand et l'état.* Paris, 1966.

Druzhinin, N. M. *Gosudarstvennye krest'iane i reforma P. D. Kiseleva* (The state peasants and the reform of P. D. Kiselëv). 2 vols. Moscow-Leningrad, 1946–1958.

Ehrhard, Marcelle. *Joukovski et le préromantisme russe.* Paris, 1938. An excellent monograph, supplying useful background on Kireevsky's family and childhood.

Evgen'ev-Maksimov, E. V., N. I. Mordovchenko, and E. G. Iampolsky, eds. *Ocherki po istorii russkoi zhurnalistiki i kritiki* (Essays on the history of Russian journalism and criticism). Vol. I. Leningrad, 1950. This volume covers half a century and is much less tendentious than Dement'ev's *Ocherki,* cited above.

Falk, Heinrich. *Das Weltbild Peter J. Tschaadaews nach seinen acht "Philosophischen Briefen".* Munich, 1954.

Fischer, Kuno. *Geschichte der neueren Philosophie.* Vol. VI. Heidel-

berg, 1872. On Schelling. Old and in some respects out of date, but still useful.

Florovsky, G. V. *Puti russkogo bogosloviia* (Paths of Russian theology). Paris, 1937.

Gershenzon, M. O. *Istoricheskie zapiski* (Historical notes). Moscow, 1910. An interesting and very often perceptive essay on Kireevsky included. Quite impressionistic and opinionated.

—— *Obrazy proshlogo* (Figures from the past). Moscow, 1912. Contains a long essay on Peter Kireevsky which includes a great deal of interesting information about the family as a whole.

Gogol', Nikolai. *Polnoe sobranie sochinenii.* 14 vols. Moscow, 1937–1952.

Golitsyn, N. V. "Chaadaev i E. A. Sverbeeva." *Vestnik Evropy,* bks. I–IV, 1918, pp. 233–250.

—— ed. and introd. *Dnevnik Elizavety Ivanovny Popovoi* (The diary of Elizaveta Ivanovna Popova). St. Petersburg, 1911. Contains a few interesting scraps of information about Kireevsky's life in the latter 1840's.

Golosovker, Ia. E. *Dostoevskii i Kant.* Moscow, 1963.

Gorodetzky, Nadejda. *St. Tikhon Zadonsky.* London, S.P.C.K., 1951.

Gratieux, Albert. *A. S. Khomiakov et le mouvement Slavophile.* 2 vols. Paris, 1939.

Grieder, Jerome. *Hu Shih and the Chinese Renaissance.* Cambridge, Harvard University Press, 1970.

Grigoryev, Apollon. *My Literary and Moral Wanderings.* Trans. Ralph Matlaw. New York, E. P. Dutton & Co., 1962.

Gudzy, N. K. *History of Early Russian Literature.* New York, Macmillan & Co., 1949.

Hauser, Arnold. *The Social History of Art.* New York, Vintage Books, 1958. Vol. I.

Hayner, Paul C. *Reason and Existence: Schelling's Philosophy of History.* Leiden, 1967.

Hegel, G. W. F. *Sämtliche Werke,* 26 vols. Stuttgart, 1927–1940.

——*The Philosophy of History.* Trans. J. Sibree. New York, Willey Book Co., 1900.

Heiler, Friedrich. *Urkirche und Ostkirche.* Munich, 1937.

Heine, Heinrich. *Sämtliche Werke.* 10 vols. Leipzig, 1910–1920.

Herder, J. G. *Sämmtliche Werke.* 33 vols. Berlin, 1877–1913.

Herzen, A. I. *Polnoe sobranie sochinenii i pisem* (Complete writings and letters). Ed. M. K. Lemke. 22 vols. Petrograd, 1915–1925.

—— *Byloe i dumy* (My past and thoughts). 2 vols. Moscow, 1962.

Hobsbawm, E. T. *The Age of Revolution.* New York, 1964.

Hunt, H. J. *Le Socialisme et le romantisme en France.* Oxford, Clarendon Press, 1935.

Iazykov, N. M. *Stikhotvoreniia. Skazki. Poemy. Dramaticheskie stseny. Pis'ma.* (Verses. Tales. Poems. Dramatic Scenes. Letters). Moscow-Leningrad, 1959.

Isaac of Nineveh. *Mystic Treatises.* Translated from Bajan's Syriac text with introd. and registers by A. J. Wensinck. Verhandelingen der Koninklijke Akademie van Wetenschappen te Amsterdam, vol. XXIII, no. 1. Amsterdam, 1923.

Ivanov-Razumnik, V. *Istoriia russkoi obshchestvennoi mysli* (The history of Russian social thought). 4th ed. 2 vols. St. Petersburg, 1914. Still valuable for background.

Kartashëv, A. V. *Ocherki po istorii russkoi tserkvi* (Essays on the history of the Russian Church). 2 vols. Paris, 1959.

Kartsov, V. G. *Dekabrist G. S. Baten'kov* (Decembrist G. S. Baten'-kov). Novosibirsk, 1965. Baten'kov was a close friend of the Elagin family.

Kavelin, K. D. *Sobranie sochinenii.* 4 vols. St. Petersburg, 1897–1900.

Kaverin, V. *Baron Brambeus: Istoriia Osipa Senkovskogo* (Baron Brambeus: The story of Osip Senkovsky). Moscow, 1966.

Khomiakov, A. S. *Polnoe sobranie sochinenii.* 8 vols. Moscow, 1900–1914.

Kierkegaard, Sören. *The Present Age.* Trans. Alexander Dru. New York, Harper & Row, 1962.

Kireevsky, Peter. *Pis'ma N. M. Iazykovu* (Letters to N. M. Iazykov). Moscow-Leningrad, 1935.

Kohn, Hans. *Panslavism: Its History and Ideology.* 2nd ed., rev. New York, Vintage Books, 1960.

Koliupanov, N. *Biografiia Koshelëva* (The biography of Koshelëv). 2 vols. Moscow, 1889–1892. A most important source on Russian intellectual life in the first half of the nineteenth century.

Konshina, E. N. "Kireevskii-Elagin arkhiv." *Zapiska Otdela rukopisei biblioteki SSSR im. Lenina,* fasc. 15, 1953, pp. 18–42.

Kornilov, A. N. *Molodye gody Mikhaila Bakunina* (The youth of Michael Bakunin). Moscow, 1917.

Koshelëv, A. I. "Moi vospominaniia ob A. S. Khomiakove" (My reminiscences about A. S. Khomiakov). *Russkii arkhiv,* 1879, no. 11, pp. 265–272.

———— *Zapiski* (Notes). Berlin, 1884. Koshelëv was Kireevsky's oldest friend, and his memoirs contain a good deal of information, especially about Kireevsky's youth.

Kovalevsky, M. "Rannie revniteli filosofii Shellinga v Rossii, Chaadaev i Ivan Kireevskii" (Early enthusiasts of Schelling's philosophy in Russia: Chaadaev and Ivan Kireevsky). *Russkaia mysl'* (Russian thought), Dec. 1916, pp. 115–135.

Koyré, Alexandre. *Etudes sur l'histoire de la pensée philosophique en Russie.* Paris, 1950. Contains a most sophisticated and interesting essay on Kireevsky's youth.

———— *La Philosophie et le problème national en Russie au début du XIX siècle.* Paris, 1929. Still a most valuable study. See, in particular, the chapter on the "young men of the archives."

———— "Russia's Place in the World: Peter Chaadaev and the Slavophiles." *Slavonic Review,* 5 (1927), 594–608.

Koz'min, B. P., ed. *Pis'ma G. S. Baten'kova, I. I. Pushchina i E. G. Tollia* (The letters of G. S. Baten'kov, I. I. Pushchin, and E. G. Tol'). Moscow, 1936. Information on the Elagin family's reaction to the Decembrist revolt.

Krieger, Leonard. *The German Idea of Freedom.* Boston, Beacon Press, 1957.

Kuhn, Annette. *Die Staats- und Gesellschaftslehre Friedrich Schlegels.* Munich, 1959.

Kuleshov, V. I. *Literaturnye sviazi Rossii i Zapadnoi Evropy v XIX veka* (Literary ties between Russia and Western Europe in the nineteenth century). Moscow, 1965. Has some value as background, but, oddly enough, Kireevsky is scarcely mentioned.

———— *Otechestvennye zapiski i literatura 40-kh godov XIX v.* (The *Annals of the Fatherland* and the literature of the 1840's). Moscow, 1958. A solid monograph.

Lanz, Henry. "The Philosophy of Ivan Kireyevsky." *Slavonic Review,* 4 (1926), pp. 594–604.

Lednicki, Waclaw, ed. *Adam Mickiewicz in World Literature.* Berkeley and Los Angeles, University of California Press, 1956.

Lemke, Mikhail. *Nikolaevskie zhandarmy i literatura* (The gendarmes of Nicholas and literature). St. Petersburg, 1909.

────── *Ocherki po istorii russkoi tzenzury* (Essays on the history of Russian censorship). St. Petersburg, 1904.

Leont'ev, Konstantin. "Otets Kliment'" (Father Clement). *Russkii vestnik*, 144 (Nov.–Dec. 1879), 5–58, 517–555.

Levin, Harry. *The Gates of Horn*. New York, Oxford University Press, 1963.

────── "What is Realism?" *Comparative Literature*, 3 (1951), 193ff.

Liaskovsky, V. *Brat'ia Kireevskie, zhizn' i trudy ikh* (The life and works of the Kireevsky brothers). St. Petersburg, 1899. Some purely biographical information.

Lichtheim, George. *The Origins of Socialism*. New York and Washington, Frederick Praeger, 1969.

Lossky, N. O. *History of Russian Philosophy*. New York, International Universities Press, 1951.

Lossky, Vladimir. *The Mystical Theology of the Eastern Church*. London, Clarke, 1957.

Löwith, Karl. *From Hegel to Nietzsche: The Revolution in Nineteenth-Century Thought*. New York-Chicago-San Francisco, Holt, Rinehart and Winston, 1964. This extremely impressive work is essential background for Eberhard Müller's treatment of Kireevsky as an important figure in the European intellectual crisis which followed the death of Hegel and the decomposition of idealism.

Lukashevich, Stephen. *Ivan Aksakov (1823–1886): A Study in Russian Thought and Politics*. Cambridge, Harvard University Press, 1965.

Makary. *Russian Letters of Direction 1834–1860*. See Isabel Beausobre.

Malia, Martin. *Alexander Herzen and the Birth of Russian Socialism*. Cambridge, Harvard University Press, 1961. This brilliant book, which provides far more than even its title suggests, is indispensable to the student of Russian social and intellectual history in the nineteenth century.

────── "Herzen and the Peasant Commune." In *Continuity and Change in Russian and Soviet Thought*, ed. Ernest Simmons. Cambridge, Harvard University Press, 1955. Pp. 197–217.

────── "Schiller and the Early Russian Left." *Harvard Slavic Studies*, 4 (1957), 169–200.

Mannheim, Karl. *Essays on Sociology and Social Psychology*. Oxford, Clarendon Press, 1953.

—— *Essays on the Sociology of Knowledge.* New York, Oxford University Press, 1952.

—— *Ideology and Utopia.* New York, Harcourt, Brace & World, 1964.

Manuel, Frank. *The Prophets of Paris.* Cambridge, Harvard University Press, 1962.

Marcuse, Herbert. *Reason and Revolution.* Boston, Beacon Press, 1960.

Masaryk, Thomas G. *The Spirit of Russia.* 2 vols. New York, Macmillan & Co., 1955.

Maximus the Confessor. *The Ascetic Life. The Four Centuries on Charity.* Trans. and annotated by Polycarp Sherwood. Westminster, Md., Newman Press, 1955.

McGrew, Roderick. *Russia and the Cholera 1823–1832.* Madison and Milwaukee, University of Wisconsin Press, 1965.

McNally, Raymond. "Chaadaev vs. Khomiakov in the late 1830's and the 1840's." *Journal of the History of Ideas,* 27 (Jan.–March 1966), 73–91.

—— "The Books in Pëtr Ja. Čaadaev's Libraries." *Jahrbücher für Geschichte Osteuropas,* Dec. 1966, pp. 495–512.

Message from Moscow by an Observer. New York, Alfred Knopf, 1969.

Meyendorff, Jean. *A Study of Gregory Palamas.* Trans. George Lawrence. London, Faith Press, 1964.

Miliukov, P. N. *Glavnyia techeniia russkoi istoricheskoi mysli* (Main currents of Russian historical thought). Moscow, 1898.

Mirsky, D. S. *A History of Russian Literature.* New York, Vintage Books, 1960.

—— *Pushkin.* New York, E. P. Dutton & Co., 1963.

Monas, Sidney. "Šiškov, Bulgarin and the Russian Censorship." *Harvard Slavic Studies,* 4 (1957), 127–148.

—— *The Third Section.* Cambridge, Harvard University Press, 1961. An intelligent and amusing book.

Müller, Adam. *Elemente der Staatskunst.* Berlin, 1807.

Müller, Eberhard. "Lorenz von Stein und Jurij Samarins Vision des absoluten Sozialstaates." *Jahrbücher für Geschichte Osteuropas,* Dec. 1967, pp. 575–596.

—— *Russischer Intellekt in europäischer Krise: Ivan V. Kireevskij.* Cologne, 1966. A thorough and highly intelligent monograph,

treating Kireevsky's ideas in the matrix of European, particularly German, intellectual history.

———— "Zwischen Liberalismus und utopischem Sozialismus." *Jahrbücher für Geschichte Osteuropas,* Dec. 1965, pp. 511–530.

Nifontow, A. S. *Russland im Jahre 1848.* Berlin, 1954. The section on the Slavophiles must be used with some discrimination.

Nikitenko, A. V. *Dnevnik v trëkh tomakh* (Diary in three volumes). Leningrad, 1955–56. A very important source on the intellectual life of mid-nineteenth-century Russia.

Nisbet, Robert. *The Quest for Community.* New York, Oxford University Press, 1953.

———— *The Sociological Tradition.* New York, Basic Books, 1967. In both the books here cited, Mr. Nisbet has shown how the insights of nineteenth-century conservatives were incorporated into the works of sociologists — such as Weber, Marx, Durckheim, Tönnies — and developed by them.

Nol'de, B. E. *Iurii Samarin i ego vremia* (Iury Samarin and his times). Paris, 1926.

Odoevsky, V. F. *Russian Nights.* Trans. Olga Koshansky-Olienikov and R. Matlaw. New York, E. P. Dutton & Co., 1965. An important document of Russian Schellingianism.

Ostaf'evskii arkhiv kniazei Viazemskikh (The Ostaf'evo archive of the Viazemsky princes). Ed. S. D. Sheremetev. 5 vols. St. Petersburg, 1899–1913.

Parilova, G. N. and A. D. Soimonov. "P. V. Kireevskii i sobrannye im pesni" (P. V. Kireevsky and the songs collected by him). *Literaturnoe nasledstvo,* 79 (1968), 9–76.

Pascal, Blaise. *Pensées.* Introd. T. S. Eliot. New York, E. P. Dutton & Co., 1958.

Peterson, Aleksandr. "Cherty starinnogo dvorianskogo byta" (Characteristics of time-honored gentry life). *Russkii arkhiv,* 1877, no. 8, pp. 479–482.

Petrovich, Michael. *The Emergence of Russian Panslavism.* New York, Columbia University Press, 1956.

Philokalia (*Writings from the Philokalia on Prayer of the Heart*). London, Fernhill, 1951–1952. This translation was made from the Russian version (the *Dobrotoliubie*) by Kadloubovsky and Palmer.

Pipes, Richard. *Karamzin's Memoir on Ancient and Modern Russia.* Cambridge, Harvard University Press, 1959.

Presniakov, A. E. *Apogei samoderzhaviia Nikolai I* (The apogee of the autocracy of Nicholas I). Leningrad, 1925.

Prilozheniia k Trudam Redaktsionnykh komissii. Svedeniia o pomeshchich'ikh imeniakh (Supplements to the works of the Editing Commissions. Information on manorial estates). 8 vols. in 6. St. Petersburg, 1860. Information on Elagin-Kireevsky landholdings and serfs.

Pushkin, A. S. *Polnoe sobranie sochinenii.* 17 vols. Moscow-Leningrad, 1937–1959. I have also used the more convenient *Polnoe sobranie sochinenii* in 10 vols., edited by B. V. Tomashevsky, 2nd ed. (Moscow-Leningrad, 1956–1958).

———— *The Letters of Alexander Pushkin.* Trans. and ed. J. Thomas Shaw. 3 vols. Bloomington and Philadelphia, Indiana University Press and the University of Pennsylvania Press, 1963.

Pypin, A. N. *Obshchestvennoe dvizhenie v Rossii pri Aleksandre I* (The social movement in Russia under Alexander I). 3rd ed. St. Petersburg, 1900. Still useful for background.

Rachinsky, S. A., ed. *Tatevskii sbornik.* St. Petersburg, 1899. A miscellaneous collection of letters, poems, and other items from the Rachinsky country house in Tatev. Of interest are: 43 dated letters from E. A. Baratynsky to Kireevsky (1829–1833) and 9 without dates; a good deal of Zhukovsky's correspondence, including the full text of his letter to D. S. Golitsyn, the Governor-general of Moscow (Feb. 22, 1832), apropos of the suppression of the *European;* and a letter from D. V. Valuev to Kireevsky of Nov. 1835.

Reissner, H. G. *Eduard Gans.* Tübingen, 1965.

Riasanovsky, Nicholas. "Khomiakov on Sobornost'." In *Continuity and Change in Russian and Soviet Thought,* ed. Ernest Simmons. Cambridge, Harvard University Press, 1955. Pp. 183–196.

———— *Nicholas I and Official Nationality in Russia.* Berkeley and Los Angeles, University of California Press, 1961.

———— "Pogodin and Shevyrëv in Russian Intellectual History." *Harvard Slavic Studies,* 4 (1957), 149–168.

———— *Russia and the West in the Teaching of the Slavophiles.* Cambridge, Harvard University Press, 1952.

Rogger, Hans. *National Consciousness in Eighteenth-Century Russia.* Cambridge, Harvard University Press, 1960.

———— and Eugen Weber. *The European Right: A Historical Profile.* Berkeley and Los Angeles, University of California Press, 1966.

Rubinstein, N. A. "Istoricheskaia teoriia slavianofilov i ee klassovye korni." In *Trudy Instituta Krasnoi Professury, Russkaia istoricheskaia literatura v klassovom osveshchenii* (The historical theory of the Slavophiles and its class roots, in The works of the Institute of the Red Professors, Russian historical literature in its class interpretation). Ed. M. N. Pokrovsky. Moscow, 1927. Pp. 53–117.

Russell, Bertrand. *A Critical Exposition of the Philosophy of Leibniz.* London, Allen & Unwin, 1937.

Sakulin, P. N. *Iz istorii russkogo idealizma. Kniaz' V. F. Odoevskii* (From the history of Russian Idealism. Prince V. F. Odoevsky). Moscow, 1913. Important source on the 1820's in particular.

Scheibert, Peter. *Von Bakunin zu Lenin.* Leiden, 1956.

Schelling, F. W. J. v. *Sämmtliche Werke.* 14 vols. Stuttgart and Augsburg, 1856–1861.

———— *Ages of the World.* Ed. Frederick Bolman. New York, AMS Press, 1942.

Schelting, A. v. *Russland und Europa im russischen Geschichtsdenken.* Bern, 1948.

Schlegel, Friedrich, *Philosophie des Lebens.* Vienna, 1928.

Schmitt, Carl. *Politische Romantik.* Leipzig, 1925. A highly intelligent polemic with most of the principal "interpreters" of romanticism. A particularly good corrective for sociological excess.

Schnabel, Franz. *Deutsche Geschichte im neunzehnten Jahrhundert.* 8 vols. Freiburg, 1965.

Seidlitz, Carl v. *Wasily Andrejewitsch Joukoffsky.* Mitau, 1870. Provides biographical background.

Semevsky, V. I. *Krestianskii vopros v Rossii* (The Peasant Question in Russia). 2 vols. St. Petersburg, 1888.

Setschkareff, Wsewolod. *Schellings Einfluss in der russischen Literatur der 20er und 30er Jahre des XIX Jahrhunderts.* Berlin, 1939. Rather weak on analysis.

Shchepkin, D. M. "Moskovskii universitet v polovine dvadtsatykh godov" (Moscow University in the middle of the twenties). *Vestnik Evropy,* 4 (1903), 226–261.

Shevyrëv, S. P. "Izvlechenie iz pisem . . . k G. Ministru Narodnogo Prosveshcheniia" (An extract from the letters . . . to the Minister of Culture). *Zhurnal Ministerstva Narodnogo Prosveshcheniia* (The journal of the ministry of culture), 1840, pt. 4, pp. 1–14.

Shtein, V. M. *Ocherki razvitiia russkoi obshchestvenno-ekonomicheskoi mysli XIX–XX vekov* (Essays on the development of Russian socioeconomic thought of the 19th and 20th centuries). Leningrad, 1948.

Smolitsch, Igor. "I. V. Kireevskij. Leben und Weltanschauung." *Jahrbücher für Kultur und Geschichte den Slaven*, Vol. IX, 1933.

———— *Leben und Lehre der Starzen.* 2nd ed., Cologne and Olten, 1952.

Soimonov, A. D. "Novye materialy o Pushkine i P. V. Kireevskom" (New material about Pushkin and P. V. Kireevsky). *Izvestiia AN SSSR, otdelenie literatury i iazyka* (News of the Academy of Sciences of the USSR, Division of Language and Literature). Vol. XX, bk. 2, 1961, pp. 143–153.

Stankevich, A. V. *T. N. Granovskii i ego perepiska* (T. N. Granovsky and his correspondence). Moscow, 1897. Vol. II.

Stender-Petersen, Ad. *Geschichte der russischen Literatur.* Munich, 1957.

Stephan, H., and M. Schmidt. *Geschichte der deutschen evangelischen Theologie.* Berlin, 1960.

Stepun, Fëdor. "Nemetskii romantizm i russkoe slavianofil'stvo" (German romanticism and Russian Slavophilism). *Russkaia mysl'*, March 1910, pp. 65–91.

Strasser, Otto. *Alexandre Vinet.* Erlenbach-Zurich, 1946.

Strémooukhoff, Dmitri. *La Poésie et l'ideologie de Tioutchev.* Strasbourg, 1937.

Struve, Gleb. "Mickiewicz in Russia." *Slavonic and East European Review*, 26 (1947–1948), 126–145.

Thaden, E. C. *Conservative Nationalism in Nineteenth-Century Russia.* Seattle, University of Washington Press, 1964.

Thompson, E. P. *The Making of the English Working Class.* New York, Vintage Books, 1963.

Thunberg, Lars. *Microcosm and Mediator: The Theological Anthropology of Maximus the Confessor. Acta Seminarii Upsaliensis.* Lund, 1965.

Tikhomirov, M. N., ed. *Istoriia Moskovskogo universiteta* (The history of Moscow University). 2 vols. Moscow, 1955.

Tillich, Paul. *Perspectives on Nineteenth and Twentieth Century Protestant Theology*. New York, Harper & Row, 1967.

Tocqueville, Alexis de. *Democracy in America*. 2 vols. New York, Schocken Books, 1961.

Tolycheva. "Rasskazy i anekdoty" (Stories and anecdotes). *Russkii arkhiv*, 1877, no. 7, pp. 361–368.

Tomashevsky, Boris. *Pushkin*. 2 vols. Moscow, 1956–1961.

Tönnies, Ferdinand. *Community and Society*. Trans. C. Loomis. New York, Harper & Row, 1963.

Treitschke, Heinrich v. *A History of Germany in the Nineteenth Century*. Trans. E. and C. Paul. 7 vols. London, Jarrolds, 1915–1919.

Tsagalov, N. A. *Ocherki russkoi ekonomicheskoi mysli perioda padeniia krepostnogo prava* (Essays on Russian economic thought in the period of the end of serfdom). Moscow, 1950.

Tschijewskij, Dmitri. "Hegel in Russland." In *Hegel bei den Slawen*. 2nd, rev. ed. Bad Homburg, 1961.

Turgenev, A. I. *Khronika russkogo* (Chronicle of a Russian). Moscow-Leningrad, 1964.

Utkinskii sbornik. Ed. A. E. Gruzinsky. Moscow, 1904. Enormously valuable for Zhukovsky's many letters to Adot'ia Petrovna Elagina, some of which go back to 1815–1817. The notes also provide considerable information on Kireevsky's life and times.

Vaillant, Janet. "Encountering the West: The Ideological Responses of Aleksei S. Khomiakov and Leopold S. Senghor." Ph.D. diss. Harvard, 1969.

Velikaia Reforma, Russkoe obshchestvo i krest'ianskii vopros v proshlom i nastoiashchem (The Great Reform, Russian society, and the Peasant Question in the past and present). Ed. A. K. Dzhivelegov, S. P. Mel'gunov, and V. I. Picheta. 6 vols. Moscow, 1911.

Venevitinov, M. "I. V. Kireevskii i tsenzura 'Moskovskogo sbornika' 1852 g." (I. V. Kireevsky and the censorship of the "Moscow Miscellany" of 1852). *Russkii arkhiv*, 1897, no. 10, pp. 287–291.

Vesin, S. *Ocherki istorii russkoi zhurnalistiki* (Essays on the history of Russian journalism). St. Petersburg, 1881. Contains useful summaries of some of the journalistic conflicts of the 1830's.

Viazemsky, P. A. *Polnoe sobranie sochinenii*. 12 vols. St. Petersburg, 1878–1896.

Vinet, Alexandre. *Essai sur la manifestation des convictions religieuses et sur la séparation de l'eglise et de l'état.* Paris, 1842.

Walicki, Andrzej. "The Paris Lectures of Mickiewicz and Russian Slavophilism." *Slavonic and East European Review,* 46 (Jan. 1968), 155–175.

———— "Personality and Society in the Ideology of Russian Slavophiles." *California Slavic Studies,* vol. II, 1962.

———— *W kręgu konserwatywnej utopii.* Warsaw, 1964. A brilliant monograph, treating the Slavophiles from the standpoint of the sociology of political romanticism.

Ware, Timothy. *The Orthodox Church.* London, Penguin Books, 1963.

Weber, Max. *Wirtschaft und Gesellschaft.* 2 vols. Tübingen, 1925.

Wellek, René. *A History of Modern Criticism,* vol. II: *The Romantic Age.* New Haven, 1955. Vol. III: *The Age of Transition.* New Haven, 1965.

Wensinck, A. J., trans. *Mystic Treatises.* See Isaac of Nineveh.

Windelband, Wilhelm. *A History of Philosophy.* Trans. J. Tufts. Vol. II. New York, Harper & Bros., 1958. Old and not much help as far as indicating relevant secondary literature is concerned, but useful. The viewpoint is neo-Kantian.

Wortman, Richard. "Koshelev, Samarin and Cherkassky and the Fate of Liberal Slavophilism." *Slavic Review,* 21 (June 1962), 261–279.

Wytrzens, Günther. *Pjotr Andreevič Vjazemskij.* Vienna, 1961.

Zamotin, I. I. *Romanticheskii idealizm v russkom obshchestve i literatura 20–30kh godov XIX stoletiia* (Romantic idealism in Russian society and the literature of the 1820's and 1830's). St. Petersburg, 1907.

Zavitnevich, V. Z. *Aleksei Stepanovich Khomiakov.* 2 vols. Kiev, 1902. Monumental, but focusing rather narrowly on Khomiakov.

Zeltner, Hermann. *Schelling.* Stuttgart, 1954.

Zenkovsky, V. V. *A History of Russian Philosophy.* 2 vols. New York and London, Columbia and Routledge & Kegan Paul, 1953.

Zhukovsky, V. A. *Polnoe sobranie sochinenii.* 12 vols. in 2. St. Petersburg, 1902. I also used the one-volume *PSS* (Moscow and St. Petersburg, 1909), which is full of most interesting photographs.

Zhukovskii, Vasilii. An edition of the magazine "Russkii bibliofil." St. Petersburg, [1913]. Several letters from Zhukovsky to A. P. Elagina.

Index

Russian Research Center Studies

* Out of print.

† Publications of the Harvard Project on the Soviet Social System.

‡ Published jointly with the Center for International Affairs, Harvard University.